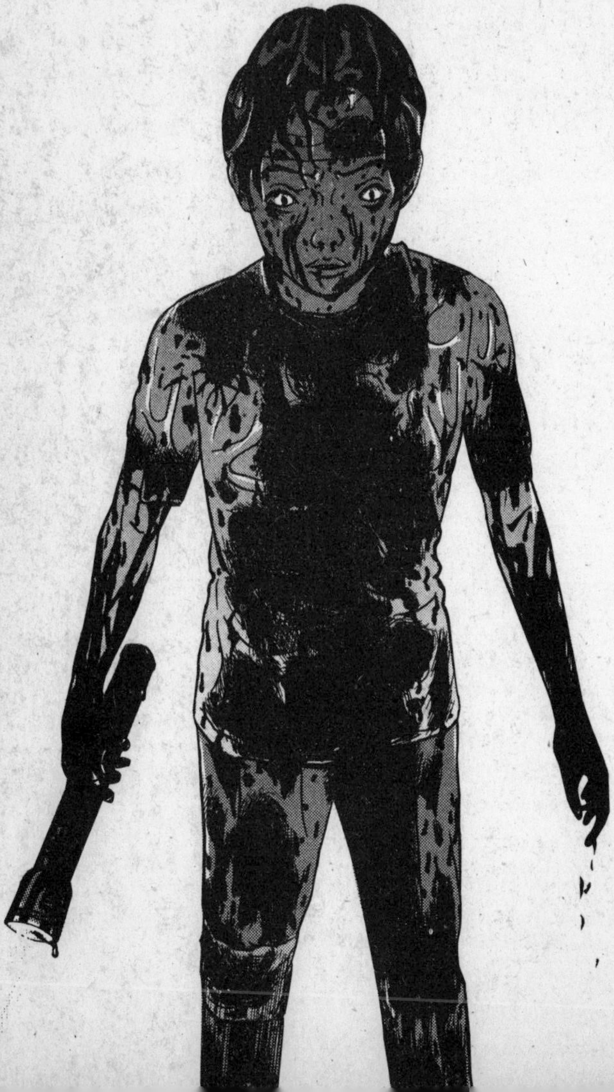

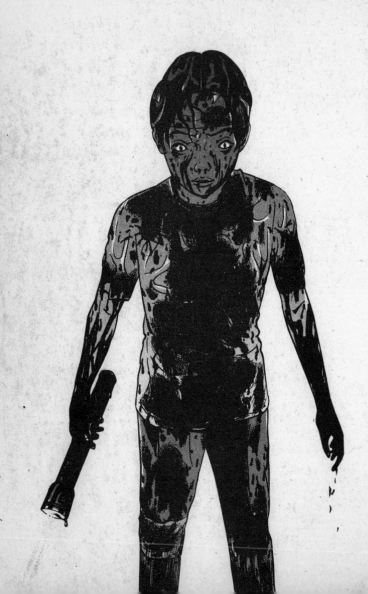

GRA
DRAGON
V. 1

# Dragon Head Vol. 1
## Created by Minetaro Mochizuki

Translation - Alexis Kirsch
English Adaptation - Aaron Sparrow
Copy Editor - Eric Althoff
Retouch and Lettering - Lucas Rivera
Production Artist - Jason Milligan
Cover Design - Jorge Negrete

Editor - Paul Morrissey
Digital Imaging Manager - Chris Buford
Production Managers - Jennifer Miller and Mutsumi Miyazaki
Managing Editor - Lindsey Johnston
VP of Production - Ron Klamert
Publisher and E.I.C. - Mike Kiley
President and C.O.O. - John Parker
C.E.O. - Stuart Levy

A  Manga

TOKYOPOP Inc.
5900 Wilshire Blvd. Suite 2000
Los Angeles, CA 90036

E-mail: info@TOKYOPOP.com
Come visit us online at www.TOKYOPOP.com

© 1995 Minetaro Mochizuki. All Rights Reserved.
First published in Japan in 1995 by Kodansha Ltd., Tokyo.
English publication rights arranged through Kodansha Ltd.

English text copyright © 2006 TOKYOPOP Inc.

ISBN: 1-59532-914-5

First TOKYOPOP printing: January 2006
10 9 8 7 6 5 4 3 2 1
Printed in the USA

# Volume 1

by
Minetaro Mochizuki

HAMBURG // LONDON // LOS ANGELES // TOKYO

# CONTENTS

DRIP

パ
ラ
ッ

DRIP

パ
ラ

DRIP

パ
ラ

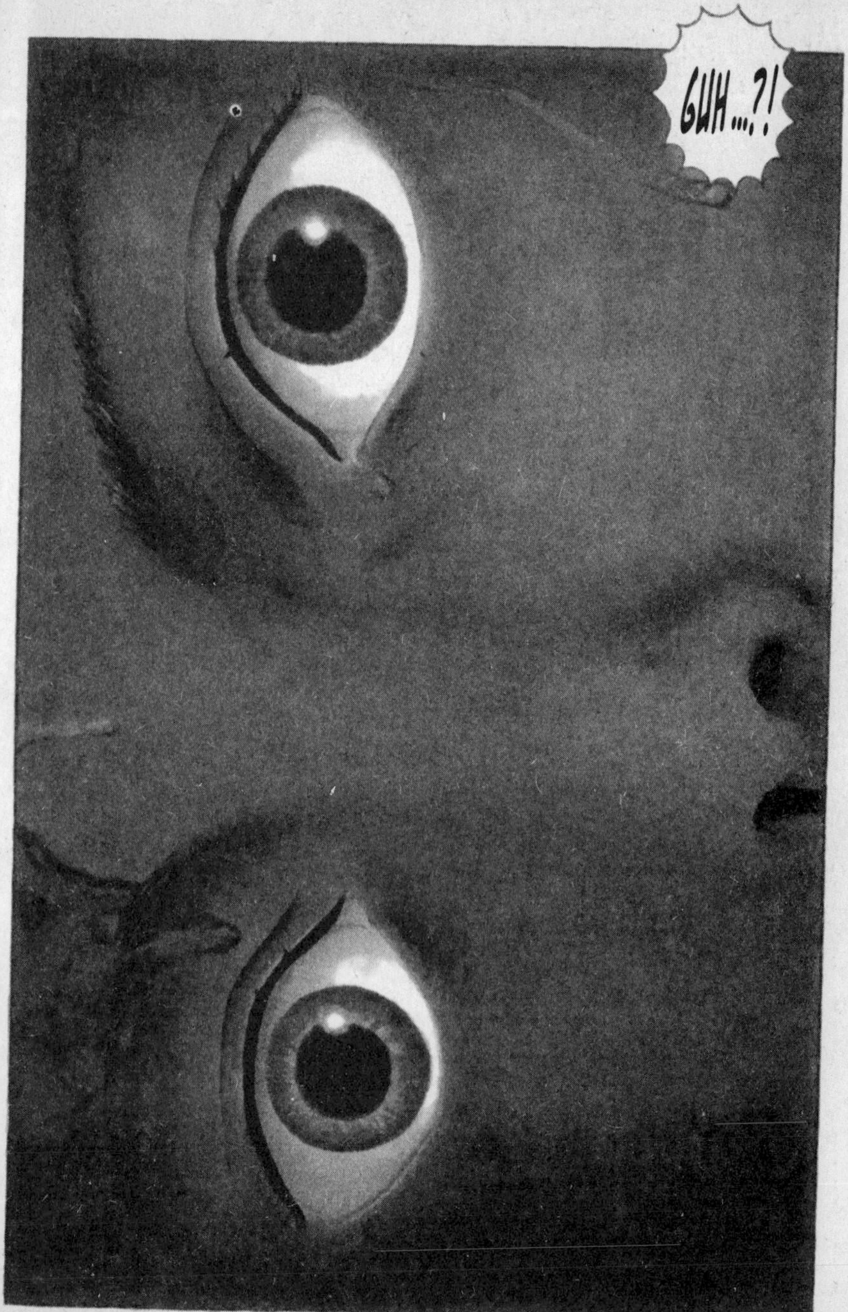
GUH...?!

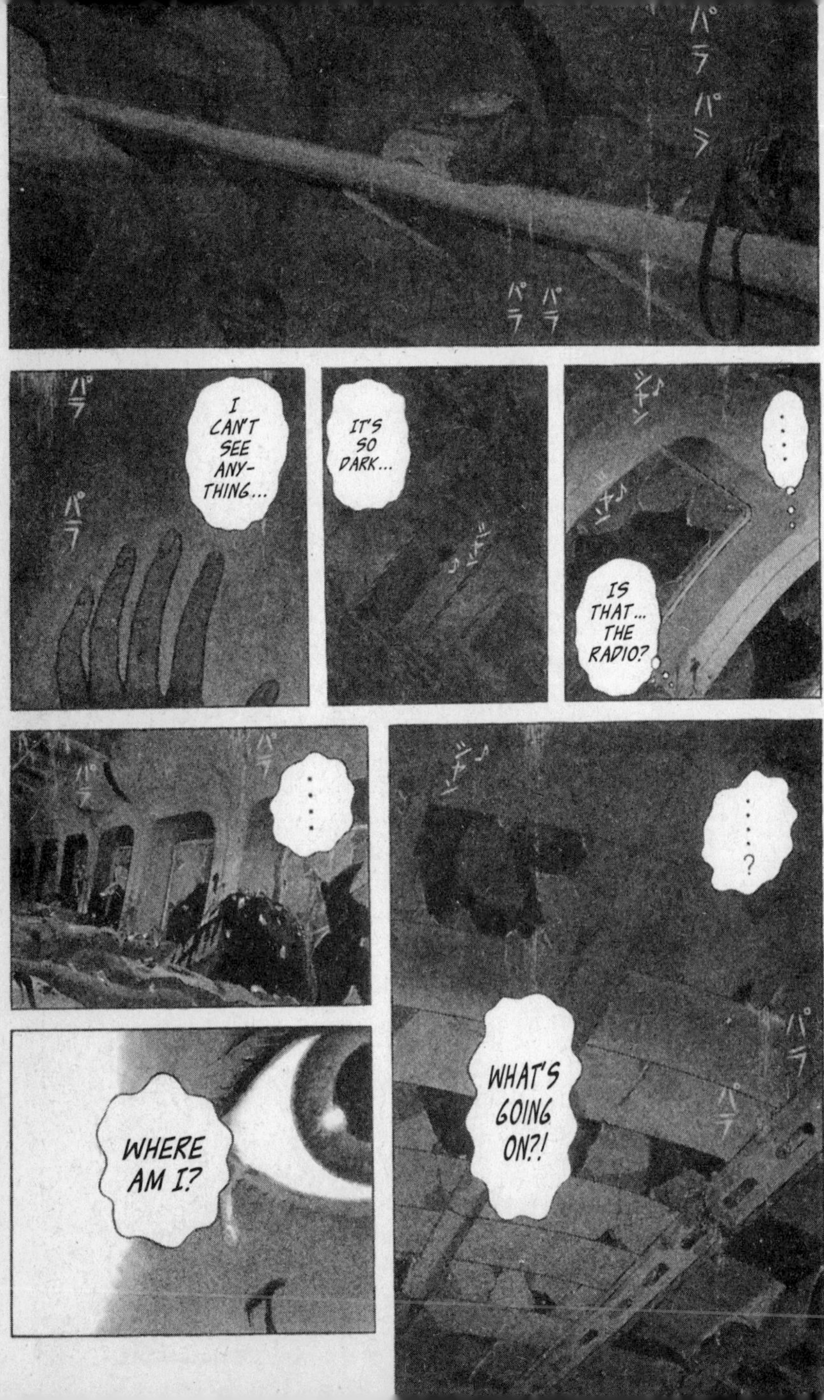

パラパラ
....
IS THAT... THE RADIO?
IT'S SO DARK...
I CAN'T SEE ANYTHING...
....?
WHAT'S GOING ON?!
....
WHERE AM I?

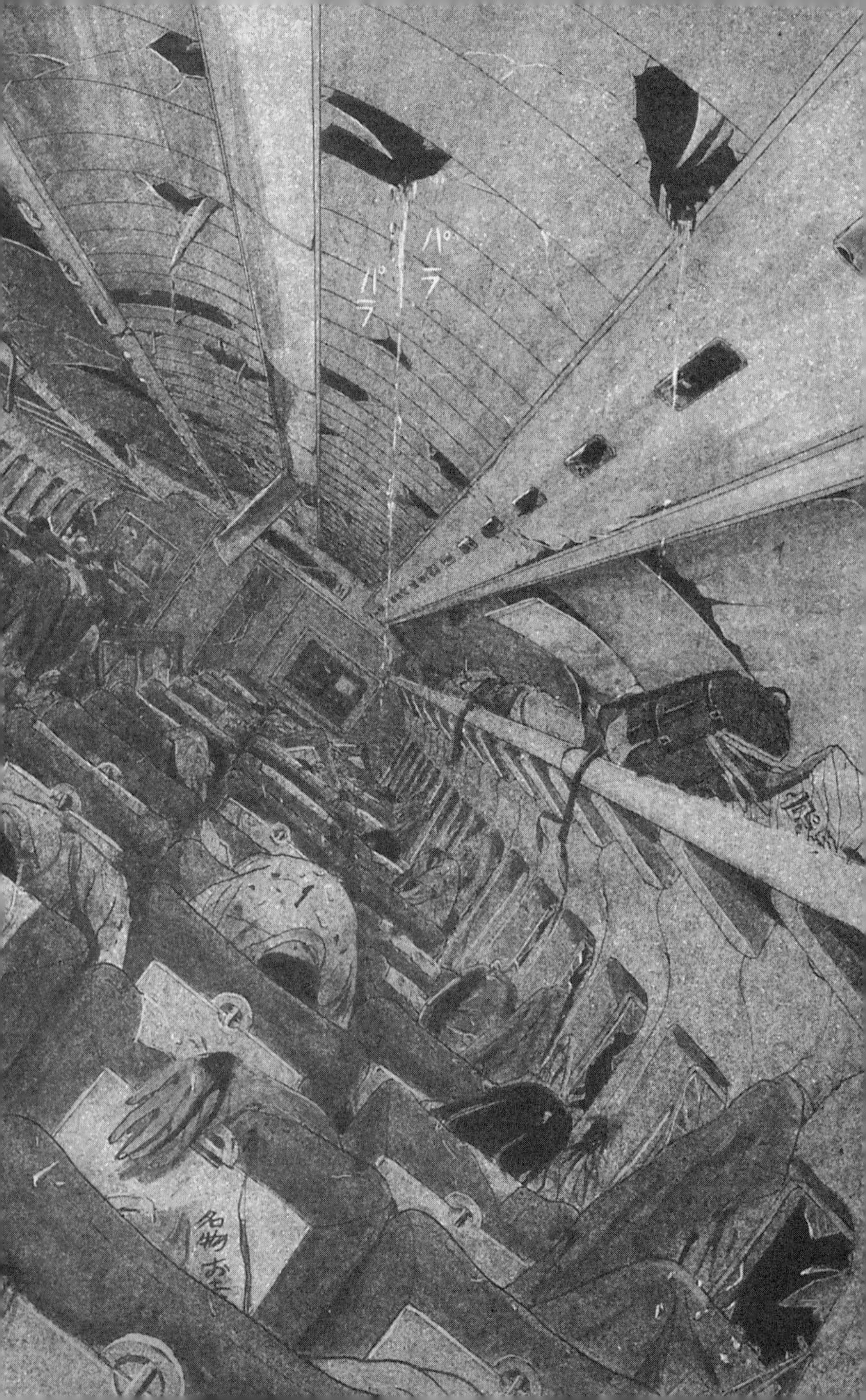
パラ
パラ

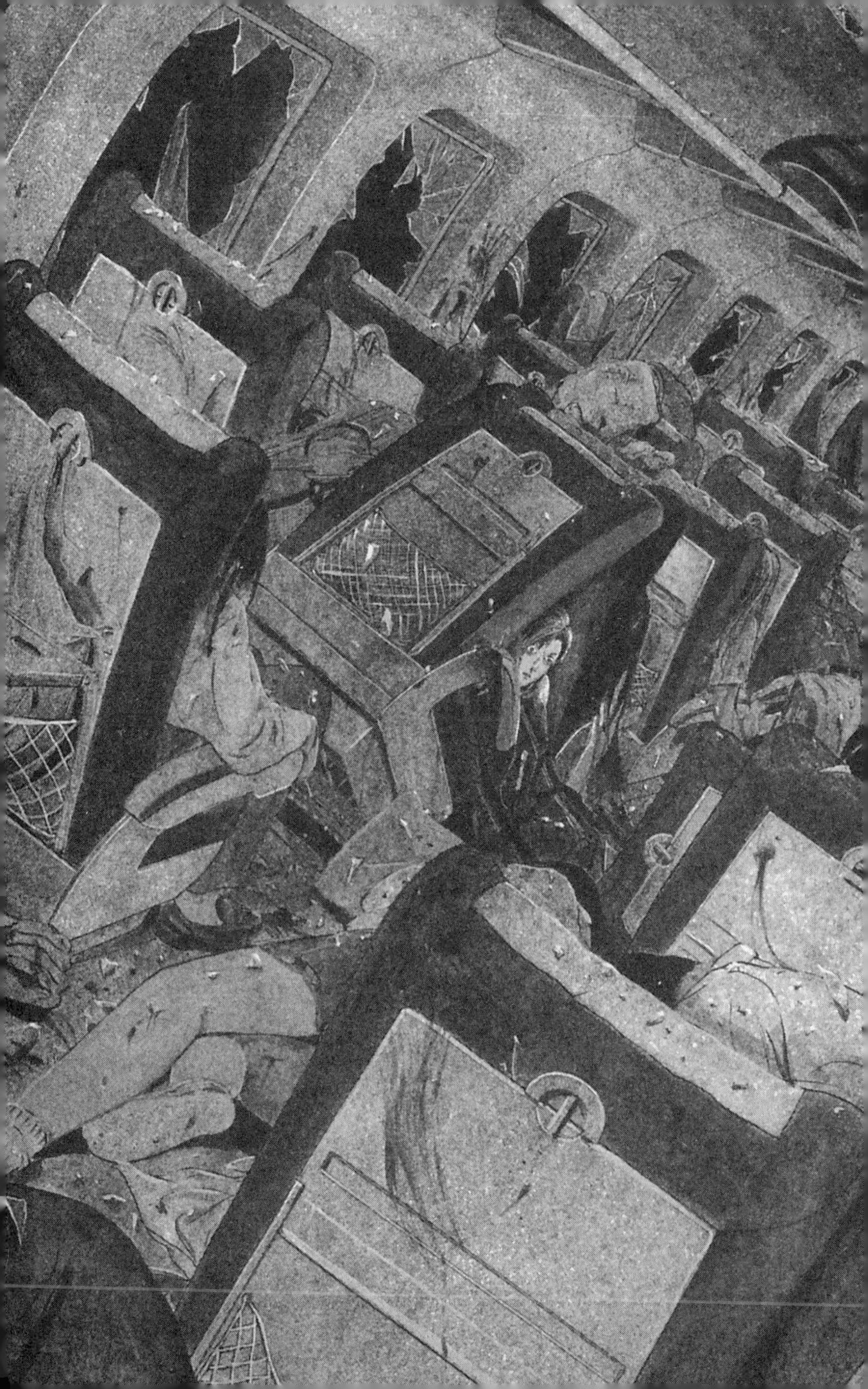

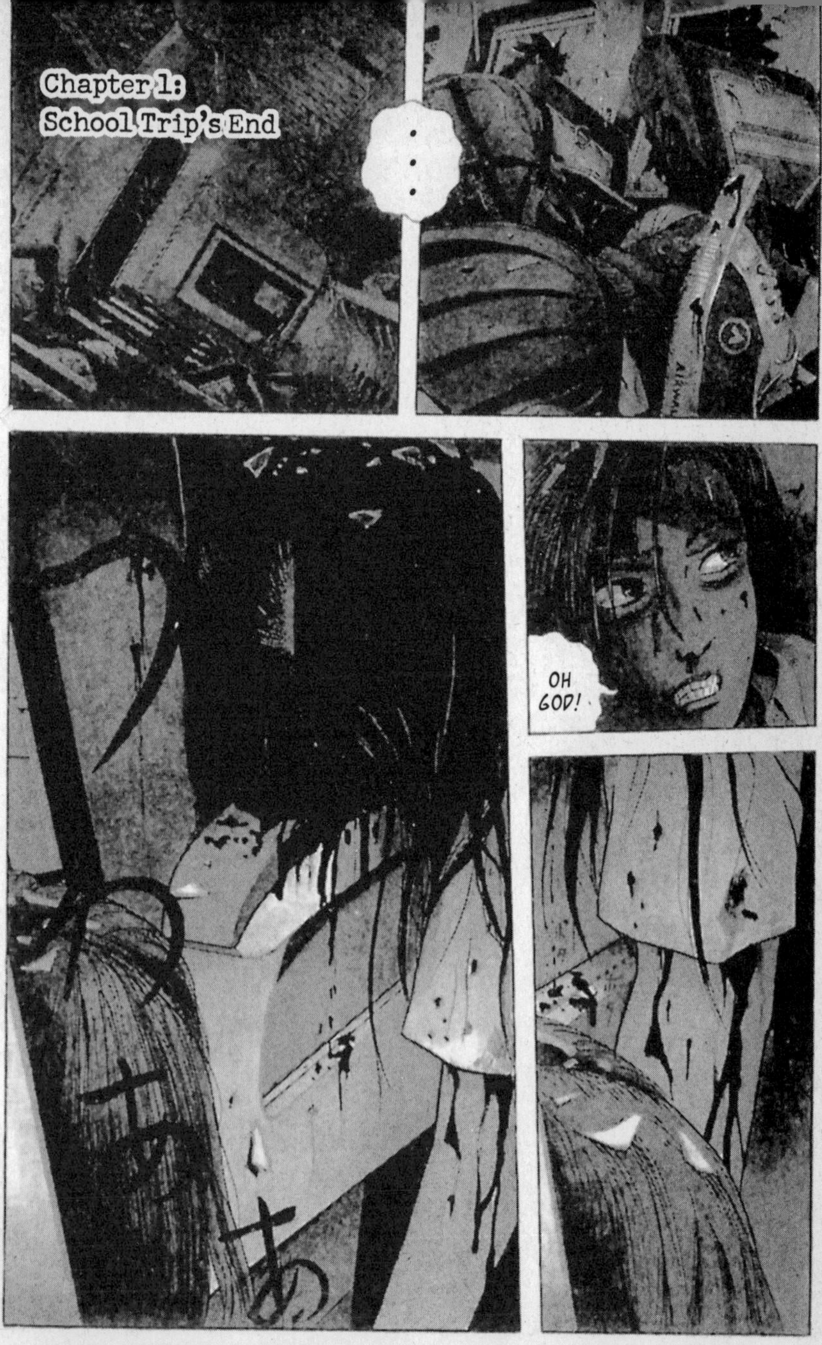
Chapter 1:
School Trip's End
...
OH GOD!

AAHHH!!! SOME-ONE HELP ME!!
HELP!!!
HEY! HEEEY!!!
おーい
おーい…
おーい…
おーい…
パラ
HELP HELP HELP HELP
パラパラ
UH...
UH...
OH SHIT. WHAT HAPPENED? A TRAIN ACCIDENT? WHEN...?
♪ニャンニャン♪

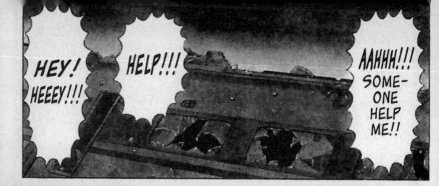

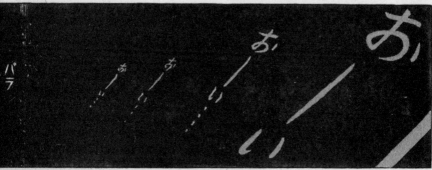

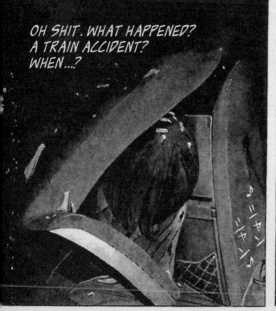

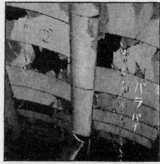

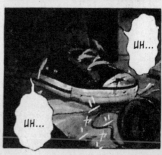

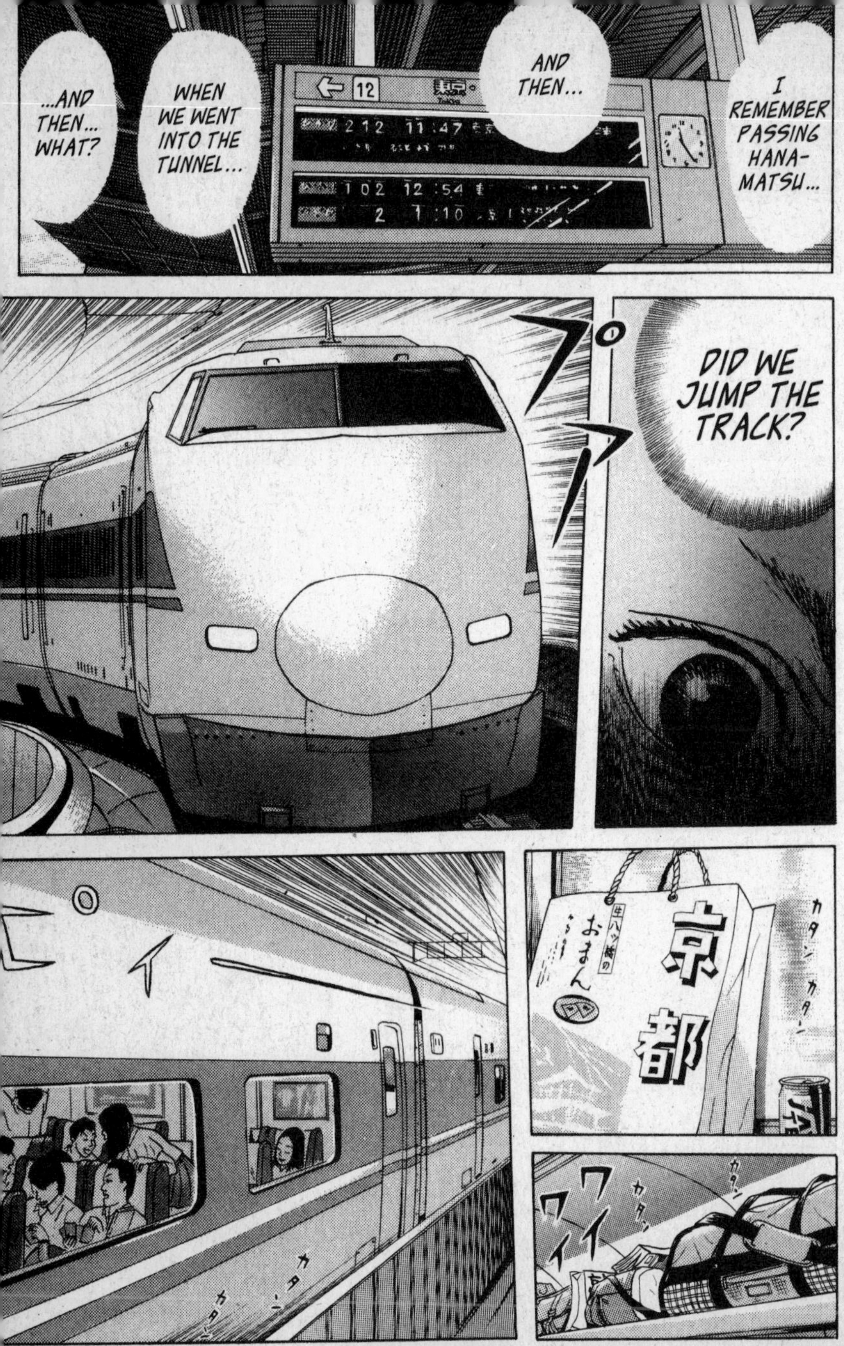
I REMEMBER PASSING HANA-MATSU...
AND THEN...
WHEN WE WENT INTO THE TUNNEL...
...AND THEN... WHAT?
DID WE JUMP THE TRACK?
京都
カタン カタン
ワイワイ
カタン カタン
カタン カタン

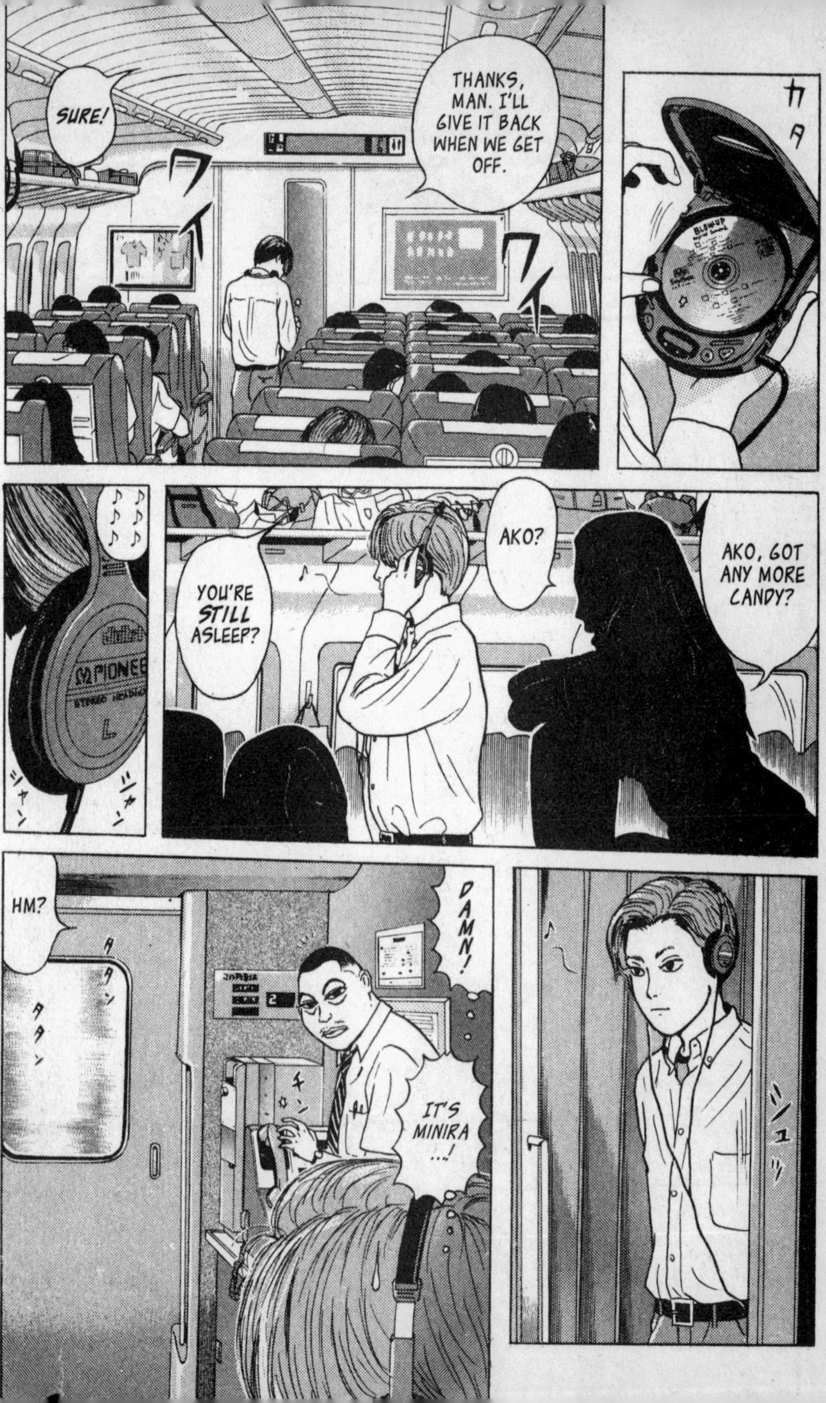
THANKS, MAN. I'LL GIVE IT BACK WHEN WE GET OFF.
SURE!
AKO, GOT ANY MORE CANDY?
AKO?
YOU'RE STILL ASLEEP?
DAMN!
HM?
IT'S MINIRA ...!

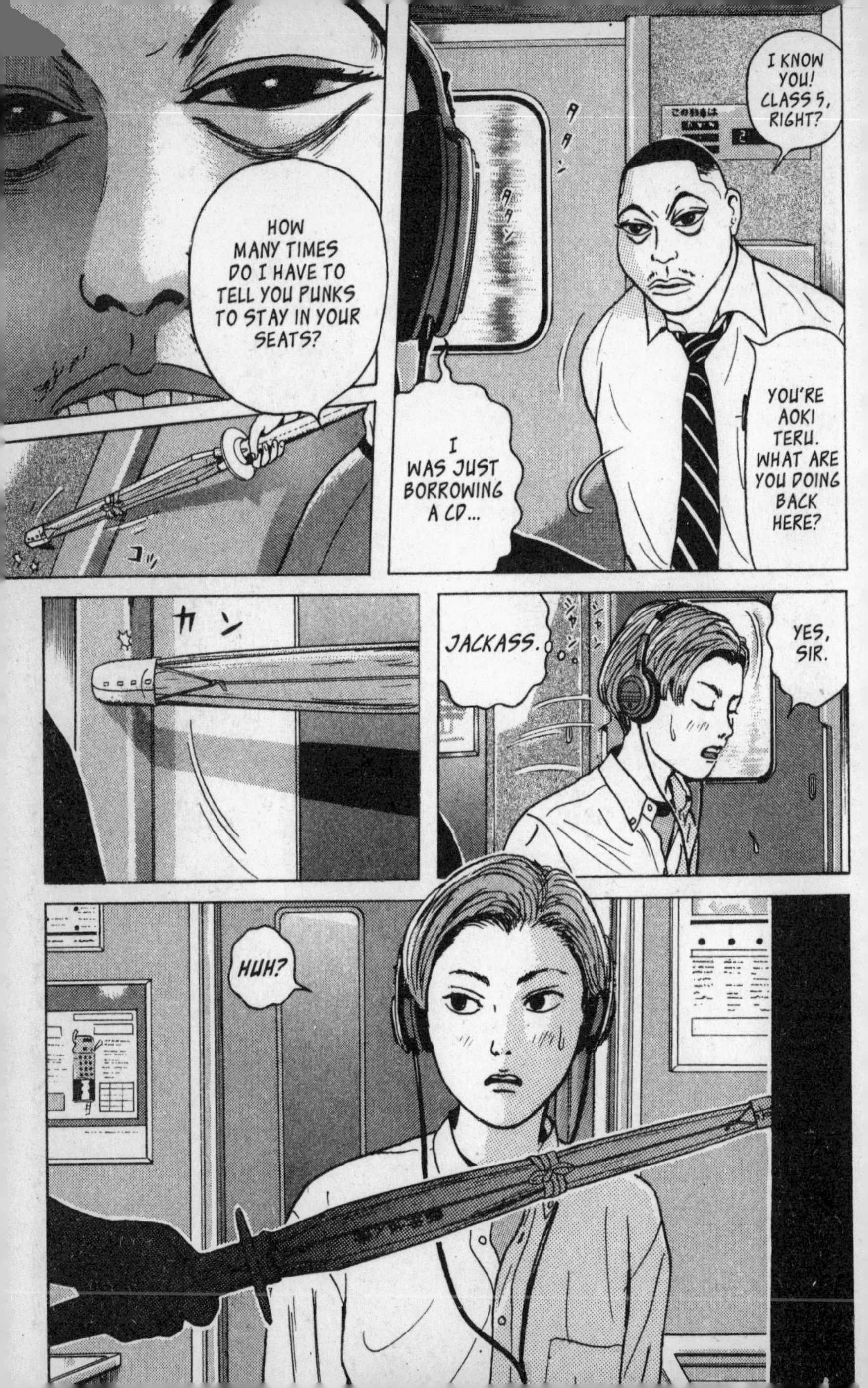
I KNOW YOU! CLASS 5, RIGHT?
YOU'RE AOKI TERU. WHAT ARE YOU DOING BACK HERE?
I WAS JUST BORROWING A CD...
HOW MANY TIMES DO I HAVE TO TELL YOU PUNKS TO STAY IN YOUR SEATS?
YES, SIR.
JACKASS.
カン
HUH?

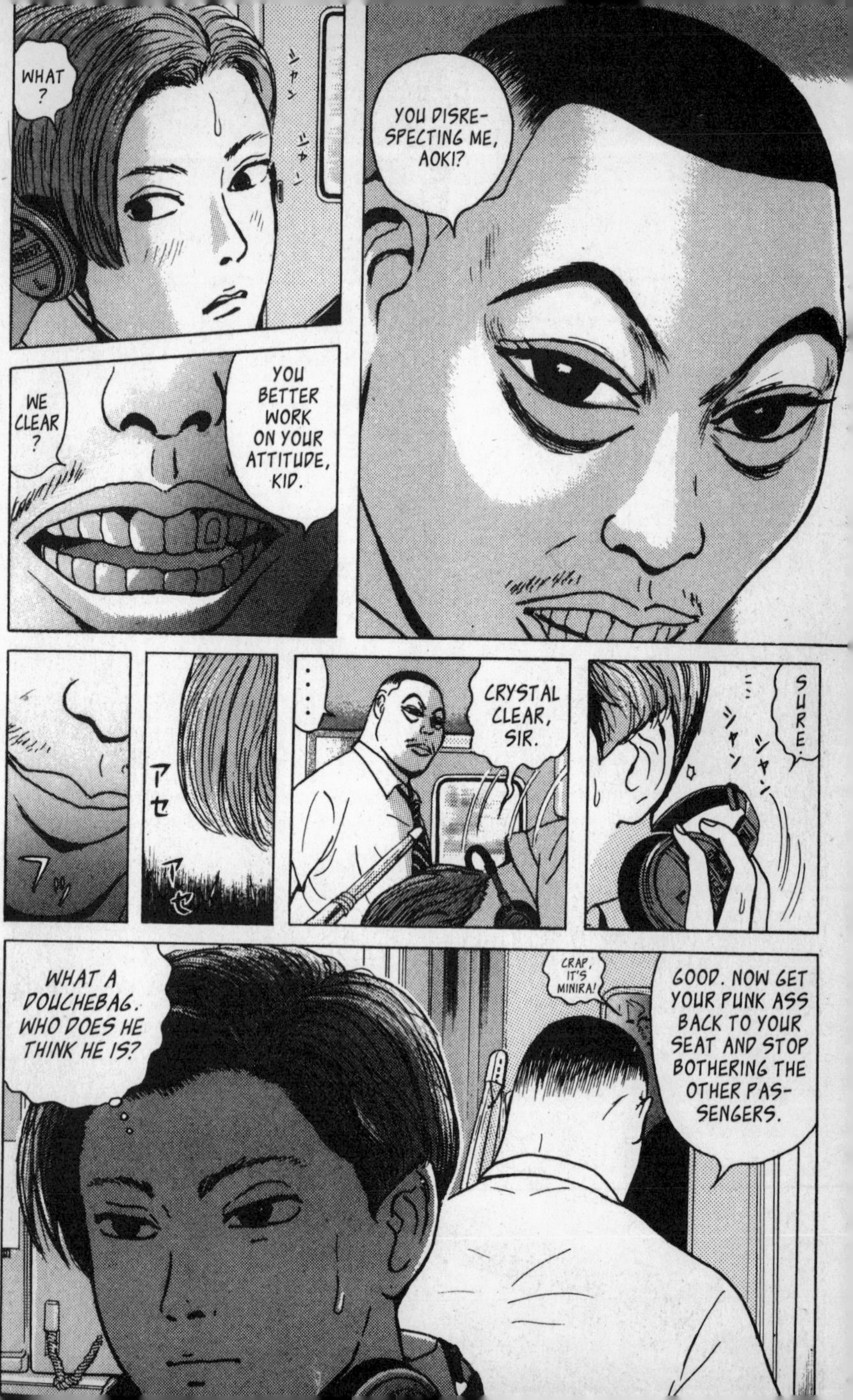

YOU DISRESPECTING ME, AOKI?
WHAT ?
シャン
シャン
YOU BETTER WORK ON YOUR ATTITUDE, KID.
WE CLEAR ?
SURE.
...
シャン シャン
CRYSTAL CLEAR, SIR.
.....
アセ
アセ
フッ
GOOD. NOW GET YOUR PUNK ASS BACK TO YOUR SEAT AND STOP BOTHERING THE OTHER PASSENGERS.
CRAP, IT'S MINIRA!
WHAT A DOUCHEBAG. WHO DOES HE THINK HE IS?

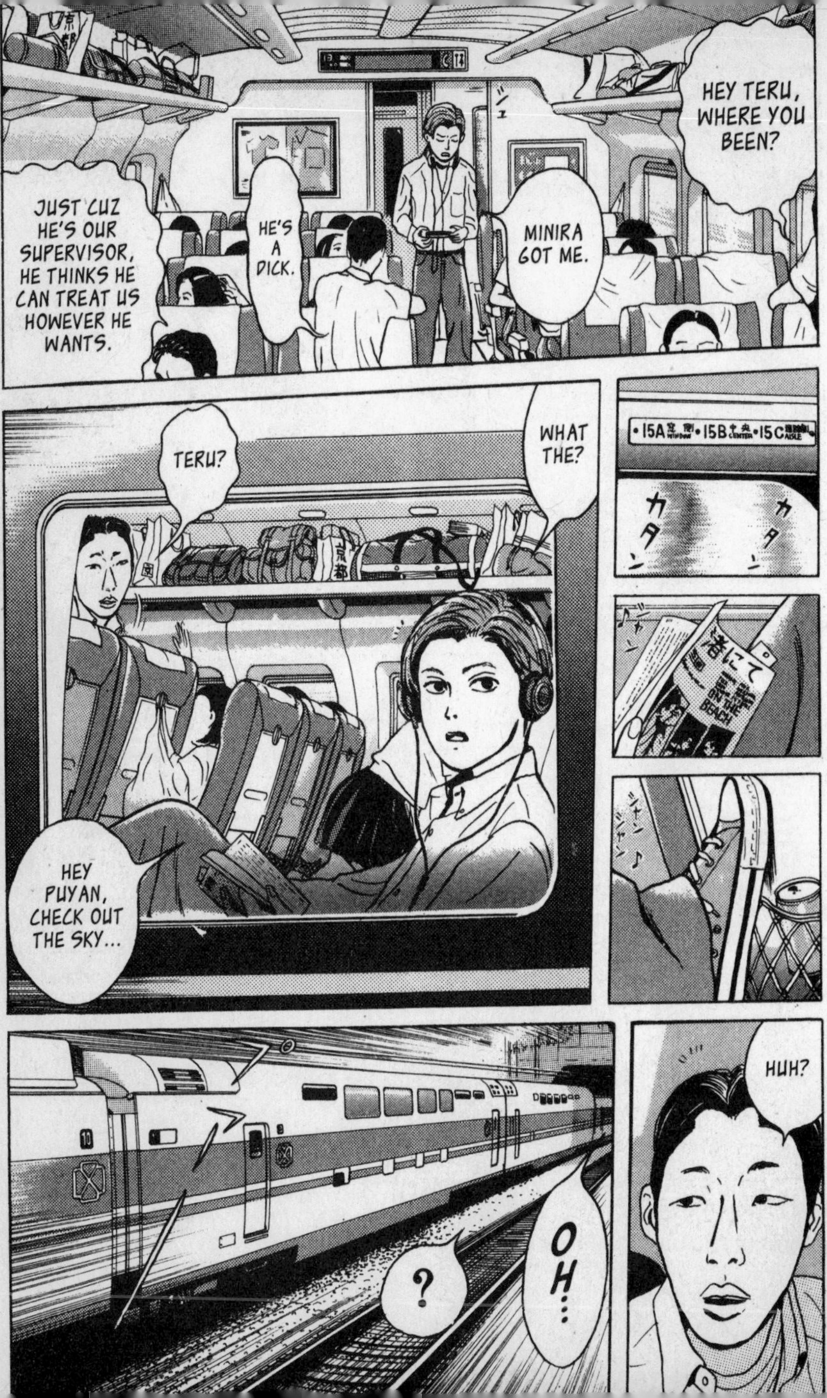
HEY TERU, WHERE YOU BEEN?
MINIRA GOT ME.
HE'S A DICK.
JUST CUZ HE'S OUR SUPERVISOR, HE THINKS HE CAN TREAT US HOWEVER HE WANTS.
•15A WINDOW •15B CENTER •15C AISLE
カタン
カタン
渚にて
BEACH
シャン
シャン
WHAT THE?
TERU?
HEY PUYAN, CHECK OUT THE SKY...
HUH?
OH...
?

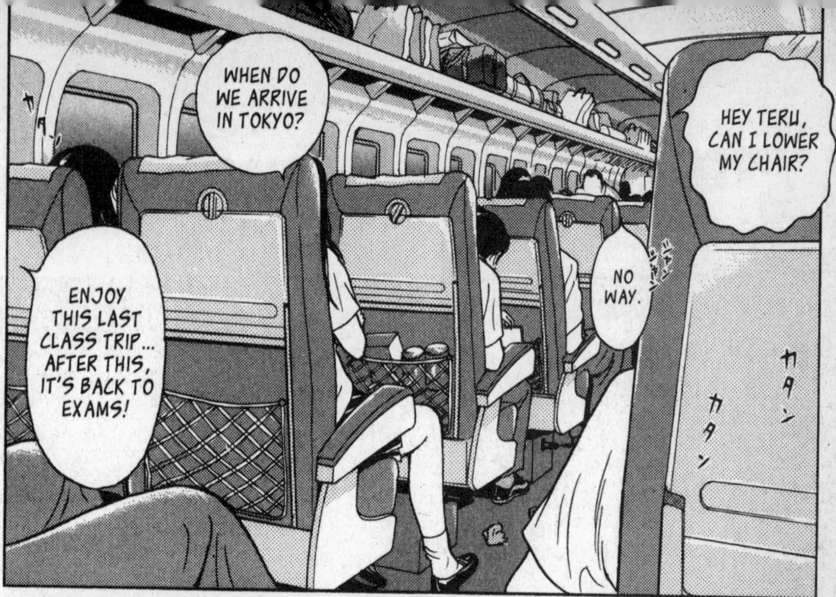
HEY TERU, CAN I LOWER MY CHAIR?
WHEN DO WE ARRIVE IN TOKYO?
NO WAY.
カタン
カタン
ENJOY THIS LAST CLASS TRIP... AFTER THIS, IT'S BACK TO EXAMS!
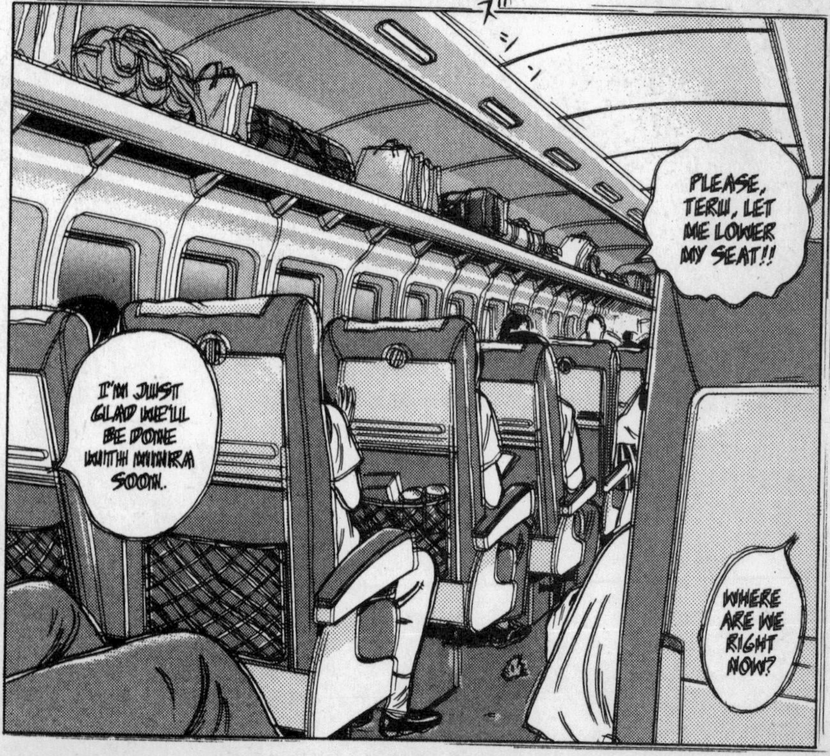
PLEASE, TERU, LET ME LOWER MY SEAT!!
I'M JUST GLAD WE'LL BE DONE WITH MIURA SOON.
WHERE ARE WE RIGHT NOW?

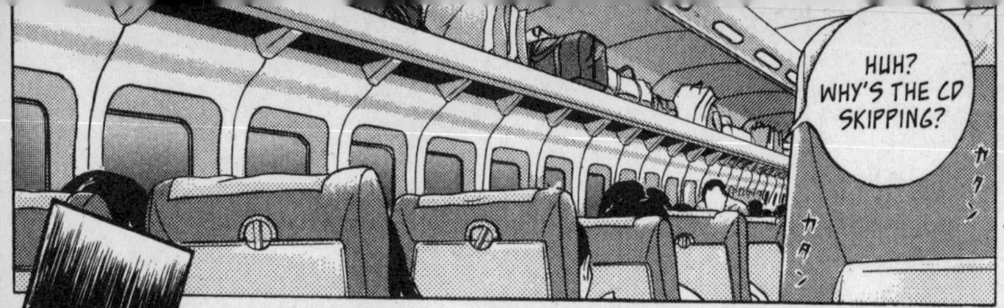
HUH? WHY'S THE CD SKIPPING?
カタン
カタン
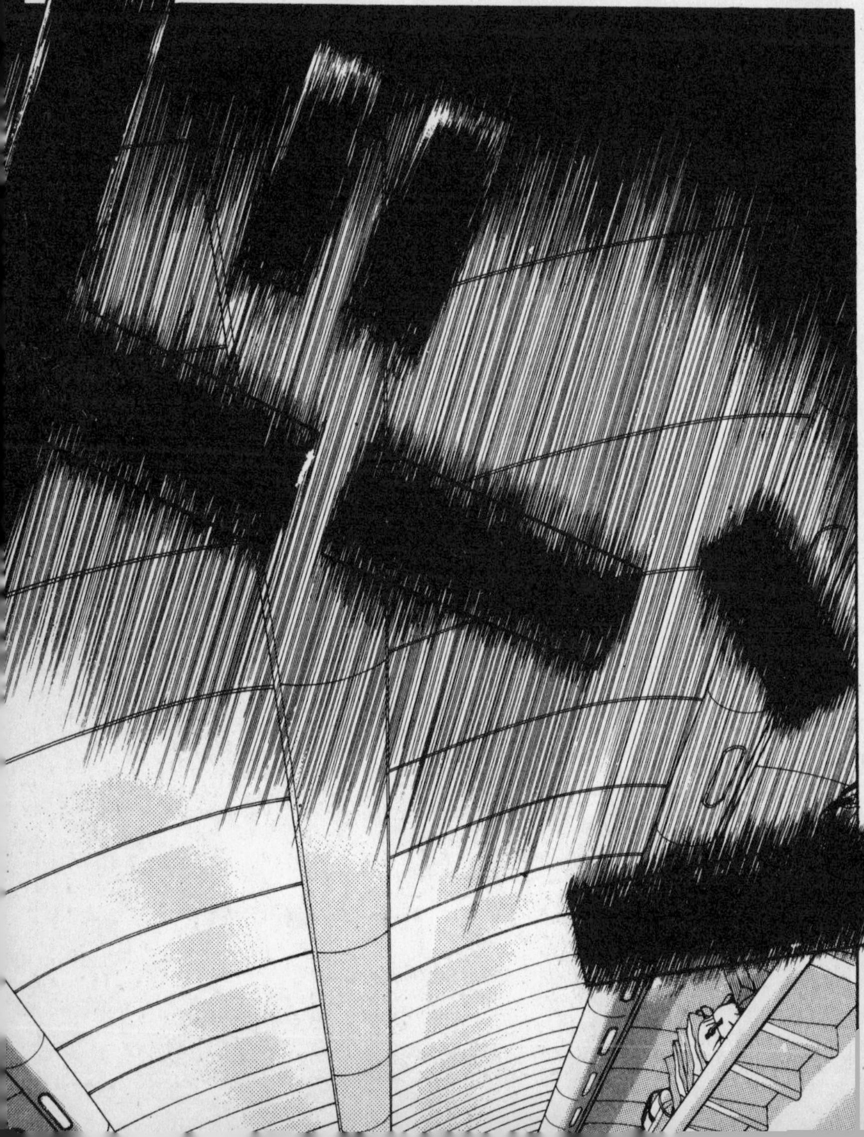

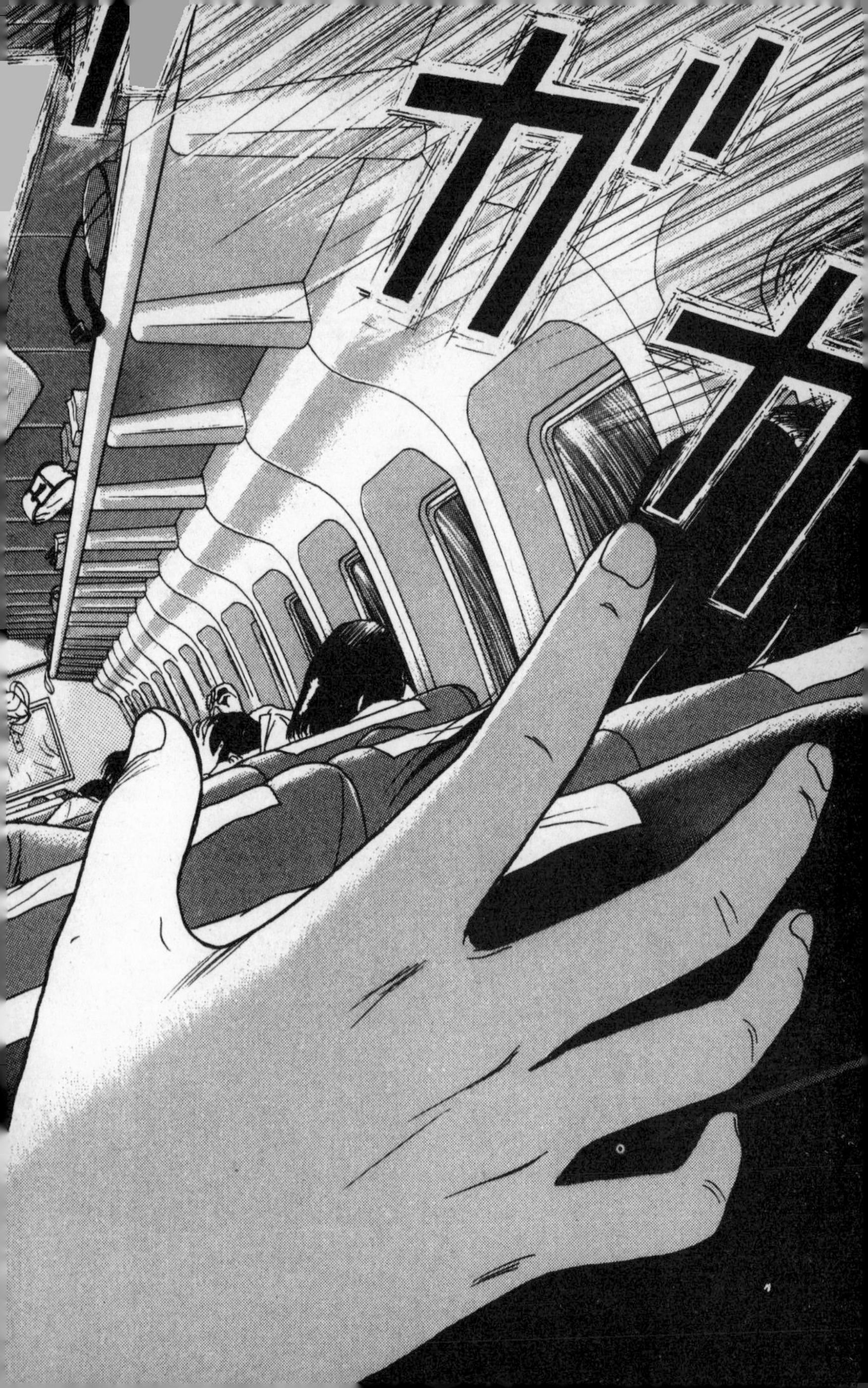
ガ

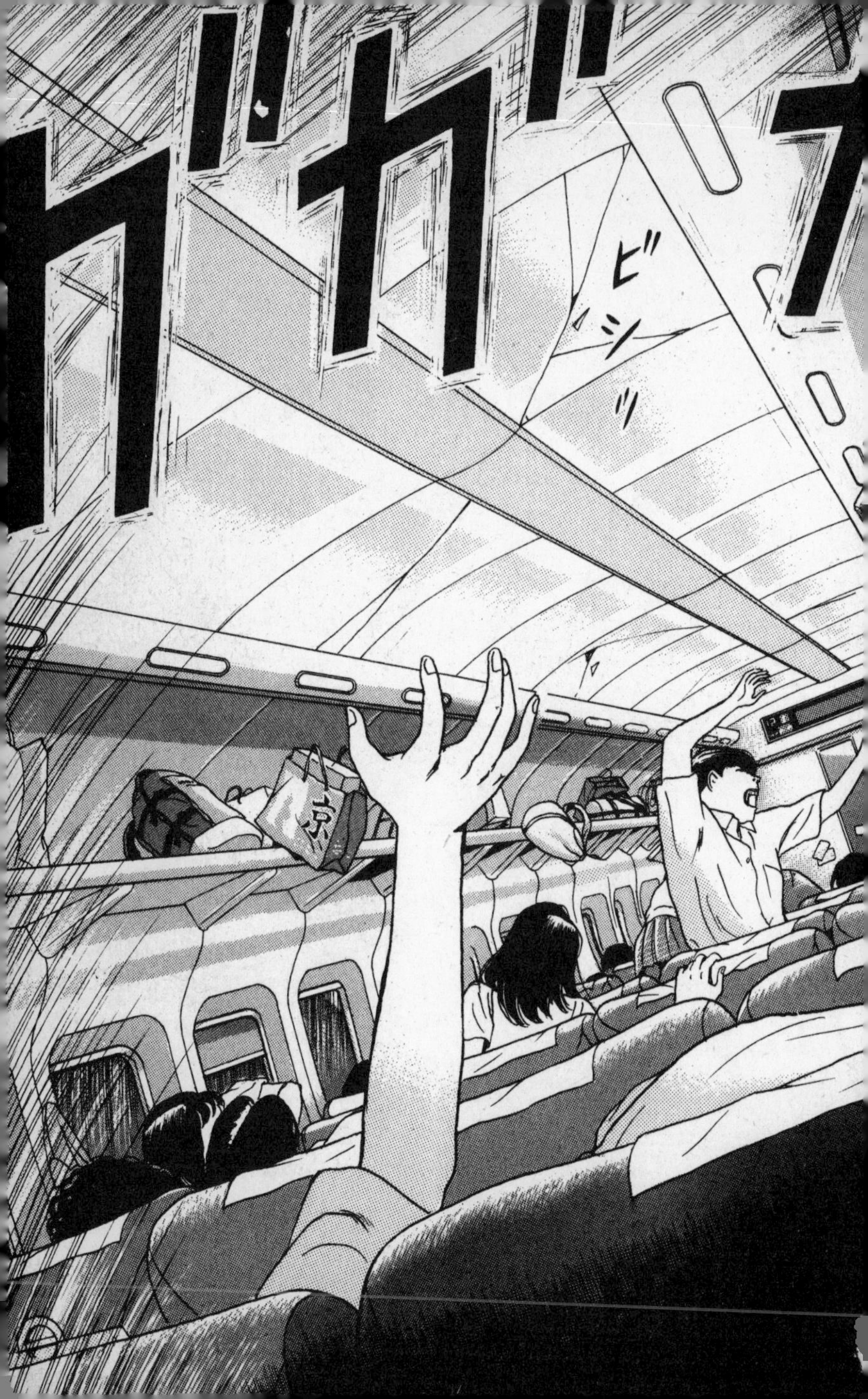
ガガ
ビシッ

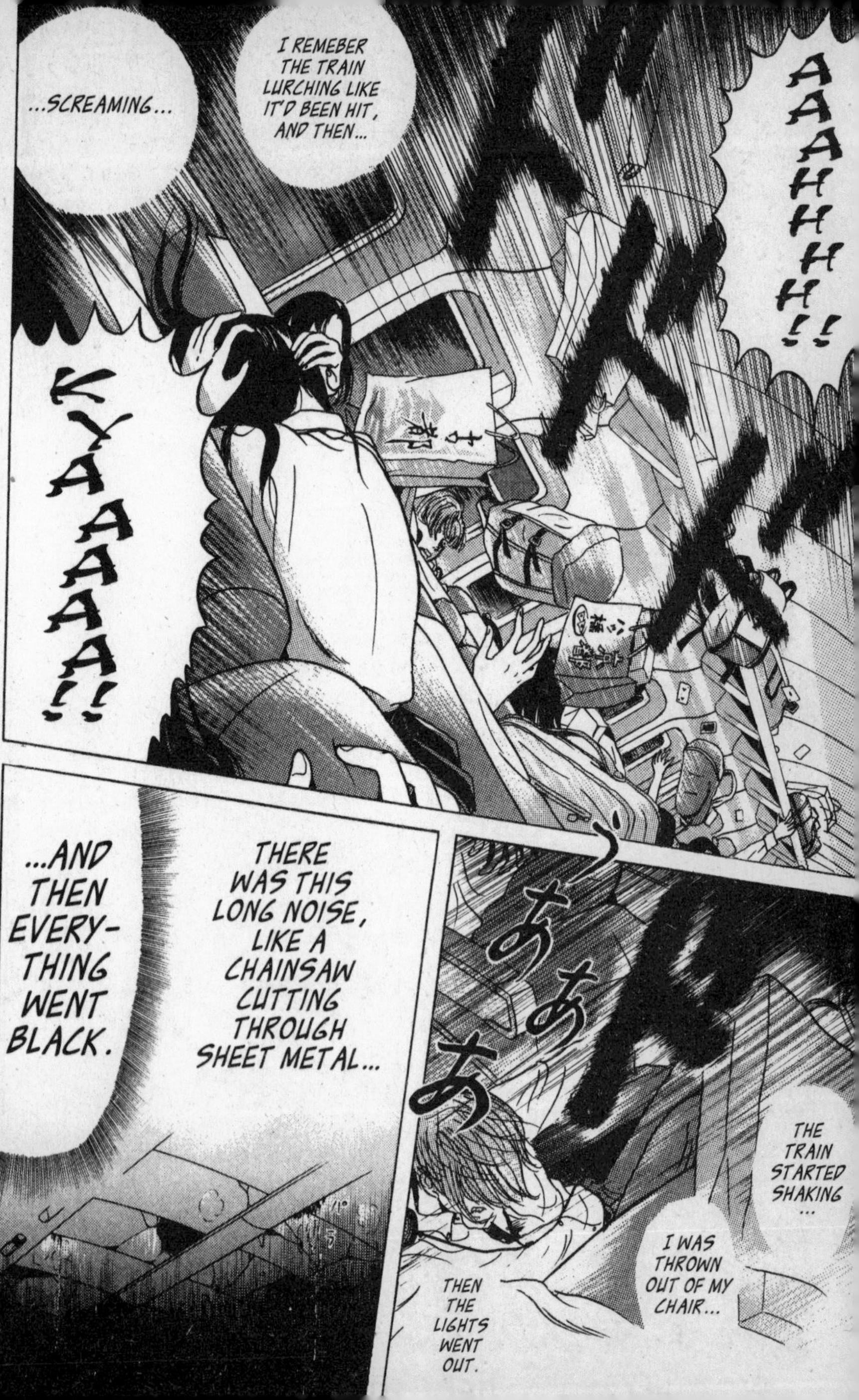
AAAAHHHHH!!
I REMEBER THE TRAIN LURCHING LIKE IT'D BEEN HIT, AND THEN...
...SCREAMING...
KYAAAAAA!!
THE TRAIN STARTED SHAKING...
I WAS THROWN OUT OF MY CHAIR...
うあああ
THEN THE LIGHTS WENT OUT.
THERE WAS THIS LONG NOISE, LIKE A CHAINSAW CUTTING THROUGH SHEET METAL...
...AND THEN EVERY-THING WENT BLACK.

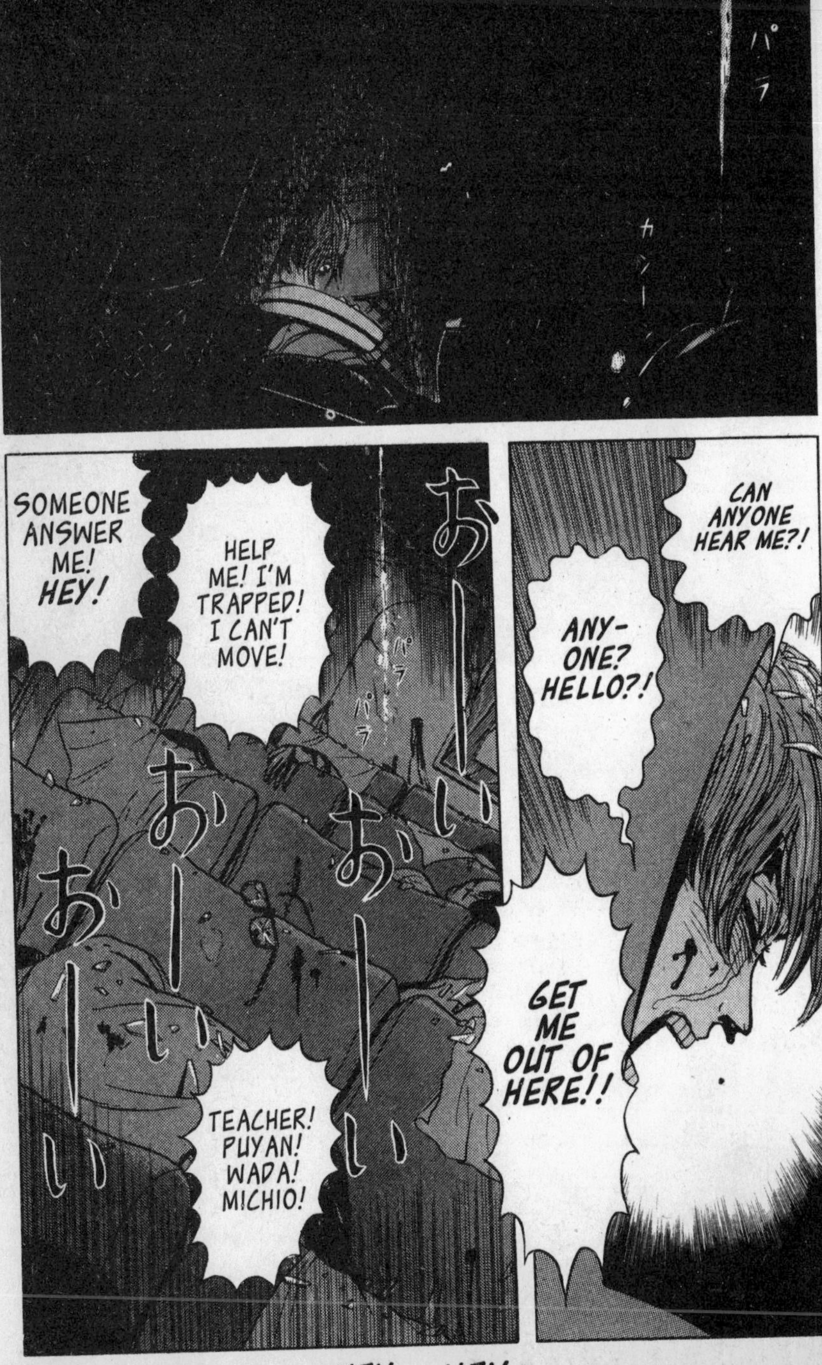
CAN ANYONE HEAR ME?!
ANY-ONE? HELLO?!
GET ME OUT OF HERE!!
おーい
おーい
HELP ME! I'M TRAPPED! I CAN'T MOVE!
SOMEONE ANSWER ME! HEY!
おーい
TEACHER! PUYAN! WADA! MICHIO!

HEY HEY HEY HEY

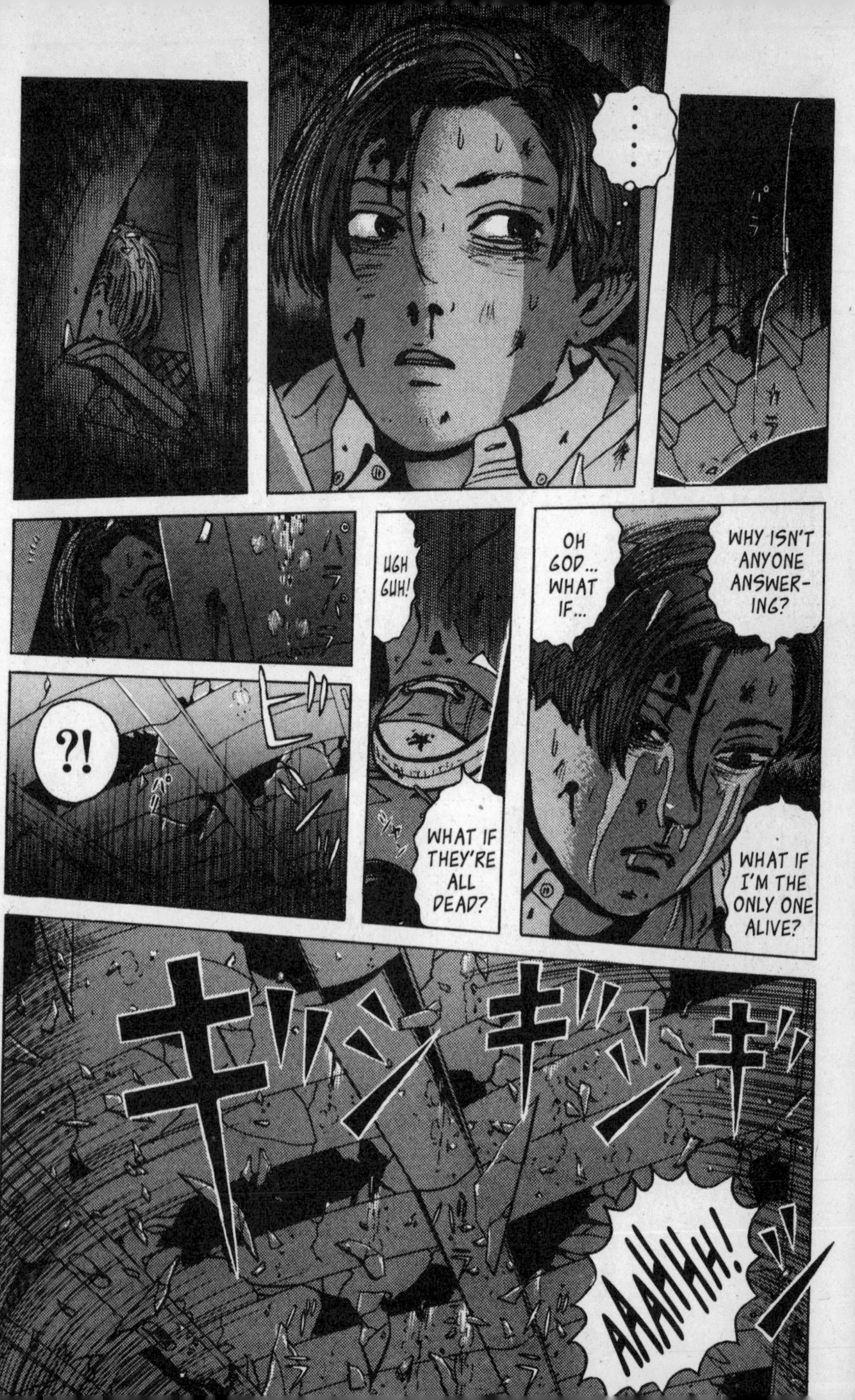
....
WHY ISN'T ANYONE ANSWERING?
OH GOD... WHAT IF...
UGH GUH!
WHAT IF THEY'RE ALL DEAD?
WHAT IF I'M THE ONLY ONE ALIVE?
?!
AAAHHH!

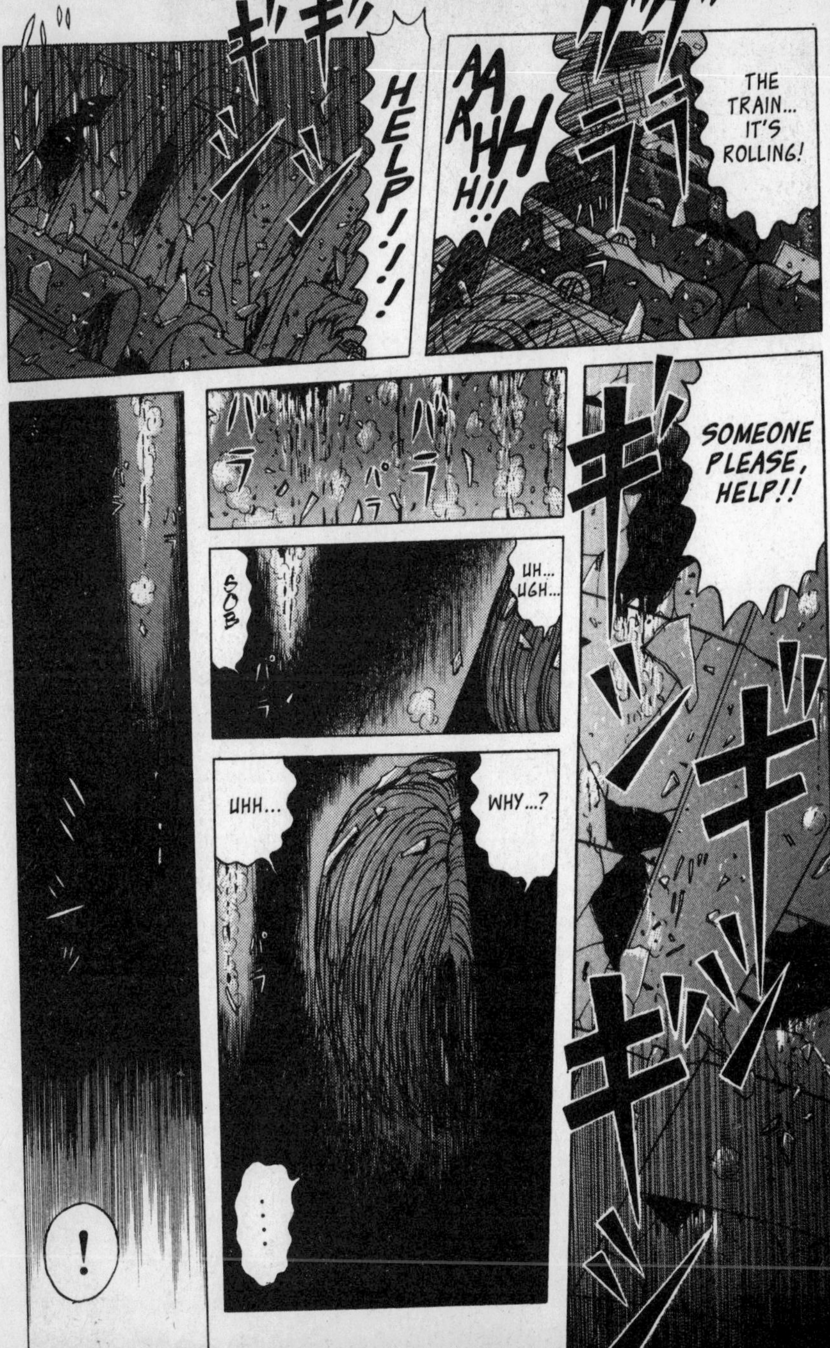
THE TRAIN... IT'S ROLLING!
AAAHHH!!
HELP!!!!
SOMEONE PLEASE, HELP!!
UH... UGH...
SOB
WHY...?
UHH...
....
!

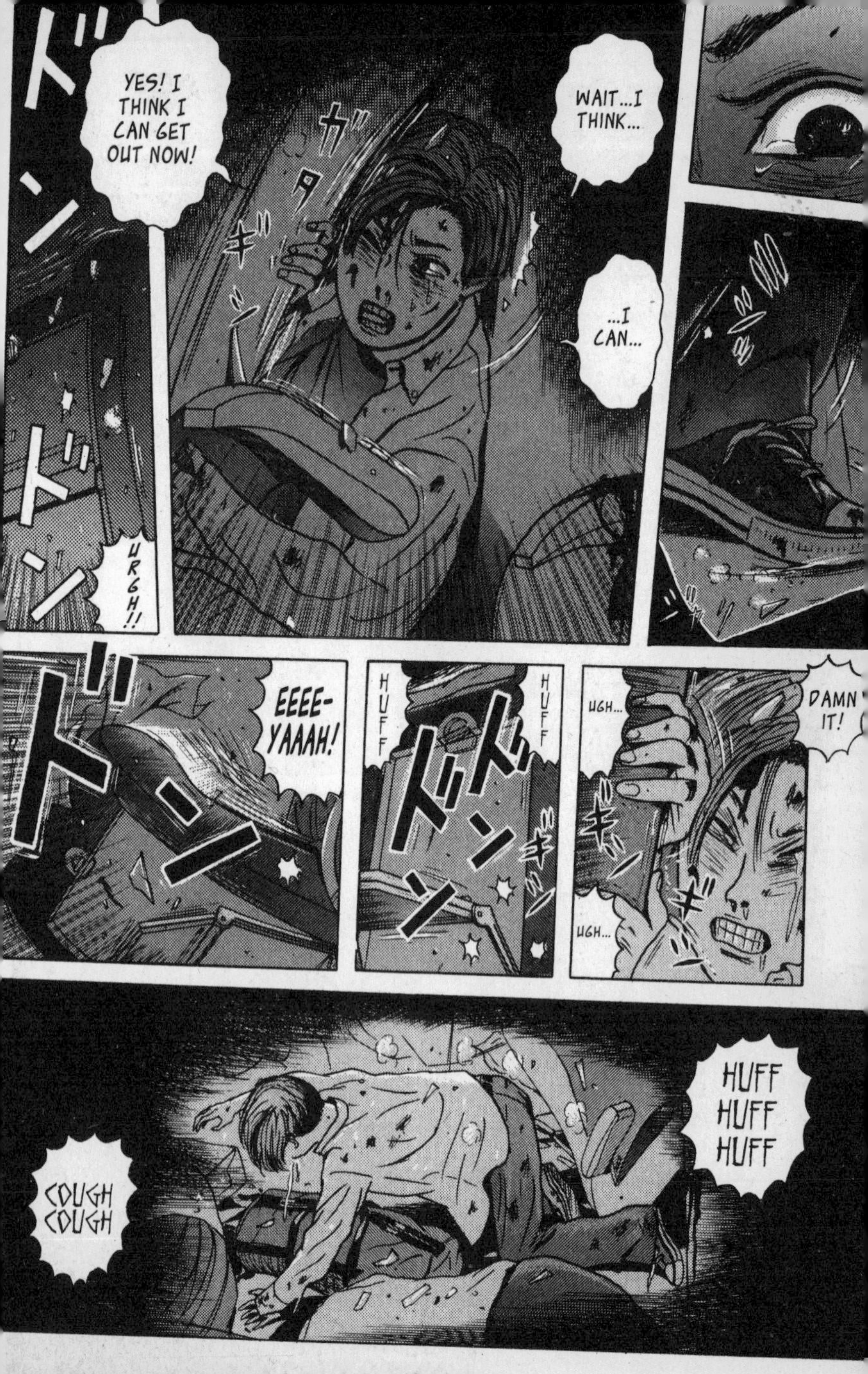
WAIT...I THINK...
...I CAN...
YES! I THINK I CAN GET OUT NOW!
URGH!!
DAMN IT!
UGH...
UGH...
HUFF
HUFF
EEEE-YAAAH!
HUFF HUFF HUFF
COUGH COUGH

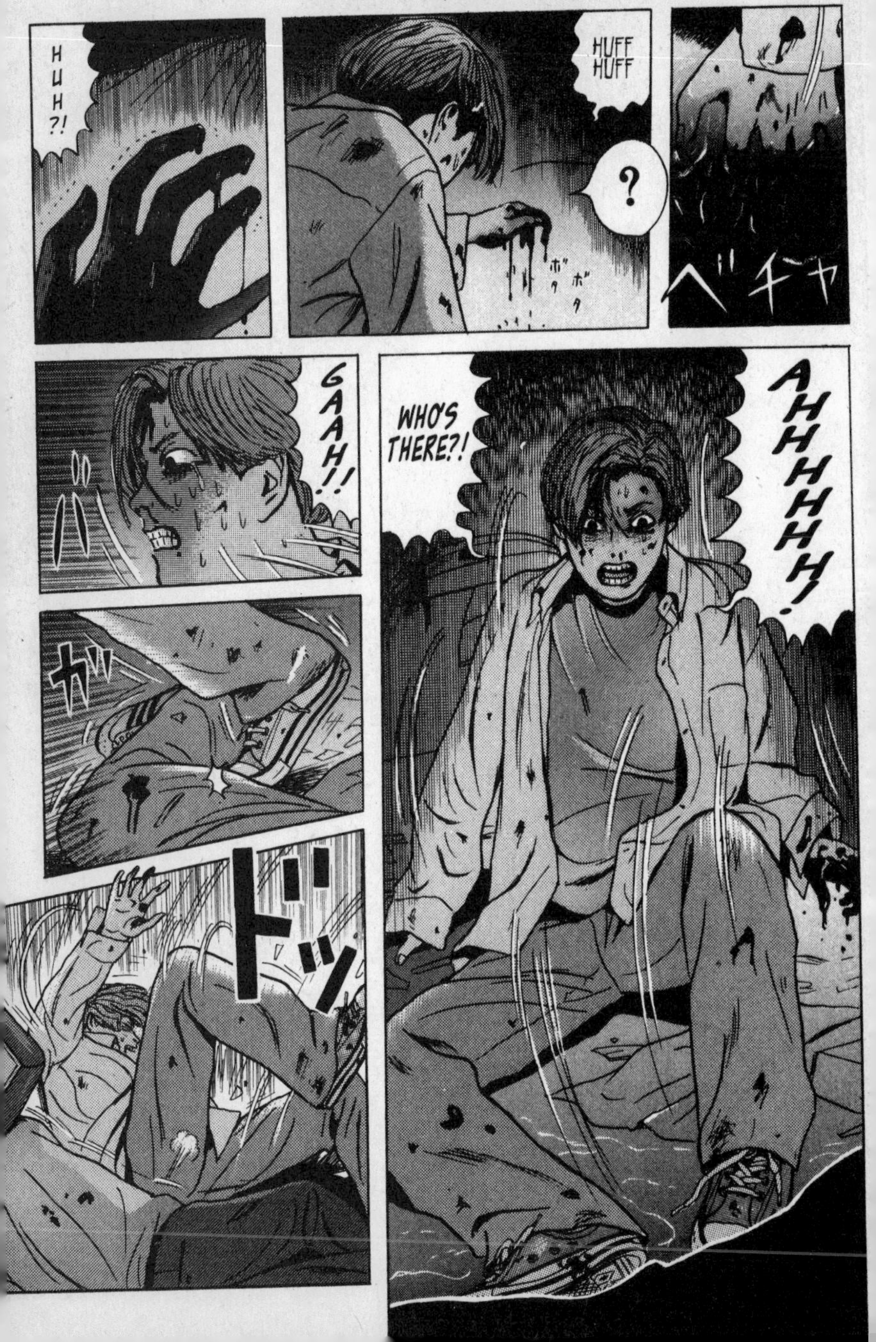

ベチャ
HUFF HUFF
?
ボタ ボタ
HUUH?!
AHHHHHHH!
WHO'S THERE?!
GAAAH!!
ガッ
ドッ

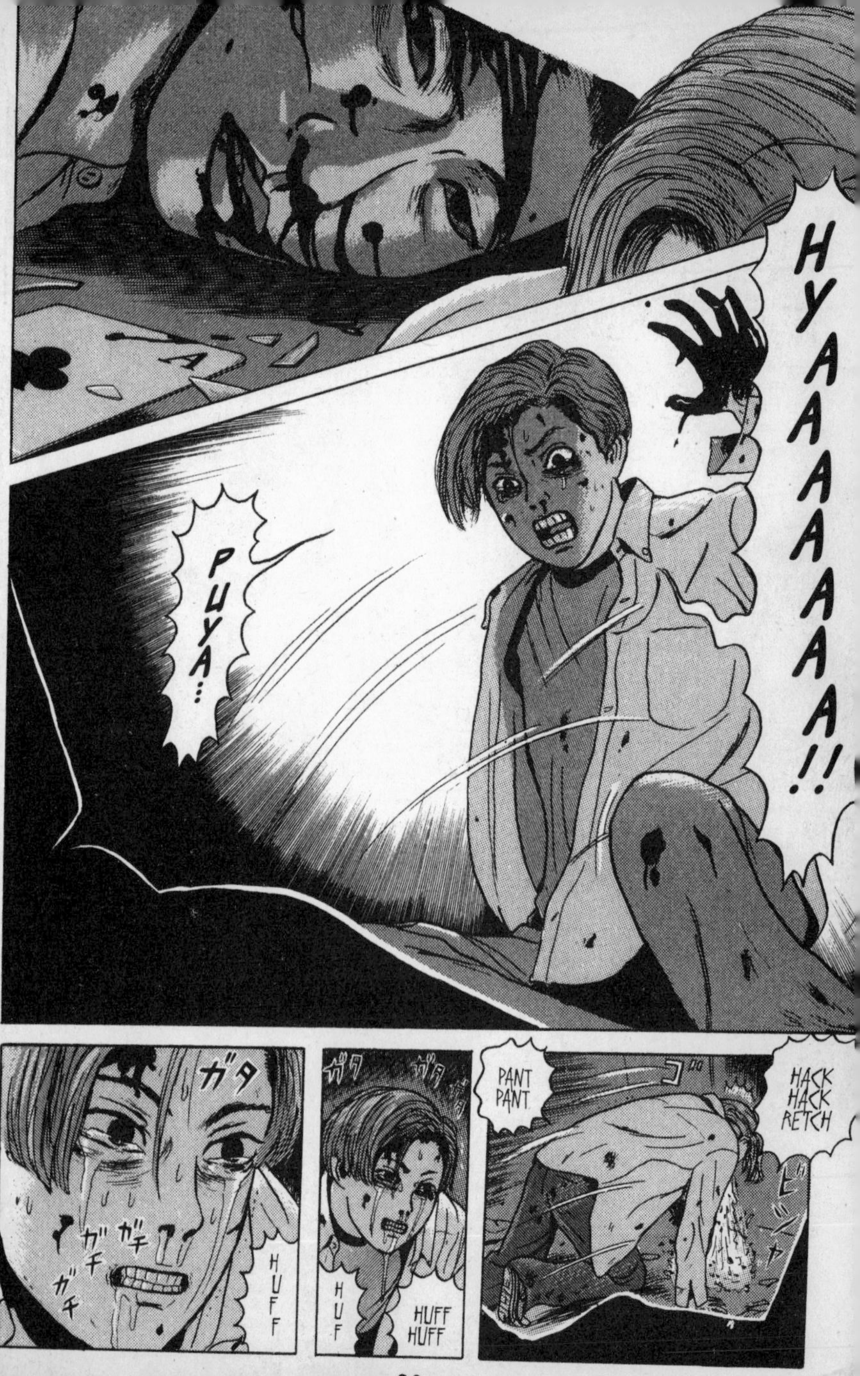
HYAAAAAAA!!
PUYA...
HACK
HACK
RETCH
PANT
PANT.
ガタ ガタ
HUFF
HUFF
HUF
ガタ
ガチ ガチ
ガチ ガチ
HUFF

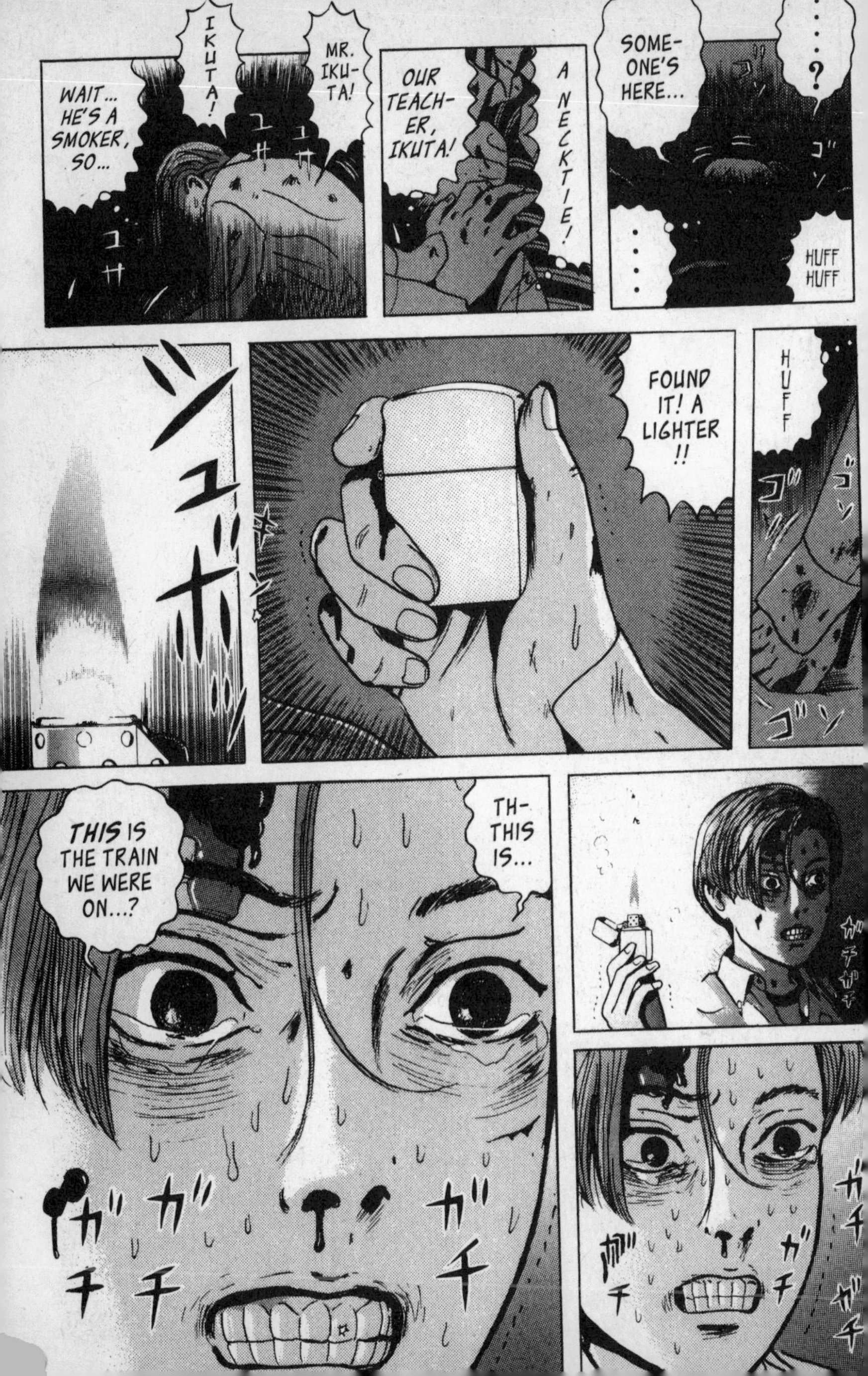
...?
SOME-ONE'S HERE...
...
HUFF HUFF
A NECKTIE!
MR. IKUTA!
OUR TEACHER, IKUTA!
IKUTA!
WAIT... HE'S A SMOKER, SO...
HUFF
FOUND IT! A LIGHTER!!
TH-THIS IS...
THIS IS THE TRAIN WE WERE ON...?

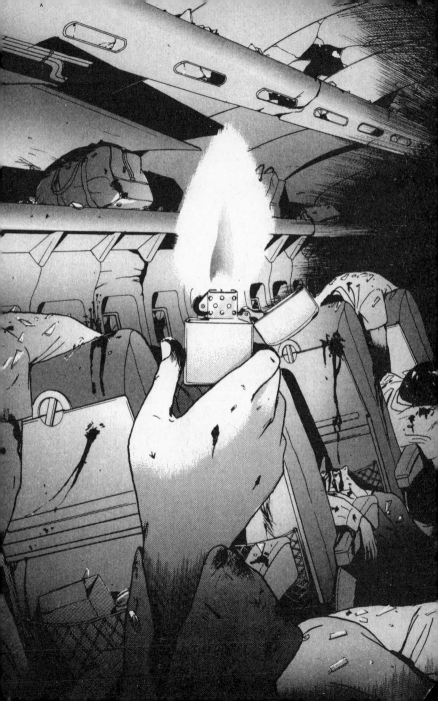

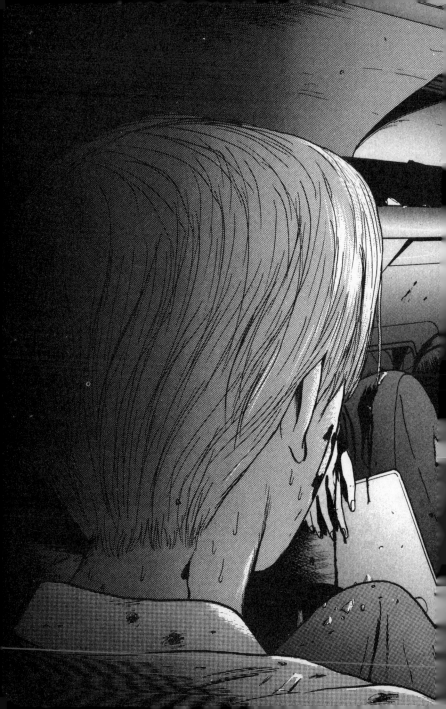

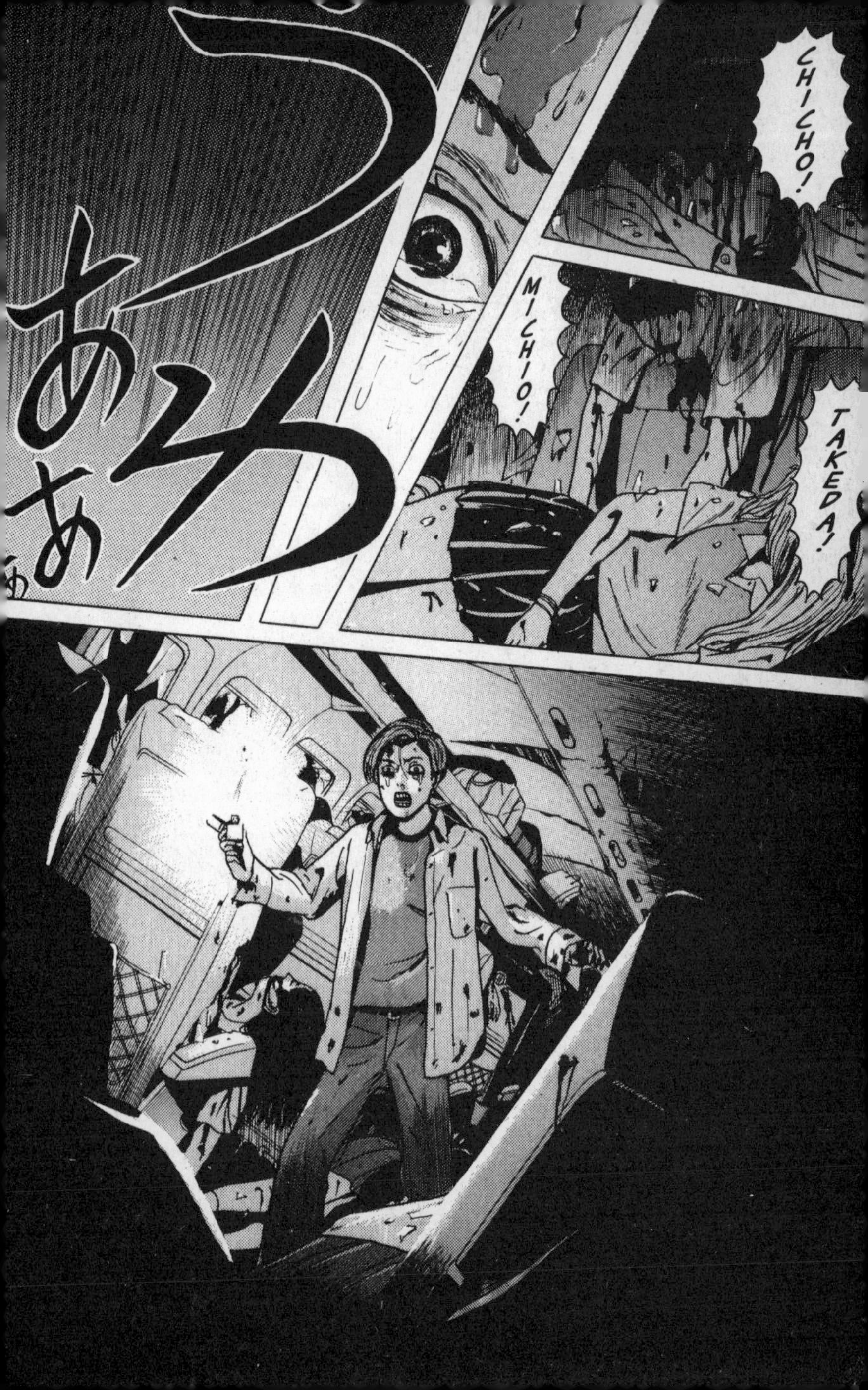
CHICHO!
TAKEDA!
MICHIO!

WE WERE
ON OUR WAY
HOME FROM THE
LAST SCHOOL TRIP
OF THE YEAR. IT
WAS SUPPOSED
TO BE FUN.

INSTEAD...

...IT WAS THE
BEGINNING OF
A NIGHTMARE
THAT JUST
YESTERDAY,
I COULD
HAVE NEVER
IMAGINED.

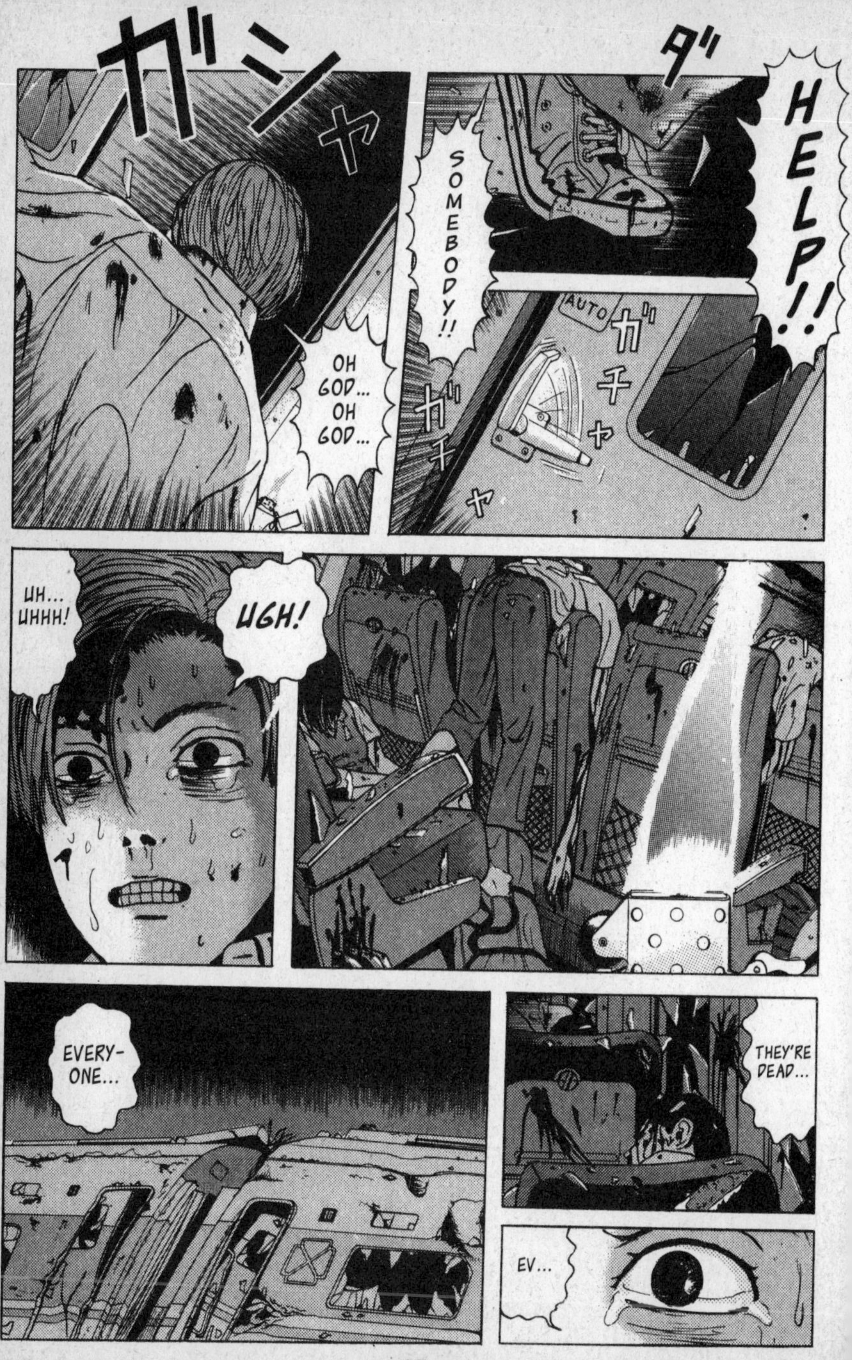
ガシャ
OH GOD... OH GOD...
ダ
SOMEBODY!!
HELP!!
AUTO
ガチャ
ガチャ
UH... UHHH!
UGH!
EVERY-ONE...
THEY'RE DEAD...
EV...

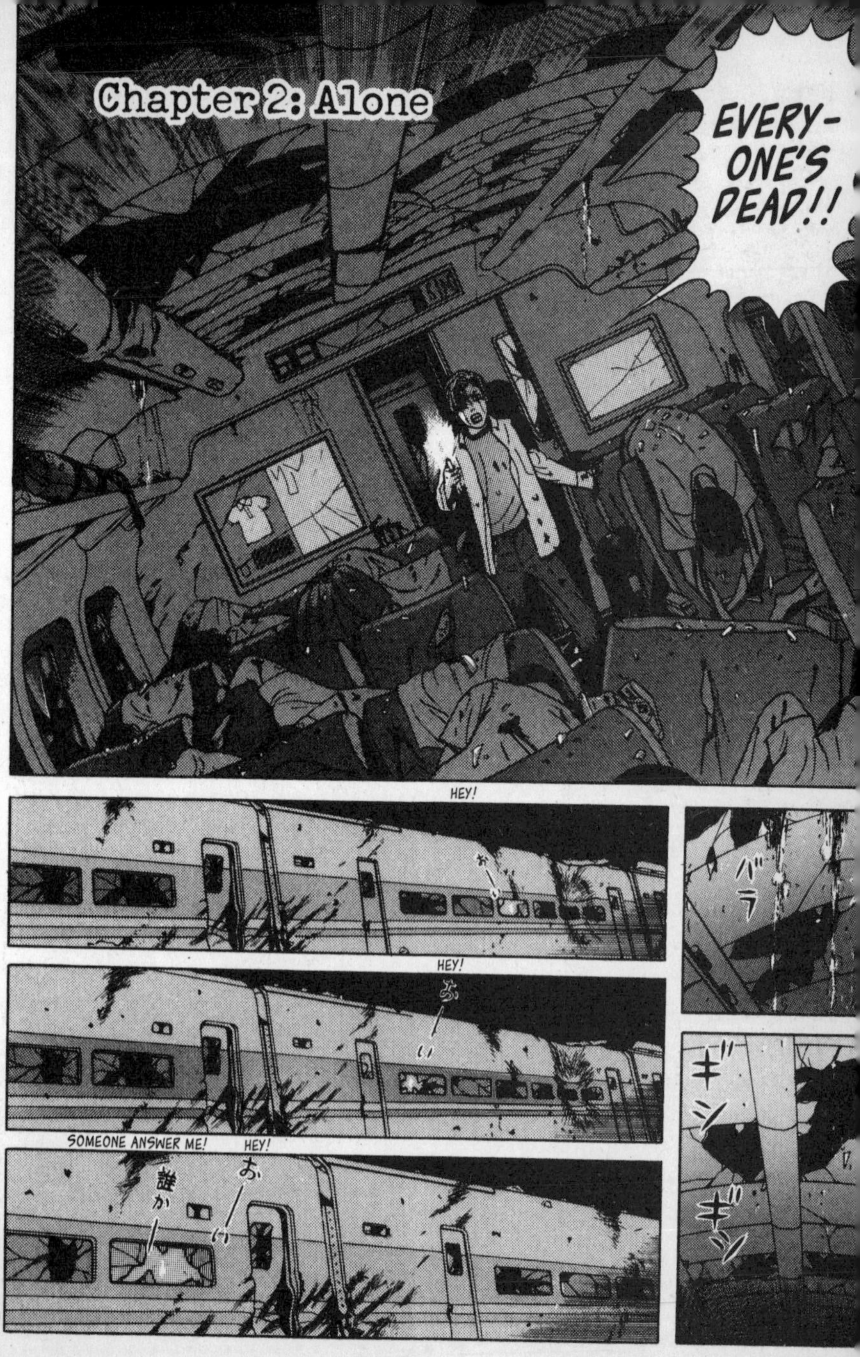
Chapter 2: Alone
EVERY-ONE'S DEAD!!
バラ
HEY!
おーい
ギシ ギシ
HEY!
おーい
SOMEONE ANSWER ME!
誰かー
HEY!
おーい

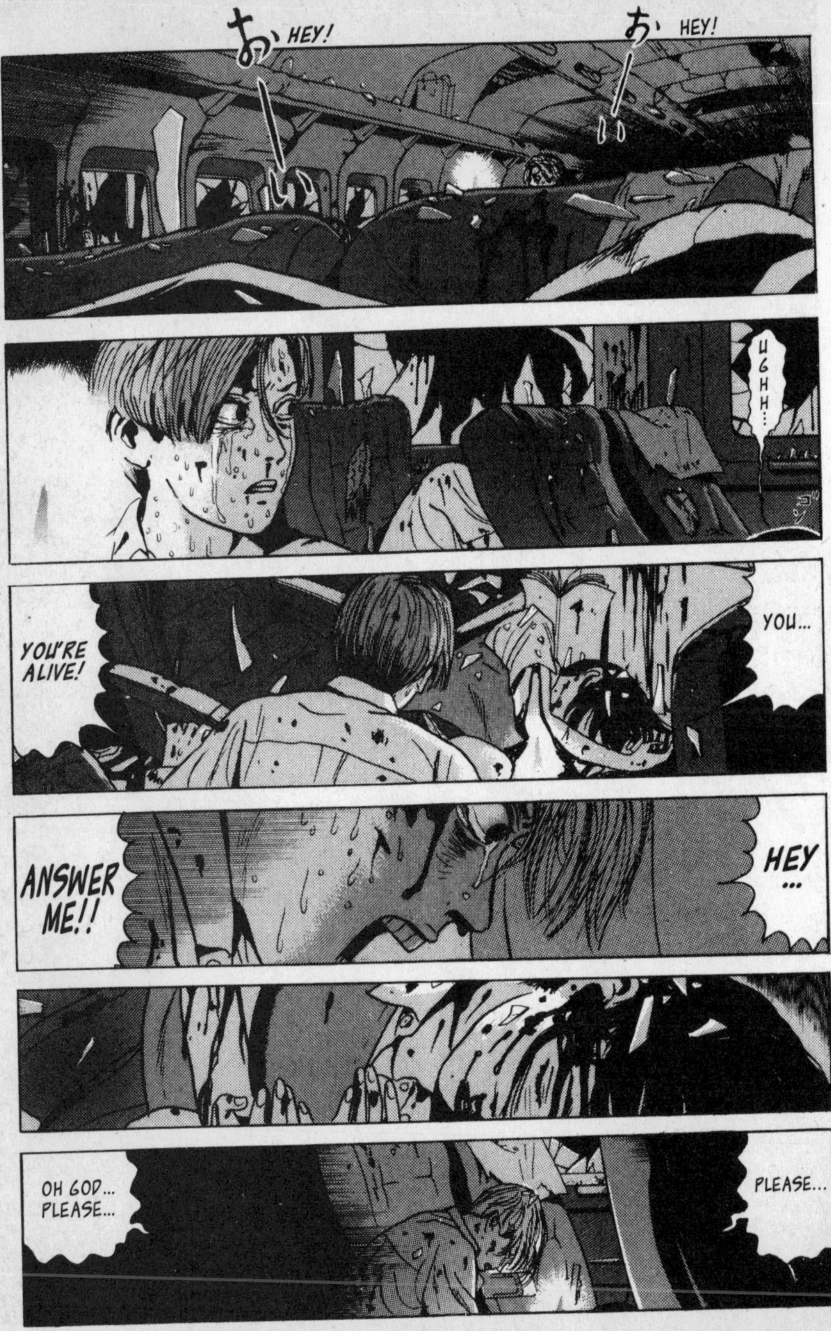
HEY!
HEY!
UGHH...
YOU...
YOU'RE ALIVE!
HEY ...
ANSWER ME!!
PLEASE...
OH GOD... PLEASE...

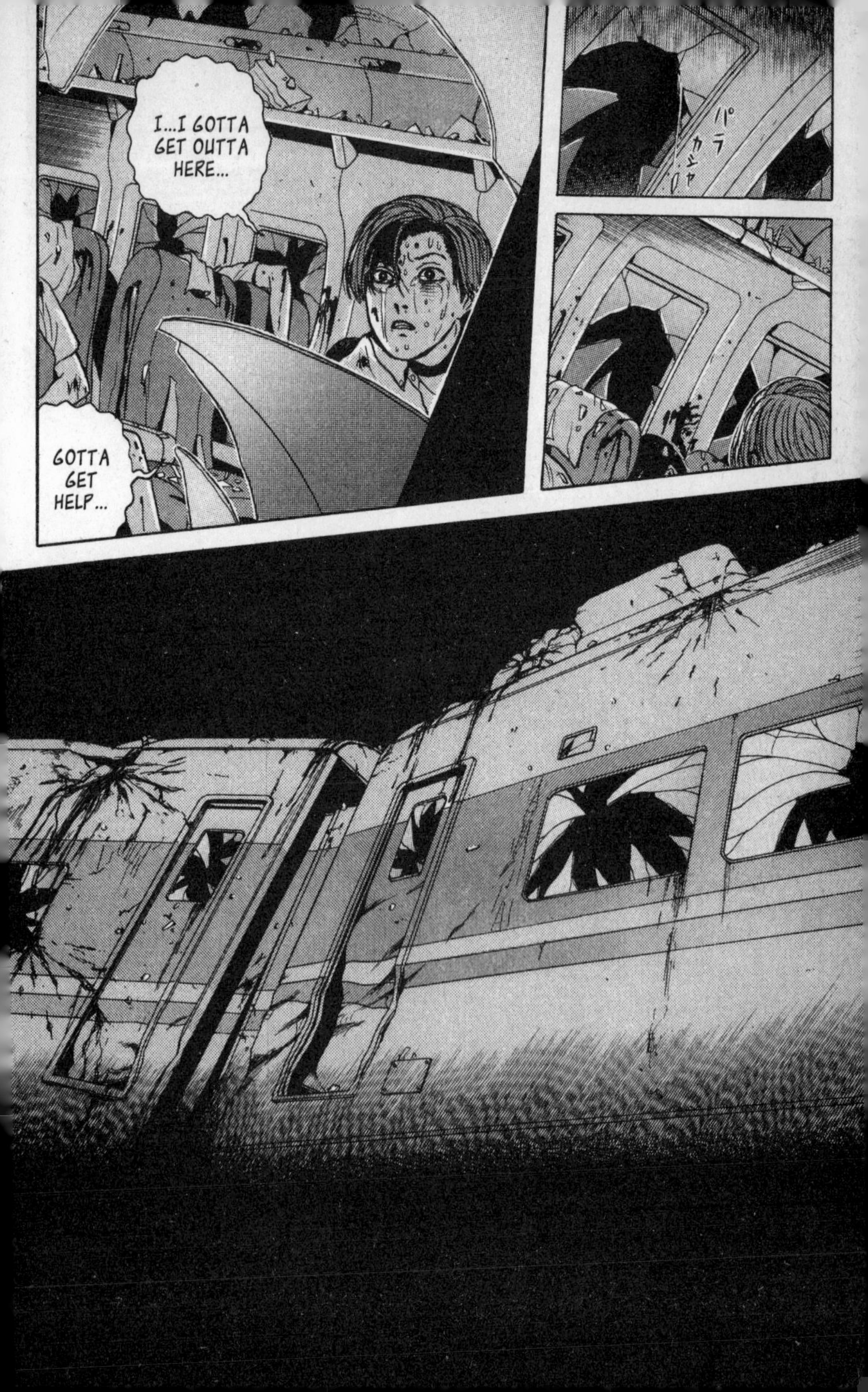
パラ
カシャ
I...I GOTTA GET OUTTA HERE...
GOTTA GET HELP...

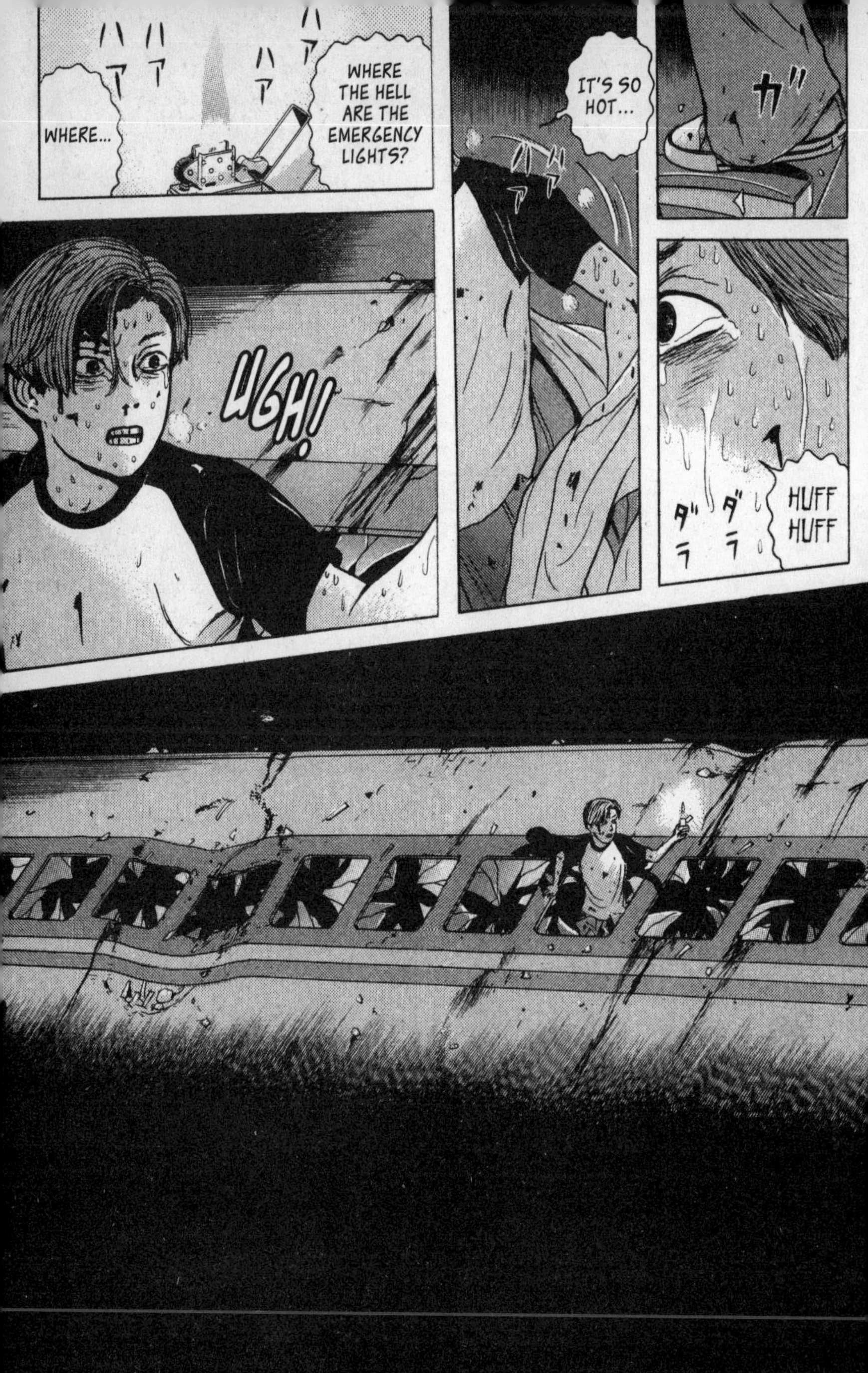
ガ
ダラ ダラ
HUFF HUFF
IT'S SO HOT...
ハァ ハァ
ハァ ハァ
WHERE THE HELL ARE THE EMERGENCY LIGHTS?
ハァ ハァ
WHERE...
UGH!

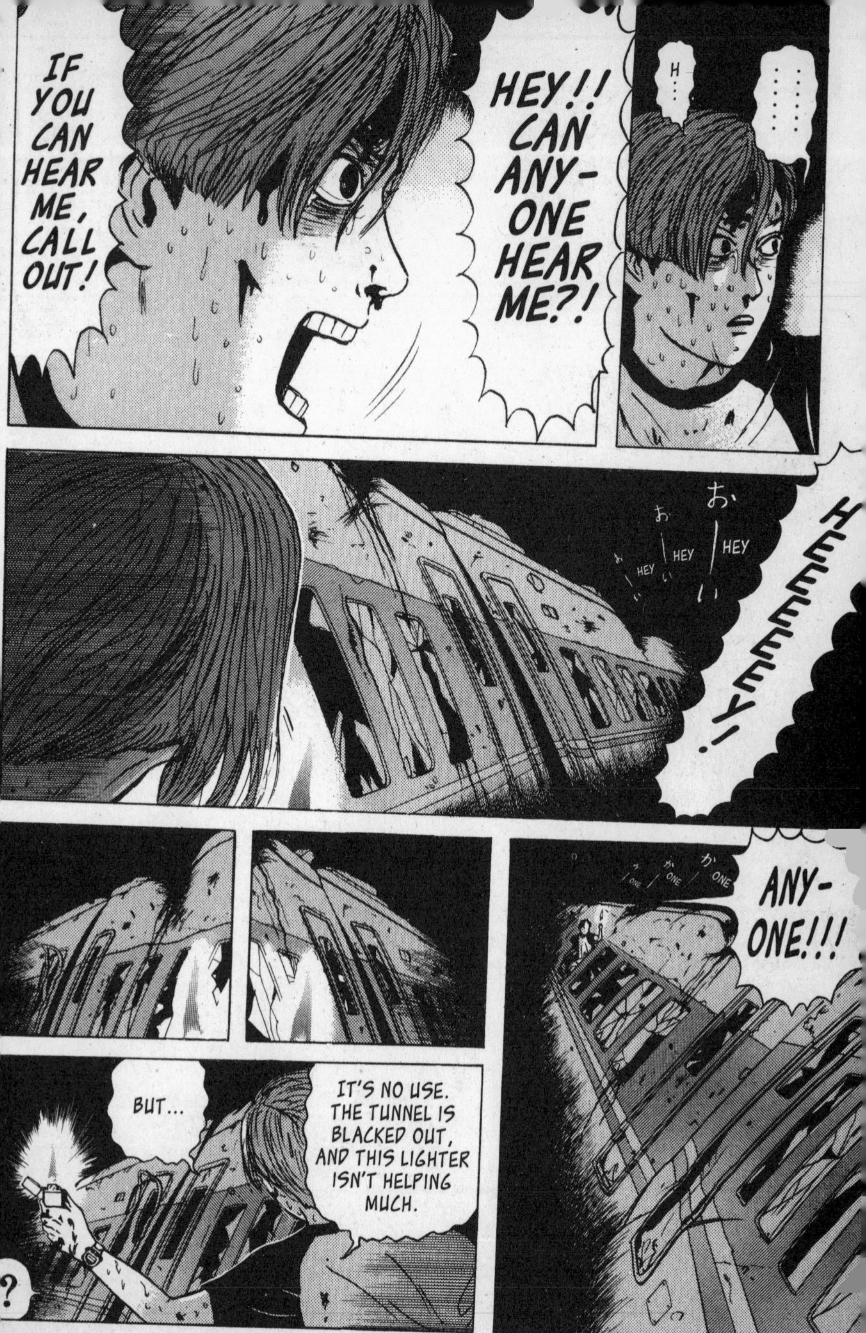
H...
......
HEY!! CAN ANY-ONE HEAR ME?!
IF YOU CAN HEAR ME, CALL OUT!
HEEEEEEY!
HEY
HEY
HEY
ANY-ONE!!!
ONE
ONE
ONE
IT'S NO USE. THE TUNNEL IS BLACKED OUT, AND THIS LIGHTER ISN'T HELPING MUCH.
BUT...
?

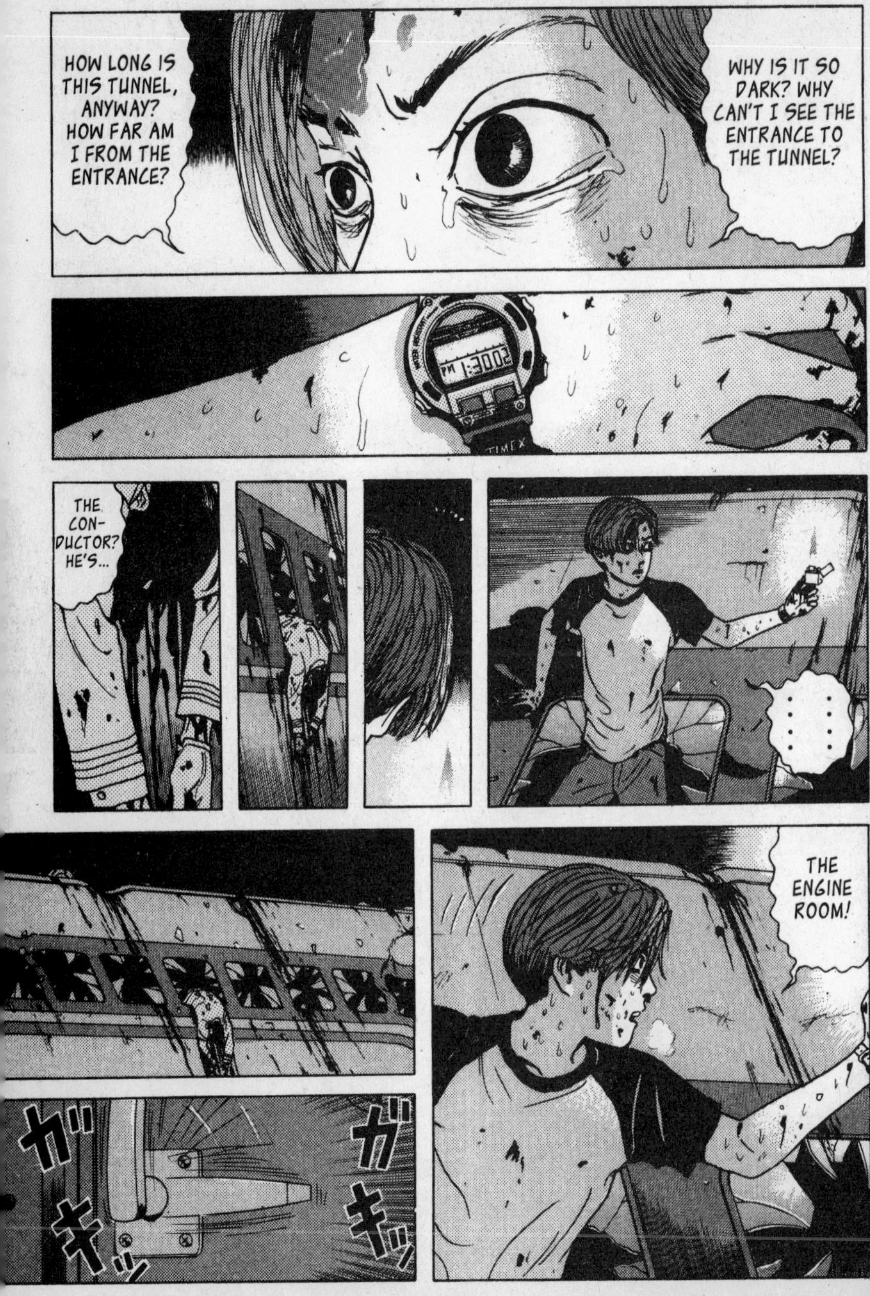
WHY IS IT SO DARK? WHY CAN'T I SEE THE ENTRANCE TO THE TUNNEL?
HOW LONG IS THIS TUNNEL, ANYWAY? HOW FAR AM I FROM THE ENTRANCE?
TIMEX
...
THE CONDUCTOR? HE'S...
THE ENGINE ROOM!
ガギッ
ガギッ

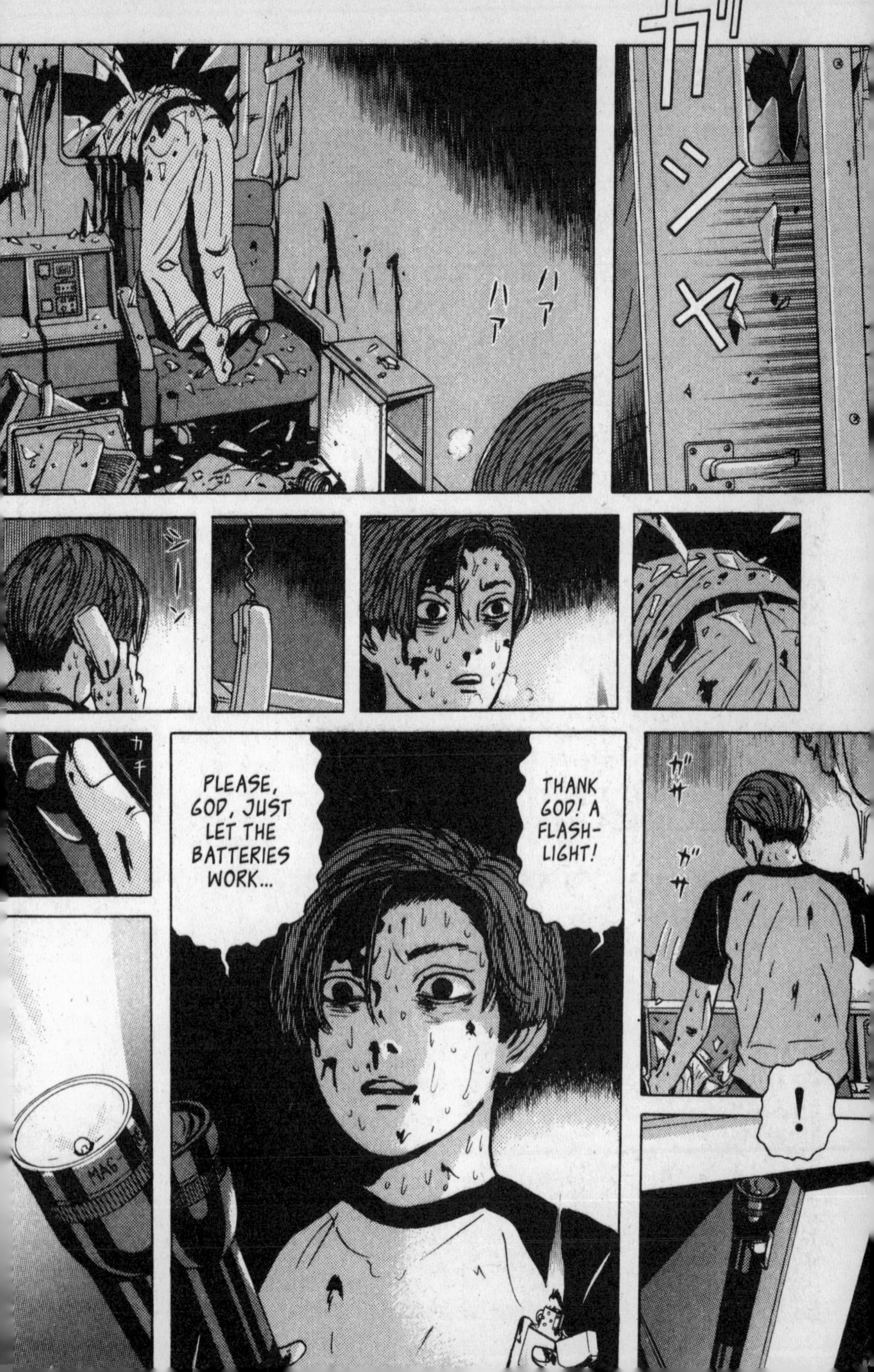
ガシャン
ハァ ハァ
ガサ ガサ
!
THANK GOD! A FLASH-LIGHT!
PLEASE, GOD, JUST LET THE BATTERIES WORK...
カチ

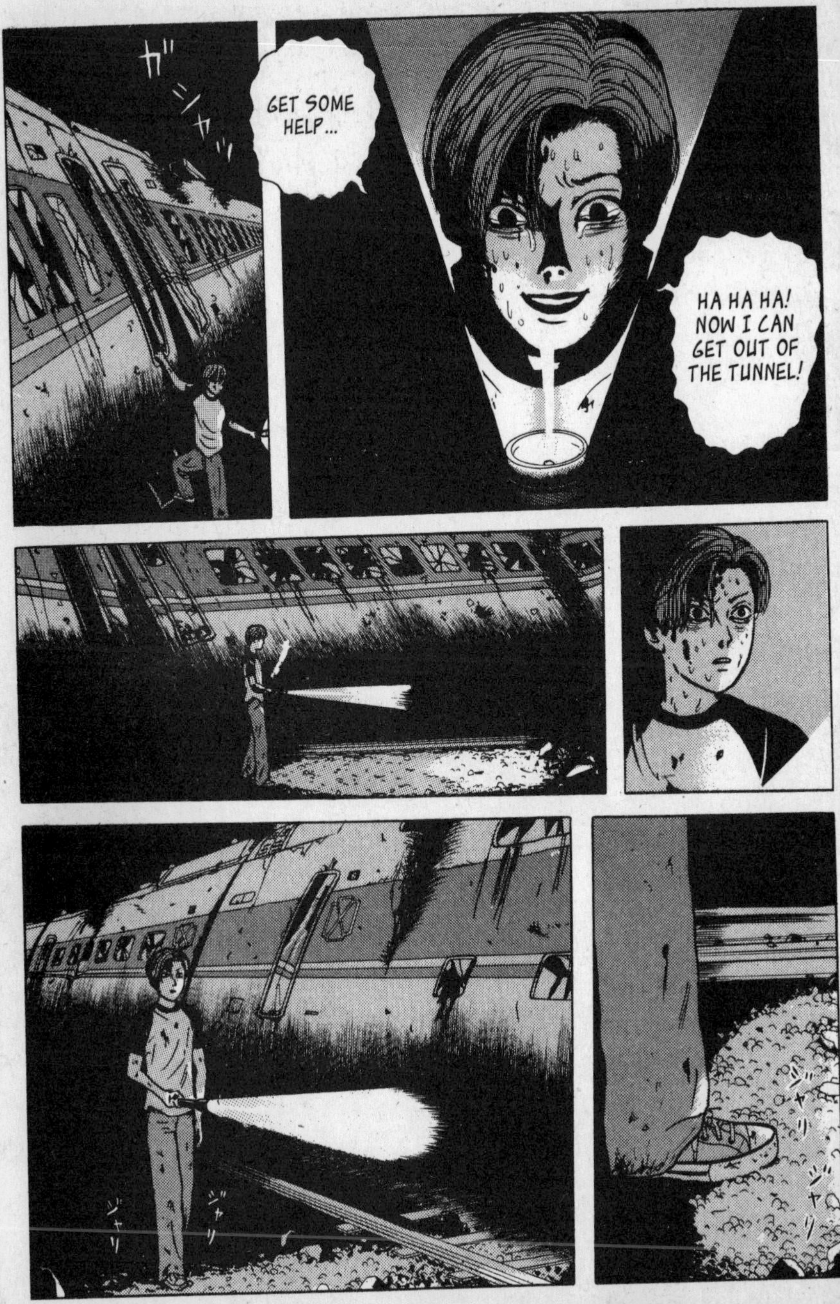
GET SOME HELP...
HA HA HA! NOW I CAN GET OUT OF THE TUNNEL!
ジャリ
ジャリ
ジャリ
ジャリ

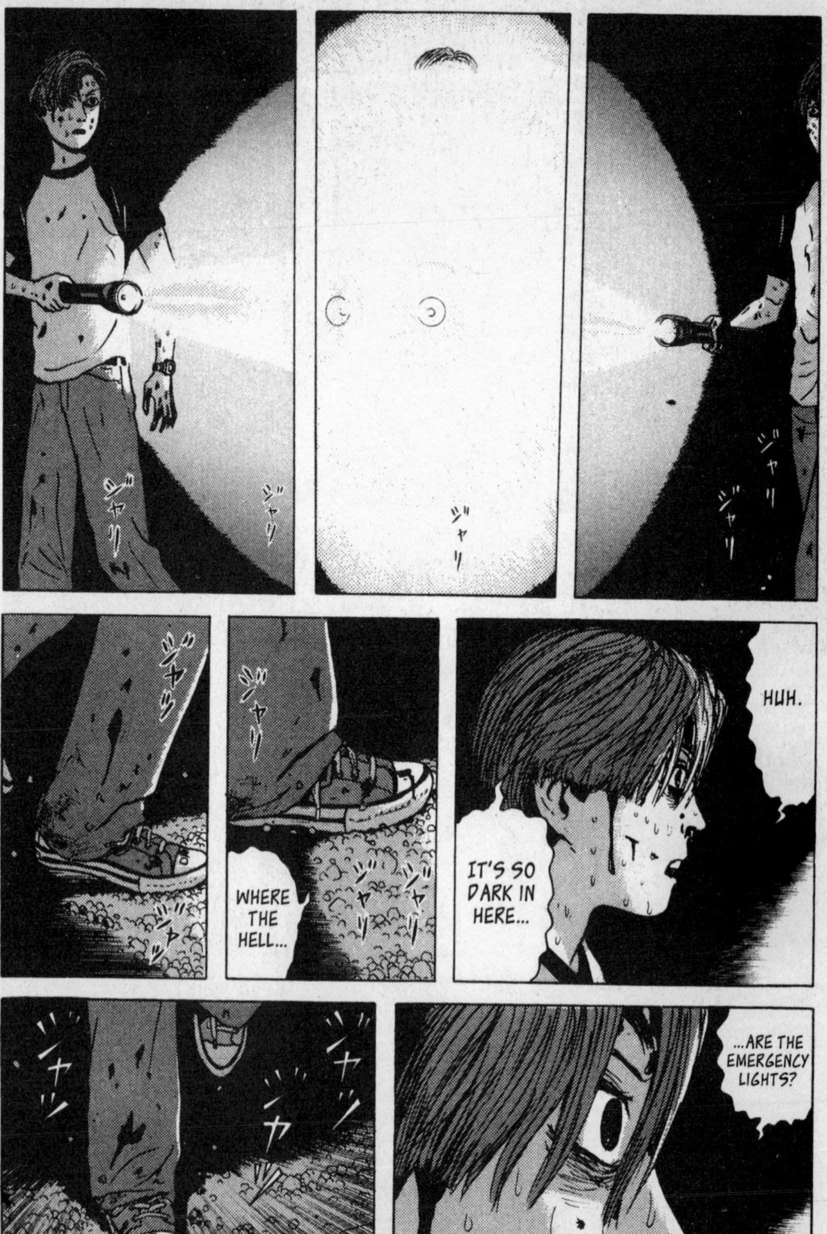
ジャリ
ジャリ
ジャリ
ジャリ
ジャリ
HUH.
IT'S SO DARK IN HERE...
ジャリ
WHERE THE HELL...
ジャリ
ジャリ
ジャッ
ジャッ
...ARE THE EMERGENCY LIGHTS?

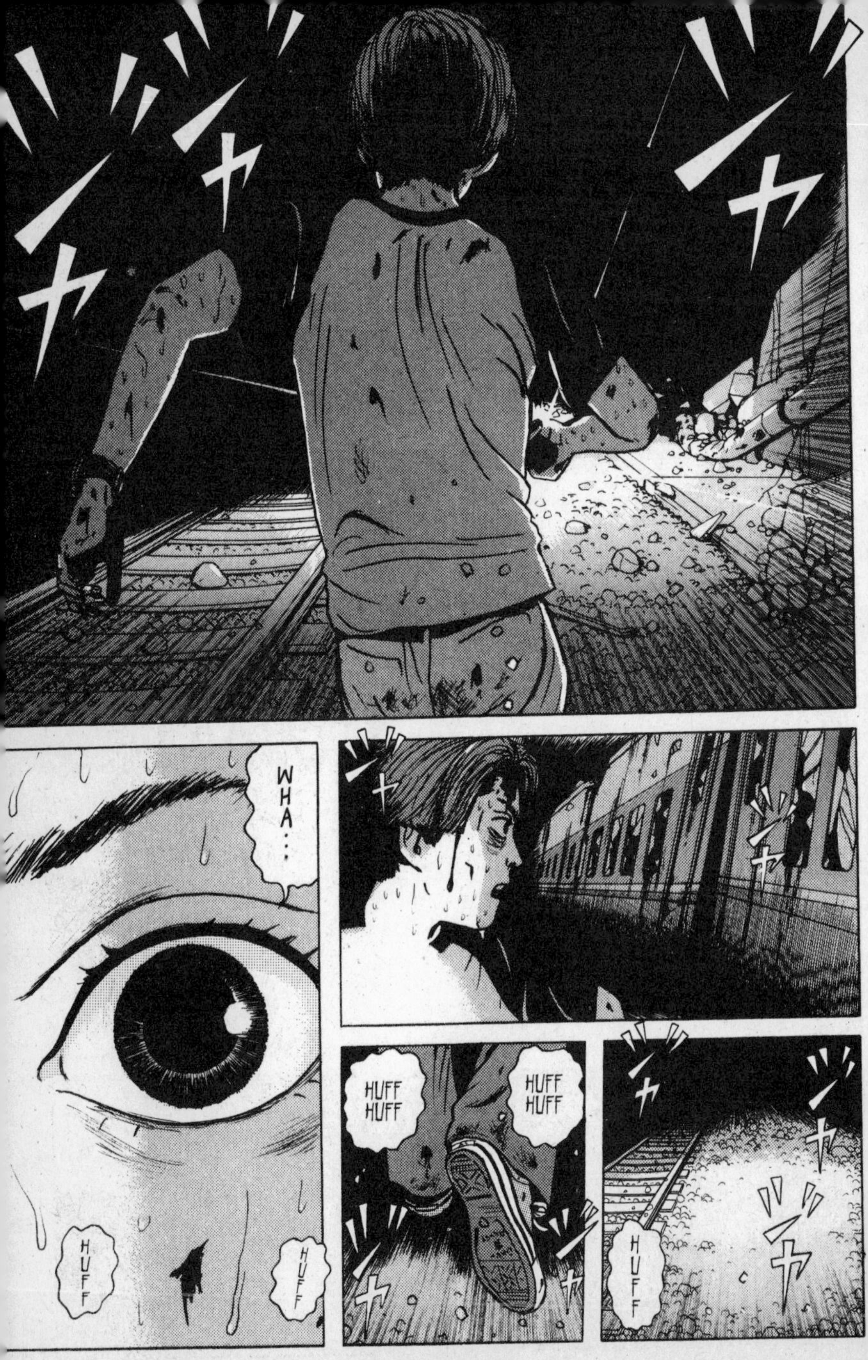
HUFF
HUFF HUFF
HUFF HUFF
WHA...
HUFF
HUFF

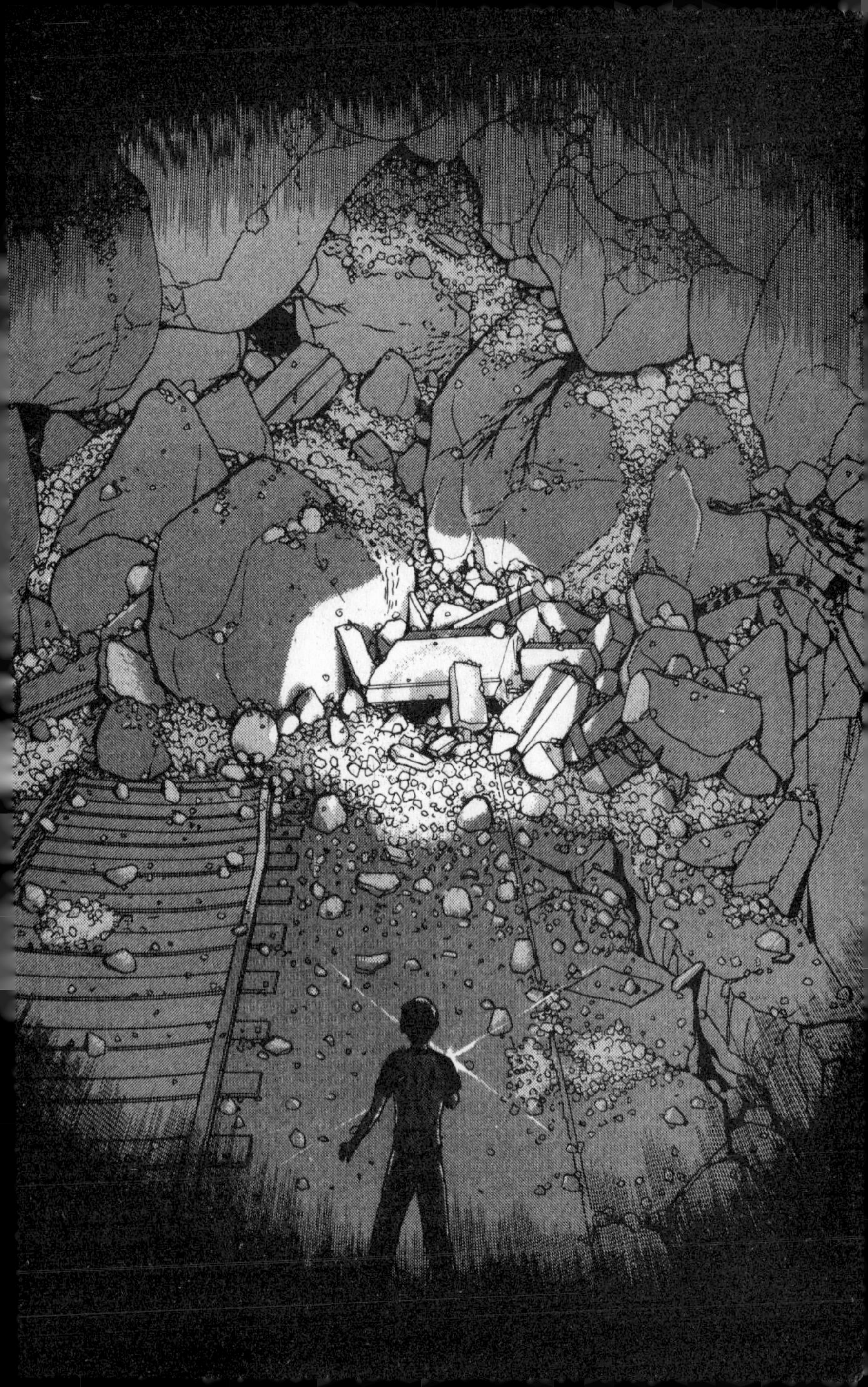

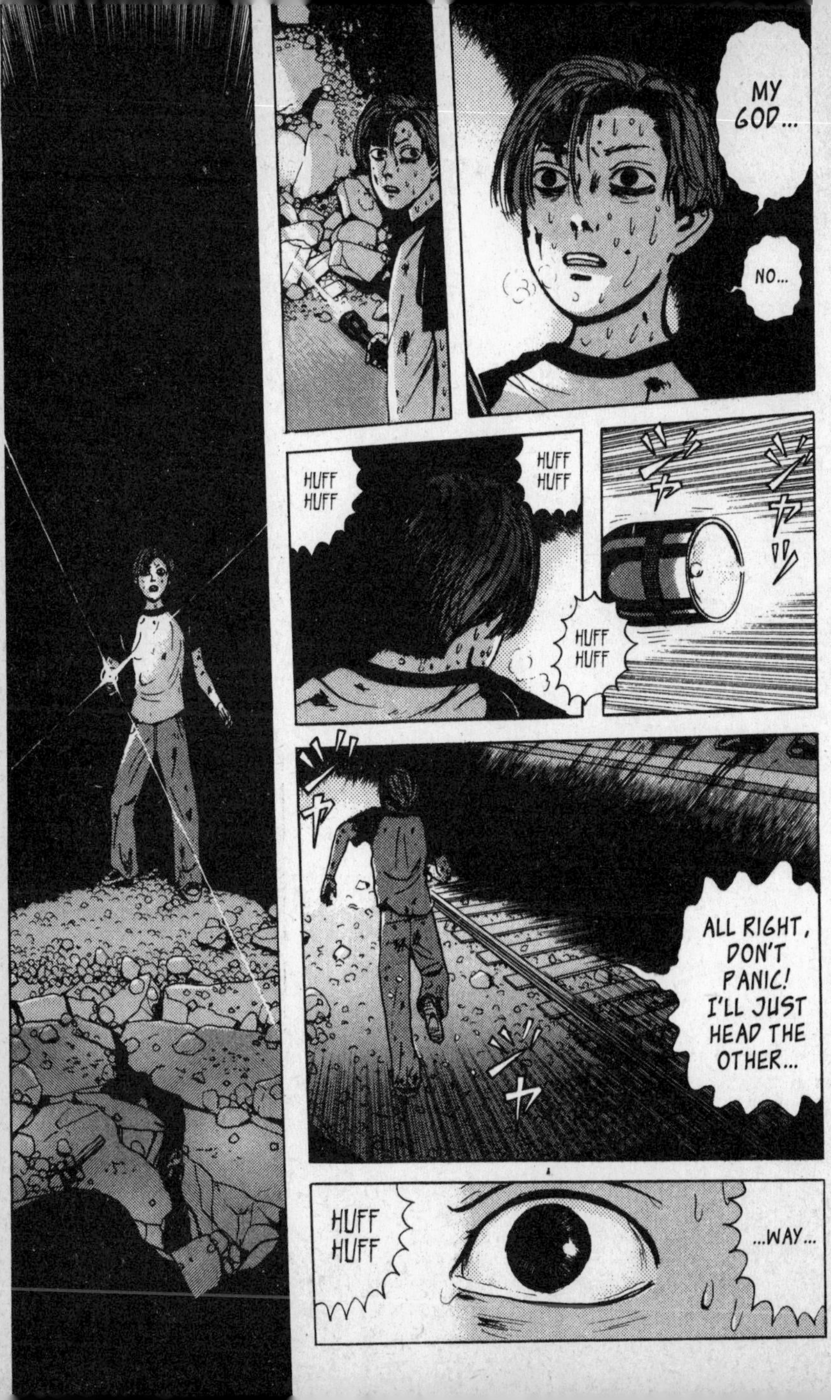
MY GOD...
NO...
HUFF HUFF
HUFF HUFF
HUFF HUFF
ALL RIGHT, DON'T PANIC! I'LL JUST HEAD THE OTHER...
...WAY...
HUFF HUFF

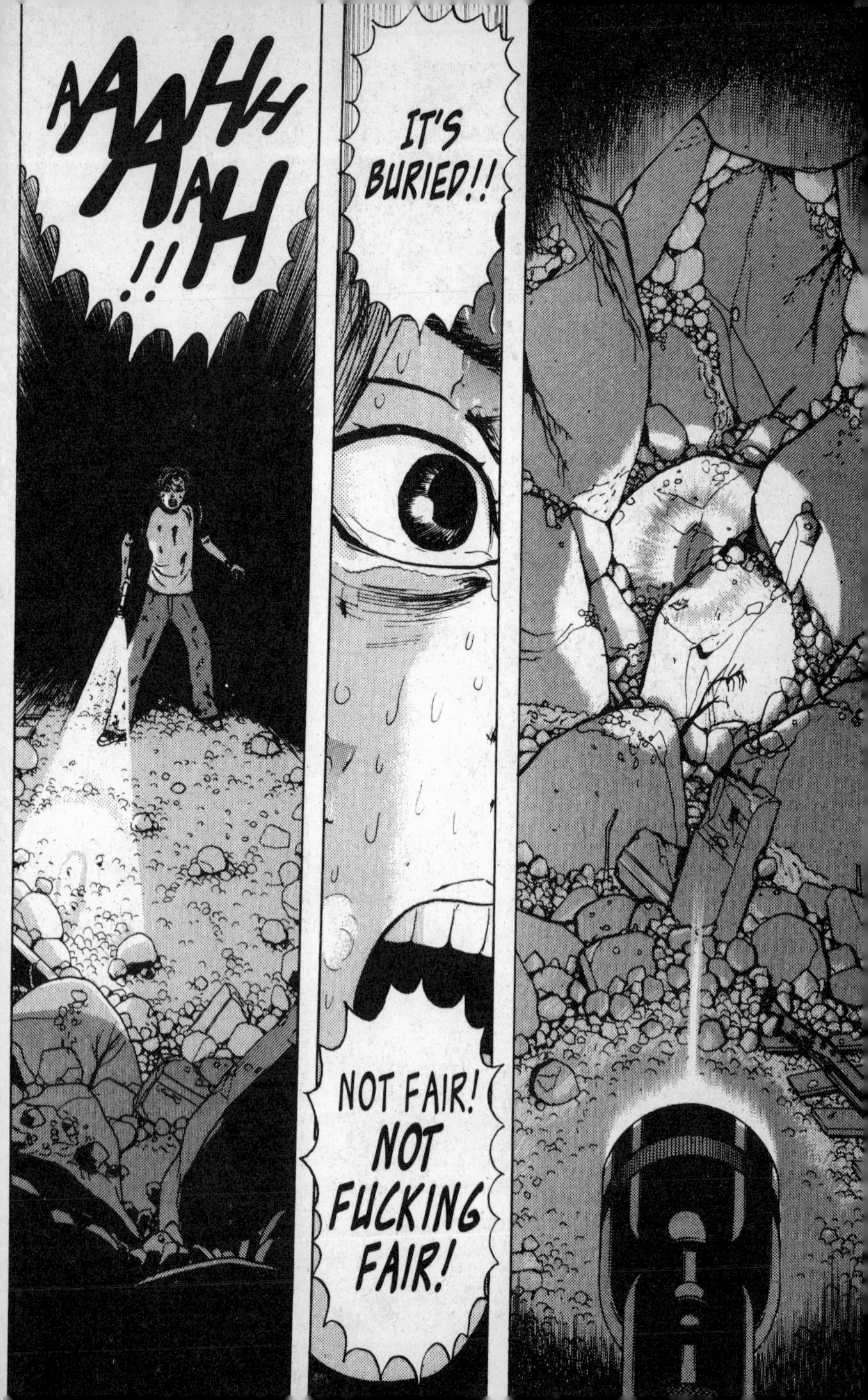
IT'S BURIED!!
NOT FAIR! NOT FUCKING FAIR!
AAAHH AAH!!

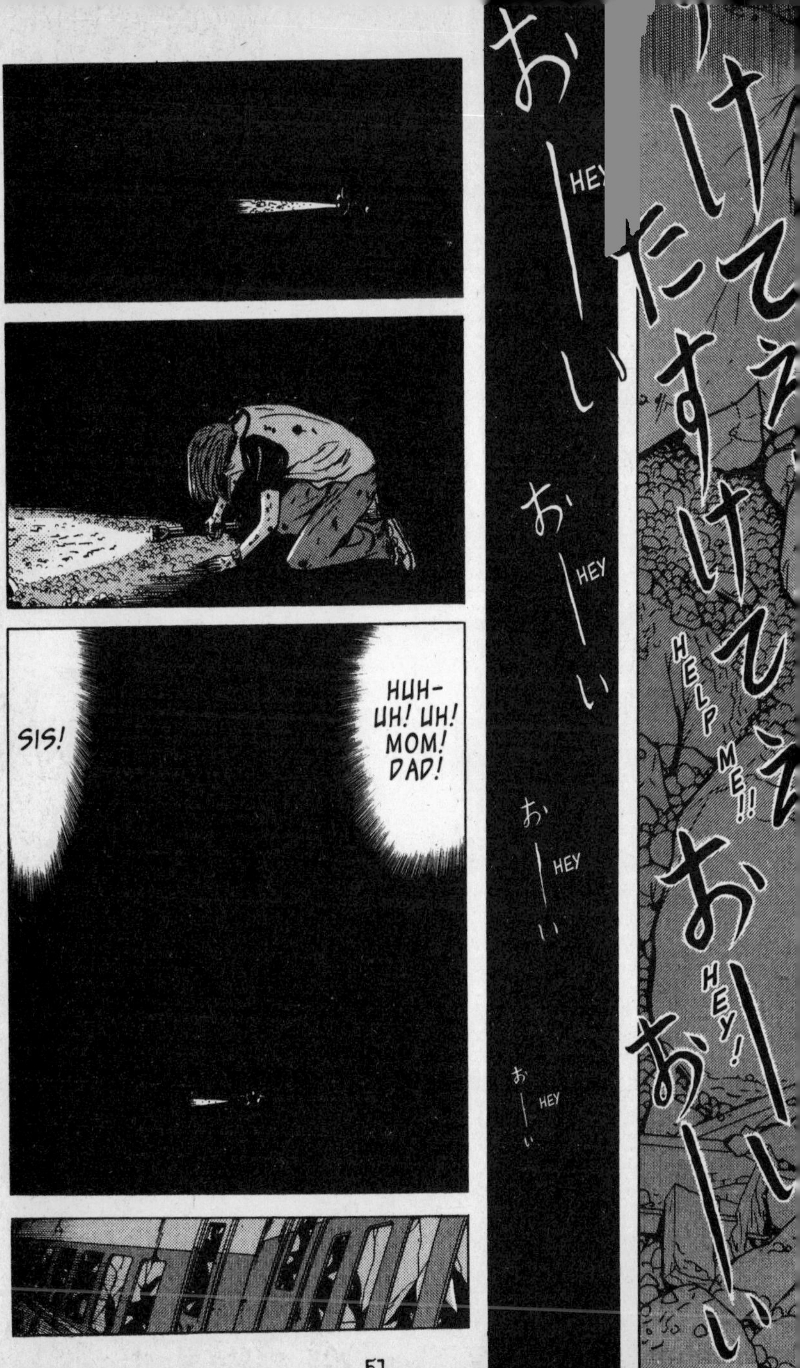

けてえええ
たすけてええ
HELP ME!!
おーい
HEY!
おーい
HEY
おーい
HEY
おーい
HEY
おーい
HEY
HUH-UH! UH! MOM! DAD!
SIS!

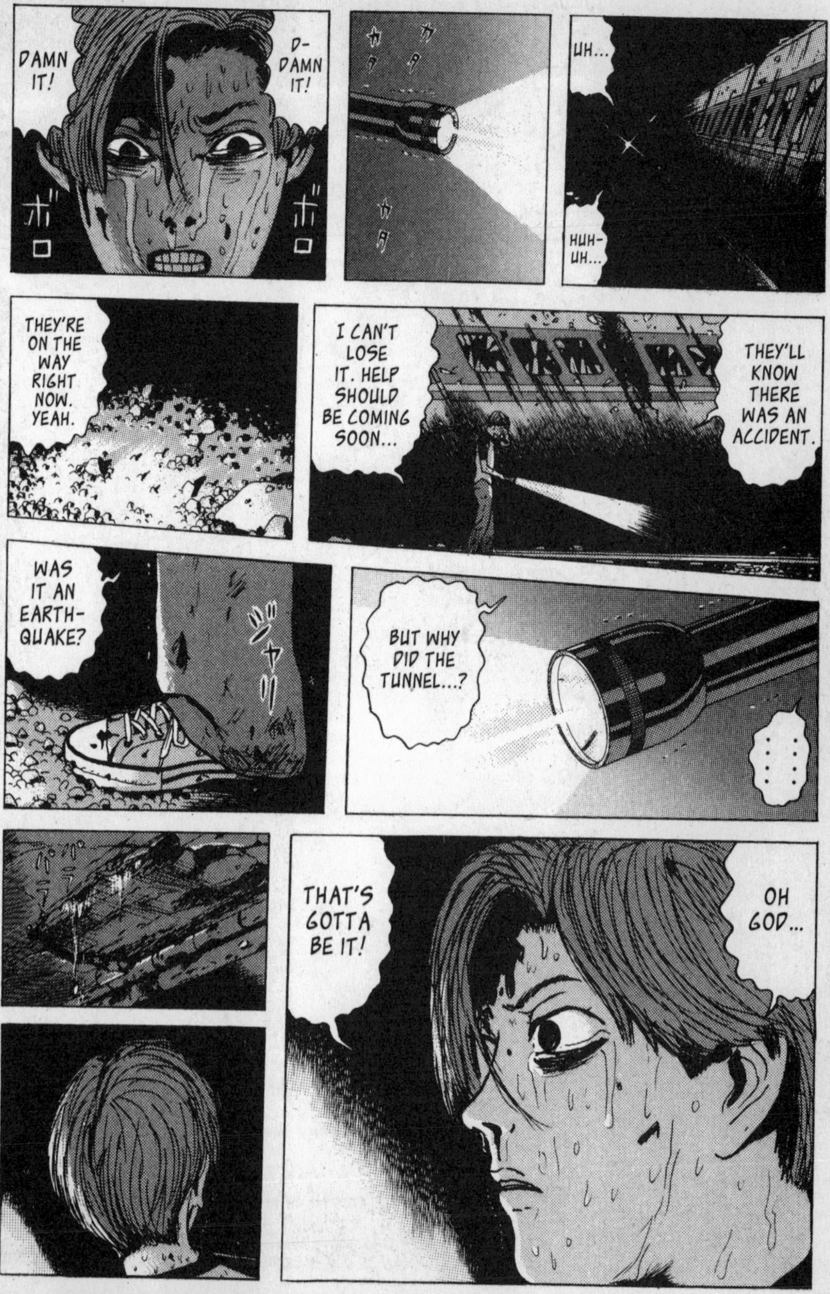
UH...
HUH-UH...
カタ
カタ
D-DAMN IT!
DAMN IT!
ボロ
ボロ
THEY'LL KNOW THERE WAS AN ACCIDENT.
I CAN'T LOSE IT. HELP SHOULD BE COMING SOON...
THEY'RE ON THE WAY RIGHT NOW. YEAH.
......
BUT WHY DID THE TUNNEL...?
ジャリ
WAS IT AN EARTH-QUAKE?
OH GOD...
THAT'S GOTTA BE IT!
パラ
パラ

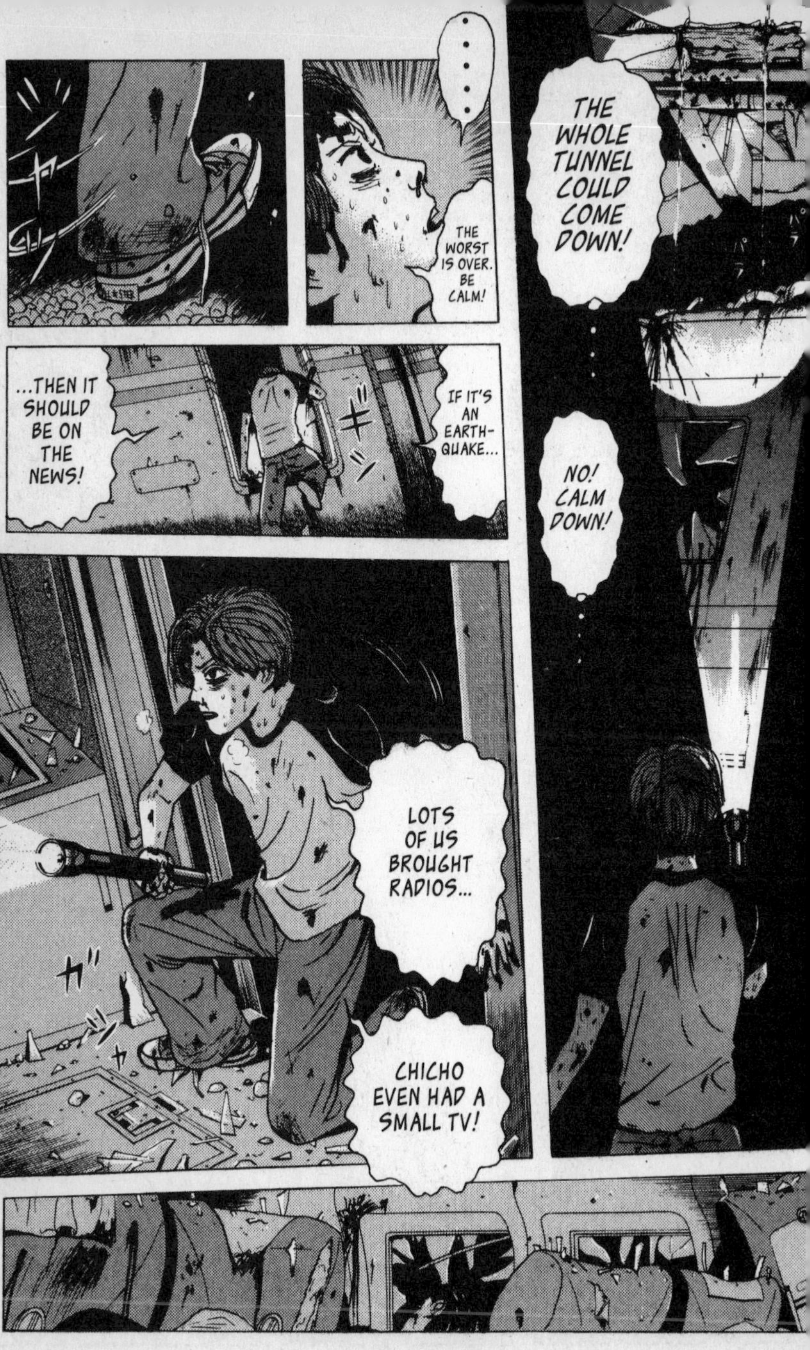
THE WHOLE TUNNEL COULD COME DOWN!
NO! CALM DOWN!
...
THE WORST IS OVER. BE CALM!
IF IT'S AN EARTHQUAKE...
...THEN IT SHOULD BE ON THE NEWS!
LOTS OF US BROUGHT RADIOS...
CHICHO EVEN HAD A SMALL TV!

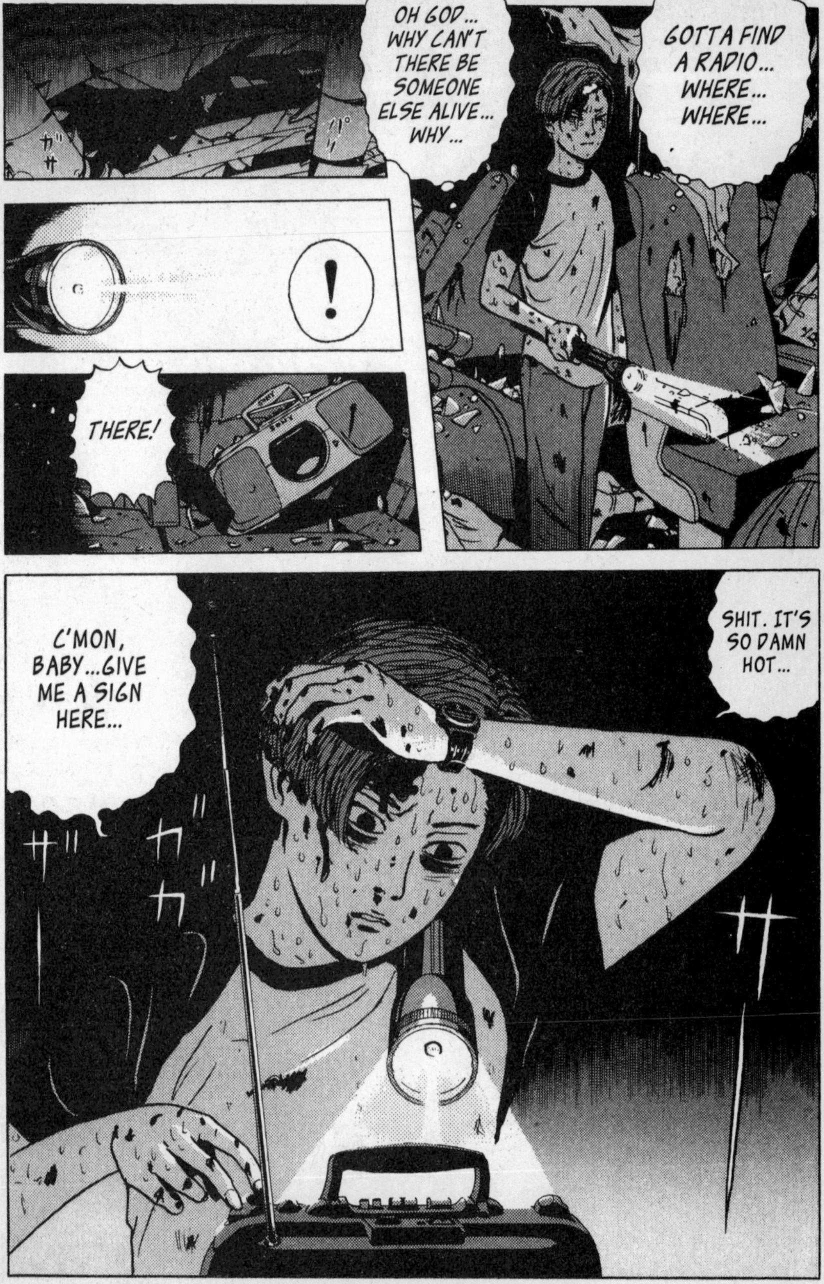
GOTTA FIND A RADIO... WHERE... WHERE...
OH GOD... WHY CAN'T THERE BE SOMEONE ELSE ALIVE... WHY...
!
THERE!
SHIT. IT'S SO DAMN HOT...
C'MON, BABY...GIVE ME A SIGN HERE...

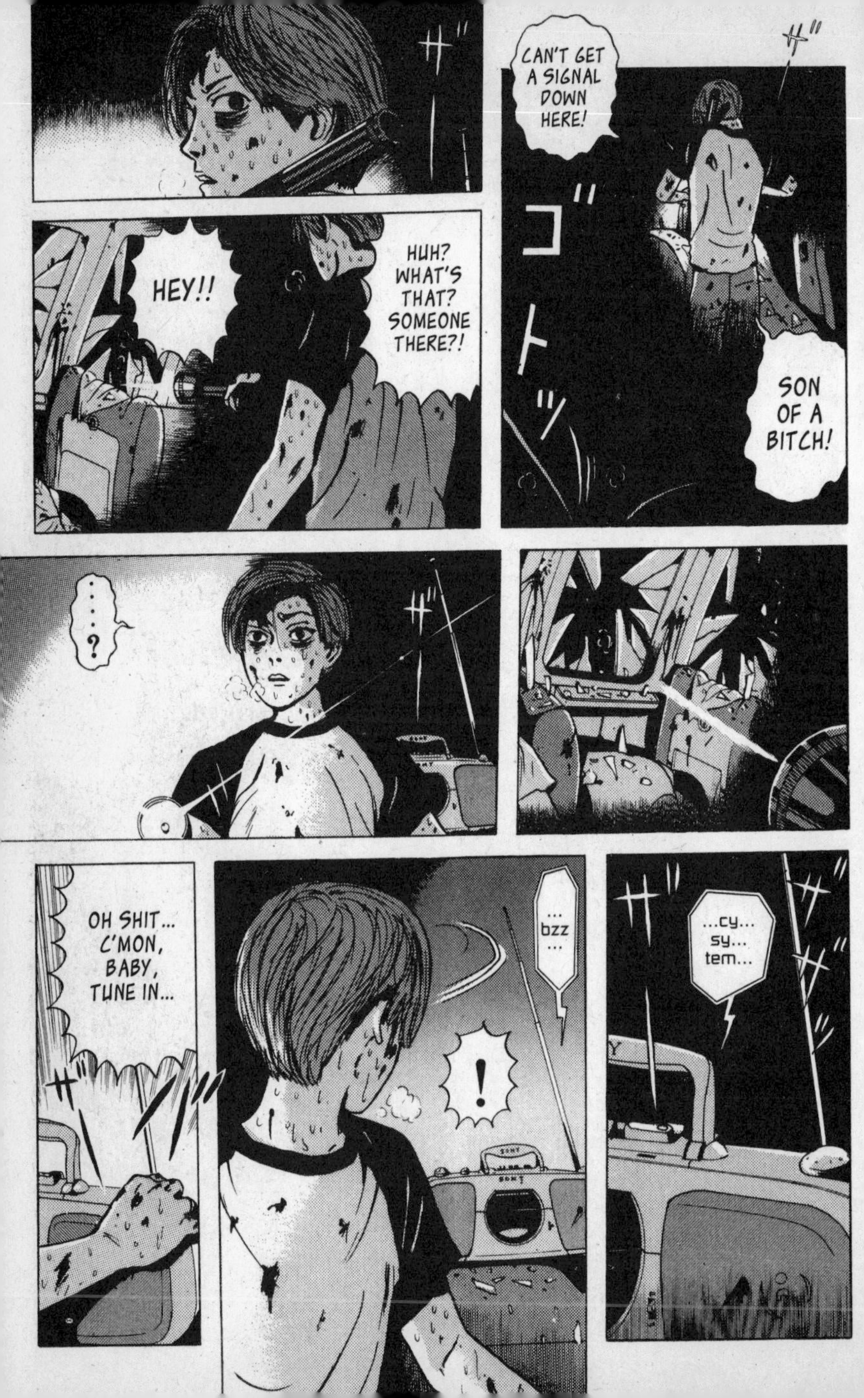
HEY!!
HUH? WHAT'S THAT? SOMEONE THERE?!
CAN'T GET A SIGNAL DOWN HERE!
SON OF A BITCH!
...?
OH SHIT... C'MON, BABY, TUNE IN...
... bzz ...
!
...cy... sy... tem...

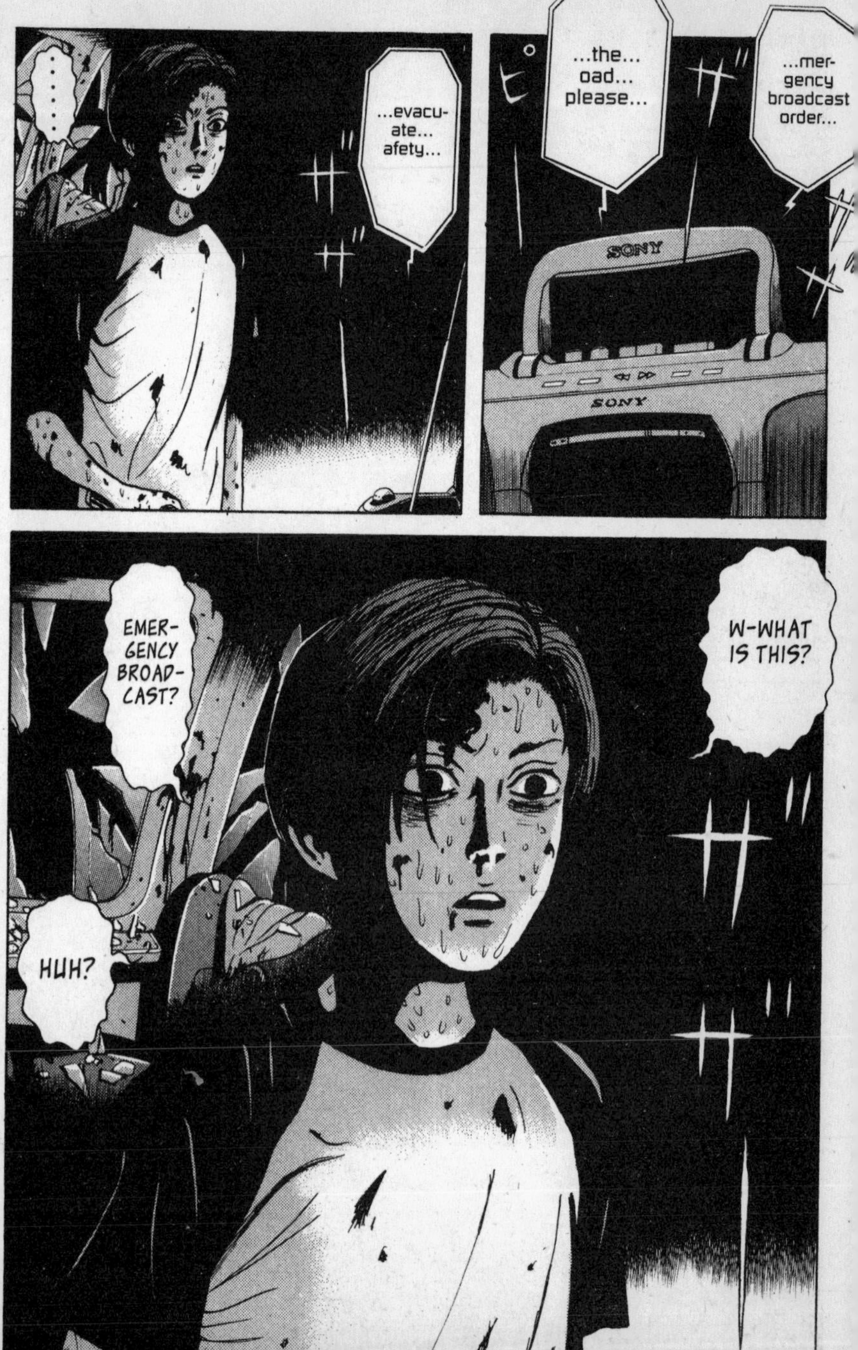
...mer-gency broadcast order...
...the... oad... please...
SONY
SONY
...evacu-ate... afety...
......
W-WHAT IS THIS?
EMER-GENCY BROAD-CAST?
HUH?

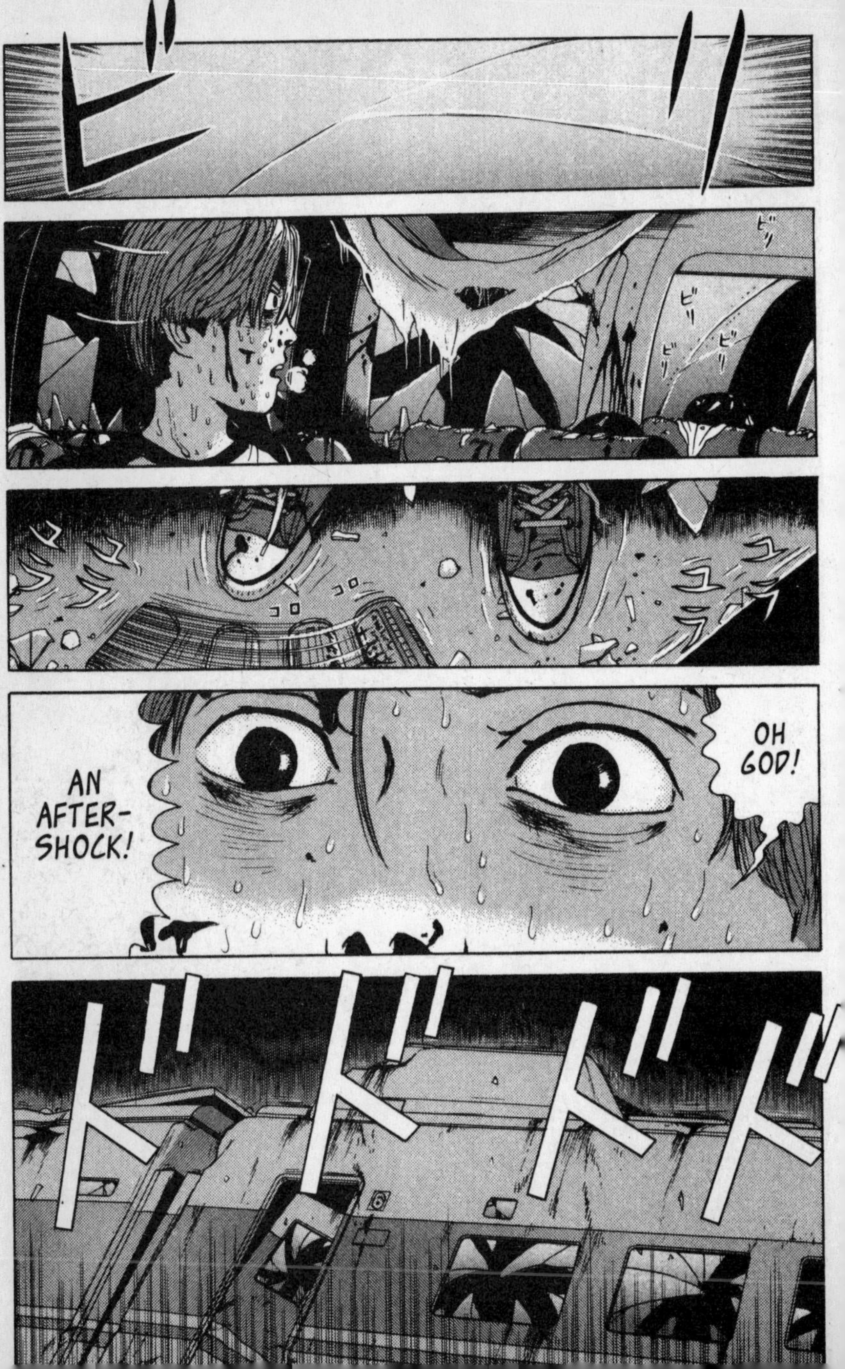

ビリ
OH GOD!
AN AFTER-SHOCK!
ドドドド

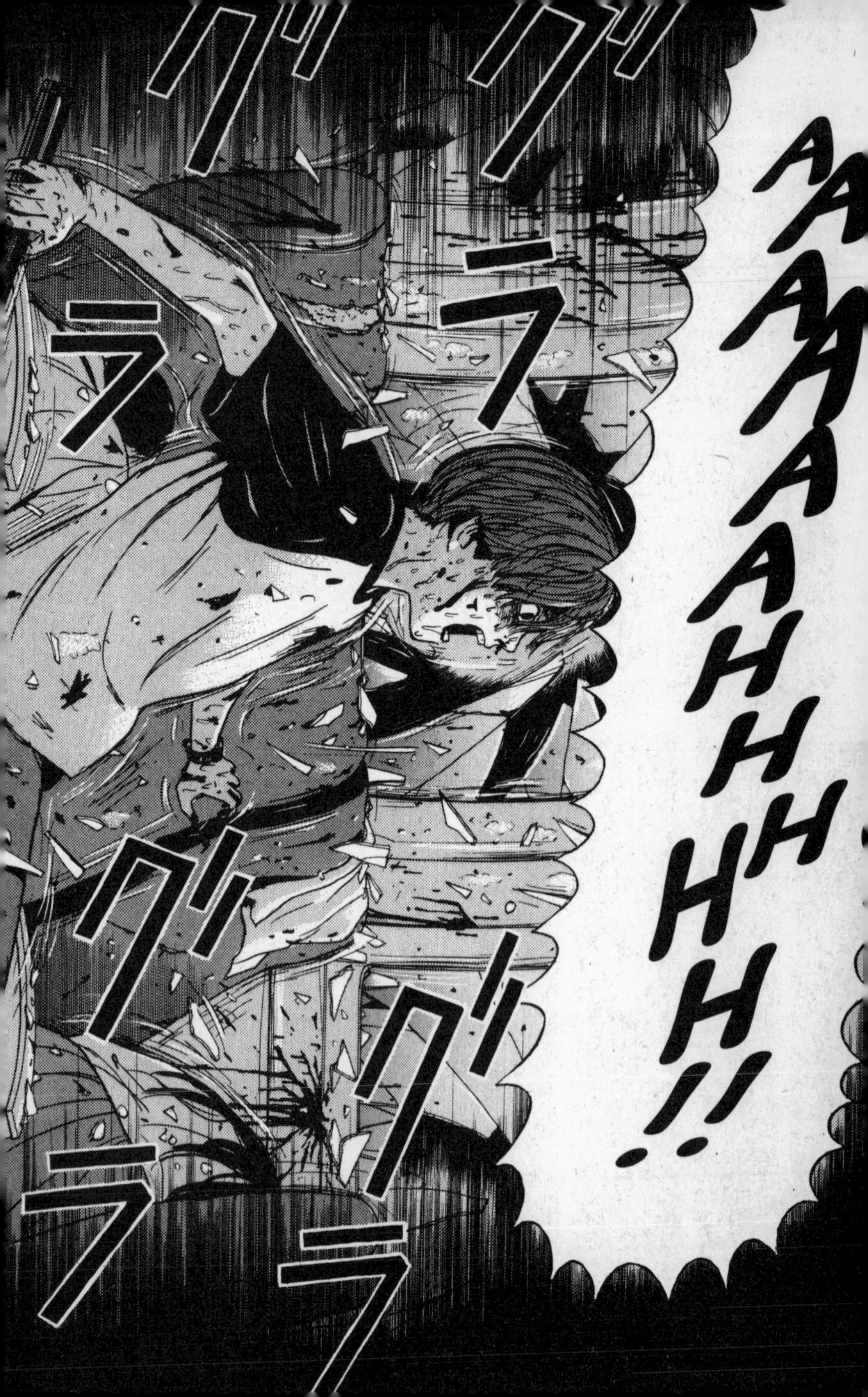
グラグラ
グラグラ
AAAAAAAHHHHH!!

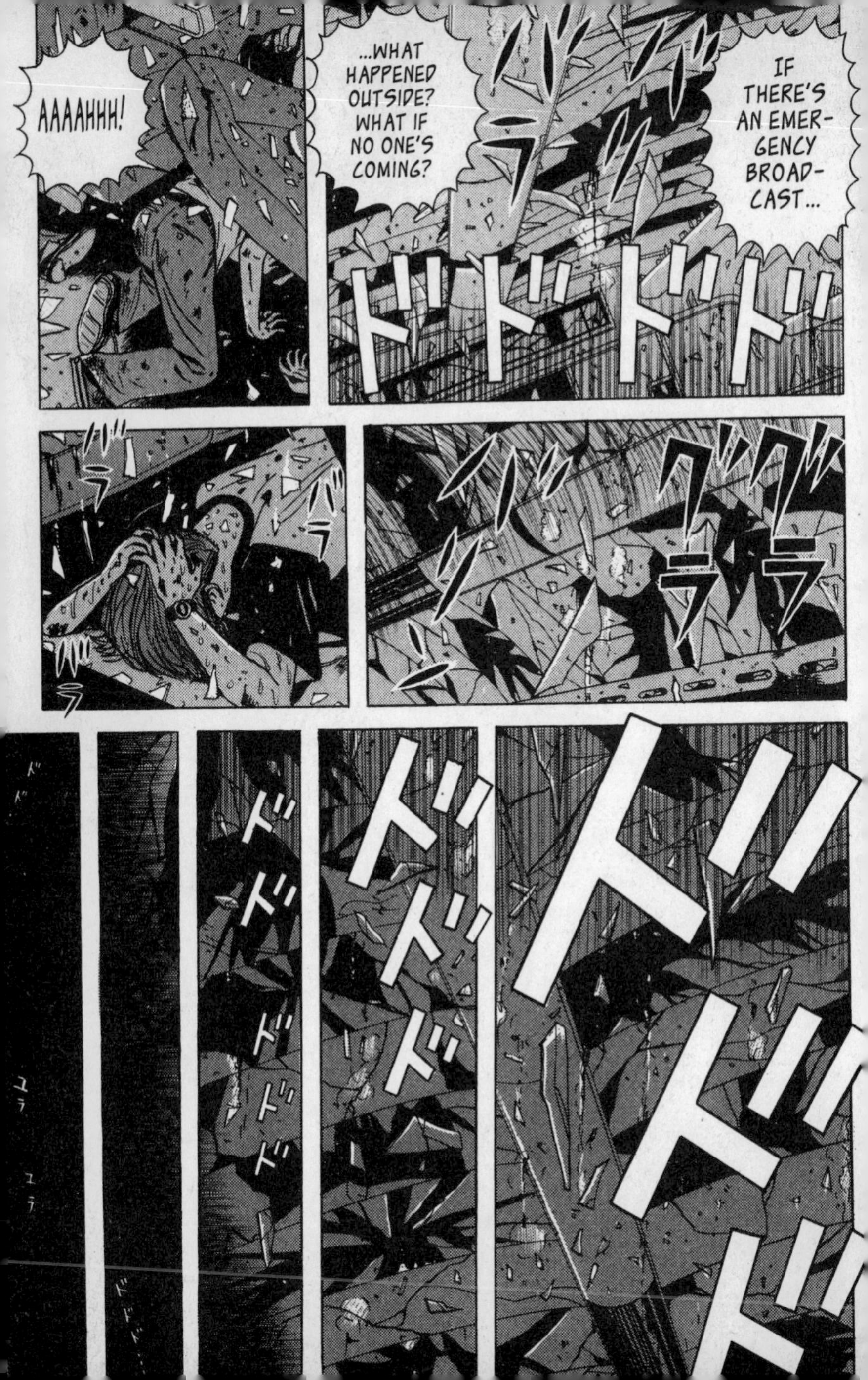
IF THERE'S AN EMERGENCY BROADCAST...
...WHAT HAPPENED OUTSIDE? WHAT IF NO ONE'S COMING?
AAAAHHH!

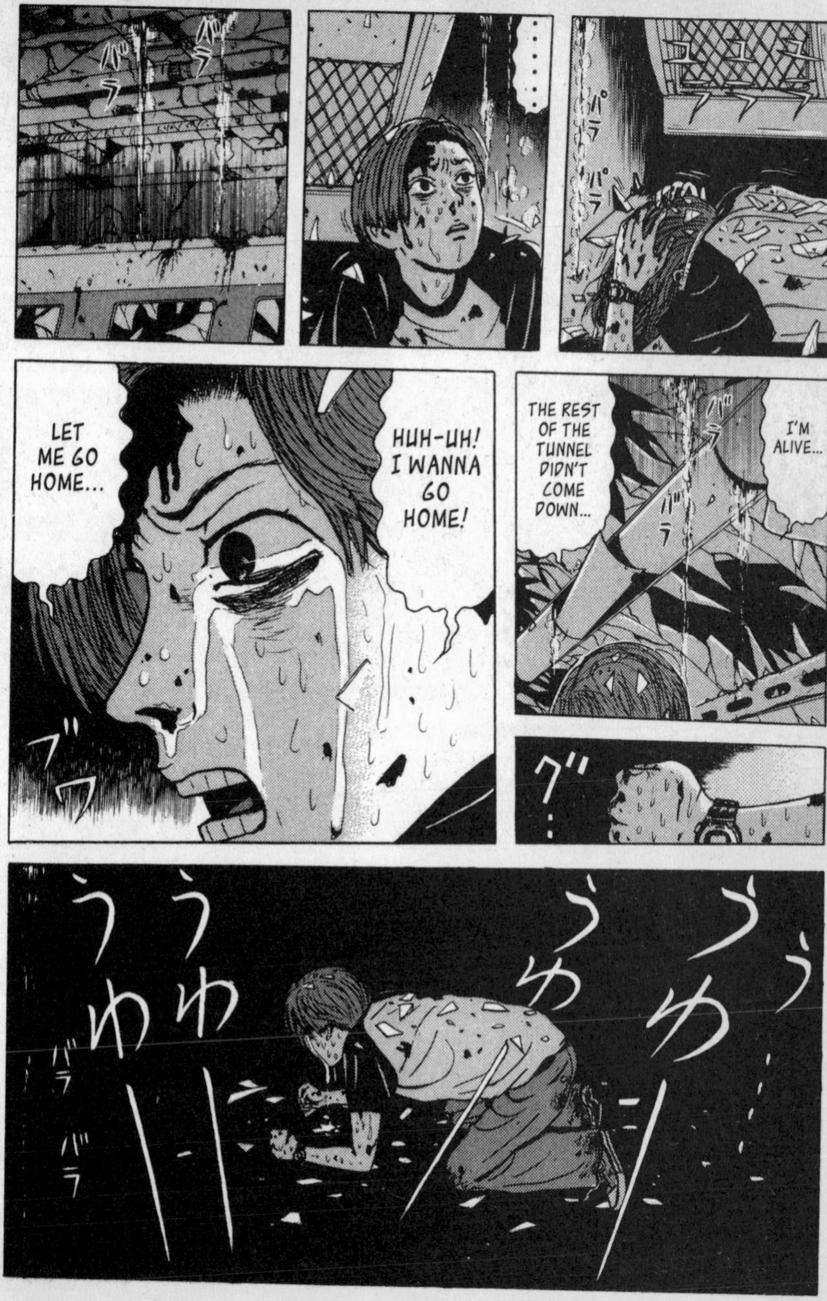
I'M ALIVE...
THE REST OF THE TUNNEL DIDN'T COME DOWN...
HUH-UH! I WANNA GO HOME!
LET ME GO HOME...

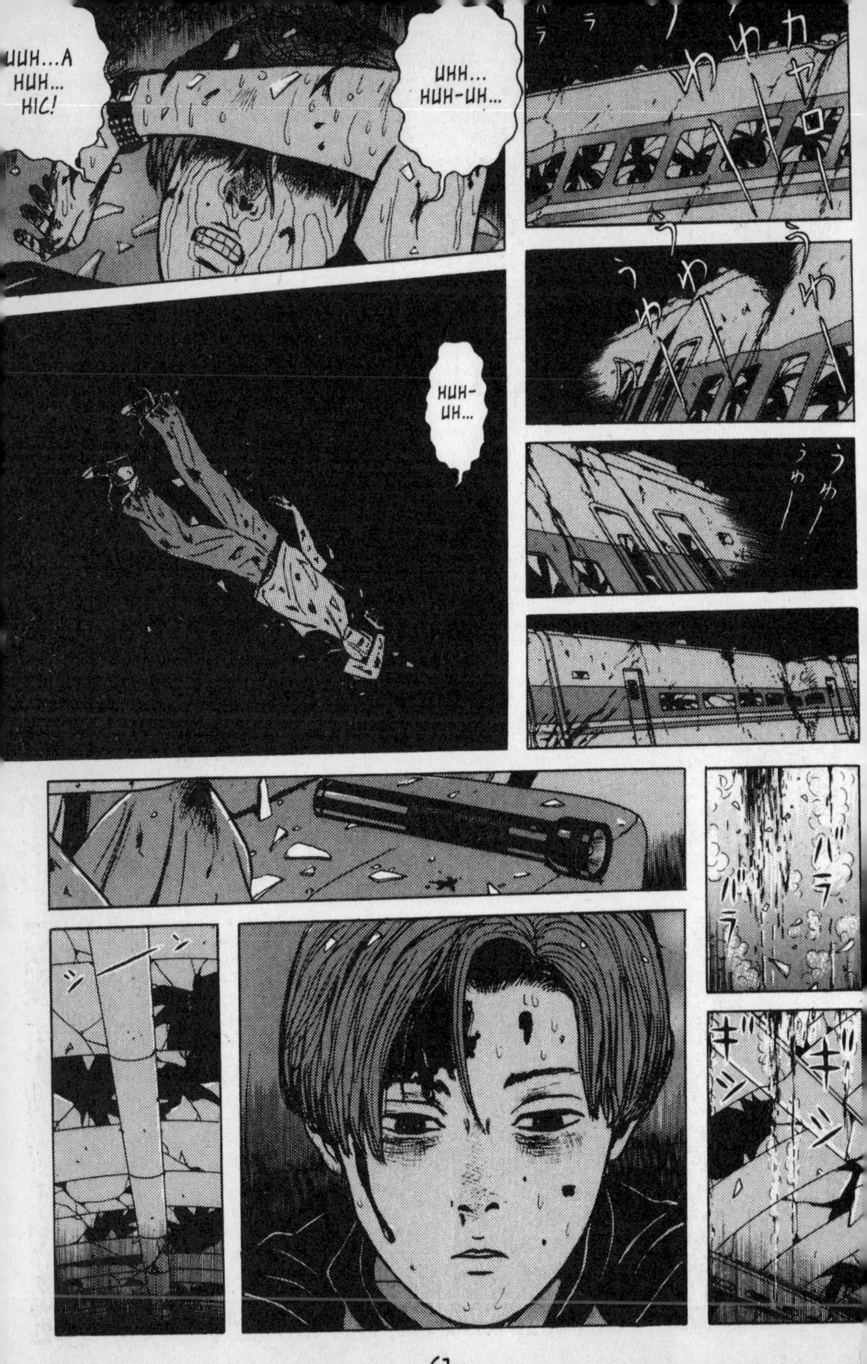
UHH... HUH-UH...
UUH...A HUH... HIC!
HUH-UH...

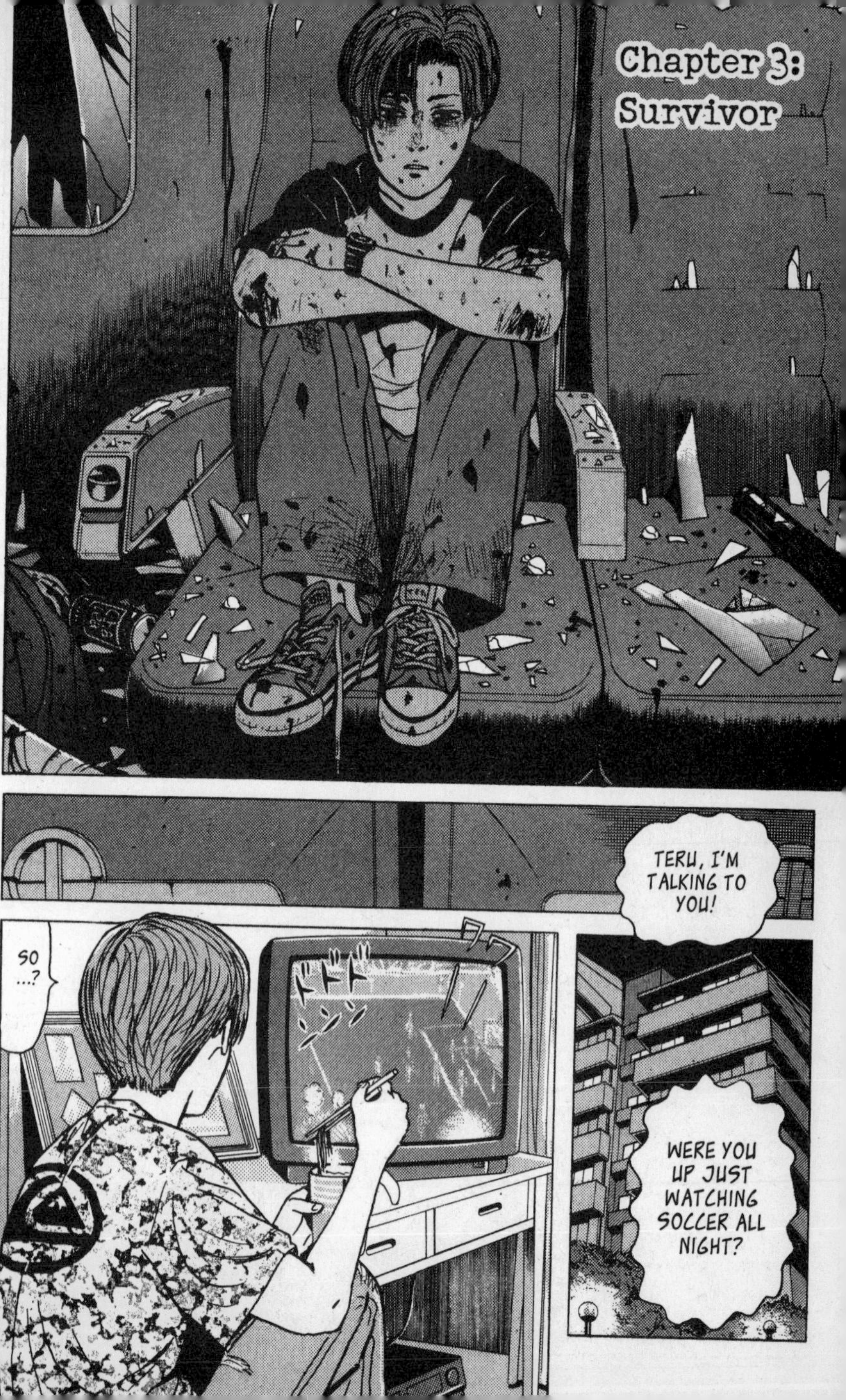
Chapter 3:
Survivor
TERU, I'M TALKING TO YOU!
WERE YOU UP JUST WATCHING SOCCER ALL NIGHT?
SO ...?

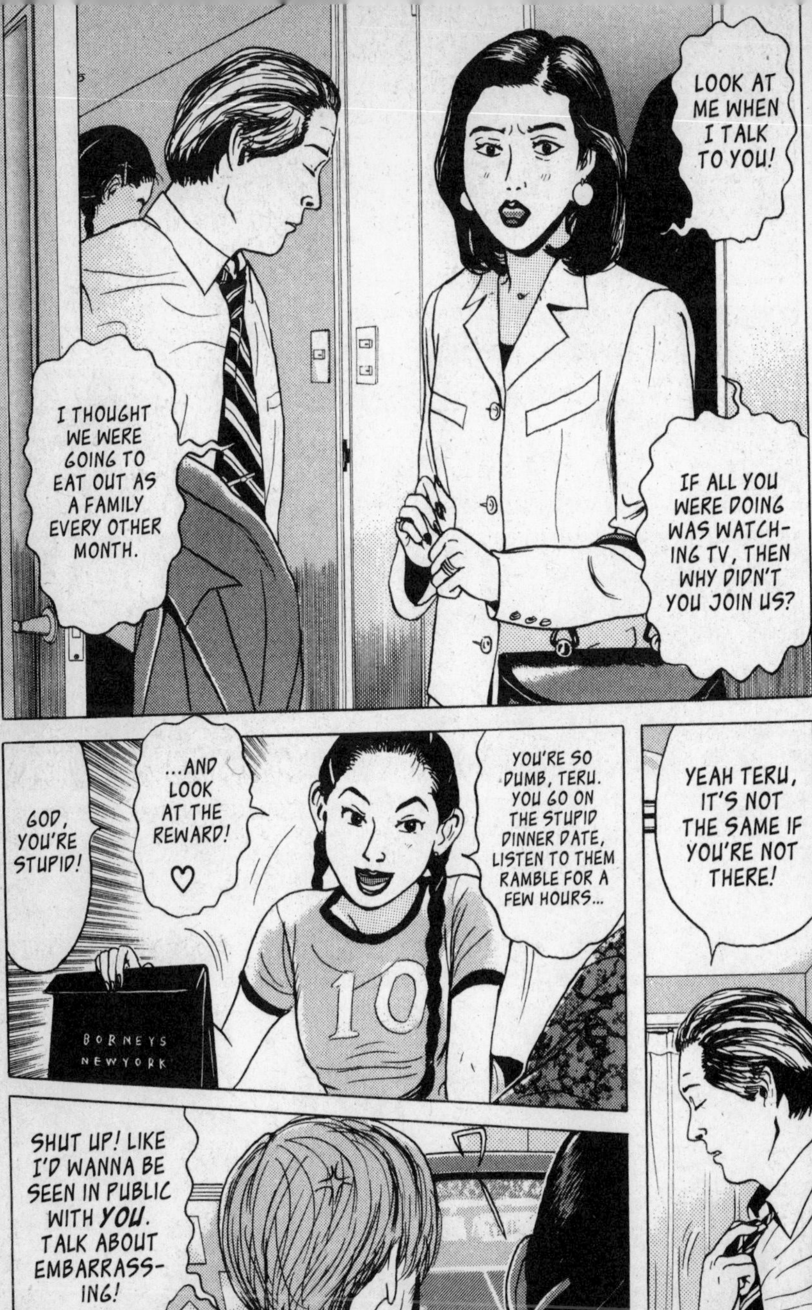
LOOK AT ME WHEN I TALK TO YOU!
IF ALL YOU WERE DOING WAS WATCHING TV, THEN WHY DIDN'T YOU JOIN US?
I THOUGHT WE WERE GOING TO EAT OUT AS A FAMILY EVERY OTHER MONTH.
YEAH TERU, IT'S NOT THE SAME IF YOU'RE NOT THERE!
YOU'RE SO DUMB, TERU. YOU GO ON THE STUPID DINNER DATE, LISTEN TO THEM RAMBLE FOR A FEW HOURS...
...AND LOOK AT THE REWARD! ♡
GOD, YOU'RE STUPID!
BORNEYS NEWYORK
SHUT UP! LIKE I'D WANNA BE SEEN IN PUBLIC WITH ***YOU***. TALK ABOUT EMBARRASSING!

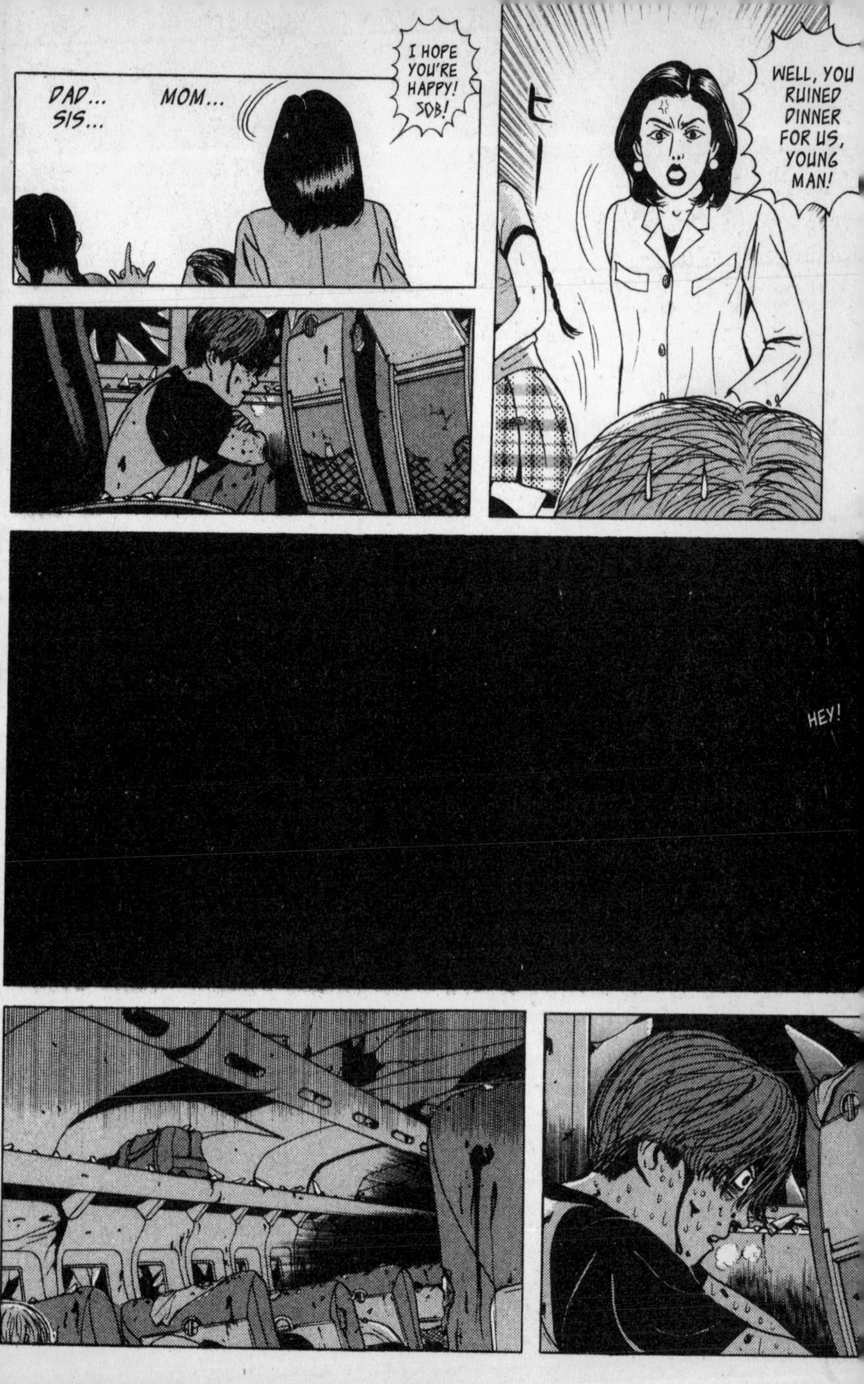
WELL, YOU RUINED DINNER FOR US, YOUNG MAN!
I HOPE YOU'RE HAPPY! SOB!
MOM...
DAD... SIS...
HEY!

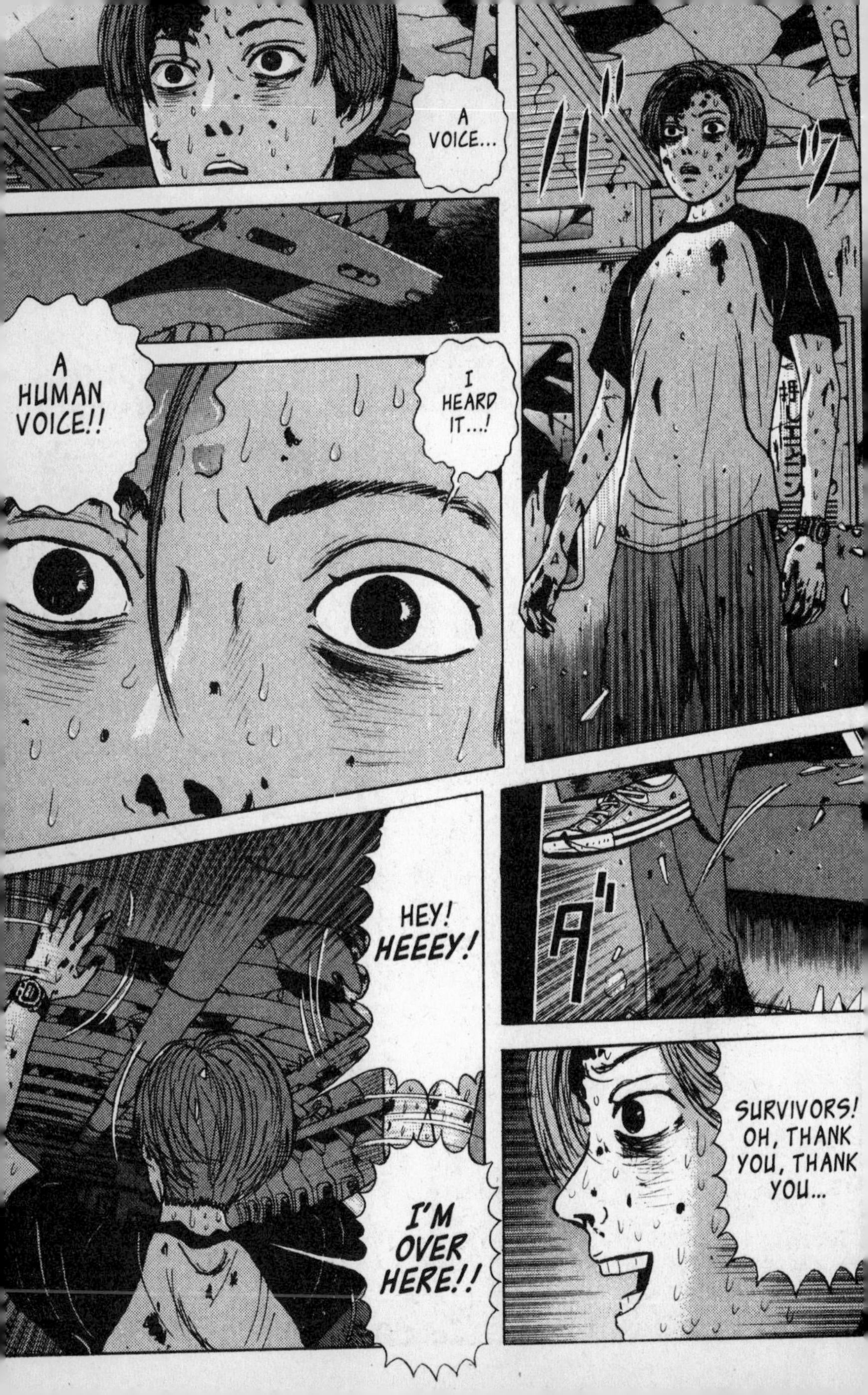
A VOICE...
A HUMAN VOICE!!
I HEARD IT...!
HEY! HEEEY!
I'M OVER HERE!!
SURVIVORS! OH, THANK YOU, THANK YOU...

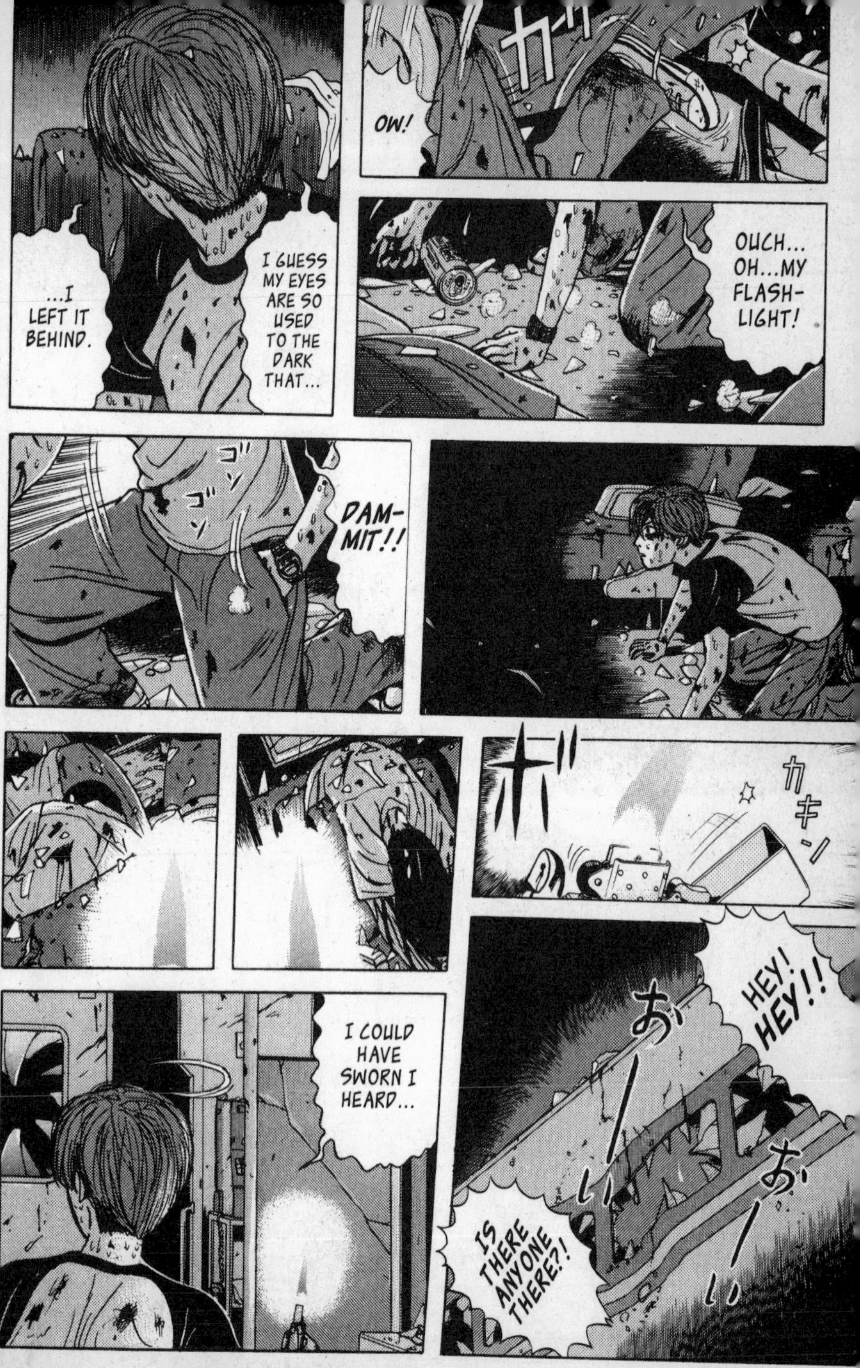
OW!
OUCH... OH...MY FLASH-LIGHT!
I GUESS MY EYES ARE SO USED TO THE DARK THAT...
...I LEFT IT BEHIND.
DAM-MIT!!
HEY! HEY!!
IS THERE ANYONE THERE?!
I COULD HAVE SWORN I HEARD...

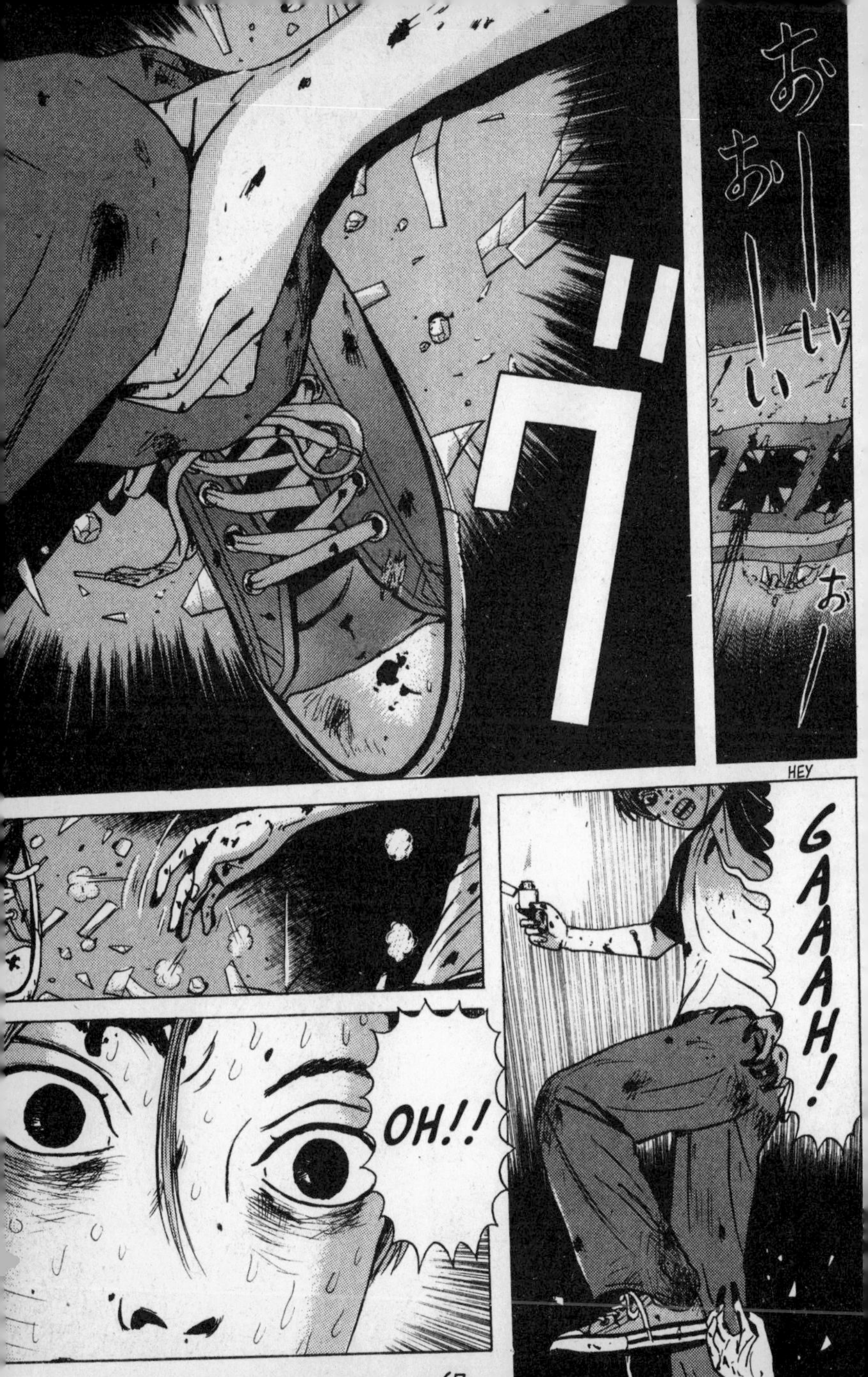
おーい
おーい
おー
ヴ
HEY
GAAAAH!
OH!!

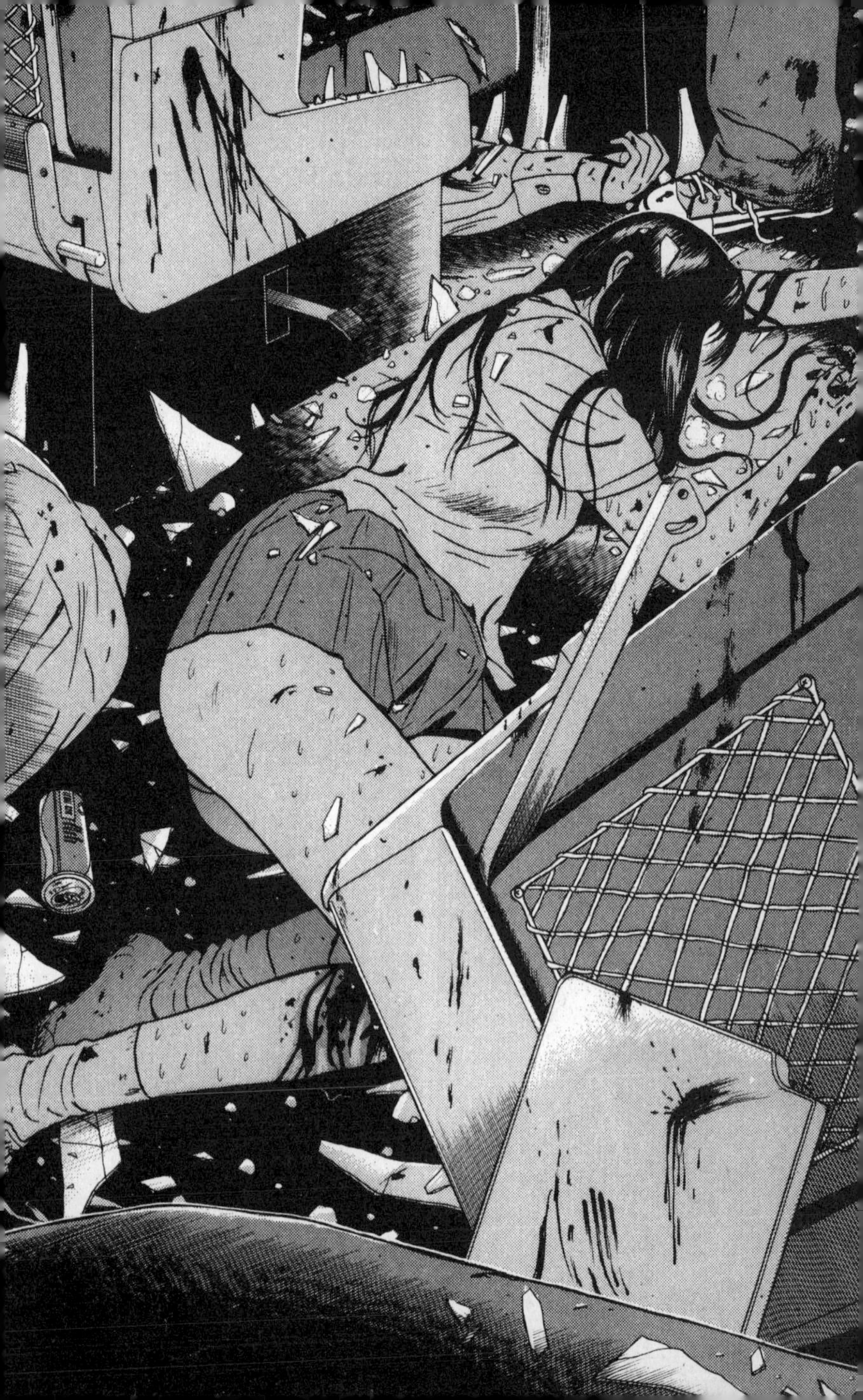

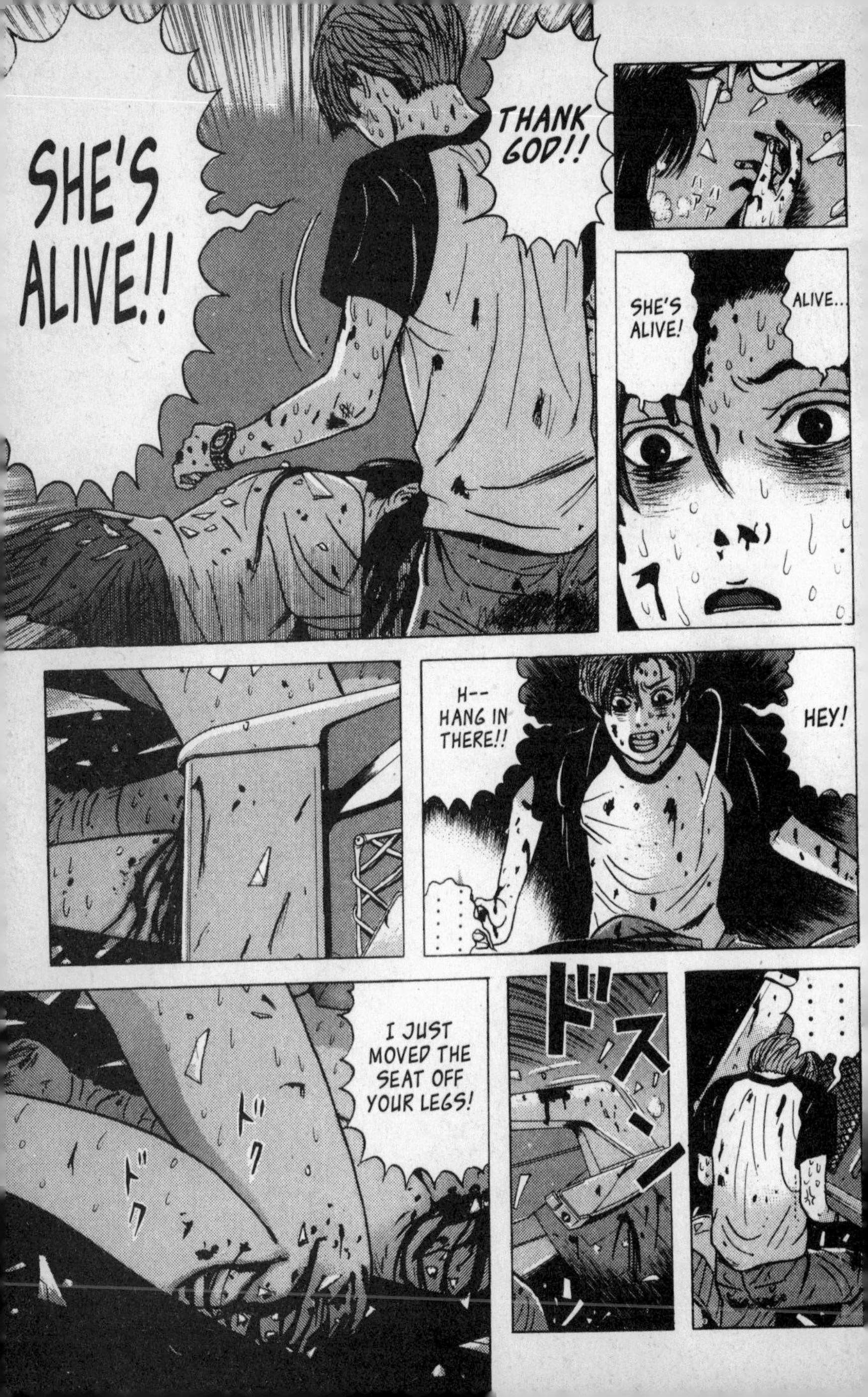
ALIVE...
SHE'S ALIVE!
THANK GOD!!
SHE'S ALIVE!!
HEY!
H-- HANG IN THERE!!
......
ドスー
I JUST MOVED THE SEAT OFF YOUR LEGS!
ドク ドク

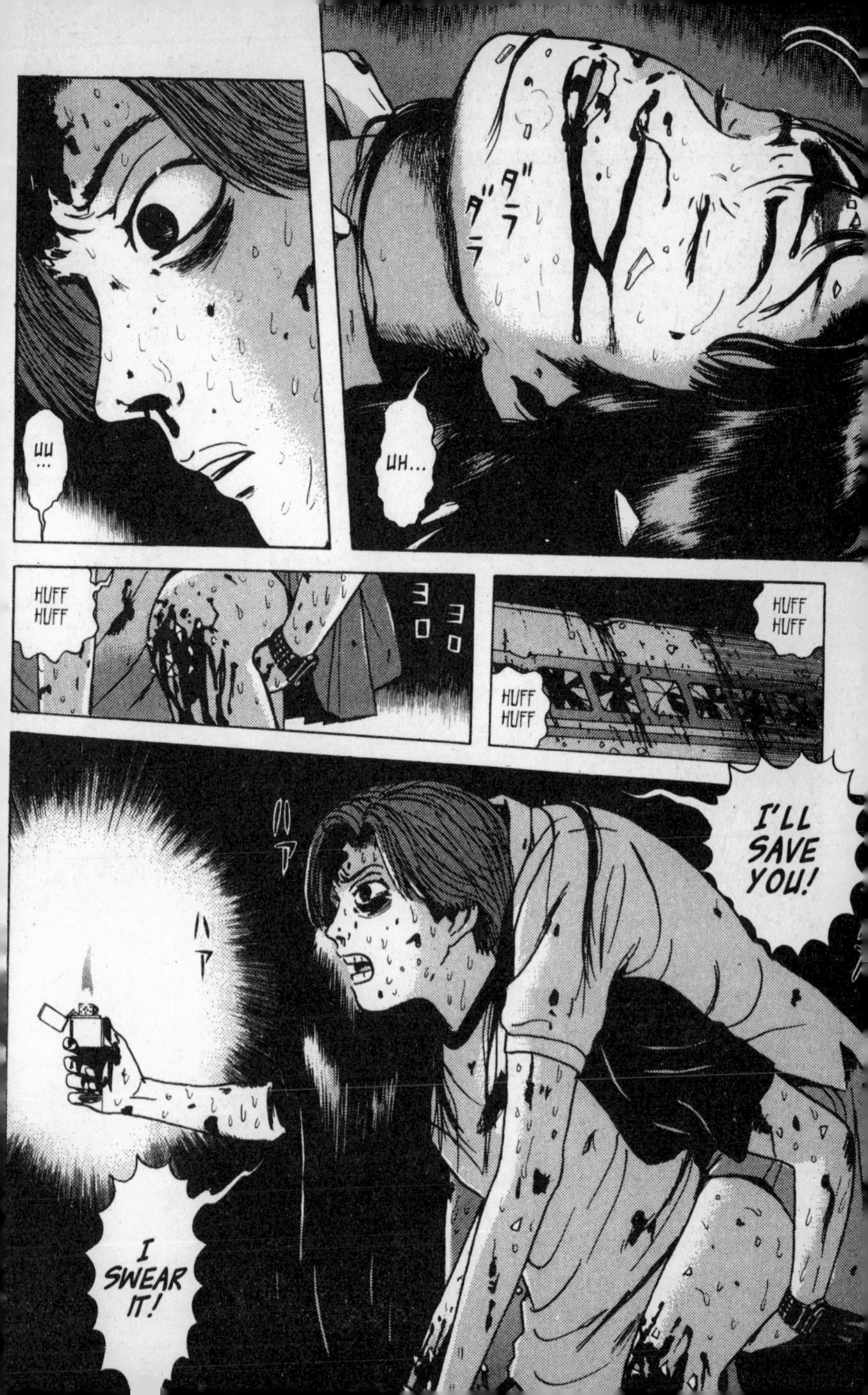
ダラダラ
UH...
UU ...
HUFF HUFF
HUFF HUFF
ヨロヨロ
HUFF HUFF
I'LL SAVE YOU!
ハァ
ハァ
I SWEAR IT!

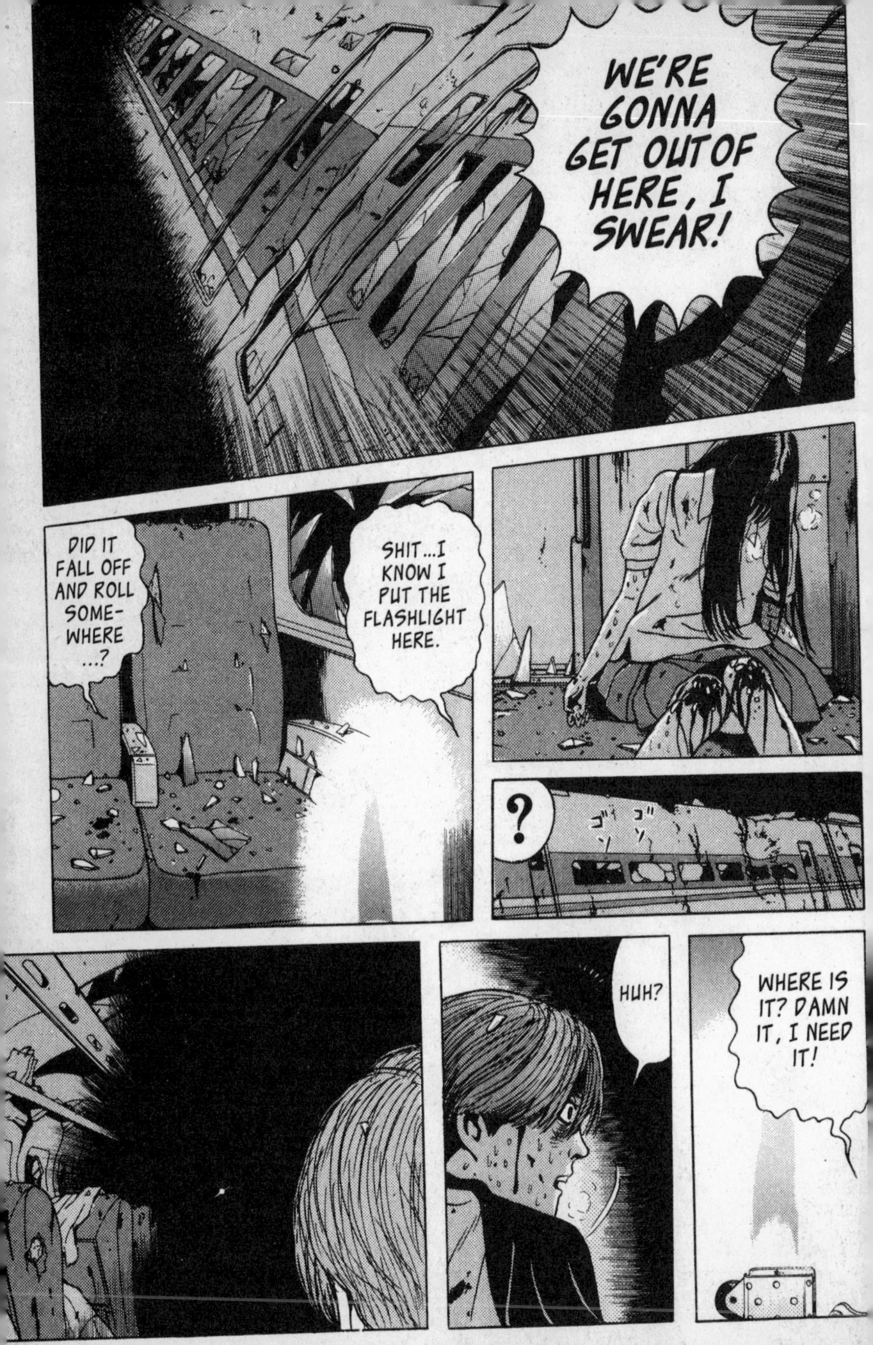

WE'RE GONNA GET OUT OF HERE, I SWEAR!
?
ゴソ ゴソ
SHIT...I KNOW I PUT THE FLASHLIGHT HERE.
DID IT FALL OFF AND ROLL SOME-WHERE ...?
WHERE IS IT? DAMN IT, I NEED IT!
HUH?

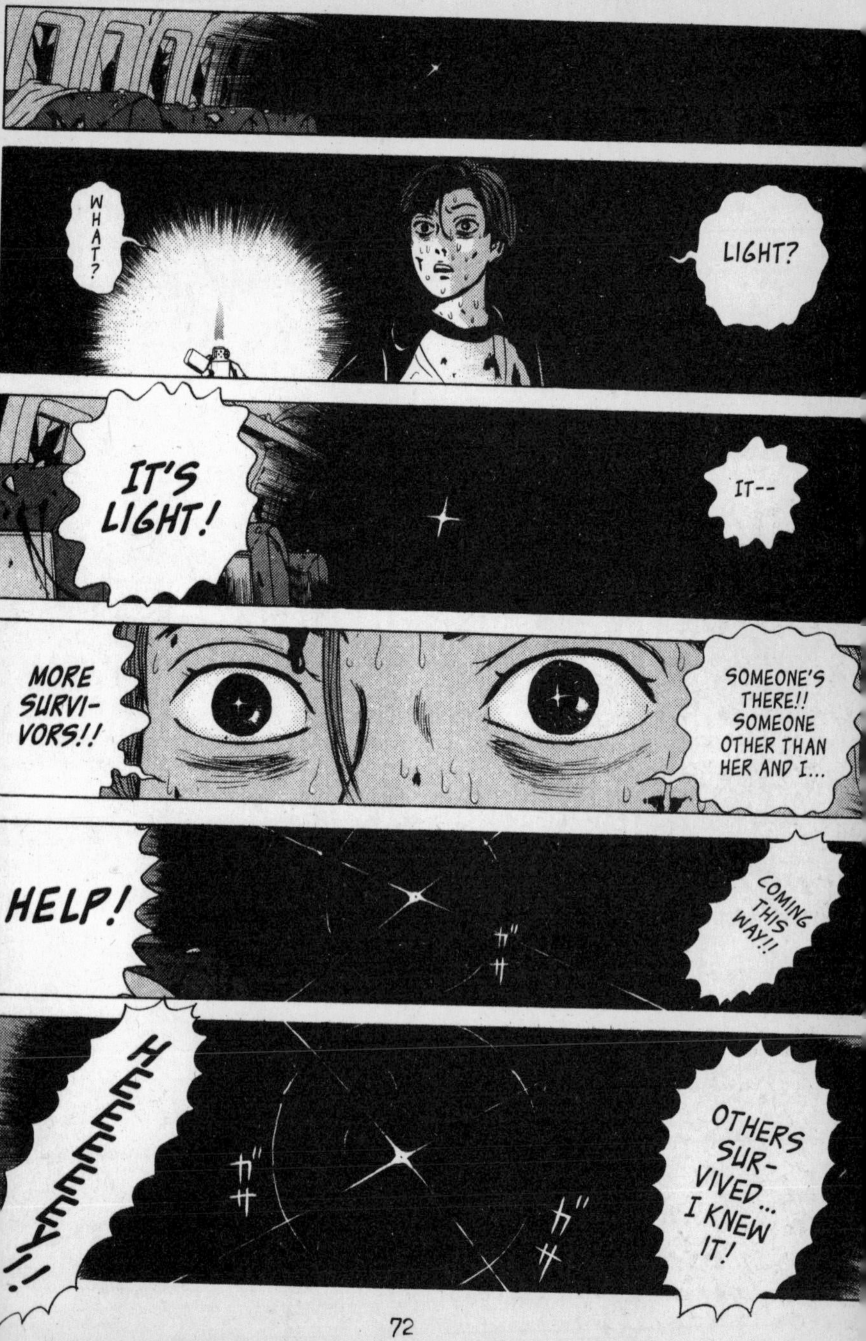
LIGHT?
WHAT?
IT--
IT'S LIGHT!
SOMEONE'S THERE!! SOMEONE OTHER THAN HER AND I...
MORE SURVIVORS!!
COMING THIS WAY!!
HELP!
OTHERS SURVIVED... I KNEW IT!
HEEEEEEY!!

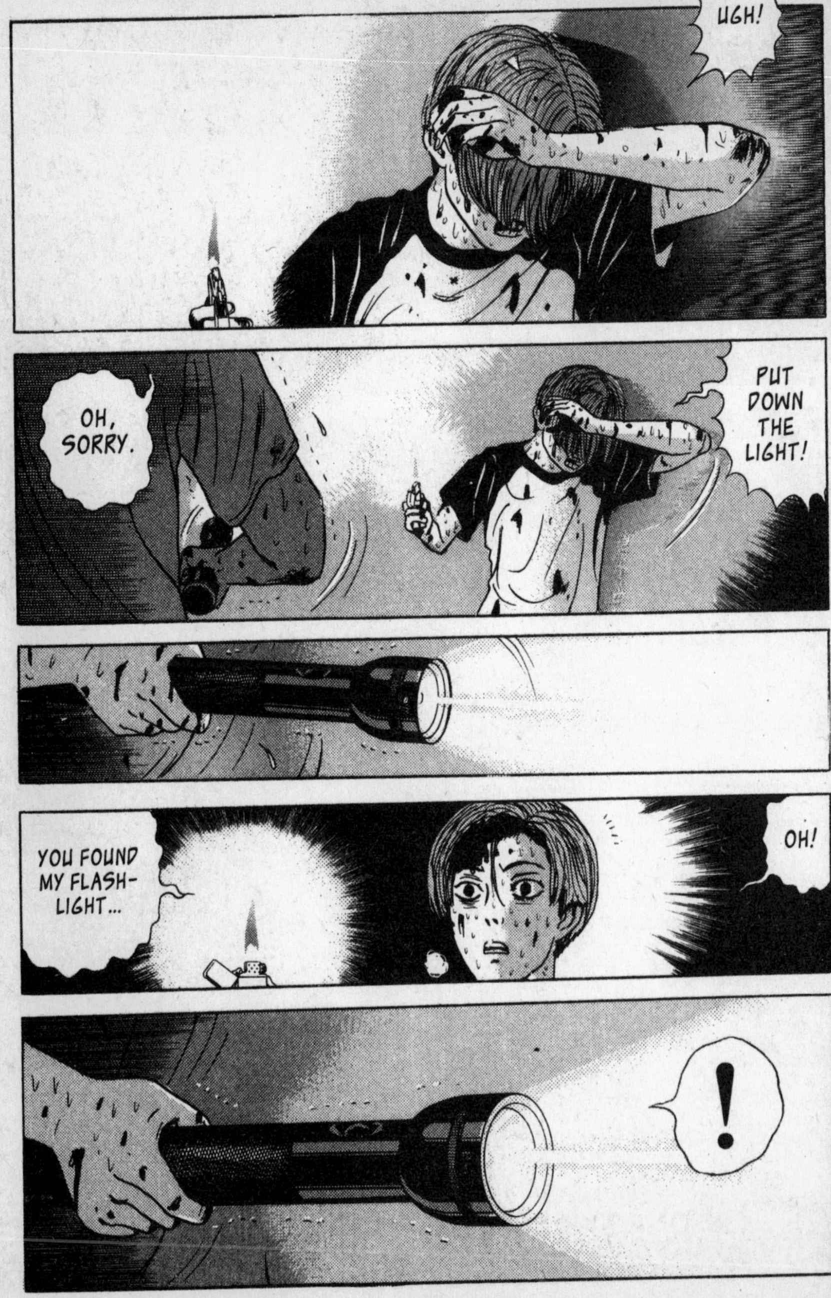
UGH!
PUT DOWN THE LIGHT!
OH, SORRY.
OH!
YOU FOUND MY FLASH-LIGHT...
!

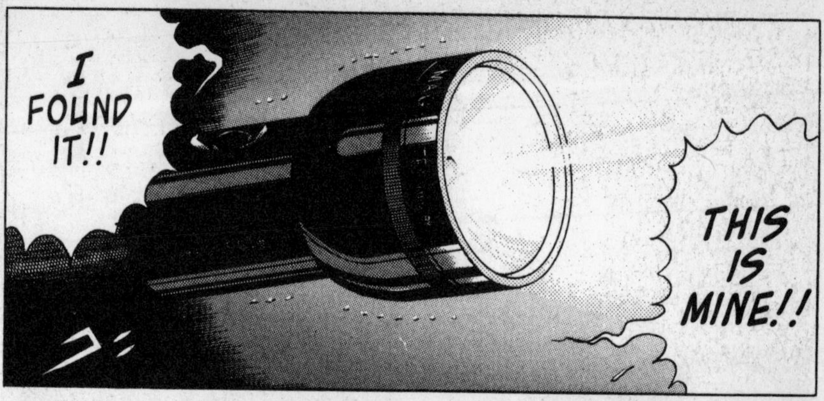
THIS IS MINE!!
I FOUND IT!!
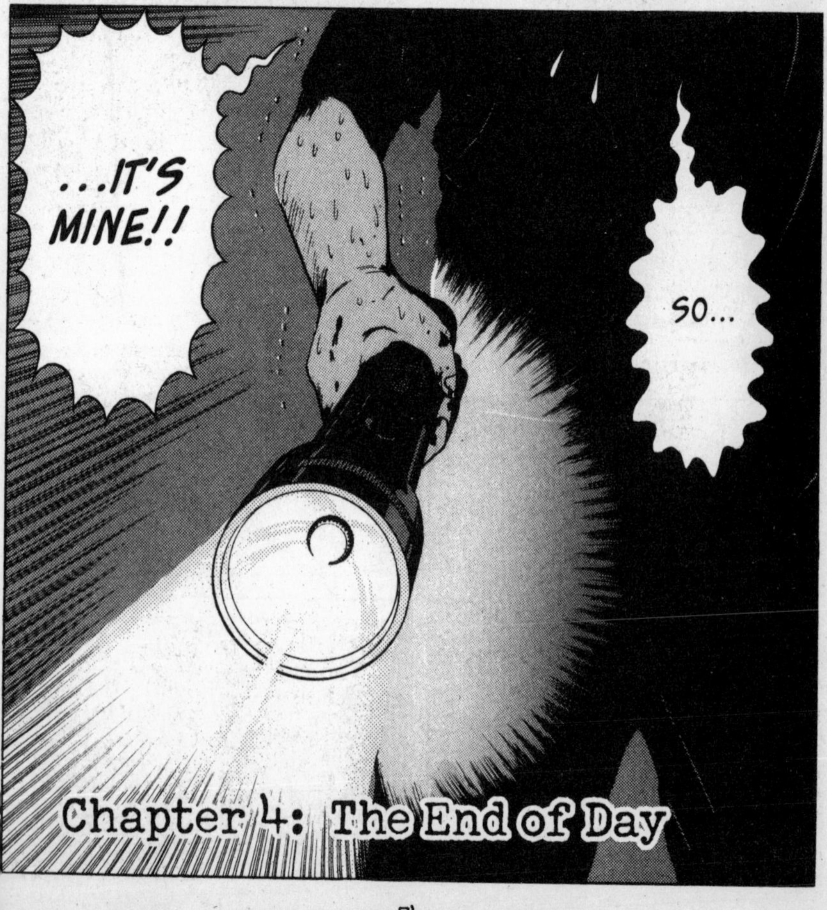
SO...
...IT'S MINE!!
Chapter 4: The End of Day

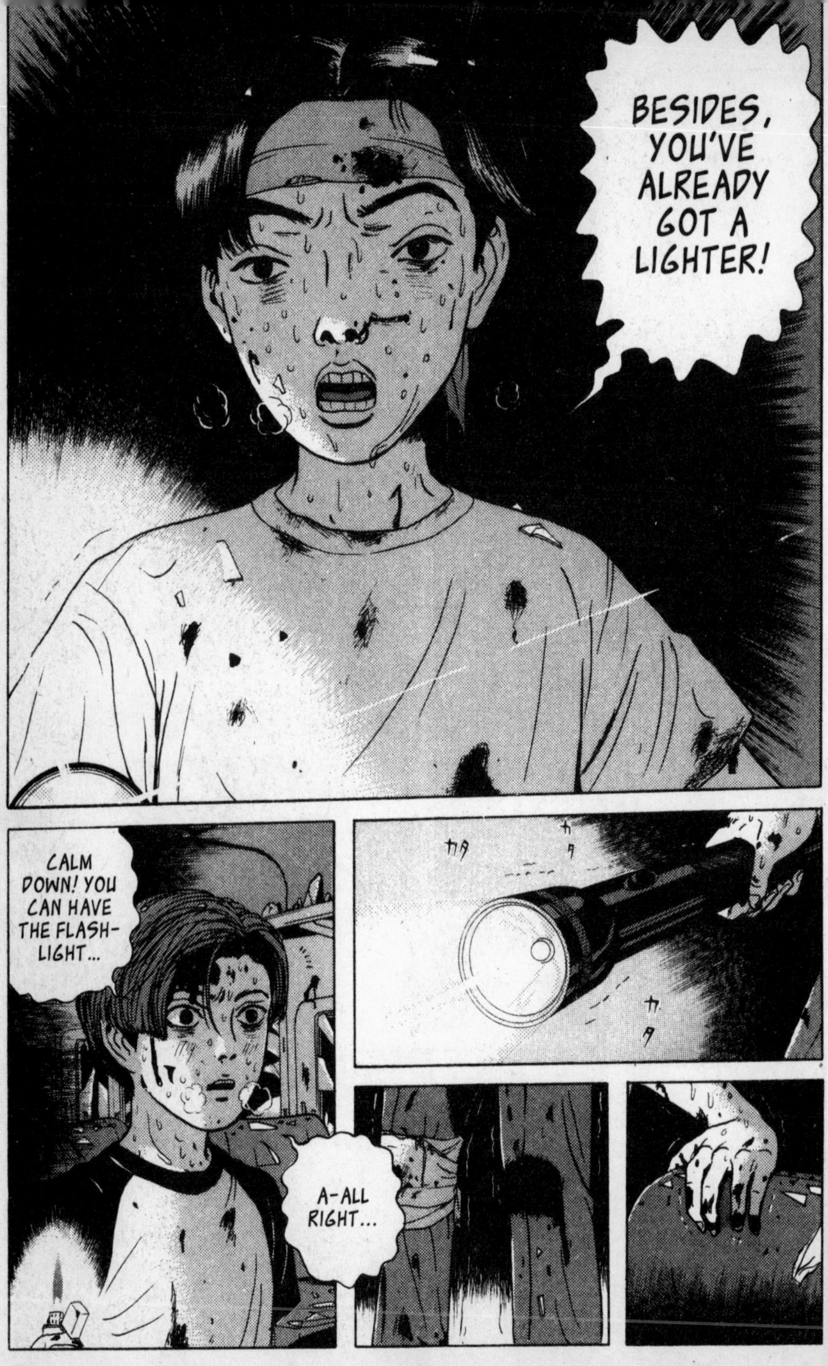
BESIDES, YOU'VE ALREADY GOT A LIGHTER!
カタ
カタ
カタ
CALM DOWN! YOU CAN HAVE THE FLASH-LIGHT...
A-ALL RIGHT...

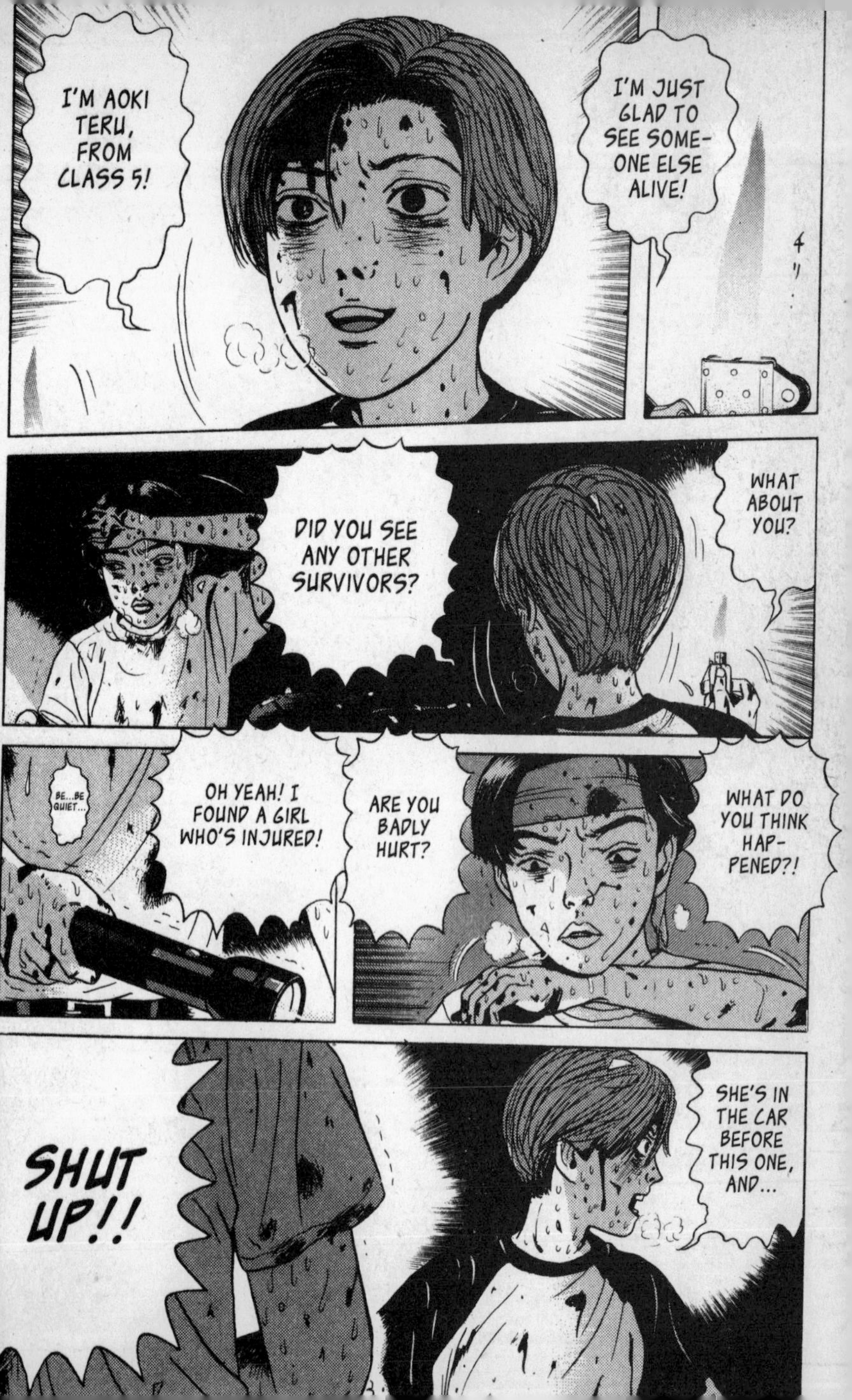
I'M JUST GLAD TO SEE SOME-ONE ELSE ALIVE!
I'M AOKI TERU, FROM CLASS 5!
WHAT ABOUT YOU?
DID YOU SEE ANY OTHER SURVIVORS?
WHAT DO YOU THINK HAP-PENED?!
ARE YOU BADLY HURT?
OH YEAH! I FOUND A GIRL WHO'S INJURED!
BE...BE QUIET...
SHE'S IN THE CAR BEFORE THIS ONE, AND...
SHUT UP!!

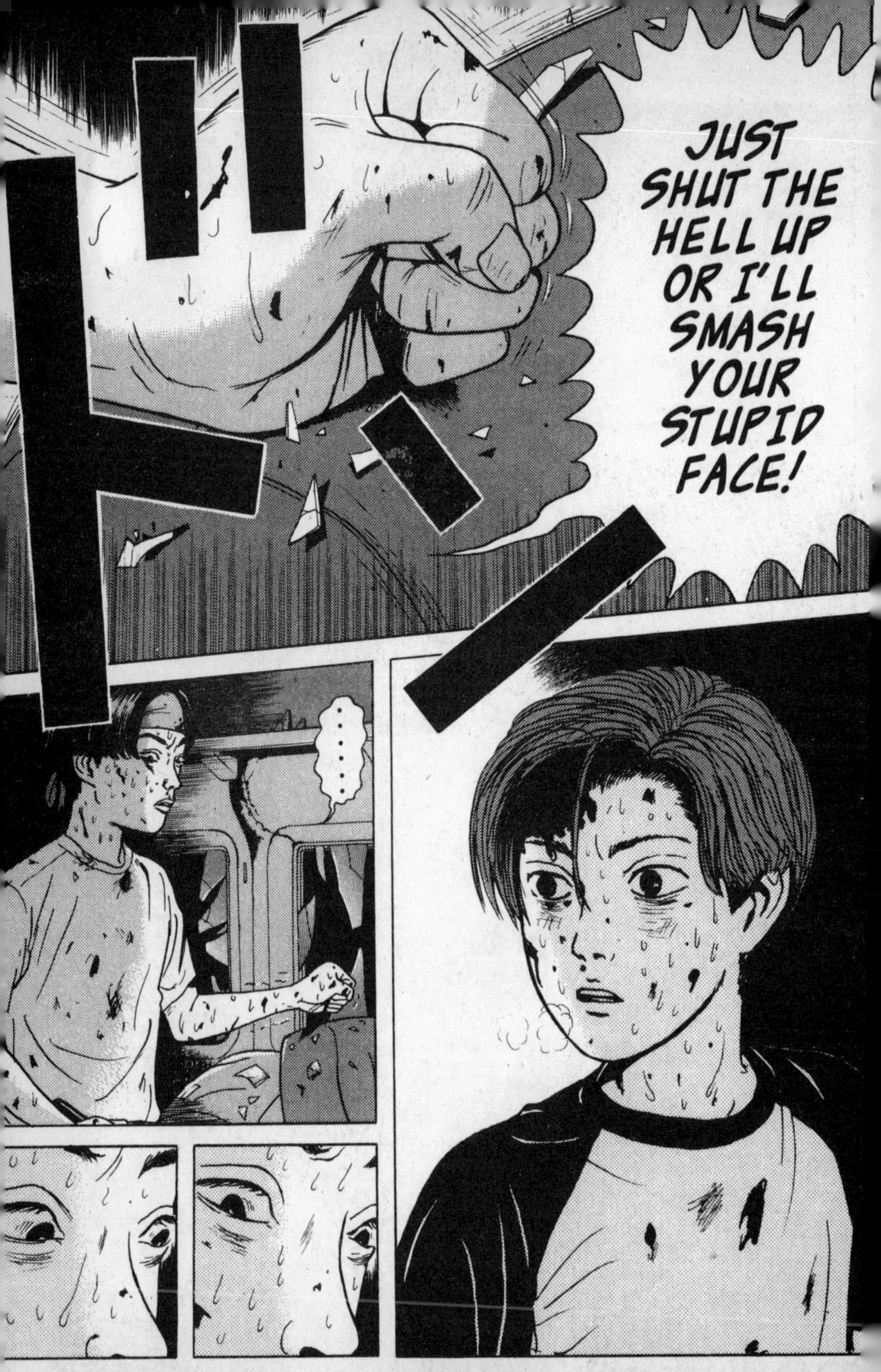
JUST SHUT THE HELL UP OR I'LL SMASH YOUR STUPID FACE!
......

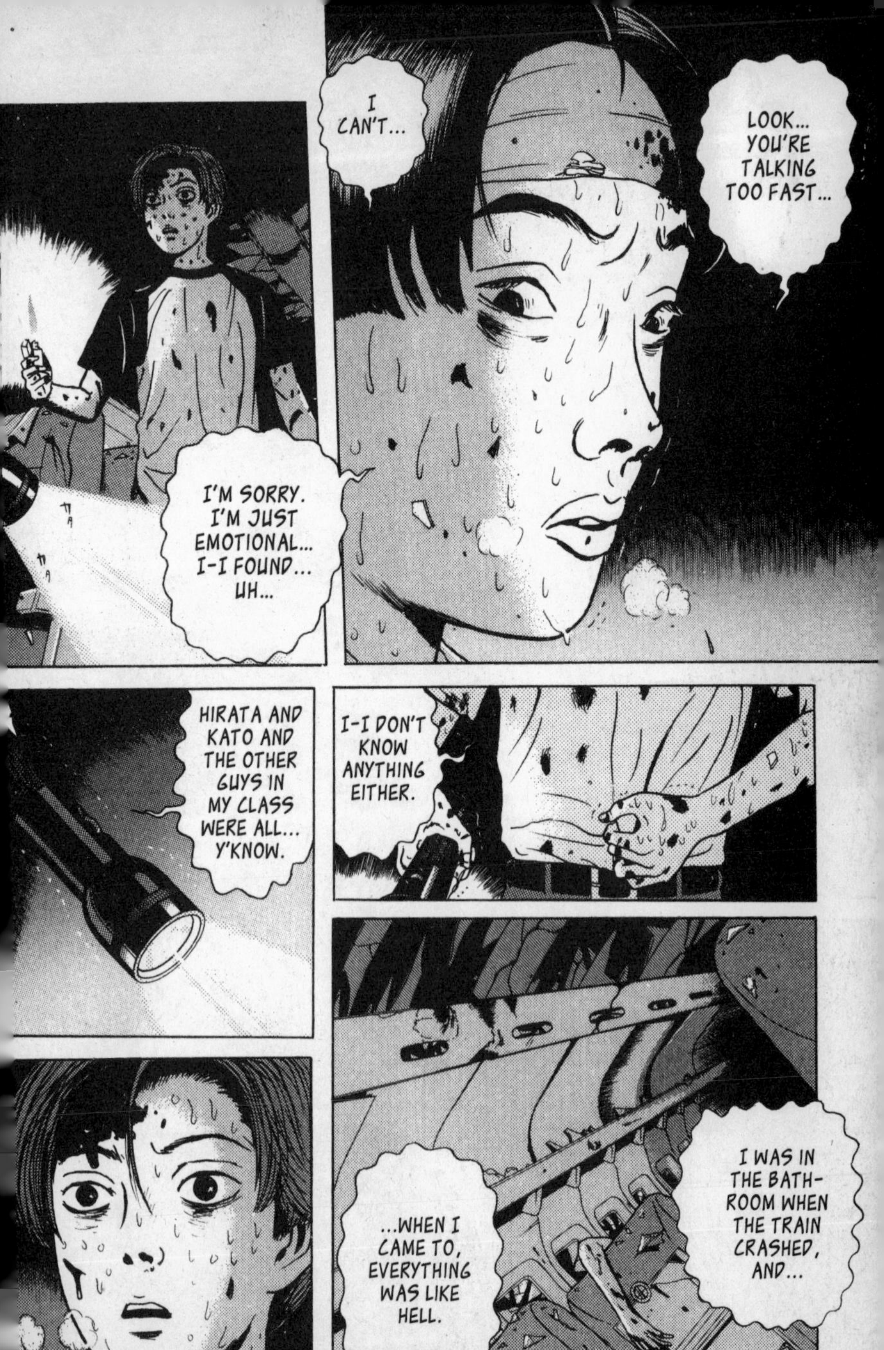
LOOK... YOU'RE TALKING TOO FAST...
I CAN'T...
I'M SORRY. I'M JUST EMOTIONAL... I-I FOUND... UH...
I-I DON'T KNOW ANYTHING EITHER.
HIRATA AND KATO AND THE OTHER GUYS IN MY CLASS WERE ALL... Y'KNOW.
I WAS IN THE BATH-ROOM WHEN THE TRAIN CRASHED, AND...
...WHEN I CAME TO, EVERYTHING WAS LIKE HELL.

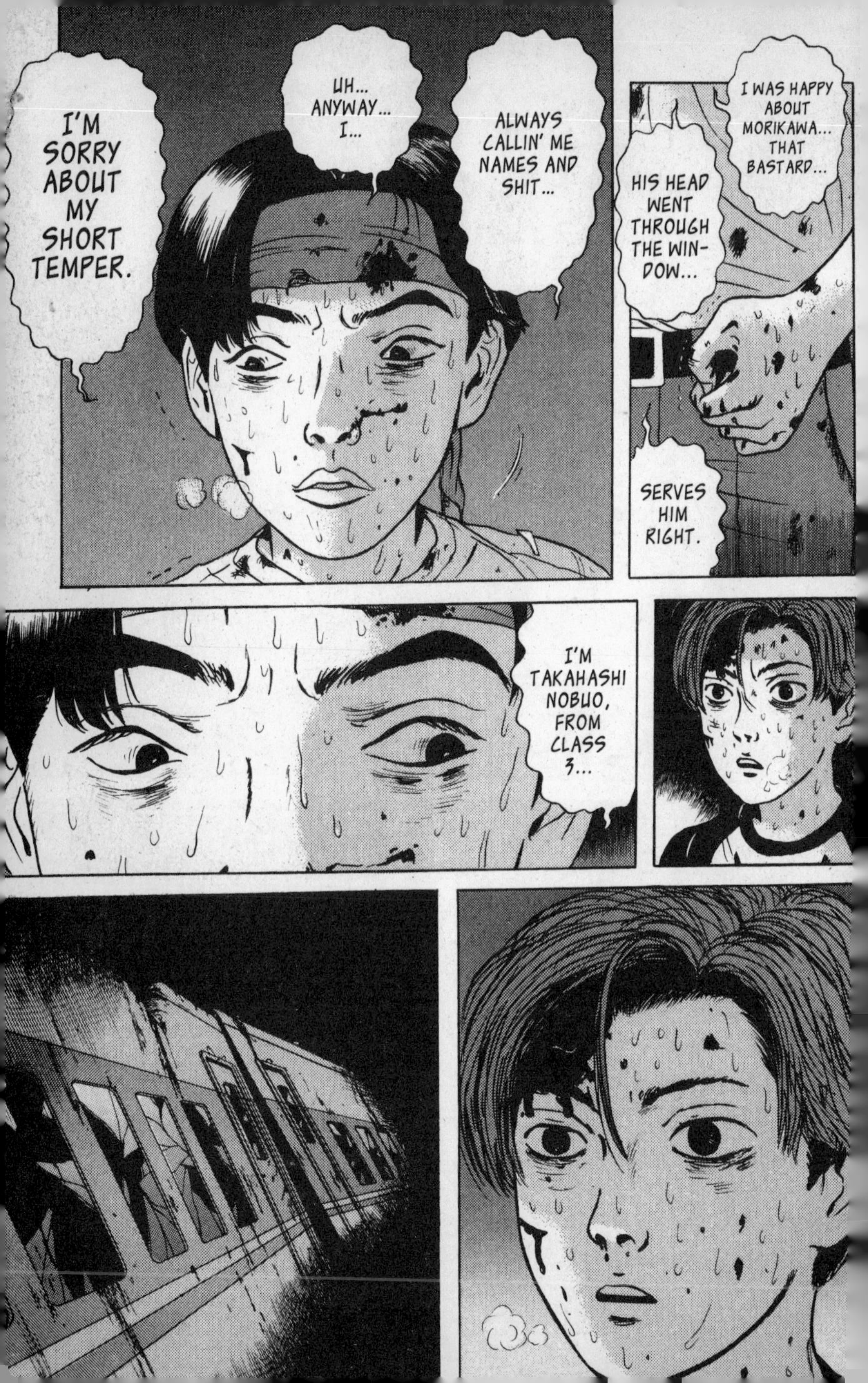
I WAS HAPPY ABOUT MORIKAWA... THAT BASTARD...
HIS HEAD WENT THROUGH THE WIN-DOW...
SERVES HIM RIGHT.
ALWAYS CALLIN' ME NAMES AND SHIT...
UH... ANYWAY... I...
I'M SORRY ABOUT MY SHORT TEMPER.
I'M TAKAHASHI NOBUO, FROM CLASS 3...

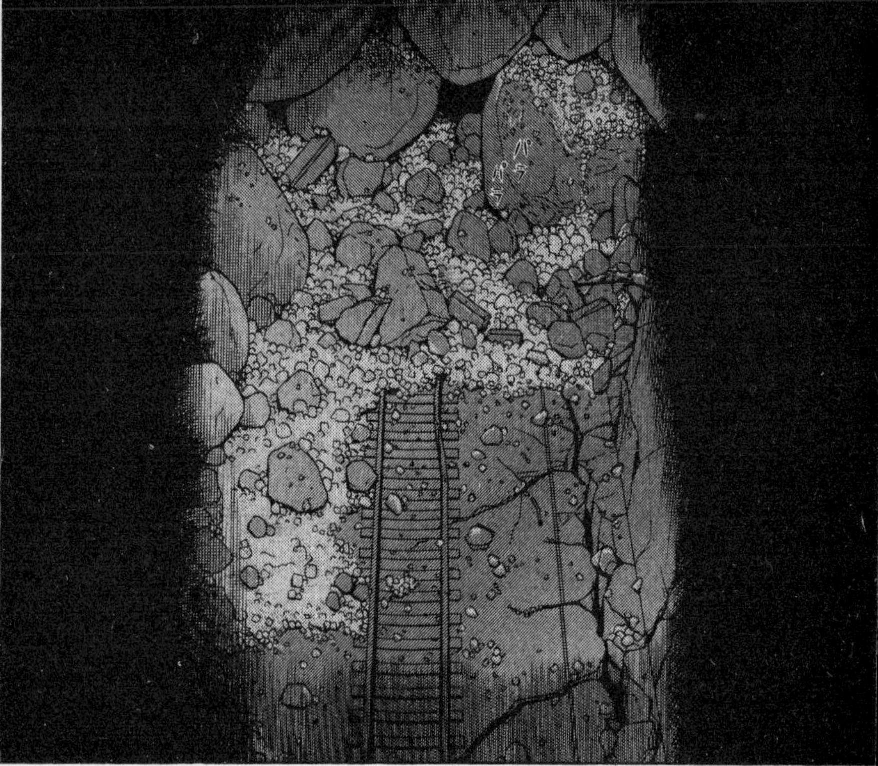
パラ
パラ
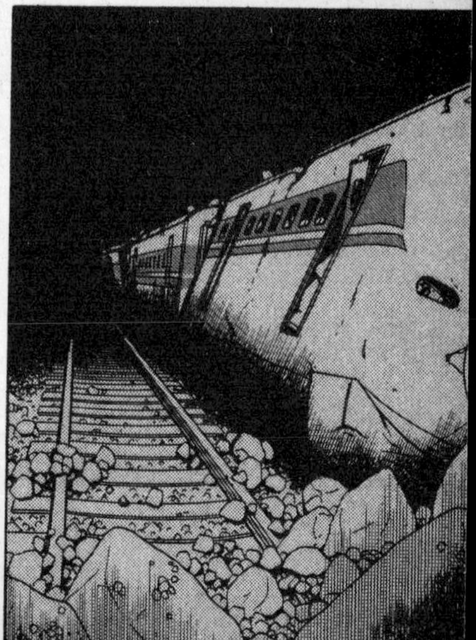
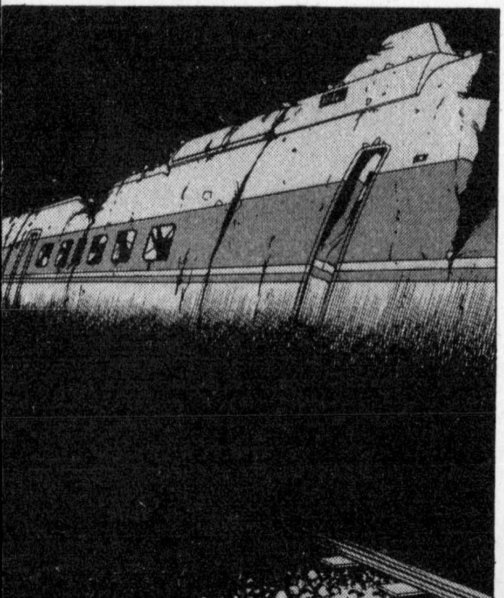

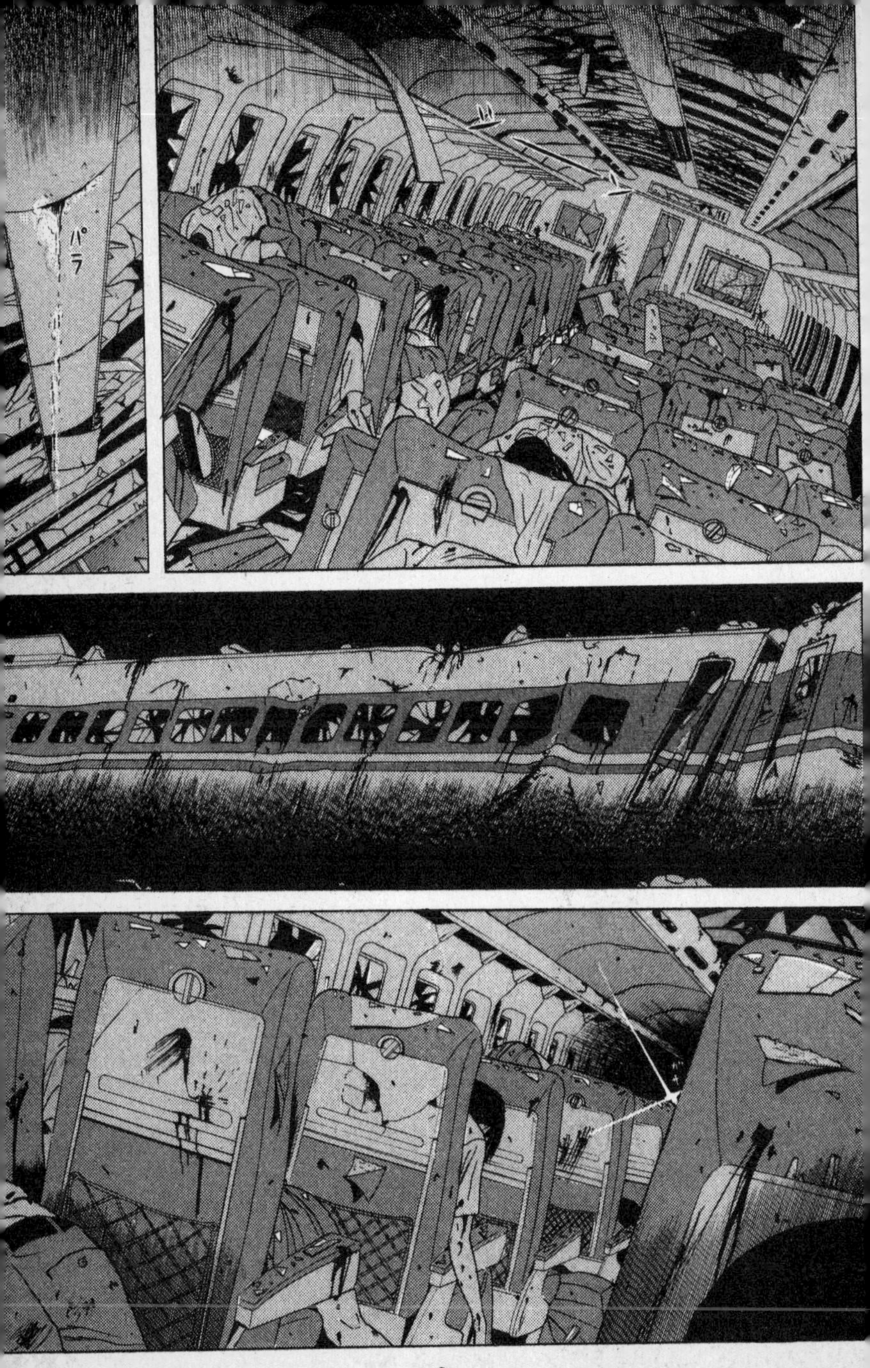
パラ

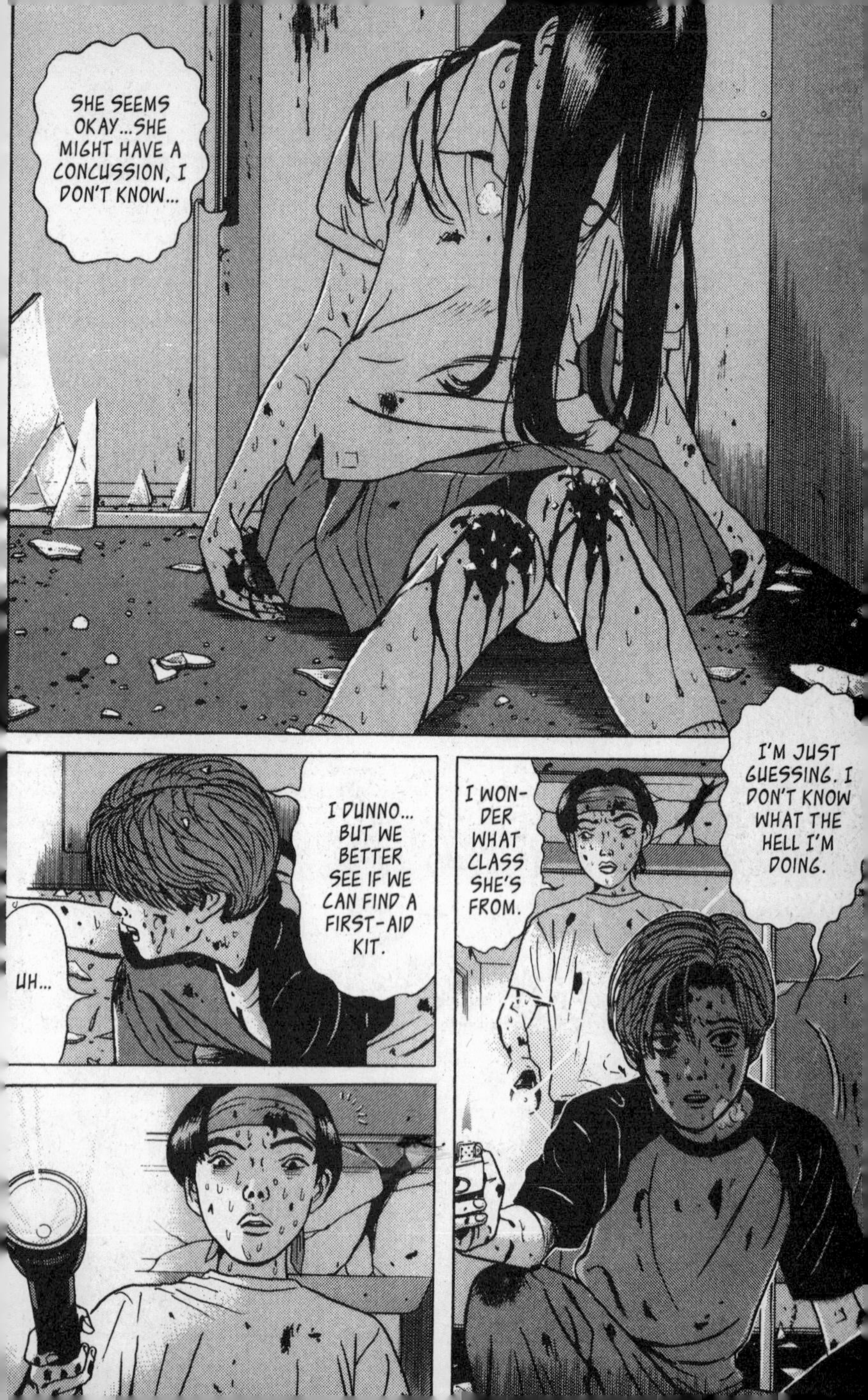
SHE SEEMS OKAY...SHE MIGHT HAVE A CONCUSSION, I DON'T KNOW...
I'M JUST GUESSING. I DON'T KNOW WHAT THE HELL I'M DOING.
I WONDER WHAT CLASS SHE'S FROM.
I DUNNO... BUT WE BETTER SEE IF WE CAN FIND A FIRST-AID KIT.
UH...

YEAH! I WAS ABOUT TO GO "SHOPPING" TOO.

GOOD THING I'VE GOT MY FLASHLIGHT.

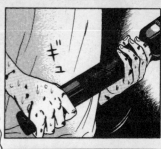

HUFF HUFF

HUFF HUFF

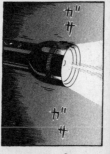

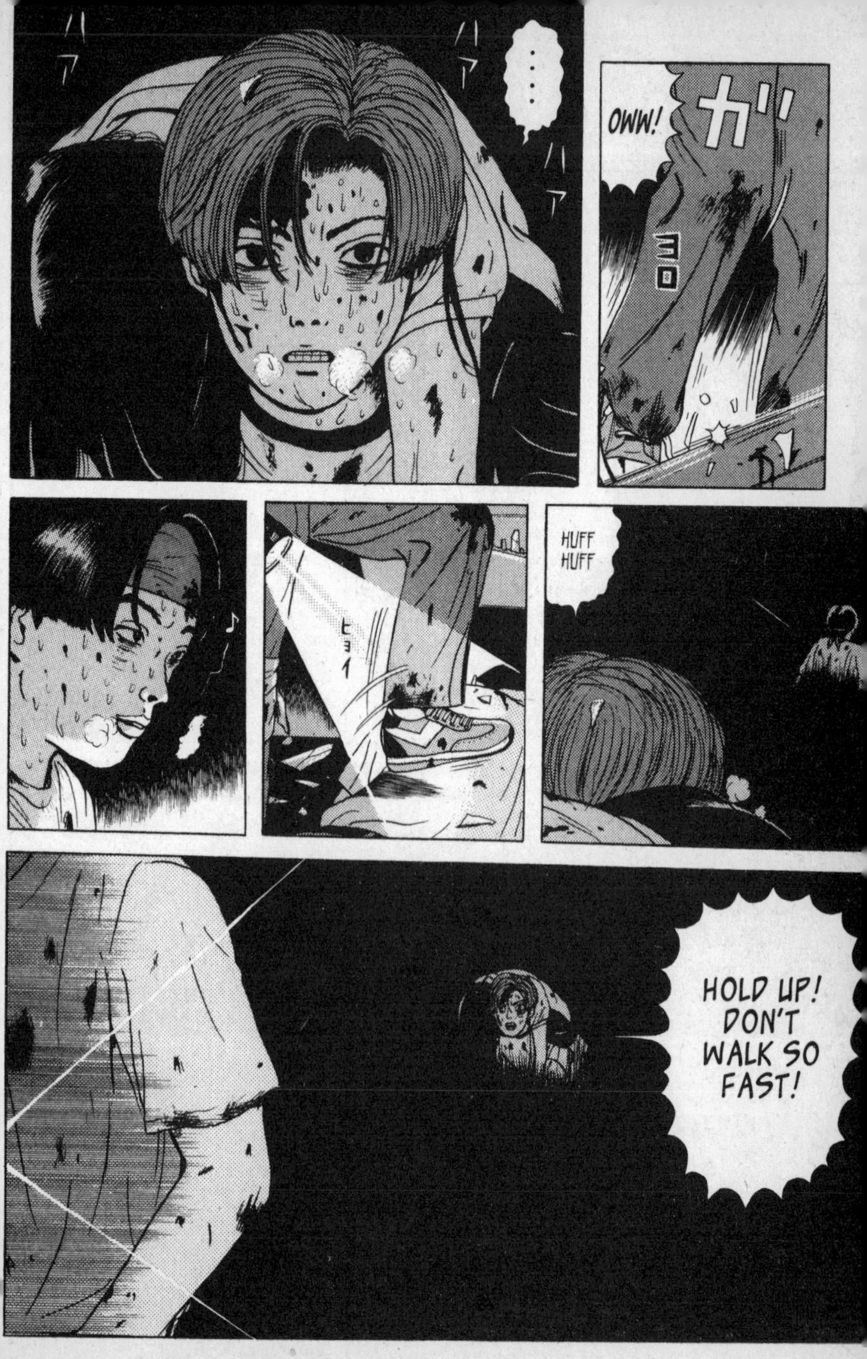
OWW!
ガッ
ヨロ
ハァ
ハァ
...
HUFF HUFF
ヒョイ
HOLD UP! DON'T WALK SO FAST!

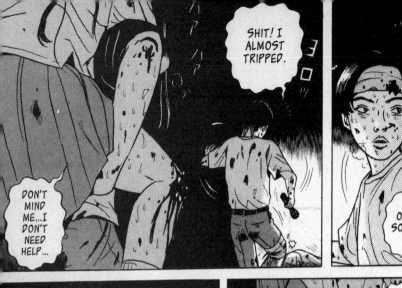

SHIT! I ALMOST TRIPPED.

OH... SORRY.

DON'T MIND ME...I DON'T NEED HELP...

WHAT'S WITH THIS GUY...?

ハァ ハァ

THE FOOD CAR!!!

THEY GOT EVERY- THING HERE!

FOOD AND DRINKS!

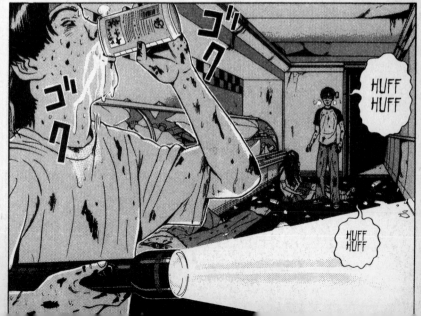

HUFF HUFF

HUFF HUFF

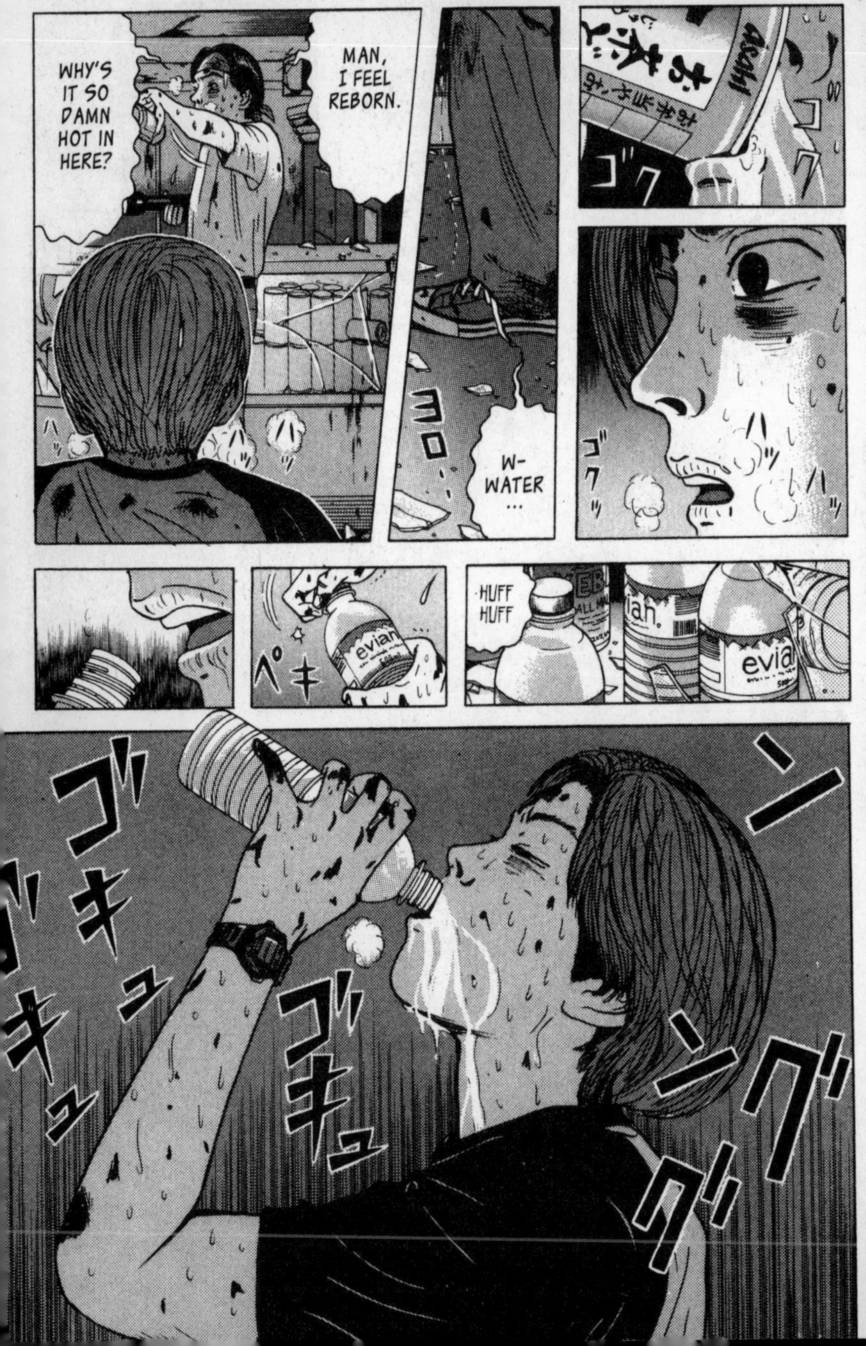
ゴク
ゴクッ
W-WATER...
ヨロ
MAN, I FEEL REBORN.
WHY'S IT SO DAMN HOT IN HERE?
HUFF HUFF
ペキ
evian
ングング
ゴキュ
ゴキュ
ゴキュ

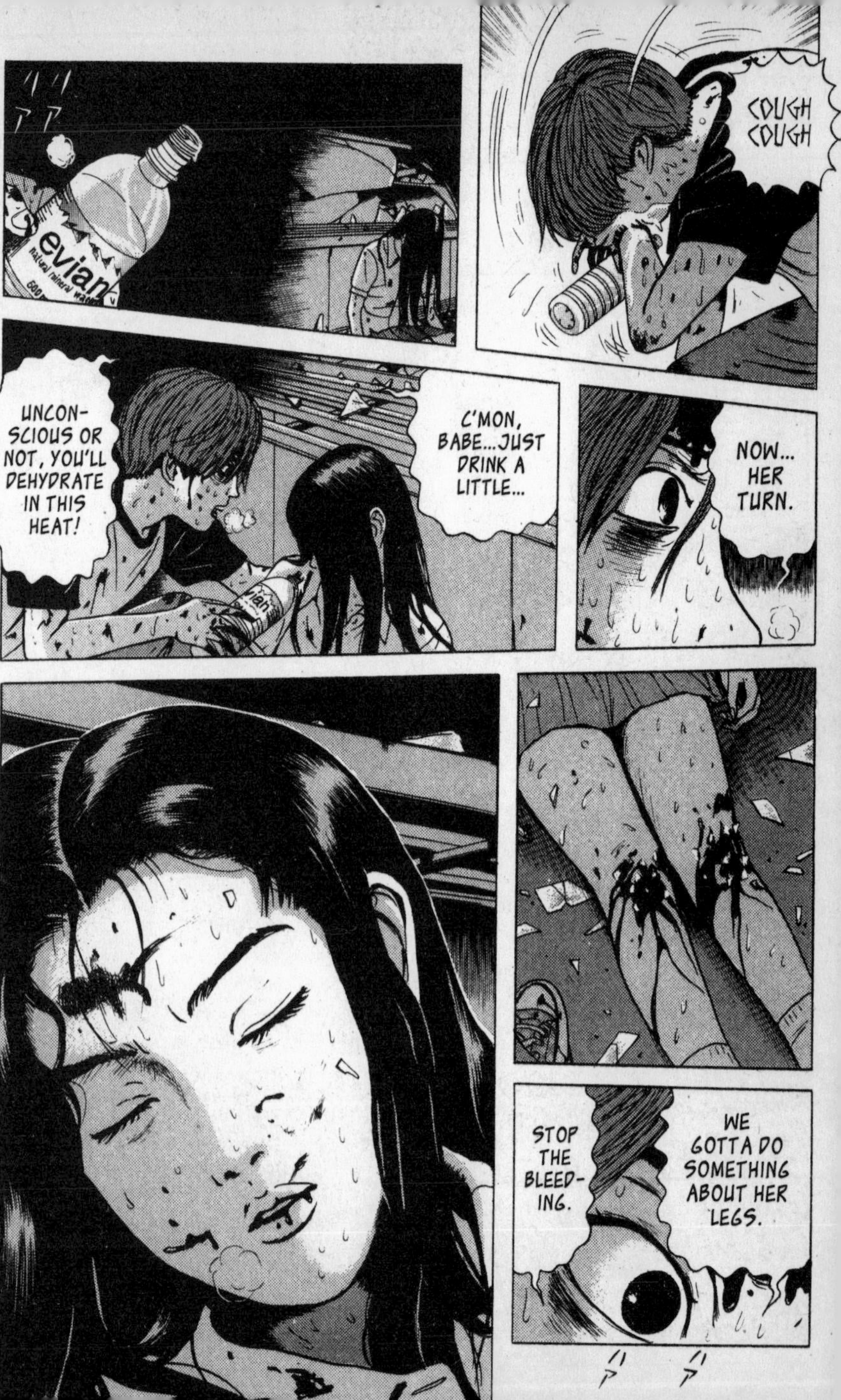
COUGH COUGH
evian
NOW... HER TURN.
C'MON, BABE...JUST DRINK A LITTLE...
UNCON-SCIOUS OR NOT, YOU'LL DEHYDRATE IN THIS HEAT!
WE GOTTA DO SOMETHING ABOUT HER LEGS.
STOP THE BLEED-ING.

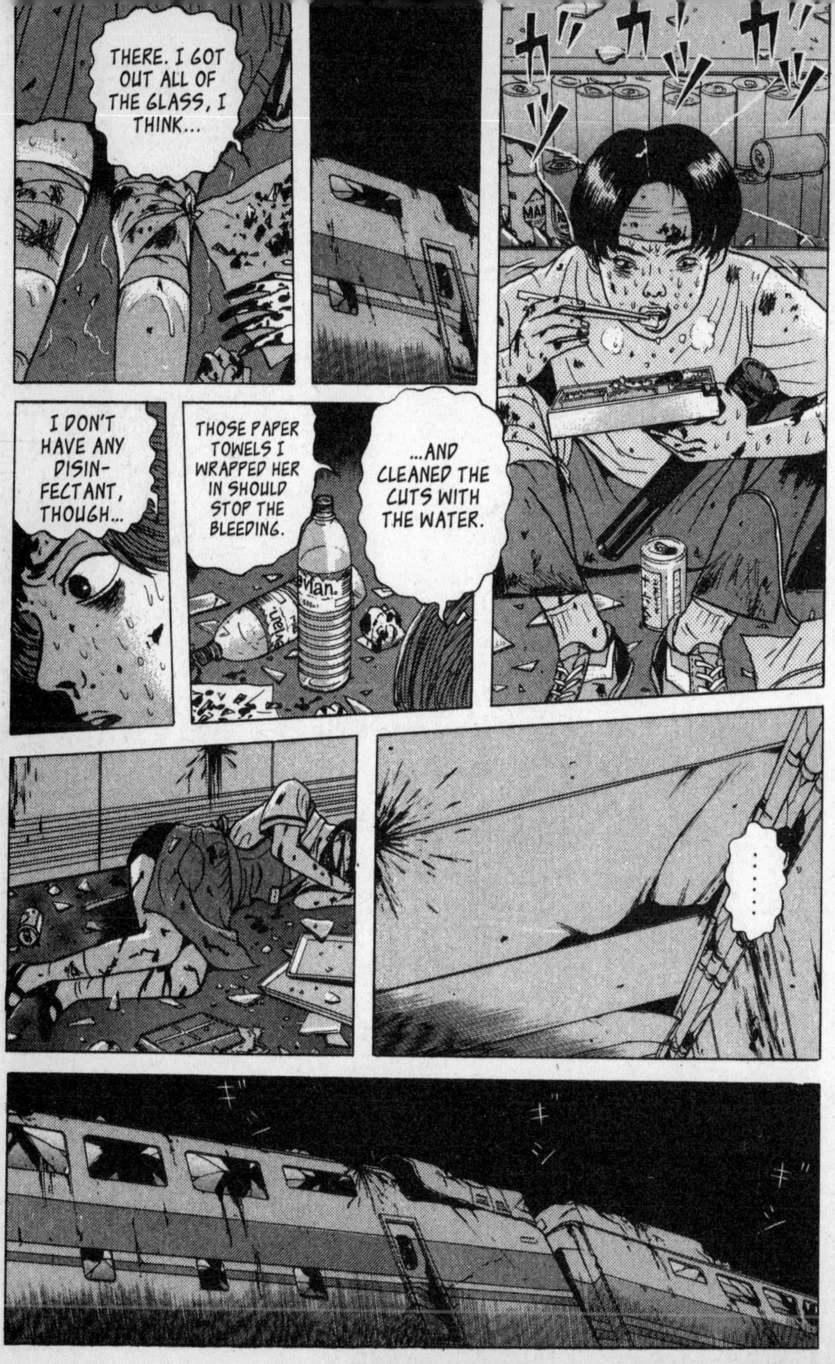
THERE. I GOT OUT ALL OF THE GLASS, I THINK...
...AND CLEANED THE CUTS WITH THE WATER.
THOSE PAPER TOWELS I WRAPPED HER IN SHOULD STOP THE BLEEDING.
I DON'T HAVE ANY DISIN-FECTANT, THOUGH...
......

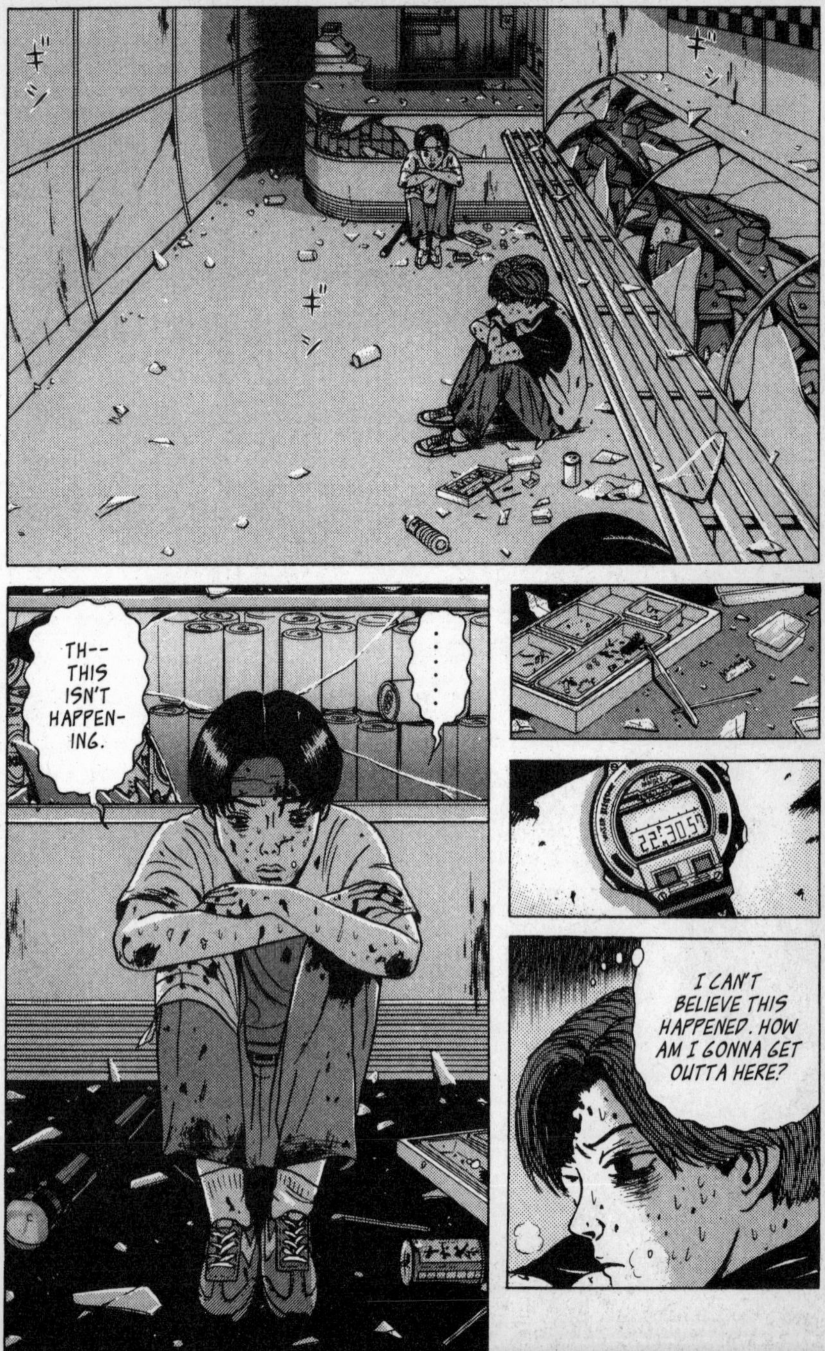

ギシ
ギシ
ギシ
22:30.57
I CAN'T BELIEVE THIS HAPPENED. HOW AM I GONNA GET OUTTA HERE?
TH-- THIS ISN'T HAPPEN-ING.
......

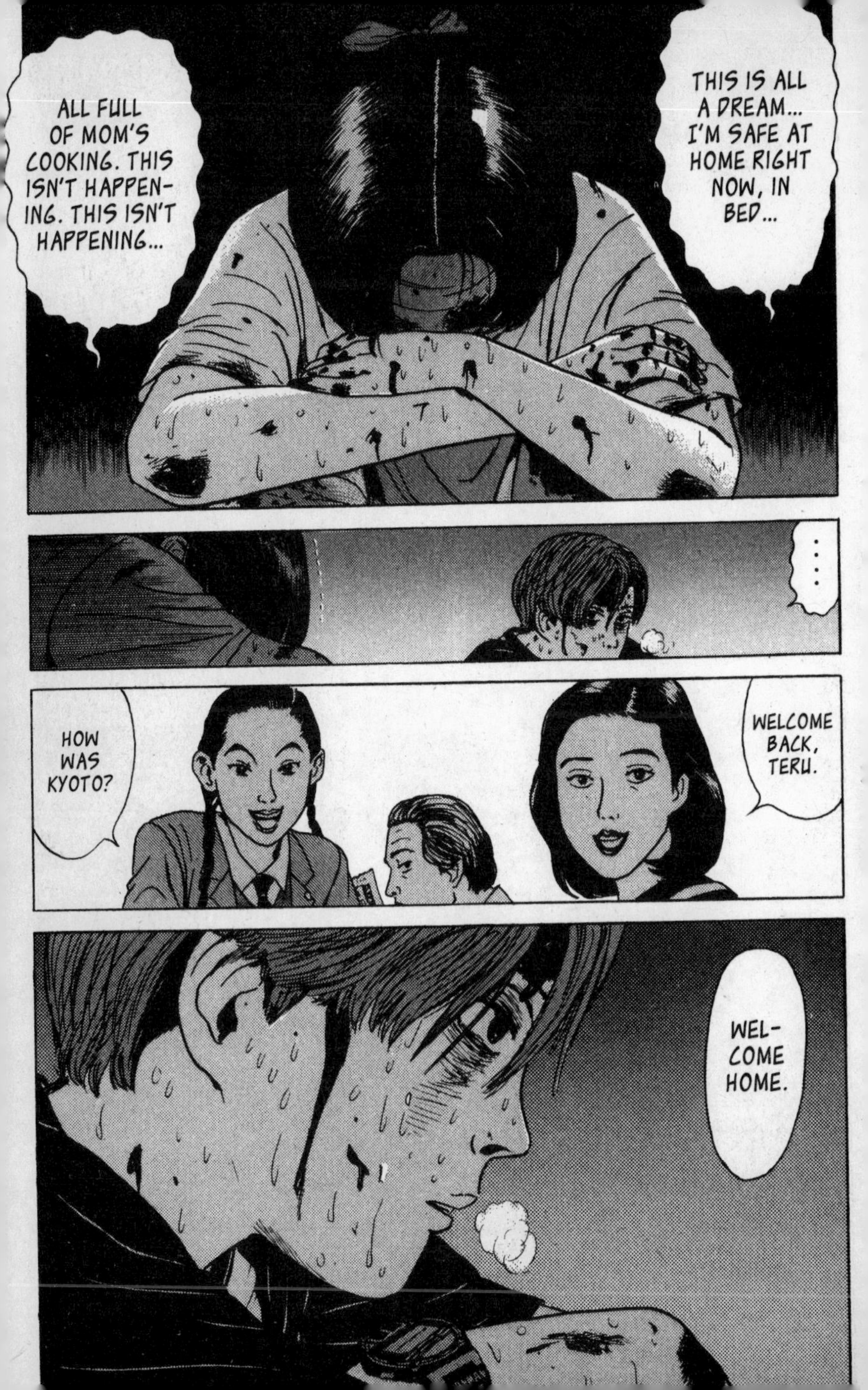
THIS IS ALL A DREAM... I'M SAFE AT HOME RIGHT NOW, IN BED...
ALL FULL OF MOM'S COOKING. THIS ISN'T HAPPEN-ING. THIS ISN'T HAPPENING...
....
WELCOME BACK, TERU.
HOW WAS KYOTO?
WEL-COME HOME.

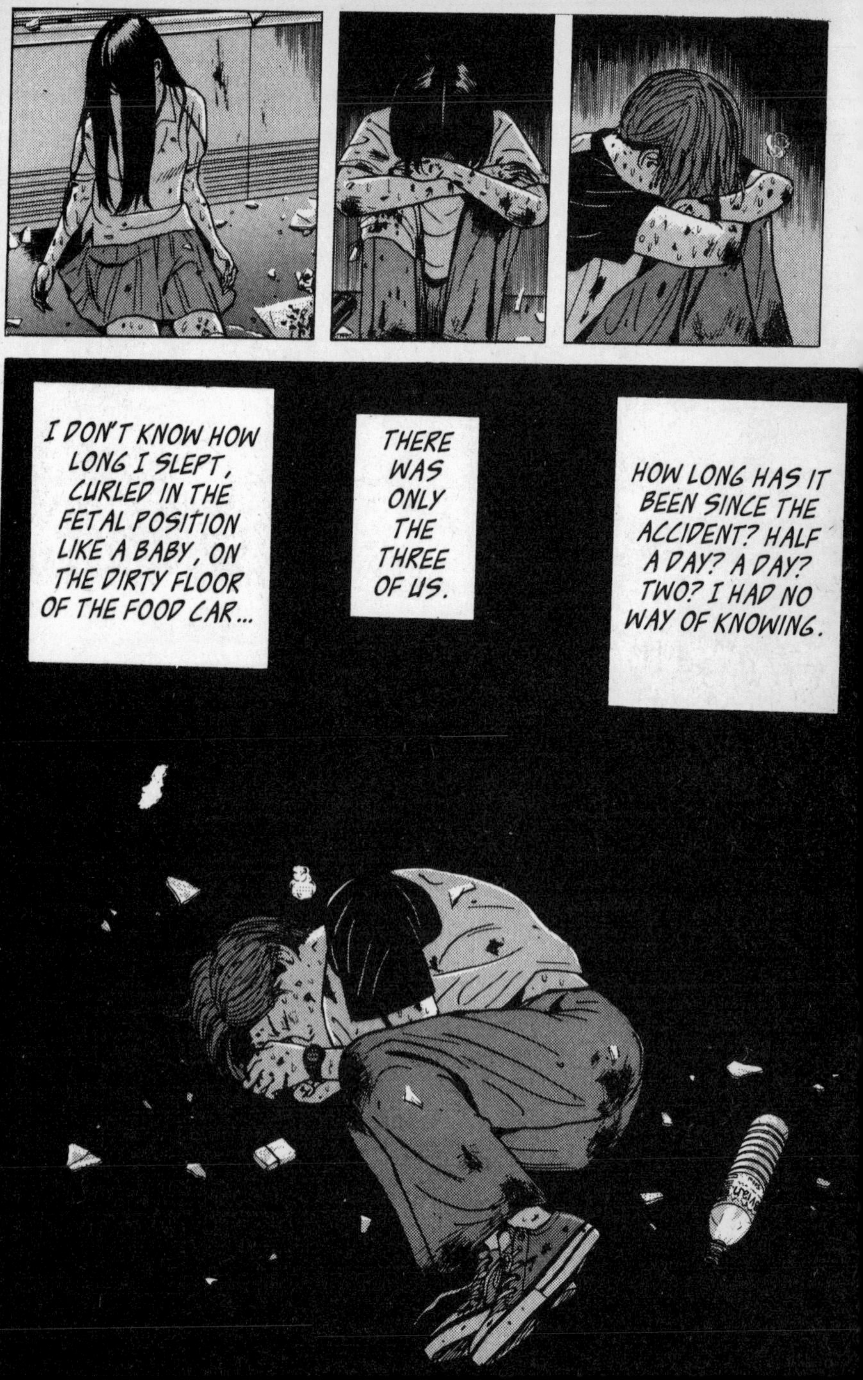
HOW LONG HAS IT BEEN SINCE THE ACCIDENT? HALF A DAY? A DAY? TWO? I HAD NO WAY OF KNOWING.
THERE WAS ONLY THE THREE OF US.
I DON'T KNOW HOW LONG I SLEPT, CURLED IN THE FETAL POSITION LIKE A BABY, ON THE DIRTY FLOOR OF THE FOOD CAR...

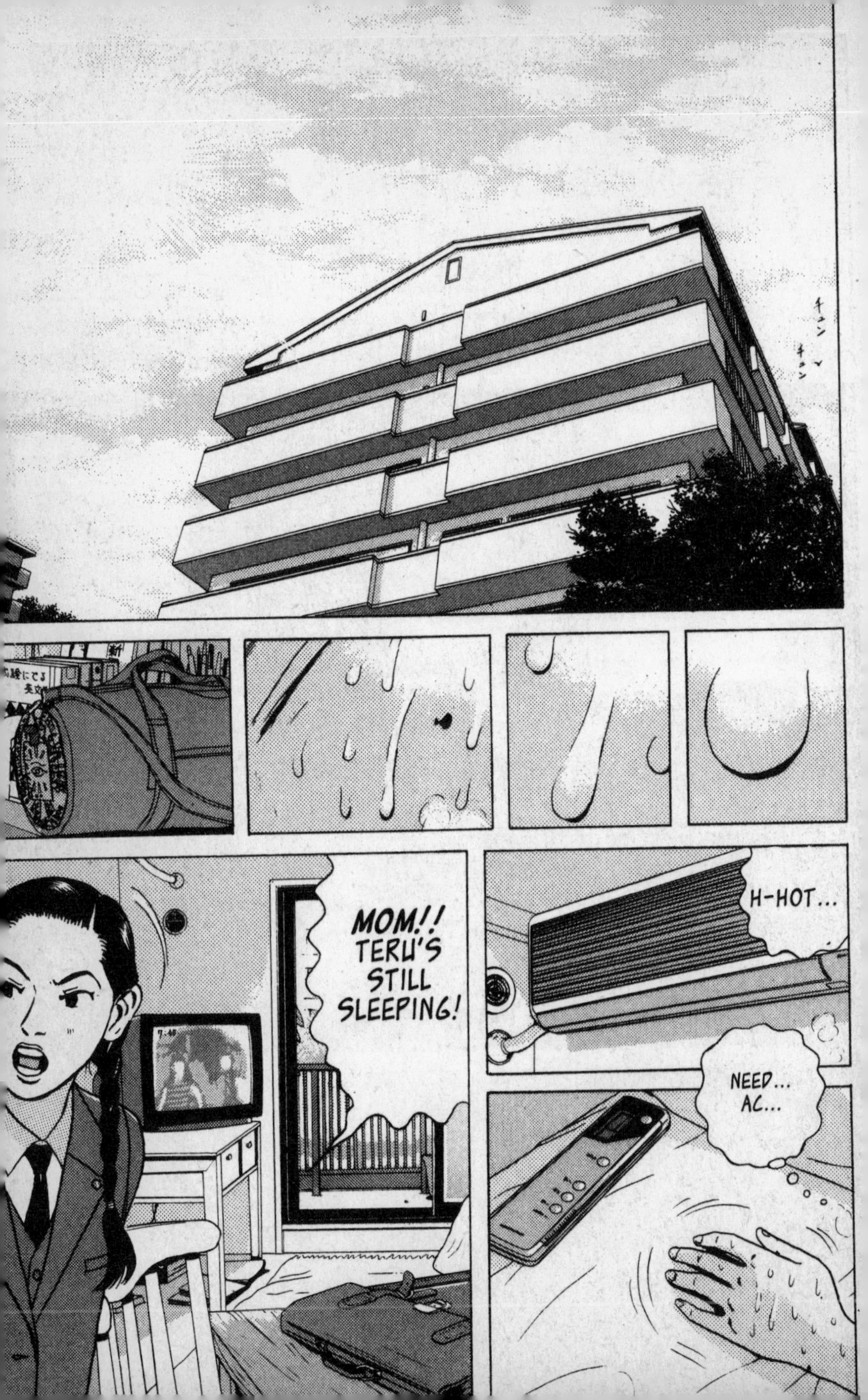
チュン
チュン
H-HOT...
NEED... AC...
MOM!! TERU'S STILL SLEEPING!

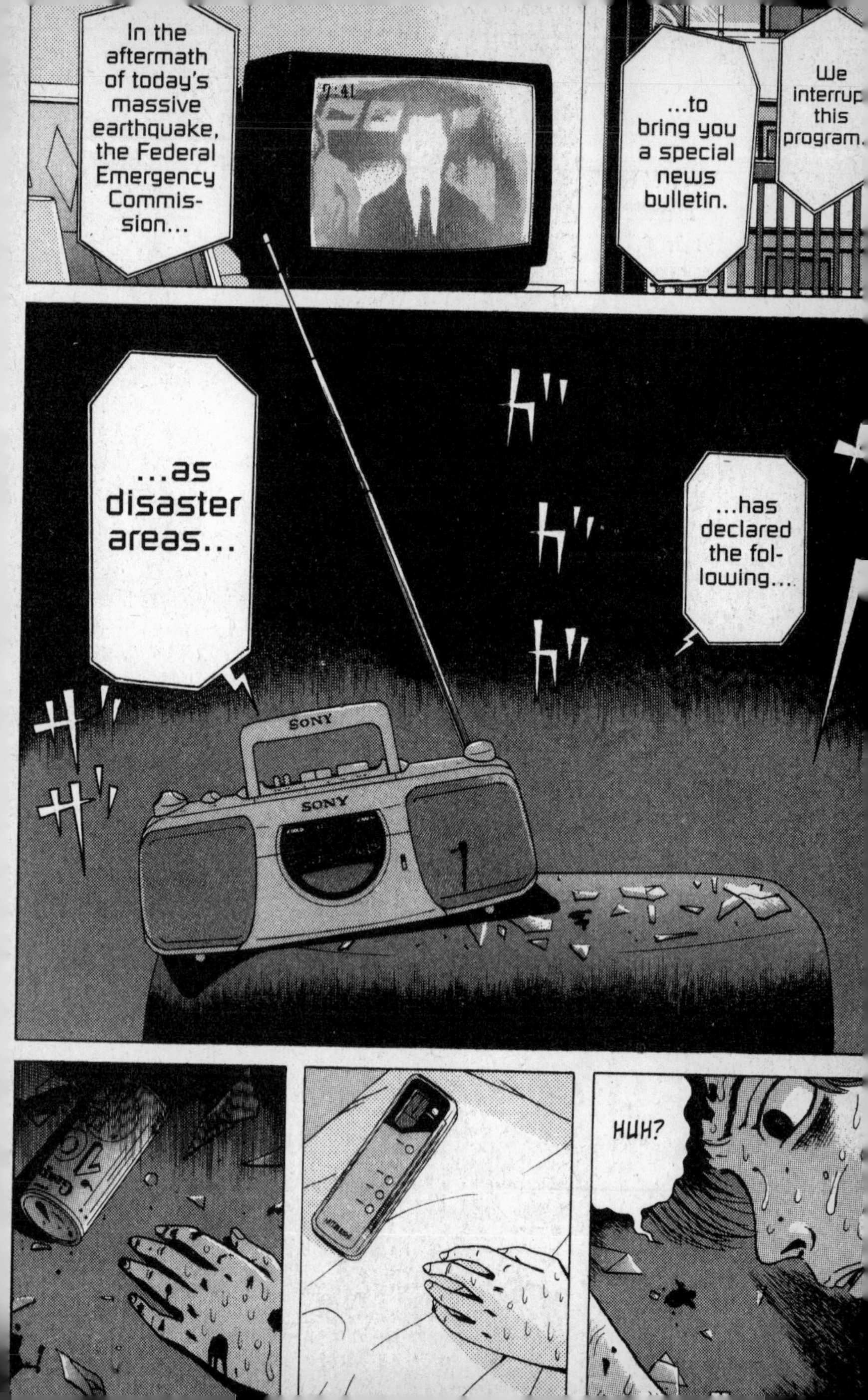
We interrup this program.
...to bring you a special news bulletin.
In the aftermath of today's massive earthquake, the Federal Emergency Commis-sion...
...has declared the fol-lowing...
...as disaster areas...
HUH?

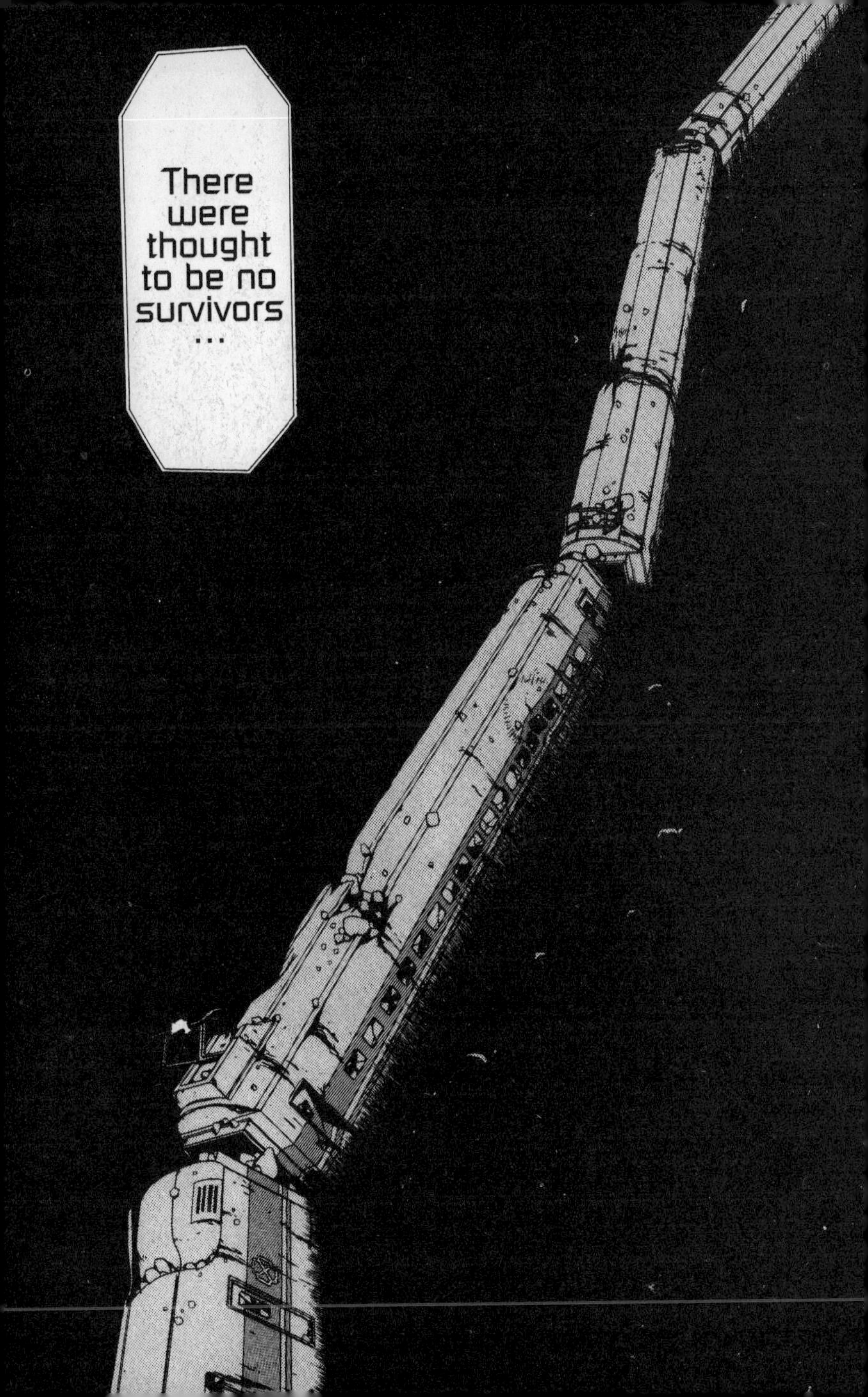
There were thought to be no survivors ...

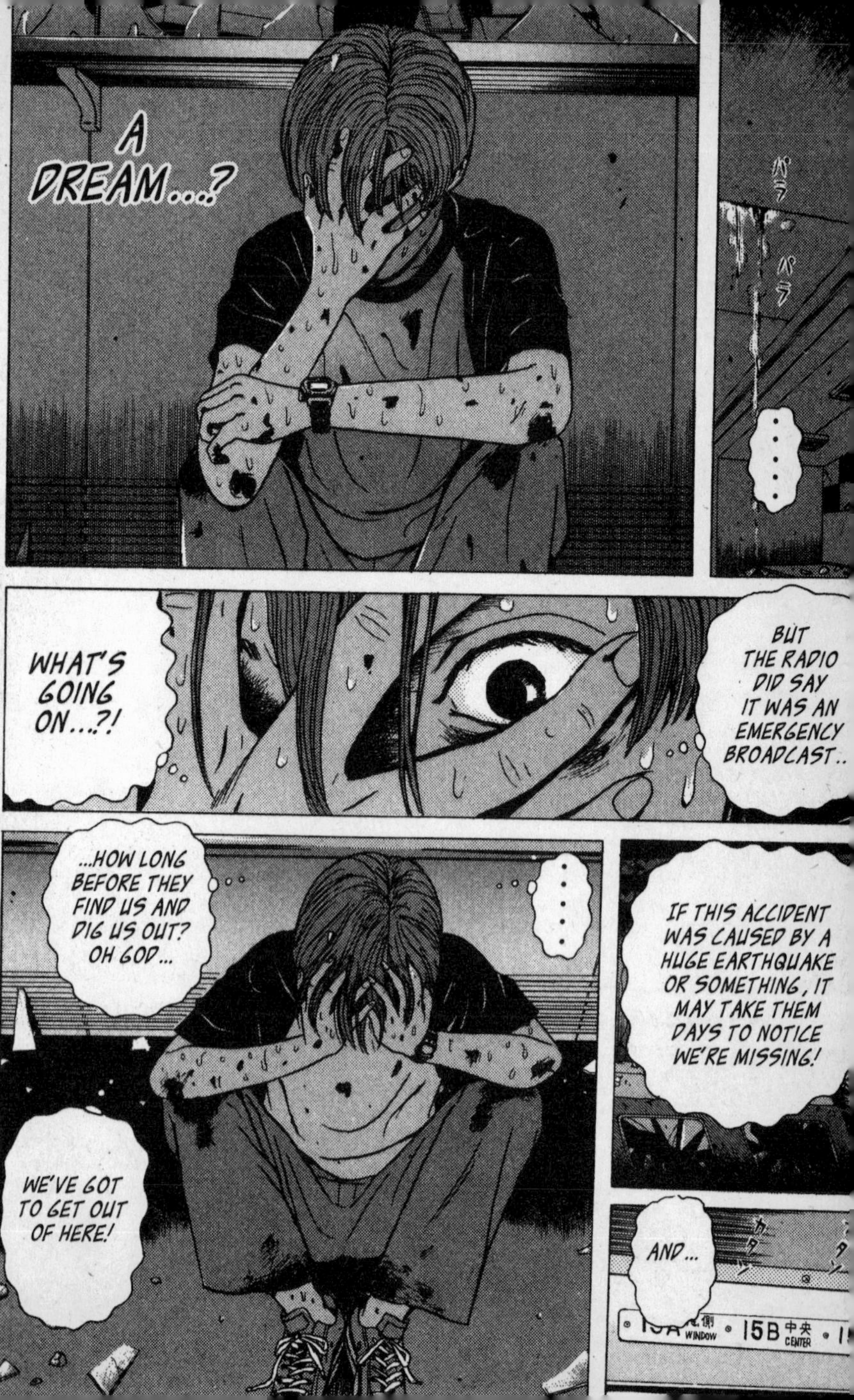
パラ パラ
......
A DREAM...?
BUT THE RADIO DID SAY IT WAS AN EMERGENCY BROADCAST..
WHAT'S GOING ON...?!
IF THIS ACCIDENT WAS CAUSED BY A HUGE EARTHQUAKE OR SOMETHING, IT MAY TAKE THEM DAYS TO NOTICE WE'RE MISSING!
......
...HOW LONG BEFORE THEY FIND US AND DIG US OUT? OH GOD...
WE'VE GOT TO GET OUT OF HERE!
カタン
AND...
WINDOW 15B 中央 CENTER

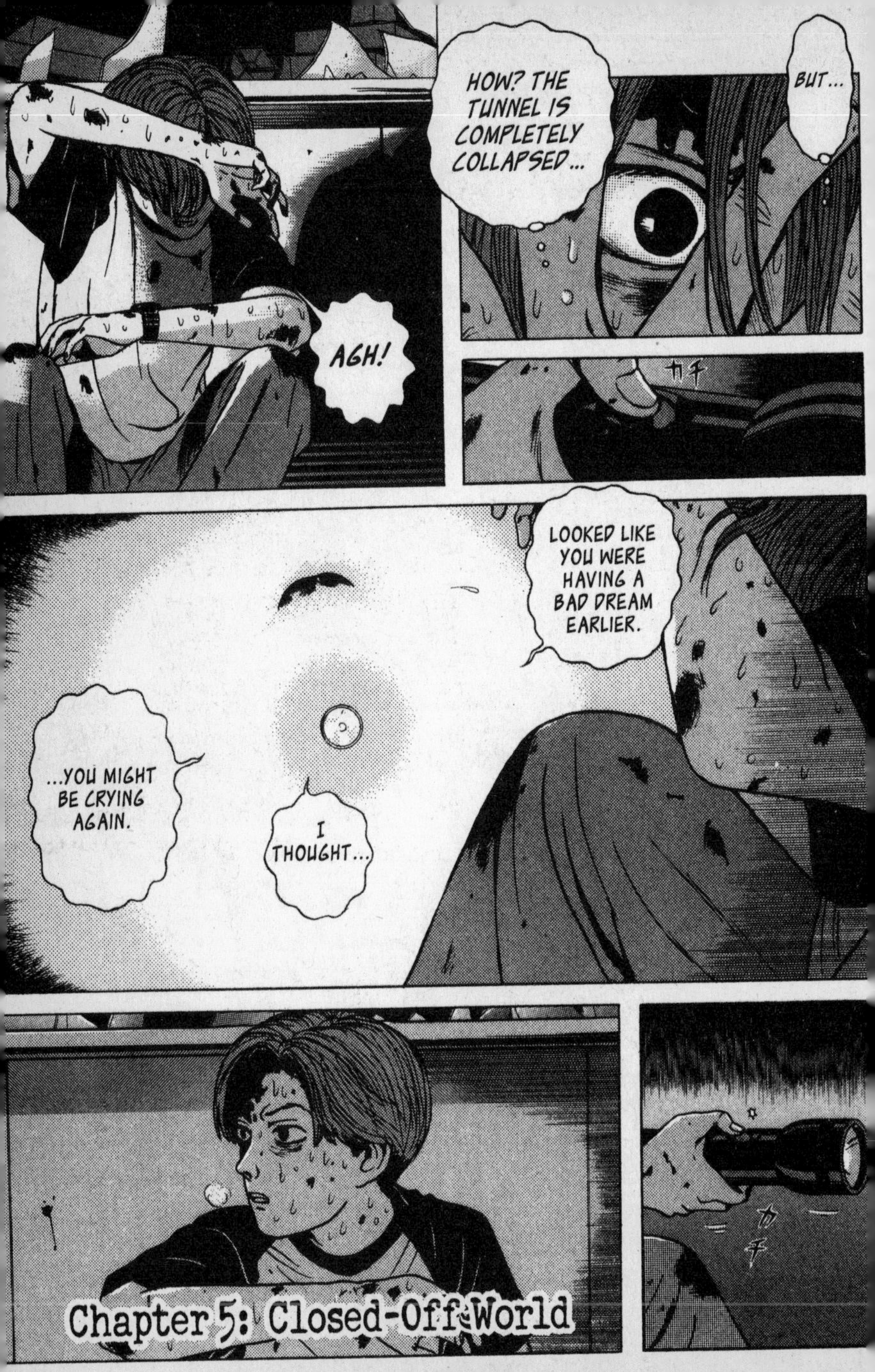
BUT...
HOW? THE TUNNEL IS COMPLETELY COLLAPSED...
カチ
AGH!
LOOKED LIKE YOU WERE HAVING A BAD DREAM EARLIER.
I THOUGHT...
...YOU MIGHT BE CRYING AGAIN.
カチ
Chapter 5: Closed-Off World

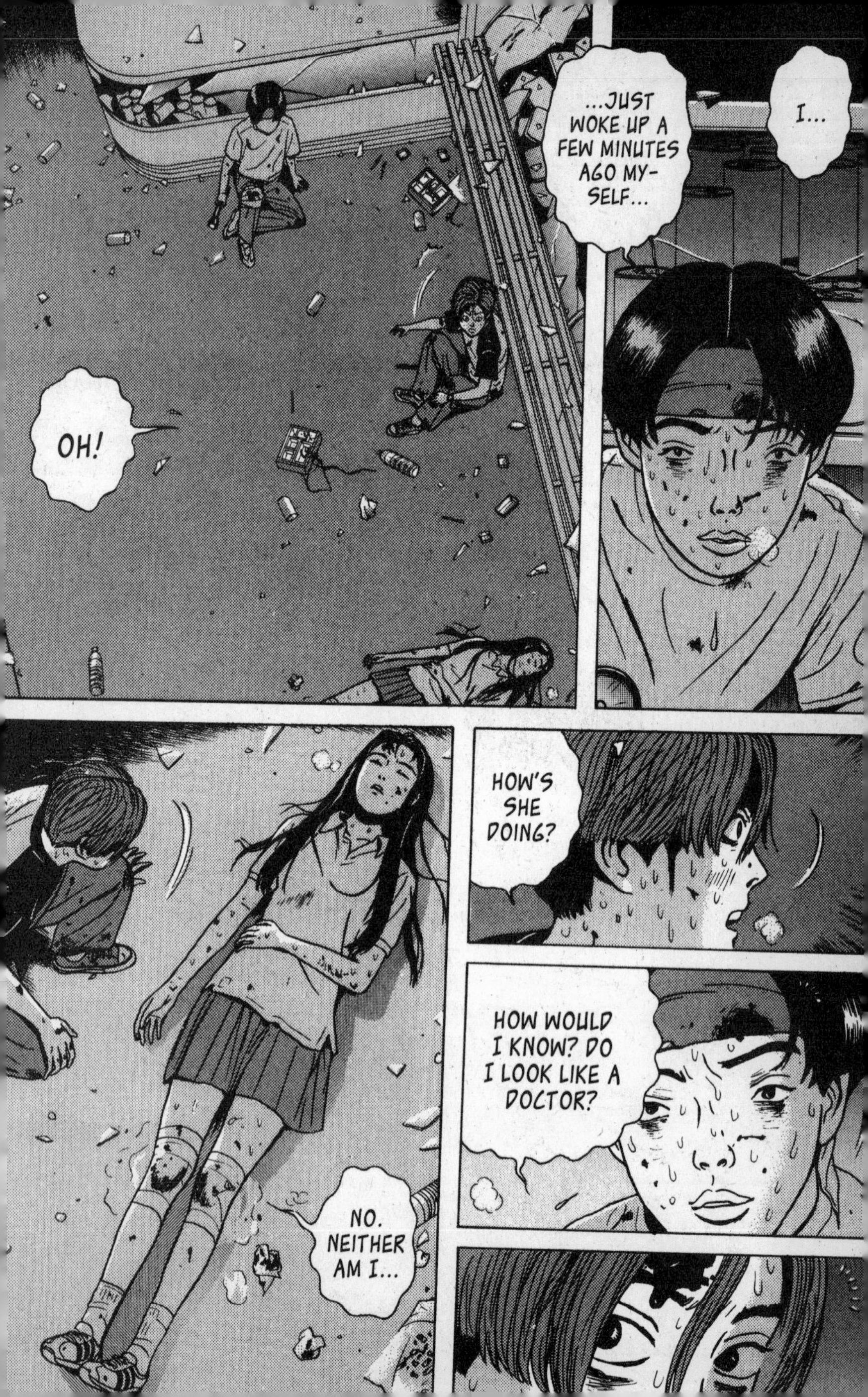
I...
...JUST WOKE UP A FEW MINUTES AGO MY-SELF...
OH!
HOW'S SHE DOING?
HOW WOULD I KNOW? DO I LOOK LIKE A DOCTOR?
NO. NEITHER AM I...

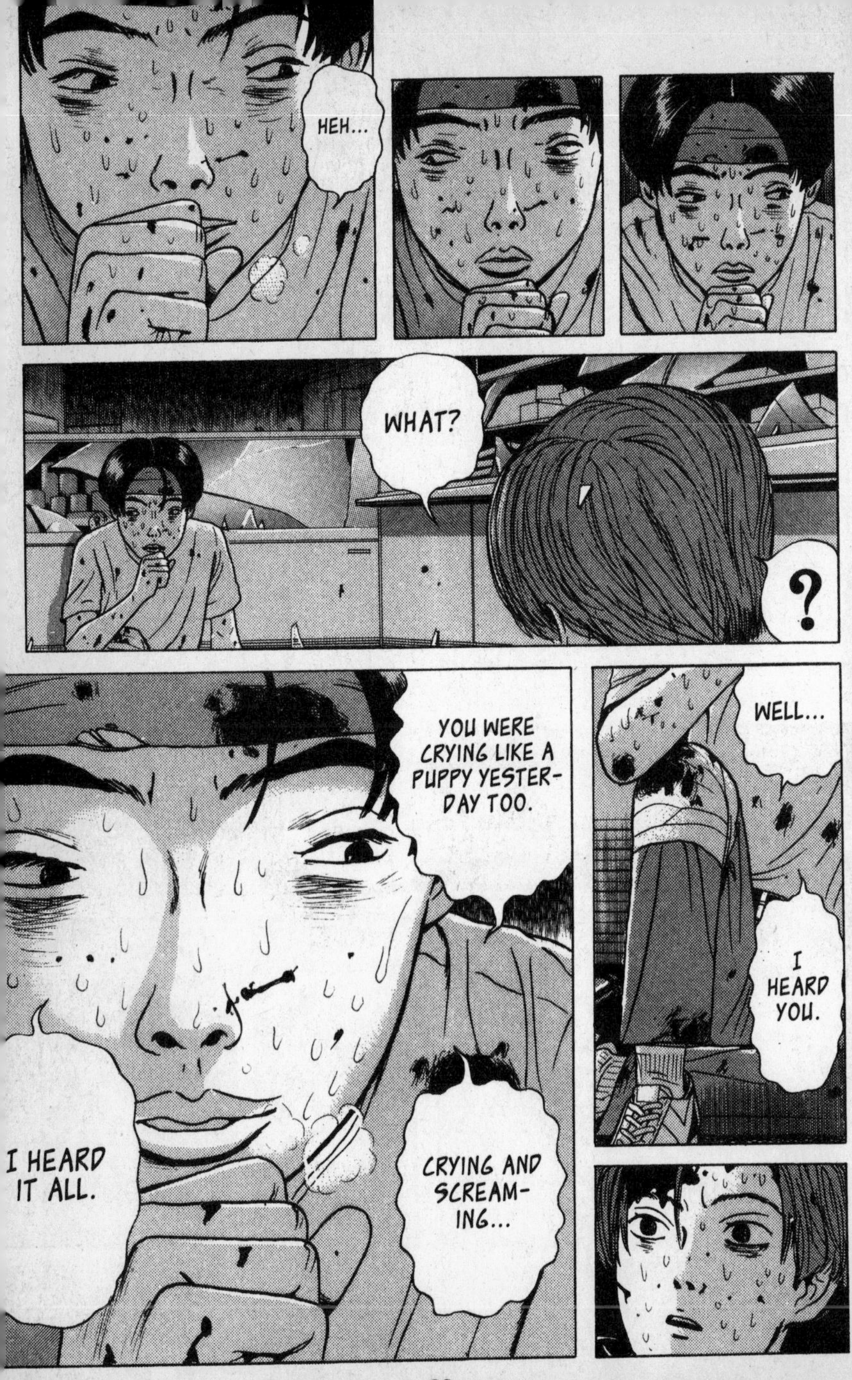
HEH...
WHAT?
?
WELL...
I HEARD YOU.
YOU WERE CRYING LIKE A PUPPY YESTER-DAY TOO.
CRYING AND SCREAM-ING...
I HEARD IT ALL.

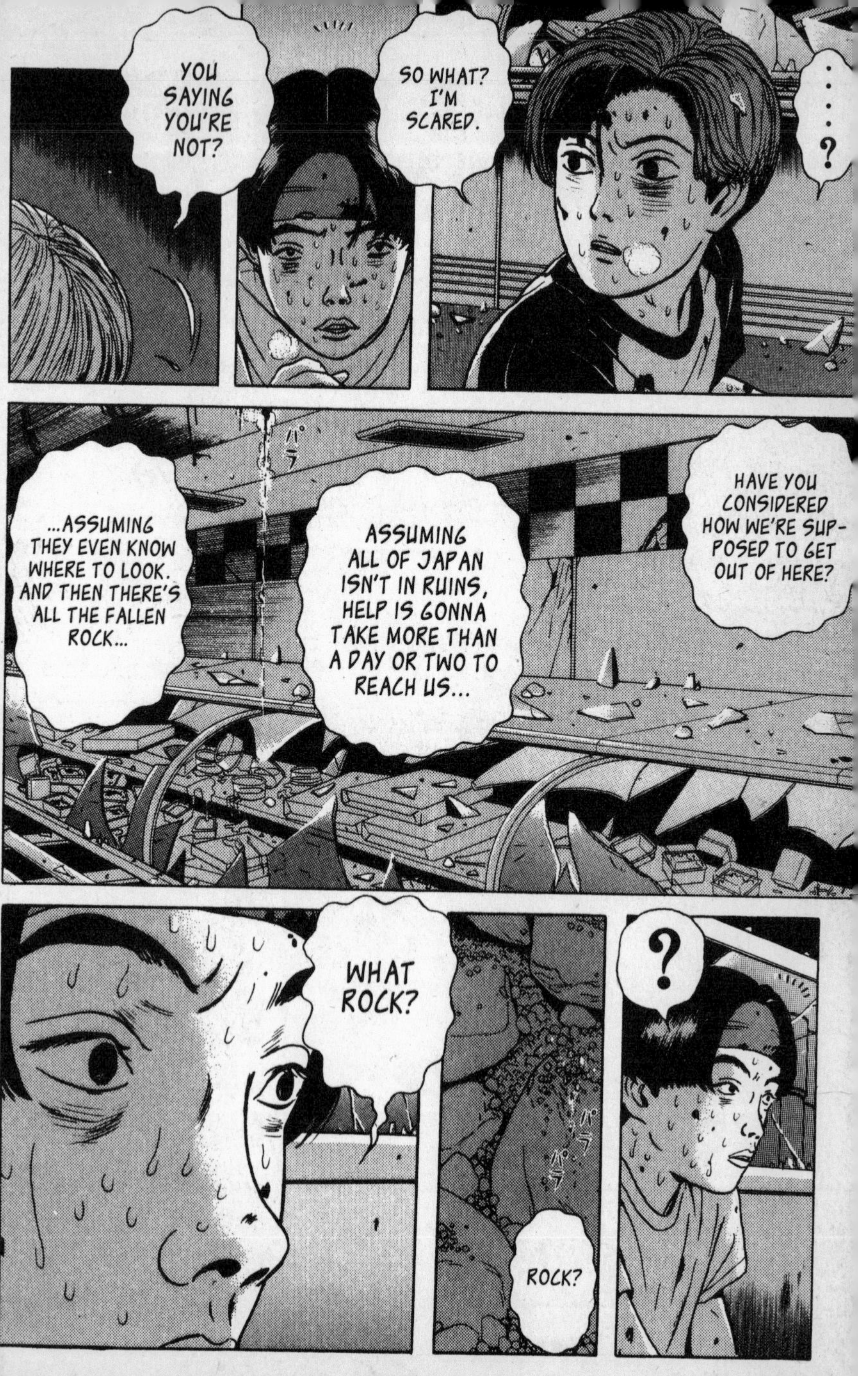
...?
SO WHAT? I'M SCARED.
YOU SAYING YOU'RE NOT?
HAVE YOU CONSIDERED HOW WE'RE SUP-POSED TO GET OUT OF HERE?
ASSUMING ALL OF JAPAN ISN'T IN RUINS, HELP IS GONNA TAKE MORE THAN A DAY OR TWO TO REACH US...
...ASSUMING THEY EVEN KNOW WHERE TO LOOK. AND THEN THERE'S ALL THE FALLEN ROCK...
?
ROCK?
WHAT ROCK?

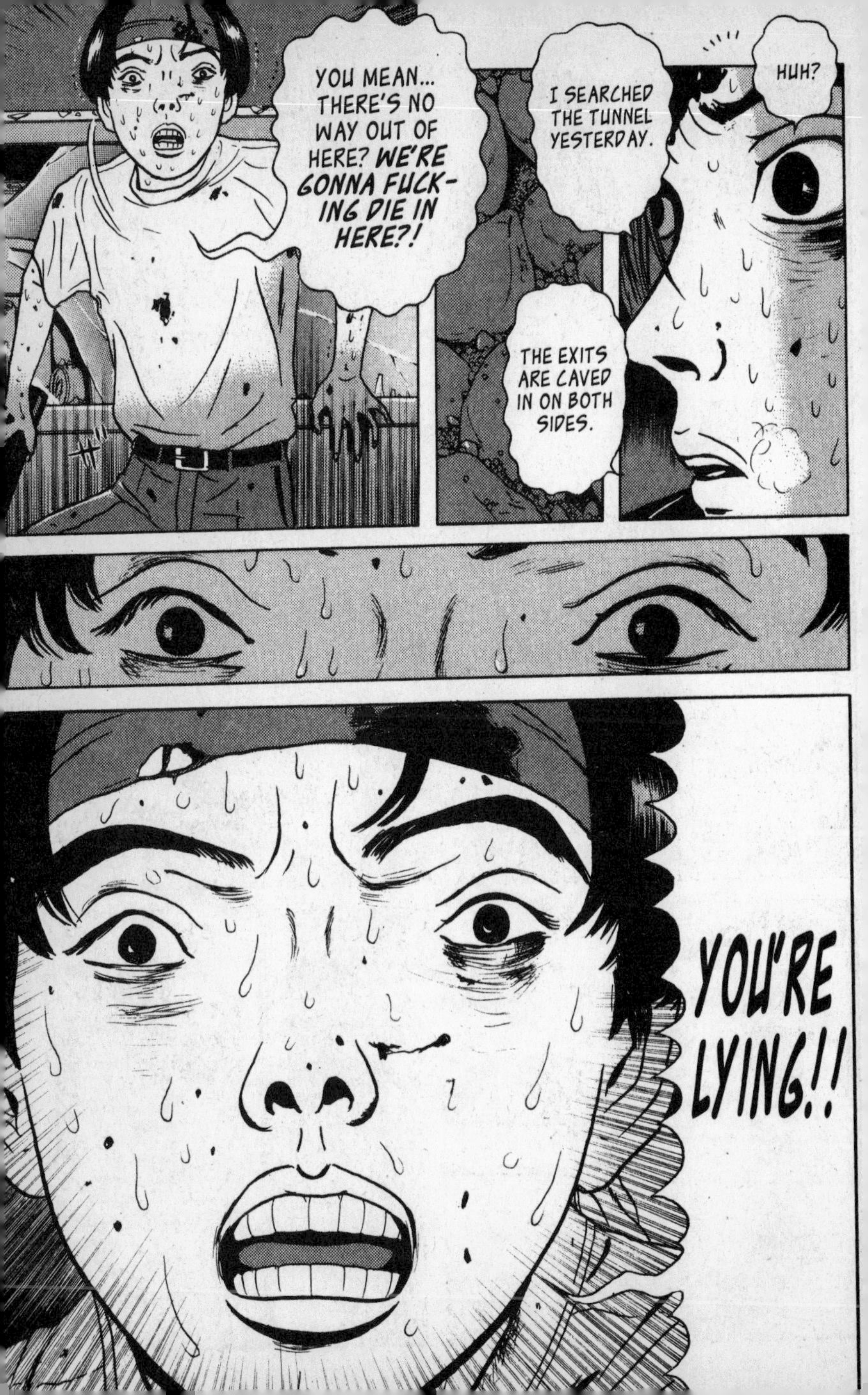
HUH?
I SEARCHED THE TUNNEL YESTERDAY.
THE EXITS ARE CAVED IN ON BOTH SIDES.
YOU MEAN... THERE'S NO WAY OUT OF HERE? WE'RE GONNA FUCKING DIE IN HERE?!
YOU'RE LYING!!

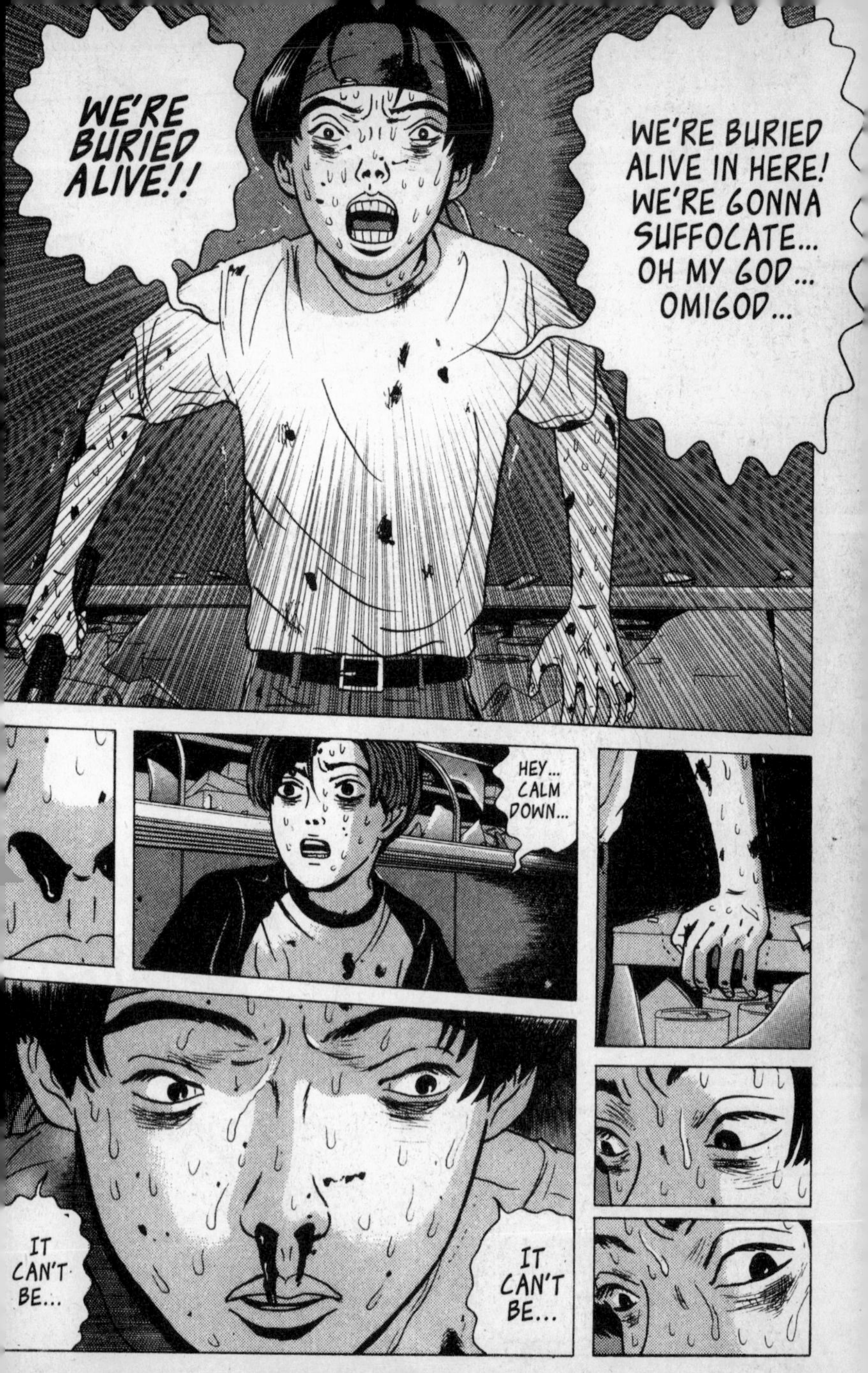
WE'RE BURIED ALIVE IN HERE! WE'RE GONNA SUFFOCATE... OH MY GOD... OMIGOD...
WE'RE BURIED ALIVE!!
HEY... CALM DOWN...
IT CAN'T BE...
IT CAN'T BE...

HEY!

ジャッ

ジャッ

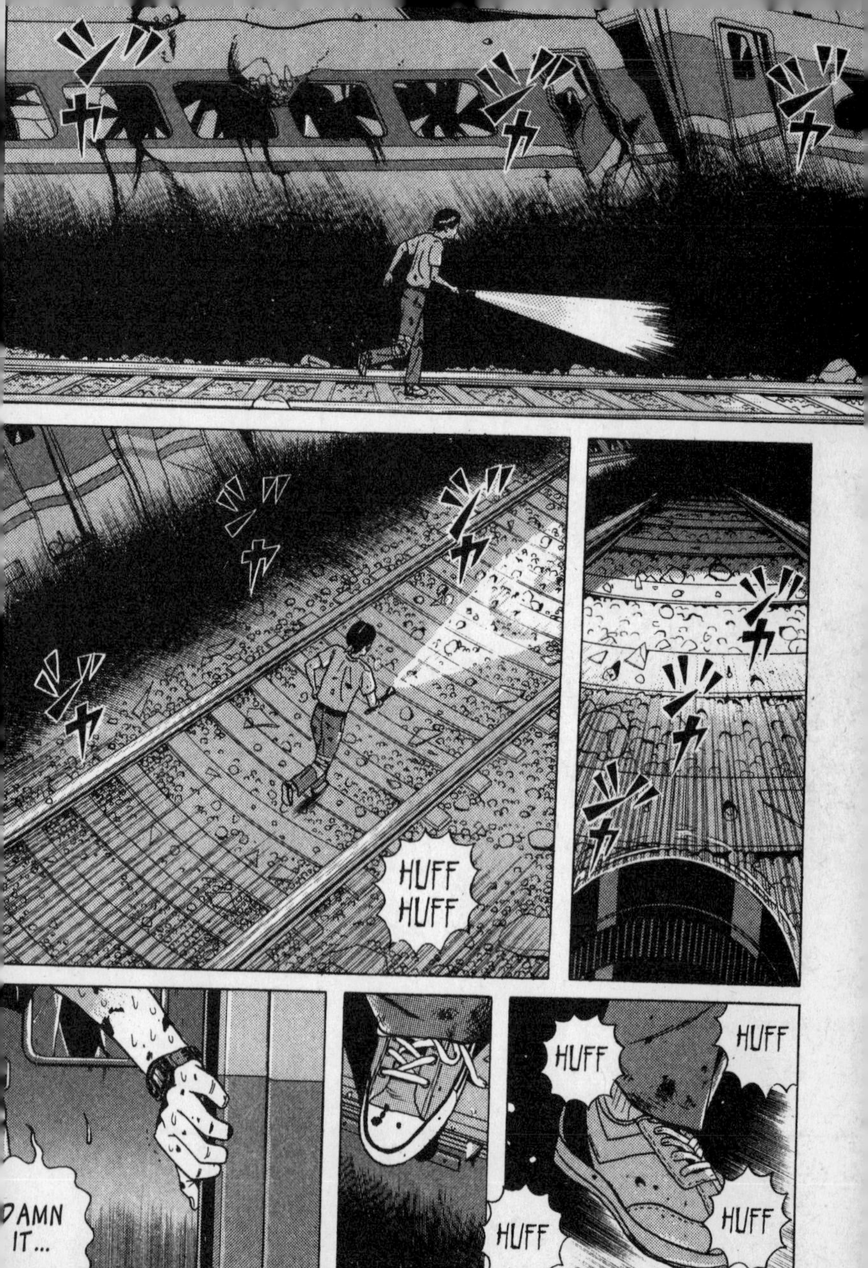
HUFF HUFF
HUFF
HUFF
HUFF
HUFF
DAMN IT...

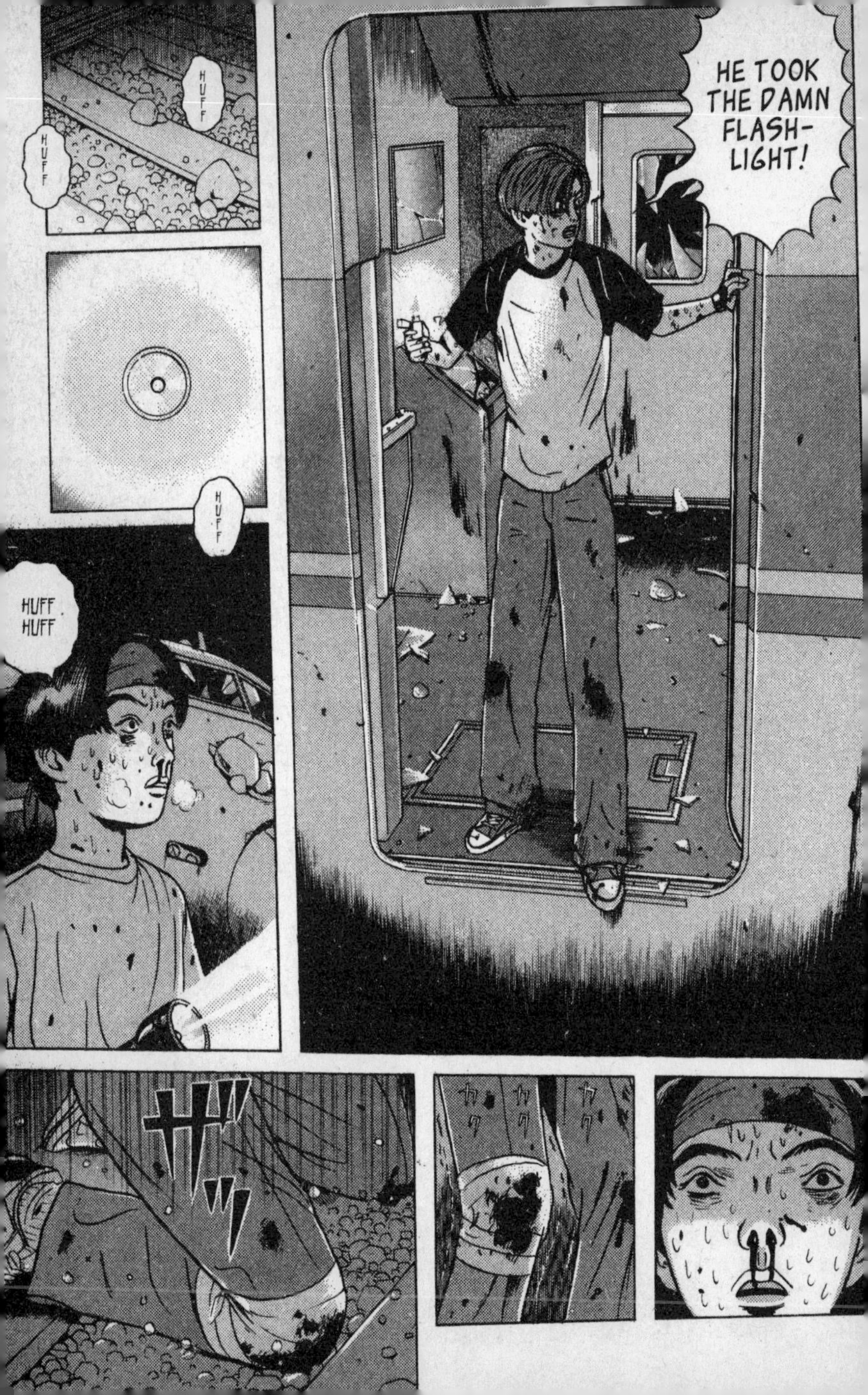
HE TOOK THE DAMN FLASH-LIGHT!
HUFF
HUFF
HUFF
HUFF HUFF

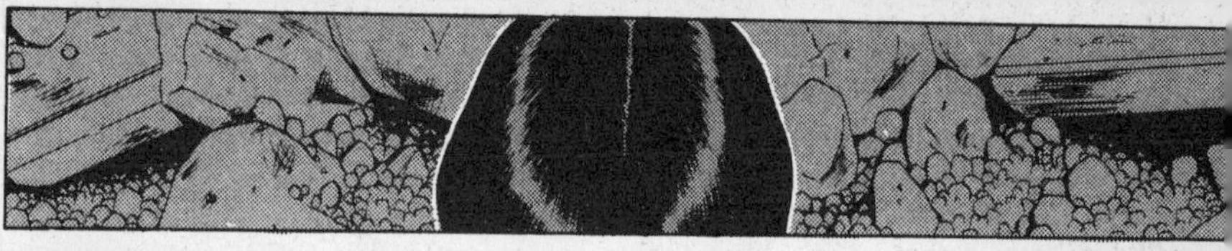
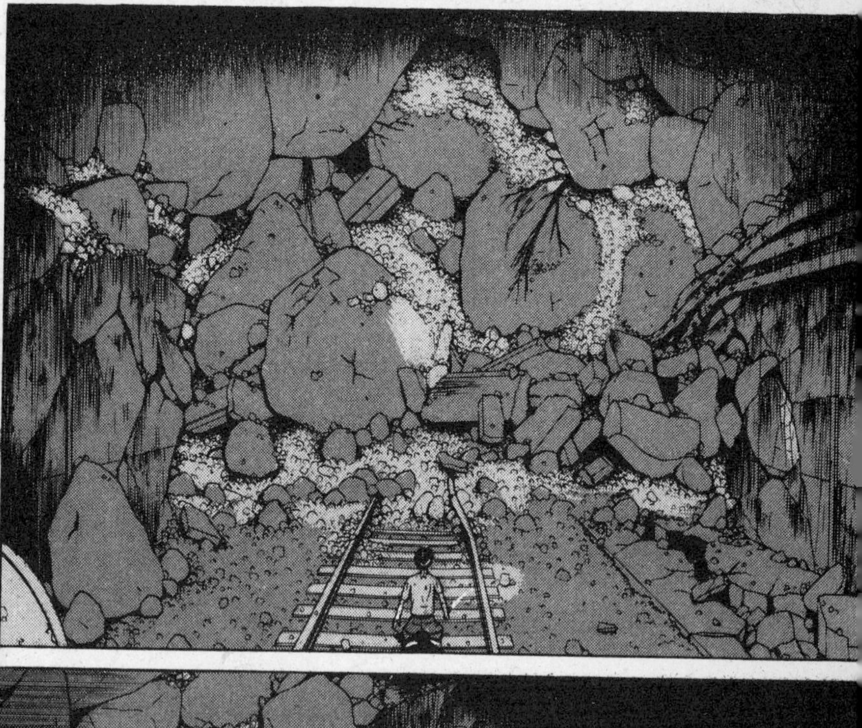
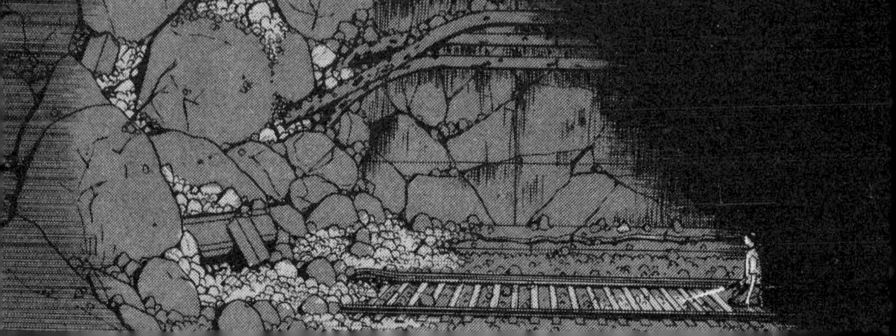

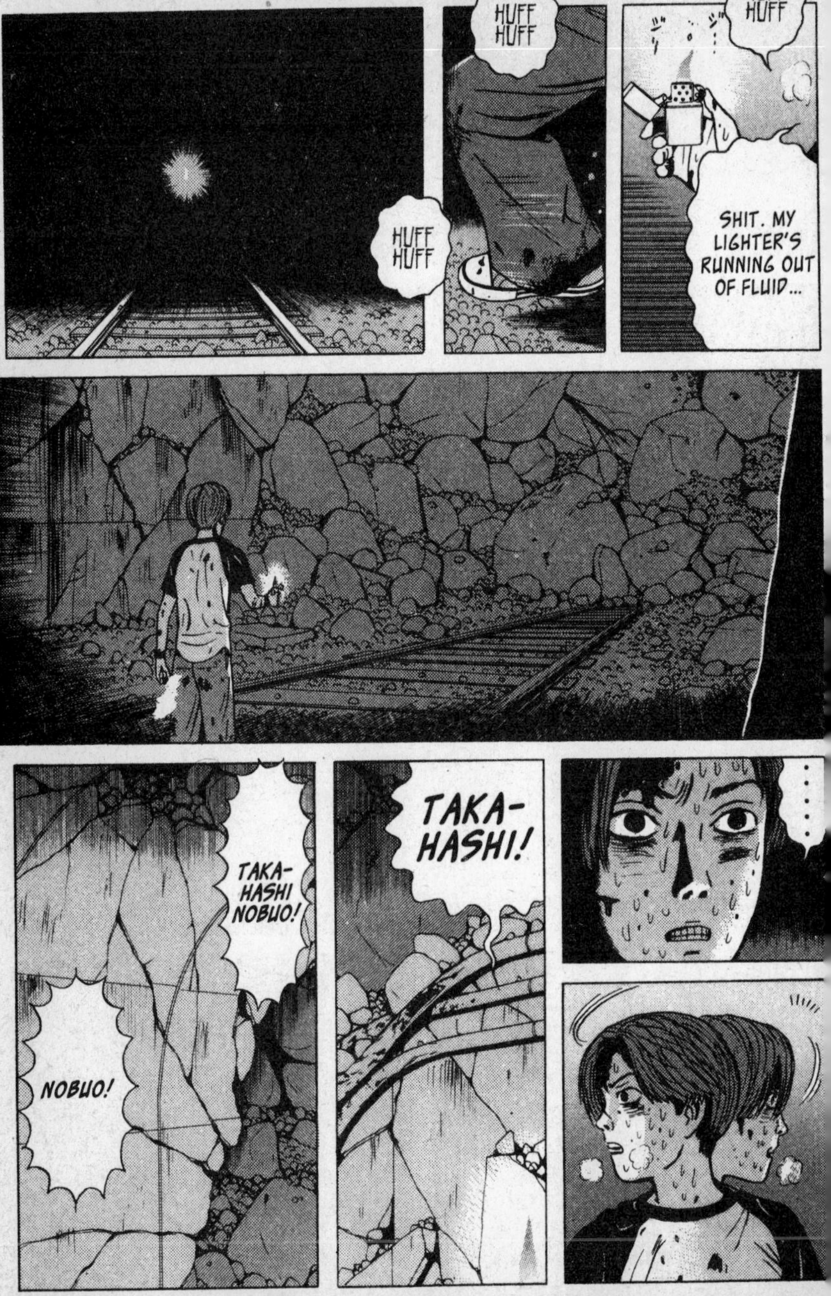
HUFF HUFF
SHIT. MY LIGHTER'S RUNNING OUT OF FLUID...
HUFF HUFF
HUFF HUFF
......
TAKA-HASHI!
TAKA-HASHI NOBUO!
NOBUO!

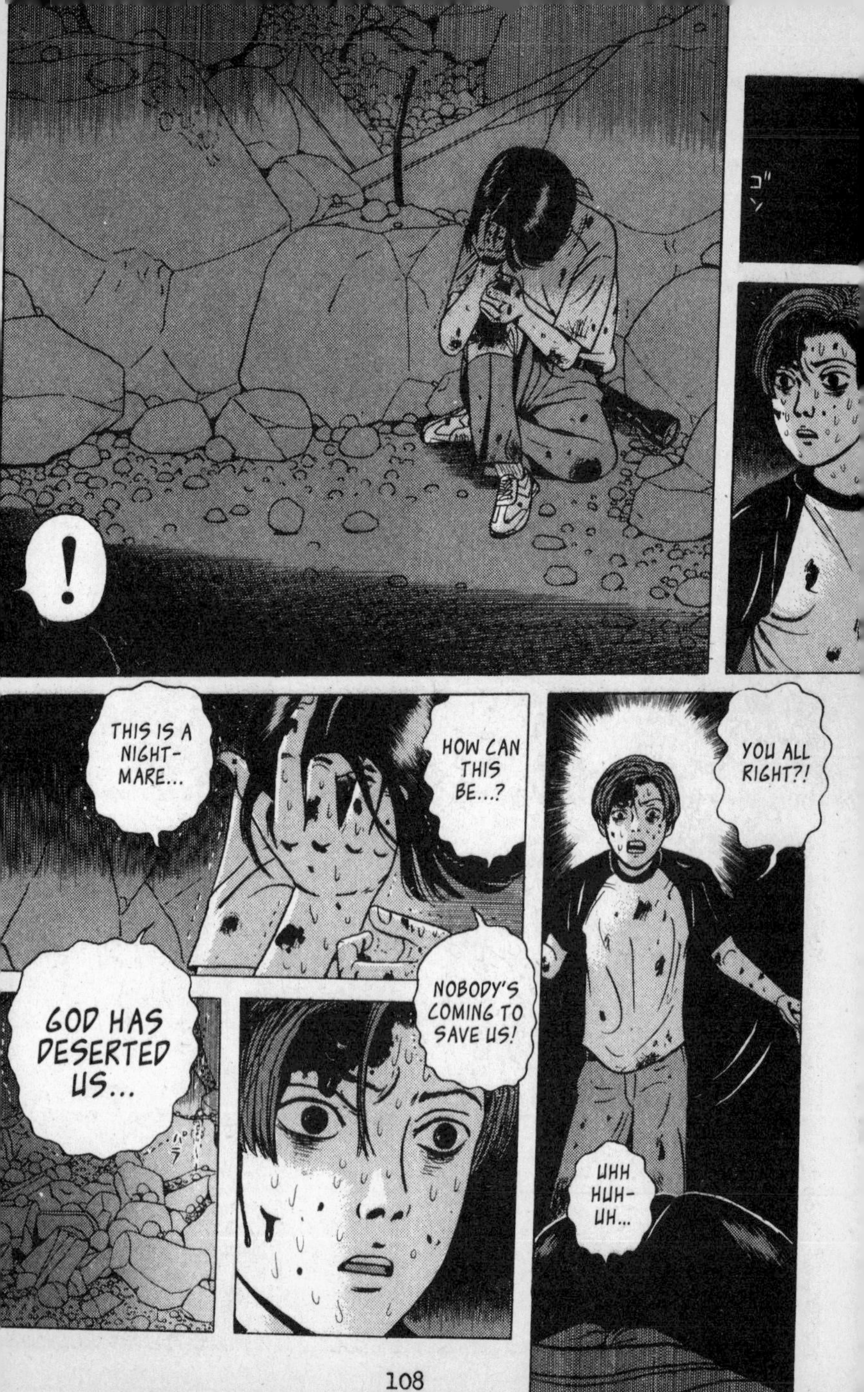
!
YOU ALL RIGHT?!
UHH HUH-UH...
HOW CAN THIS BE...?
THIS IS A NIGHT-MARE...
NOBODY'S COMING TO SAVE US!
GOD HAS DESERTED US...

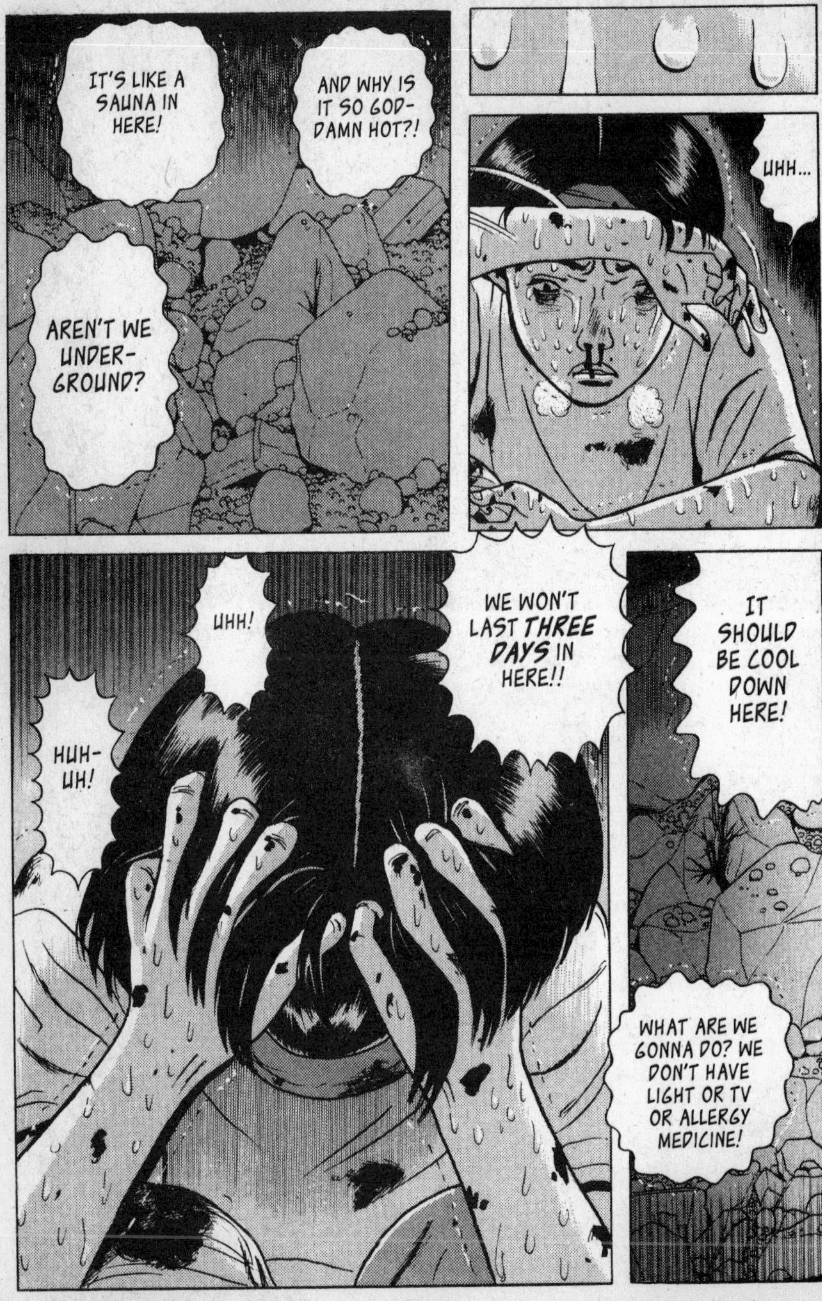
UHH...
AND WHY IS IT SO GOD-DAMN HOT?!
IT'S LIKE A SAUNA IN HERE!
AREN'T WE UNDERGROUND?
IT SHOULD BE COOL DOWN HERE!
WHAT ARE WE GONNA DO? WE DON'T HAVE LIGHT OR TV OR ALLERGY MEDICINE!
WE WON'T LAST THREE DAYS IN HERE!!
UHH!
HUH-UH!

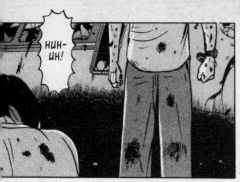

HUH-UH!

SOB

WE JUST NEED TO SIT TIGHT UNTIL HELP COMES...

. . .

IT'LL BE OKAY...

WE'RE--

HELP ISN'T COMING!

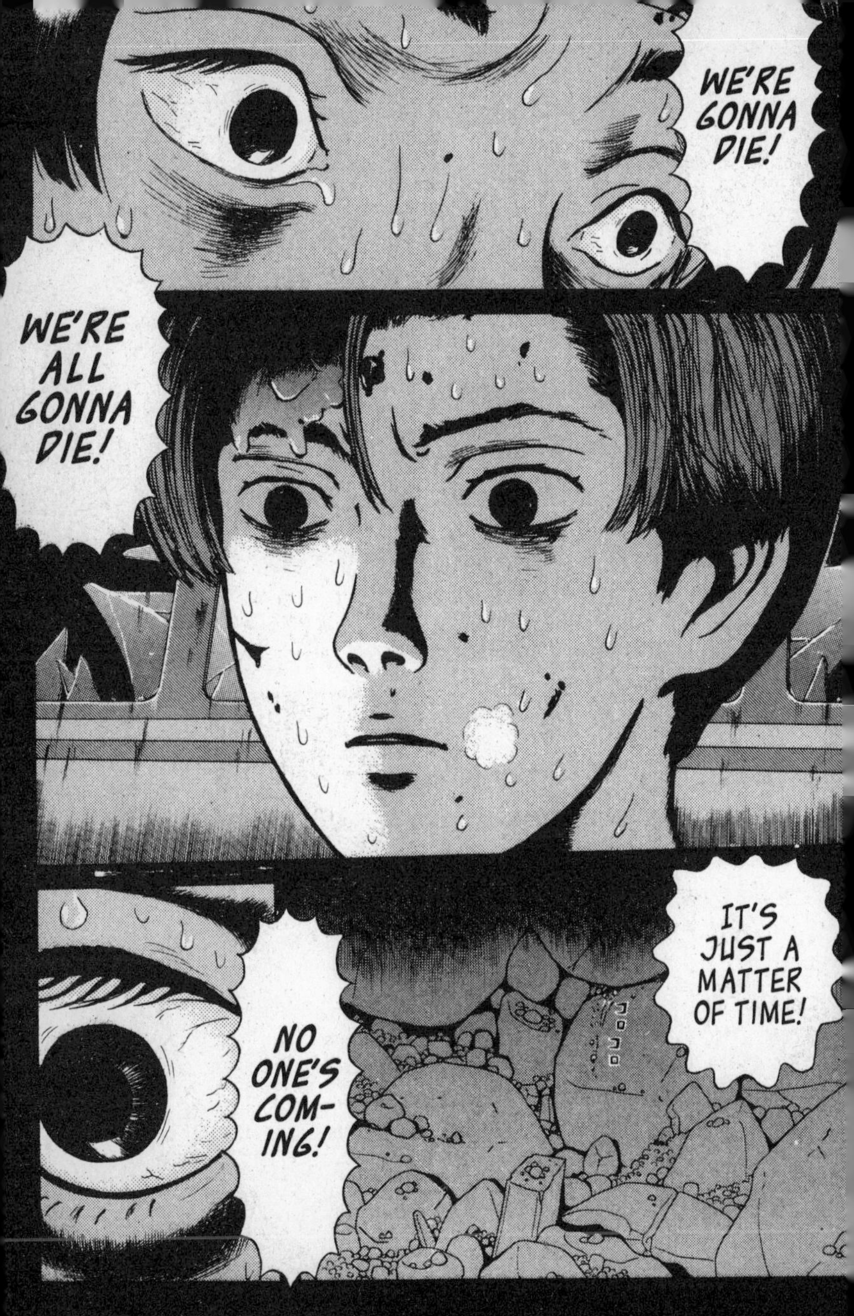
WE'RE GONNA DIE!
WE'RE ALL GONNA DIE!
IT'S JUST A MATTER OF TIME!
NO ONE'S COM-ING!

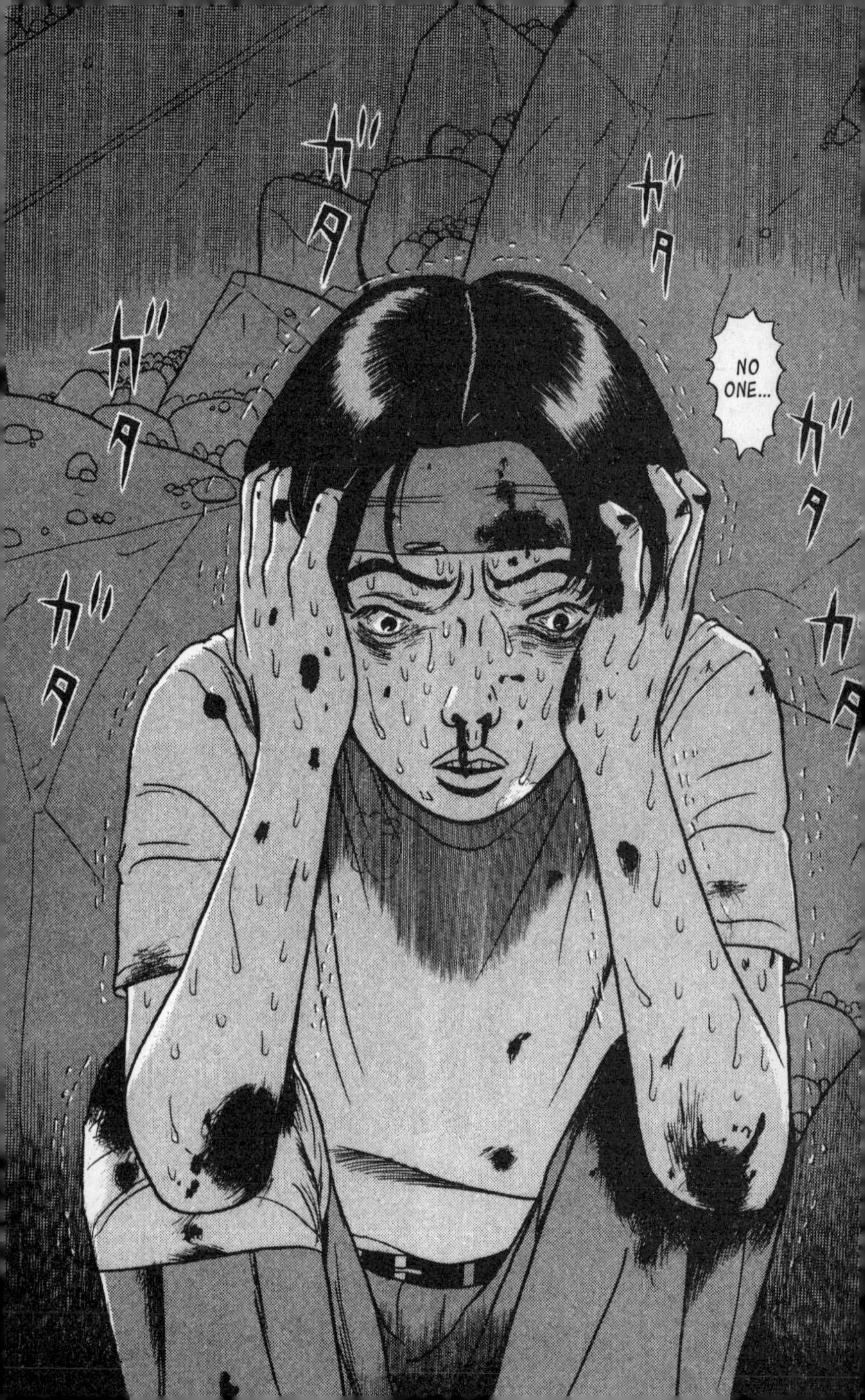
ガタ
ガタ
NO ONE...
ガタ
カタ
ガタ
ガタ

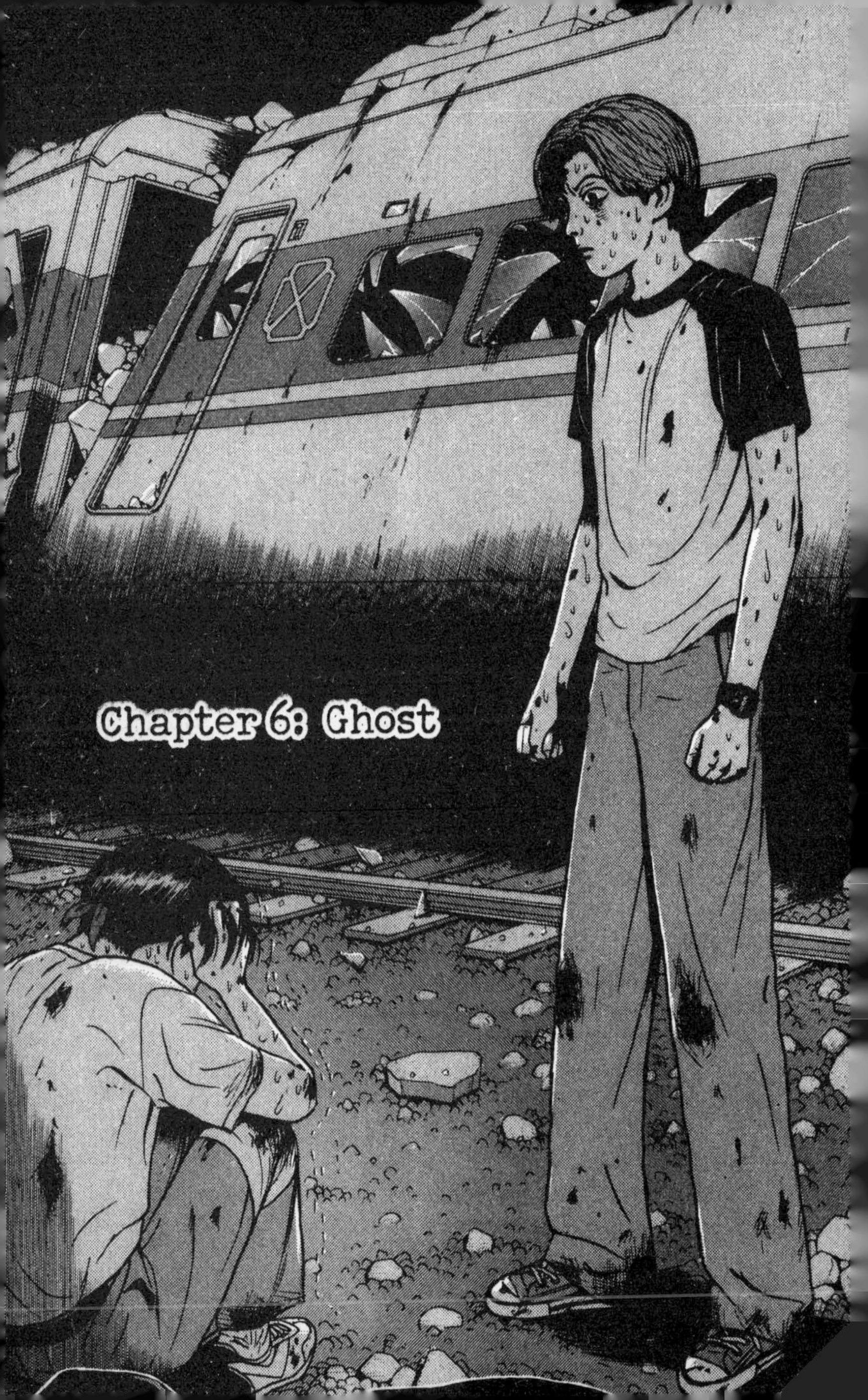
Chapter 6: Ghost

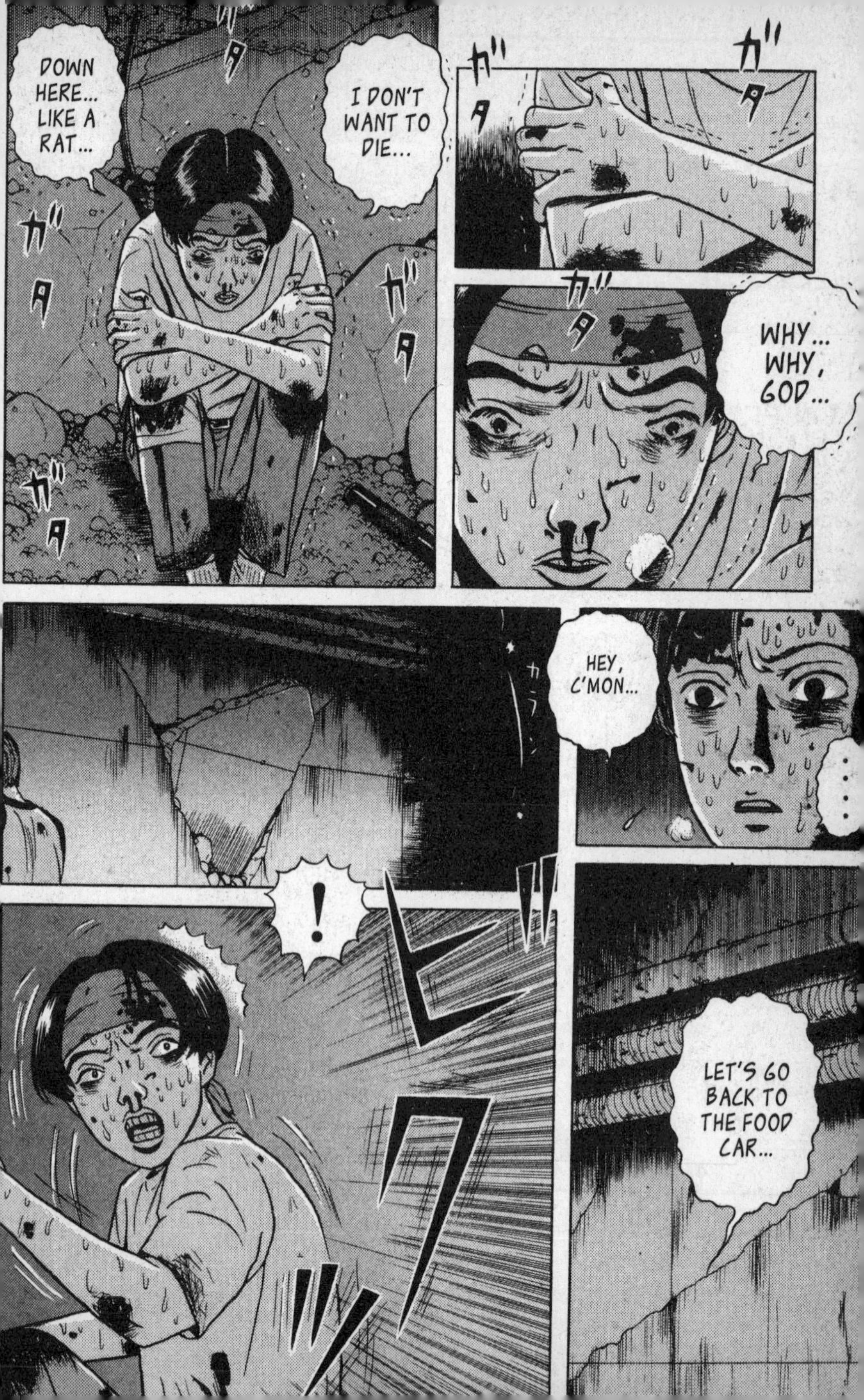
ガタ
ガタ
WHY... WHY, GOD...
I DON'T WANT TO DIE...
DOWN HERE... LIKE A RAT...
ガタ
ガタ
ガタ
HEY, C'MON...
...
カラン
LET'S GO BACK TO THE FOOD CAR...
!
ビクッ

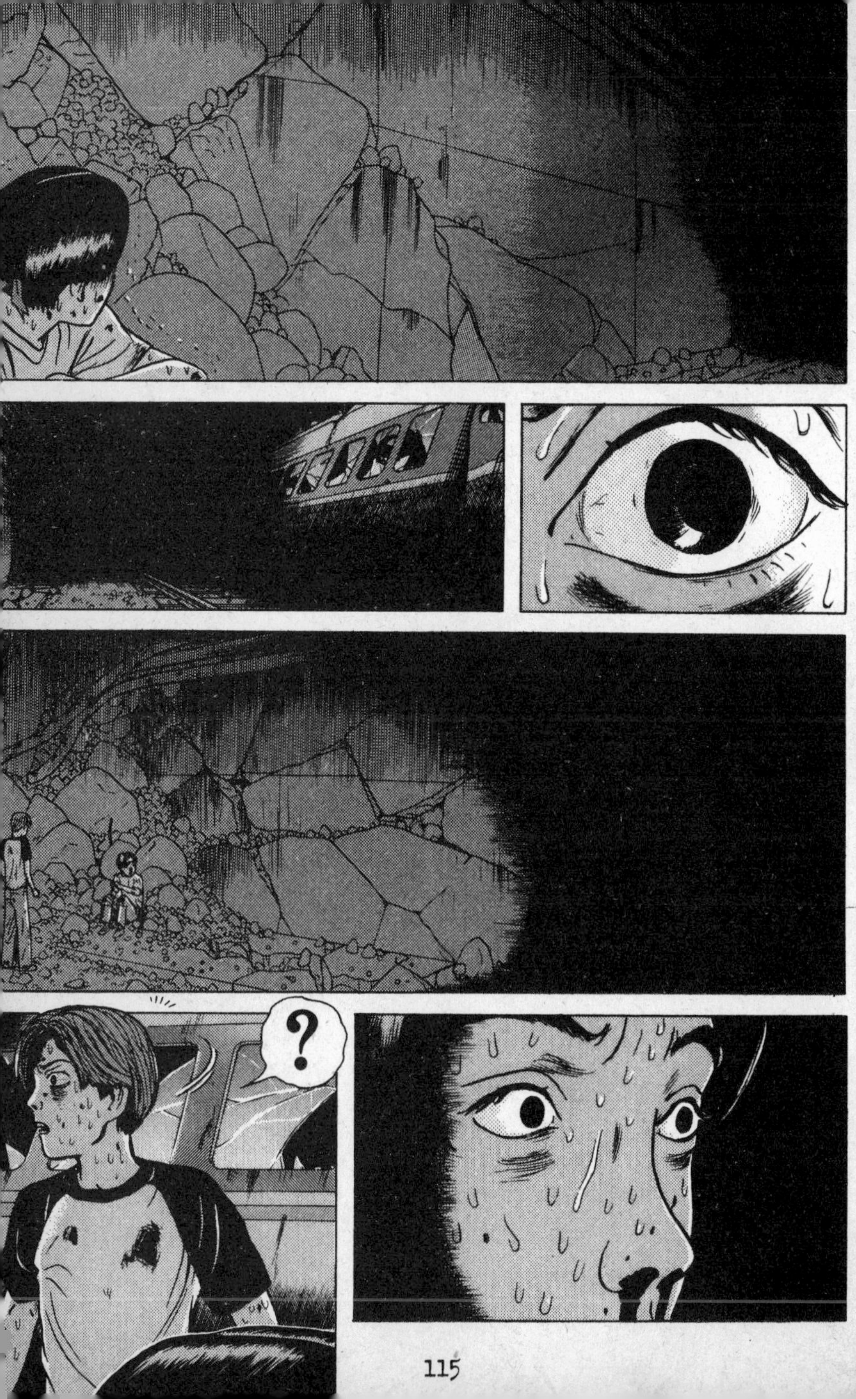
?

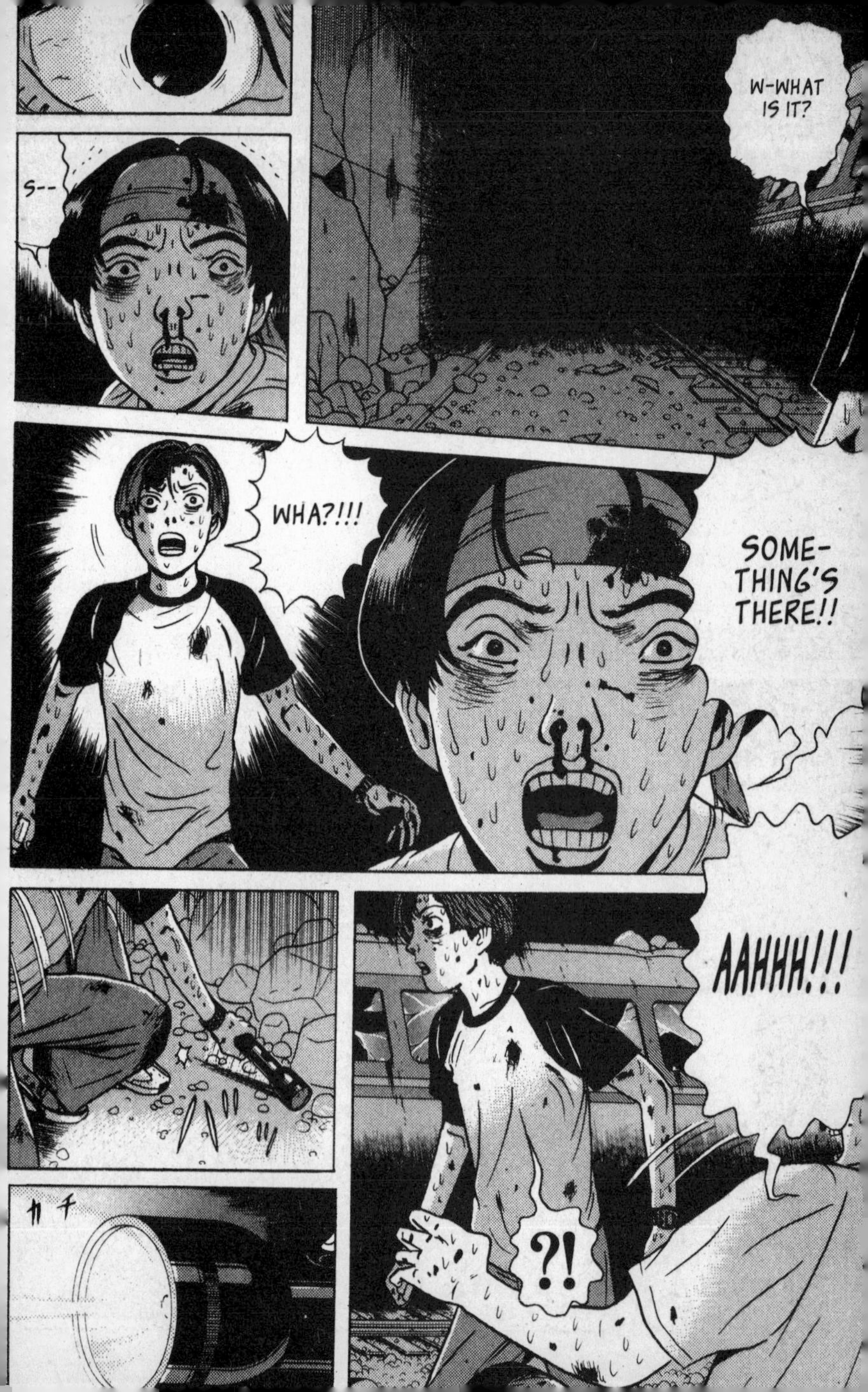
W-WHAT IS IT?
S--
SOME-THING'S THERE!!
WHA?!!!
AAHHH!!!
?!
カチ

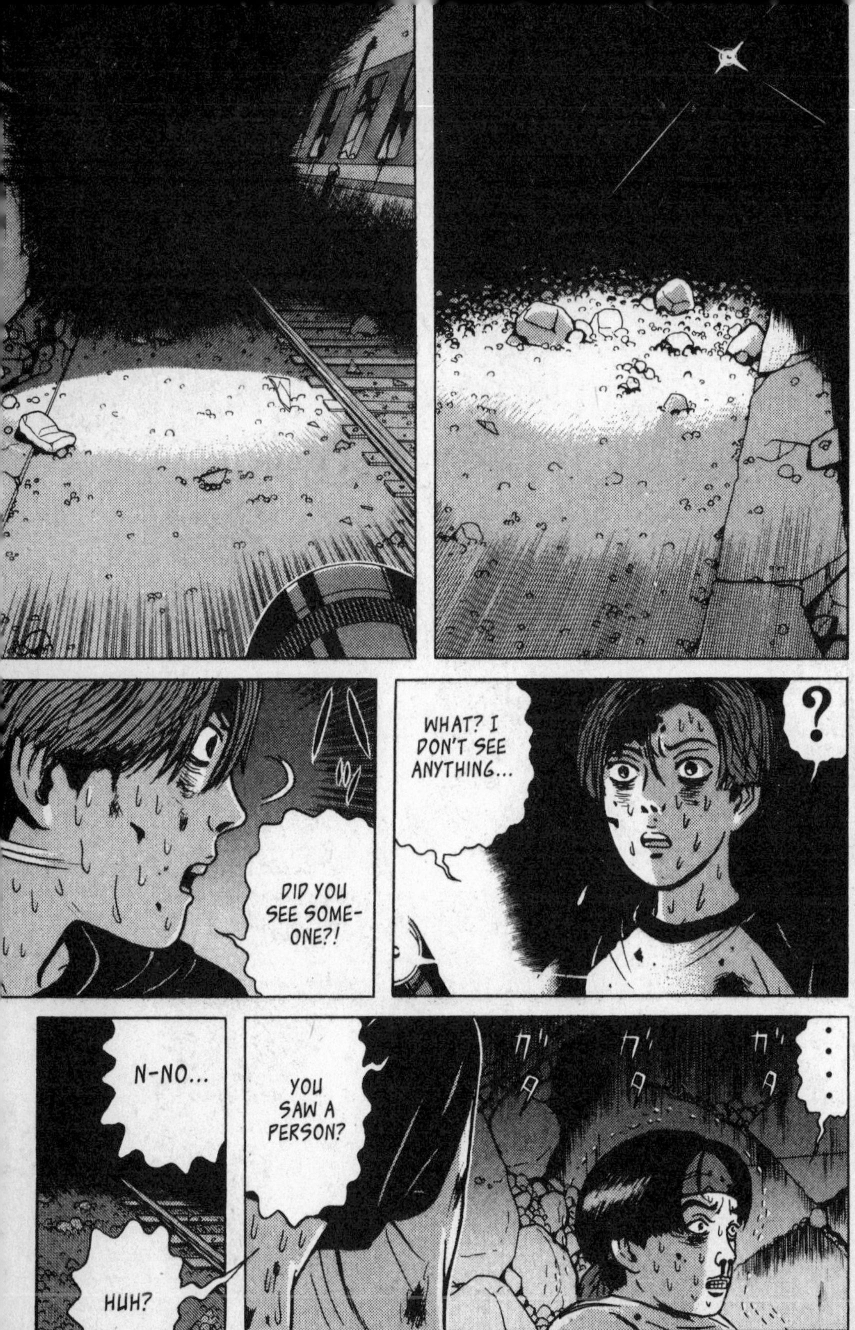
?
WHAT? I DON'T SEE ANYTHING...
DID YOU SEE SOME-ONE?!
. . . .
YOU SAW A PERSON?
N-NO...
HUH?

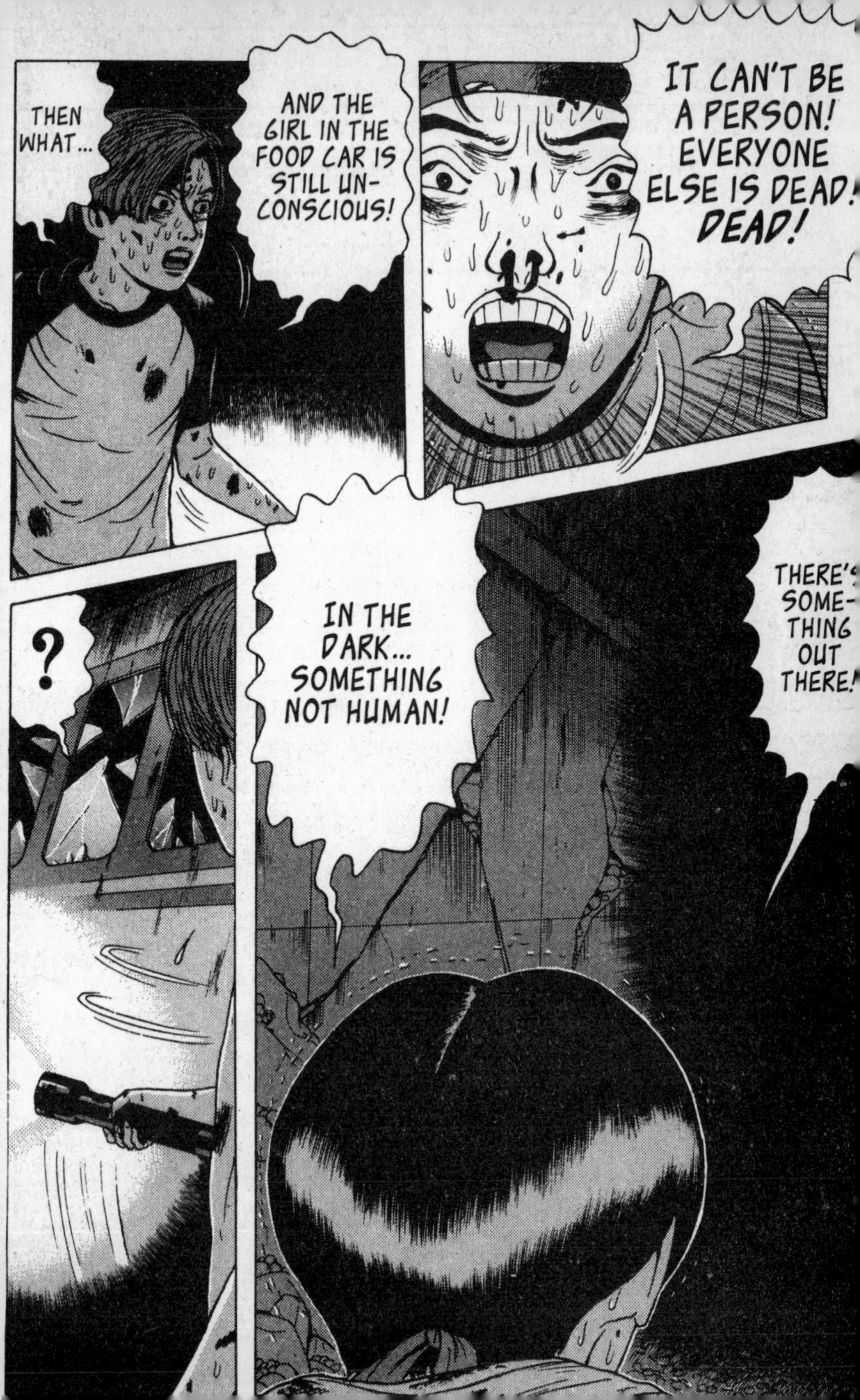
IT CAN'T BE A PERSON! EVERYONE ELSE IS DEAD! DEAD!
AND THE GIRL IN THE FOOD CAR IS STILL UN-CONSCIOUS!
THEN WHAT...
THERE'S SOME-THING OUT THERE!
IN THE DARK... SOMETHING NOT HUMAN!
?

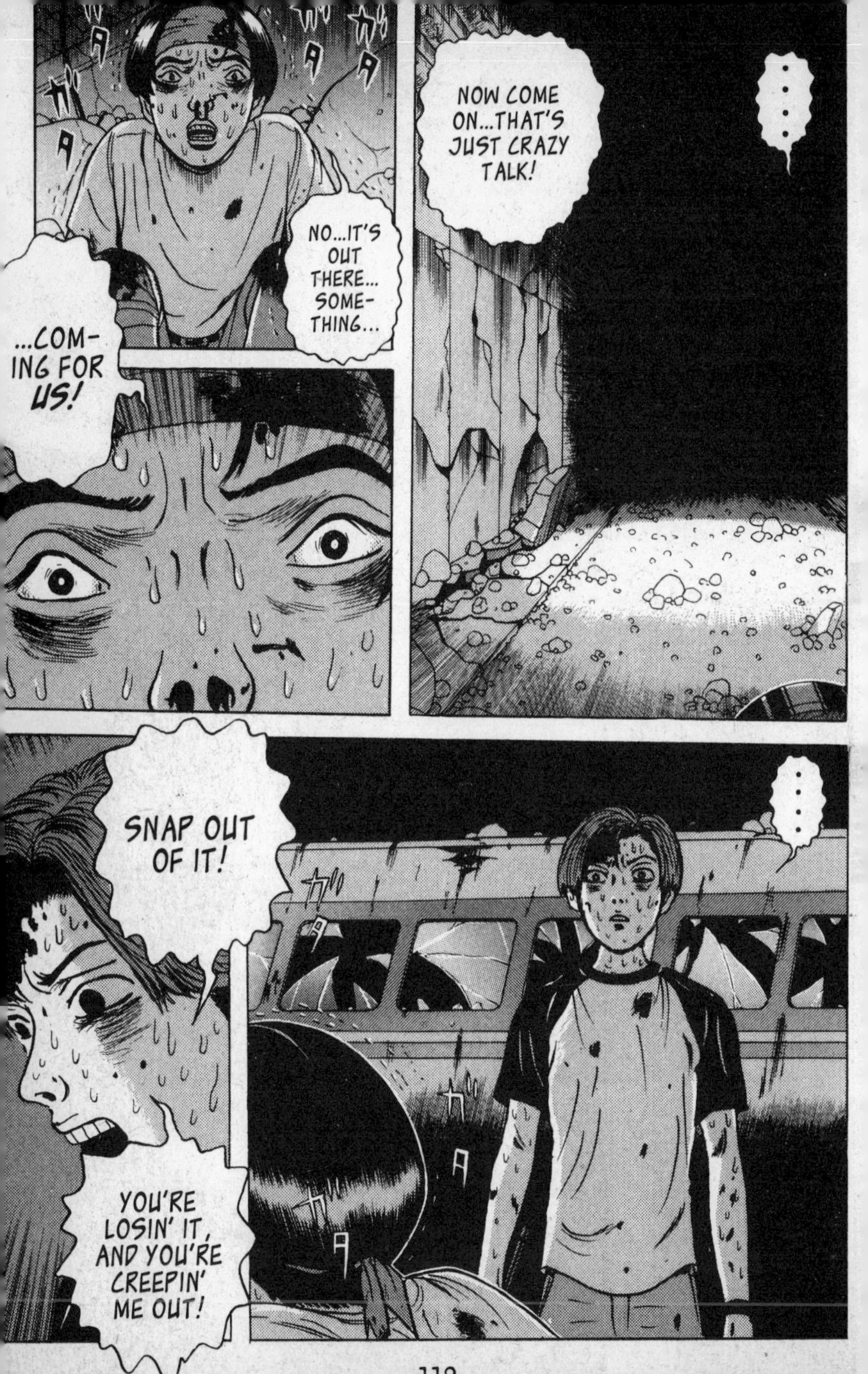
....
NOW COME ON...THAT'S JUST CRAZY TALK!
NO...IT'S OUT THERE... SOME-THING...
...COM-ING FOR US!
....
SNAP OUT OF IT!
YOU'RE LOSIN' IT, AND YOU'RE CREEPIN' ME OUT!

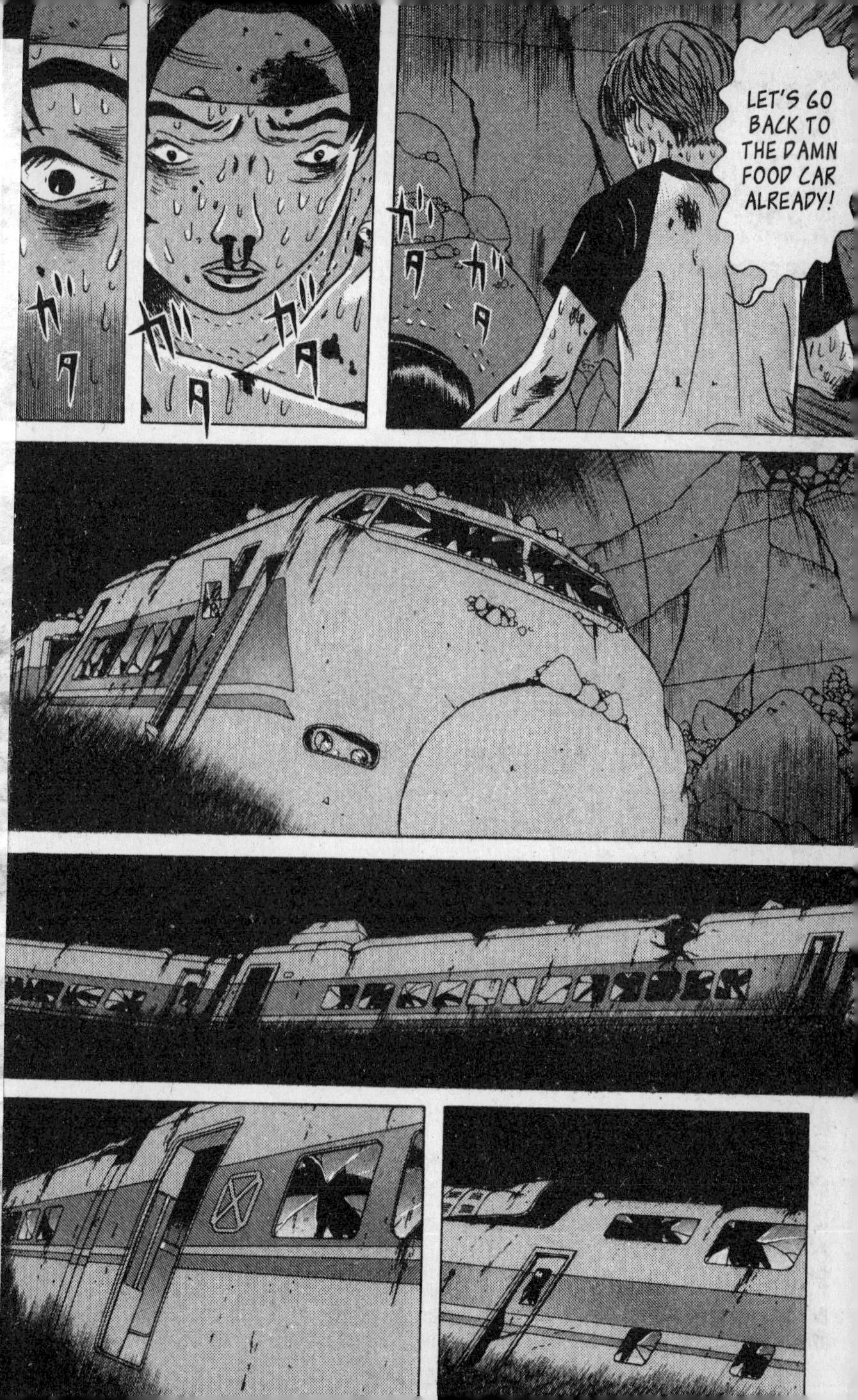
LET'S GO BACK TO THE DAMN FOOD CAR ALREADY!

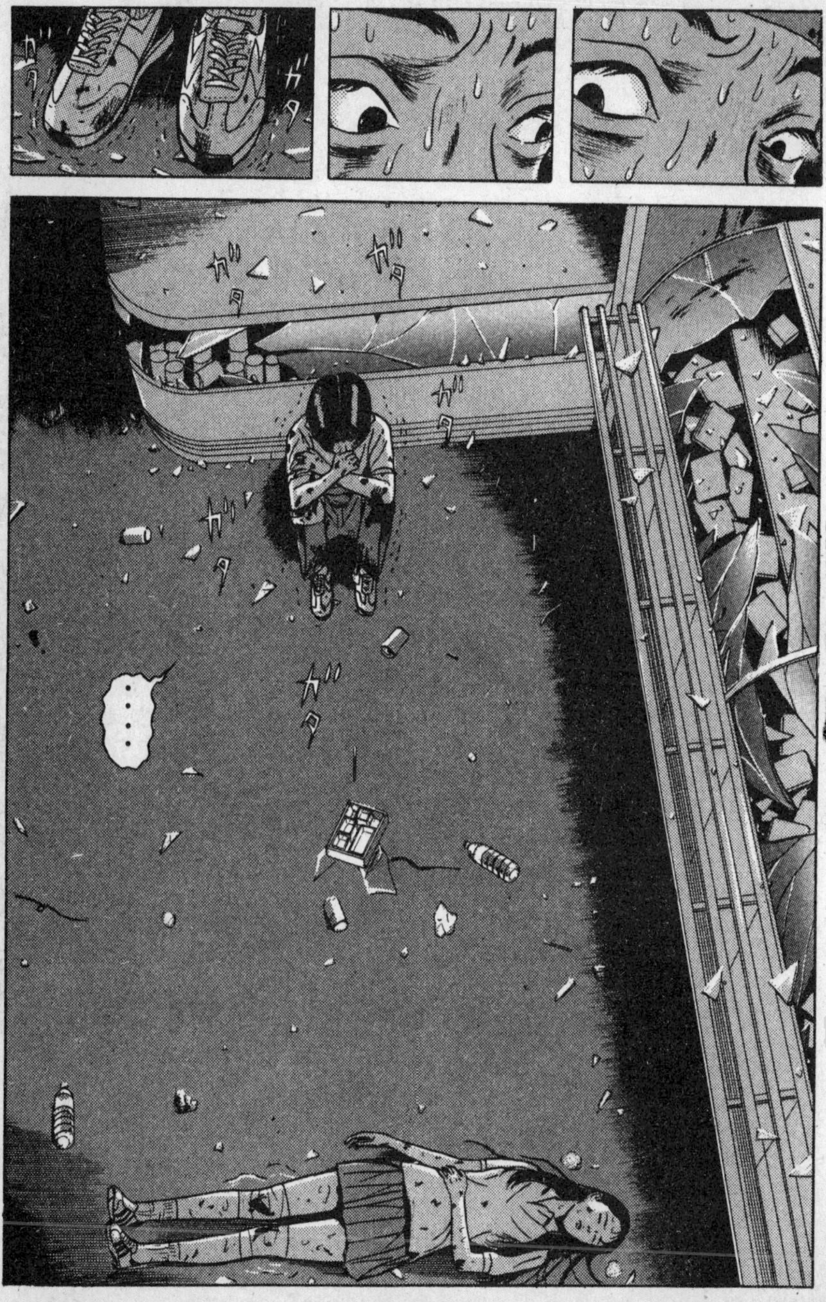
ガタ
ガタ
ガタ
ガタ
ガタ
ガタ
ガタ
....

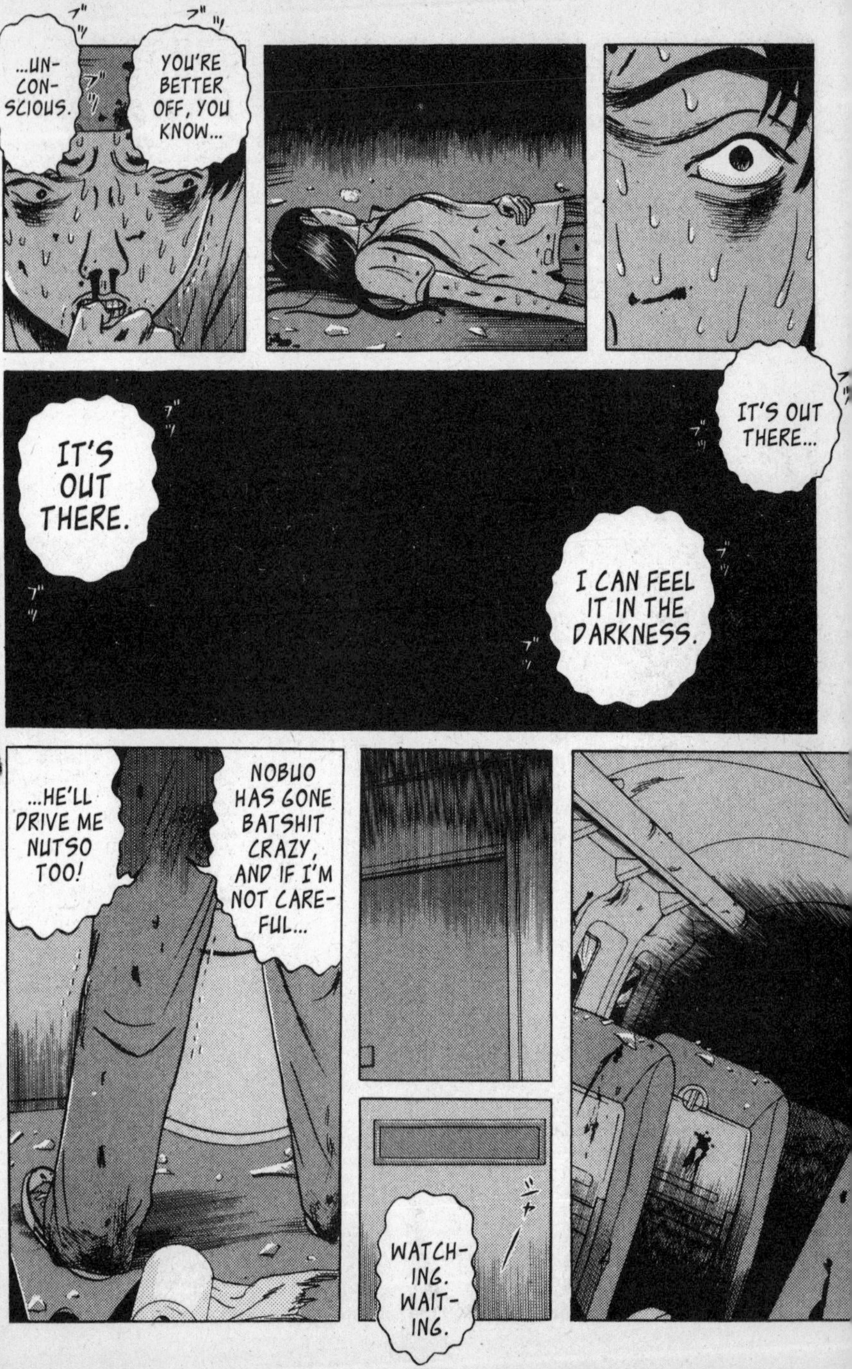
YOU'RE BETTER OFF, YOU KNOW...
...UN-CONSCIOUS.
IT'S OUT THERE...
I CAN FEEL IT IN THE DARKNESS.
IT'S OUT THERE.
WATCHING. WAITING.
NOBUO HAS GONE BATSHIT CRAZY, AND IF I'M NOT CAREFUL...
...HE'LL DRIVE ME NUTSO TOO!

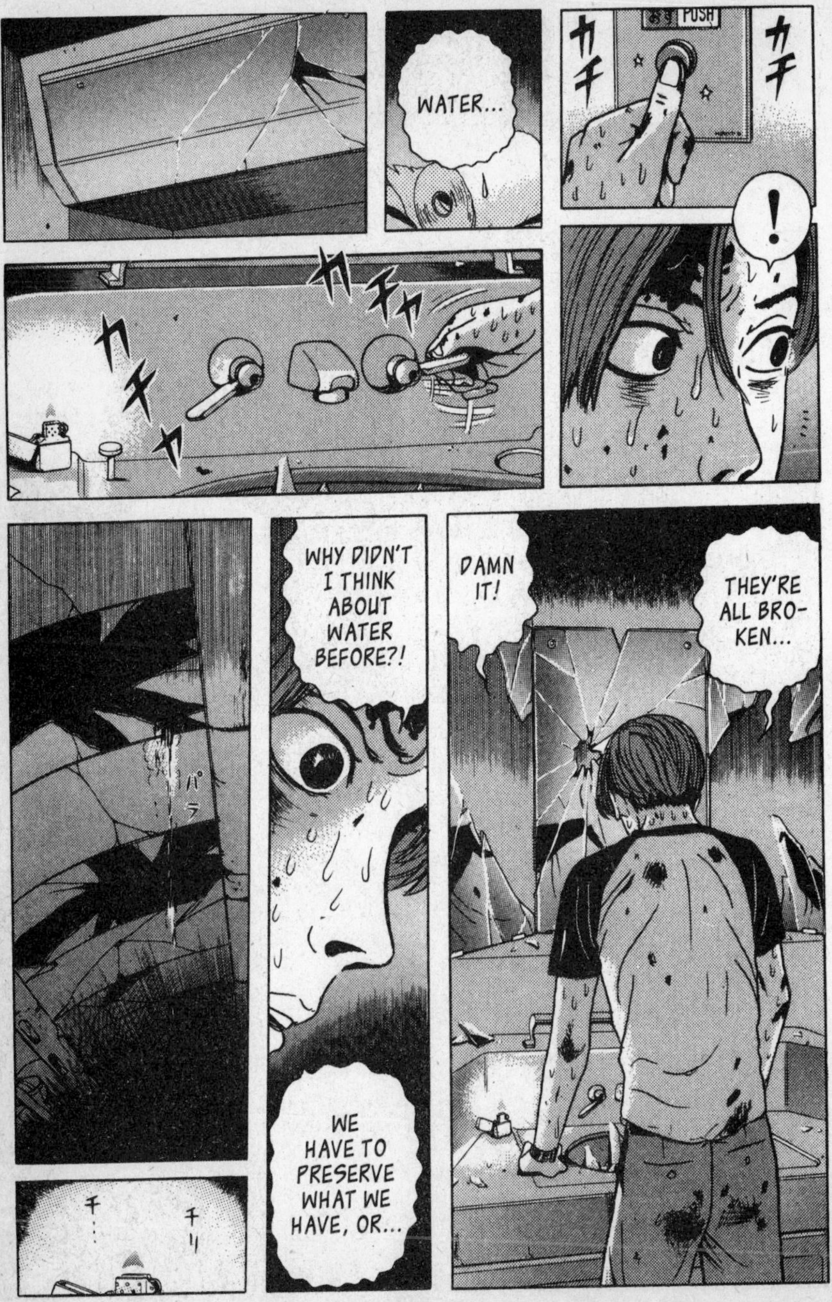

PUSH
カチ
カチ
WATER...
!
ガチャ
カチャ
THEY'RE ALL BRO- KEN...
DAMN IT!
WHY DIDN'T I THINK ABOUT WATER BEFORE?!
WE HAVE TO PRESERVE WHAT WE HAVE, OR...
パラ
チ…
チリ

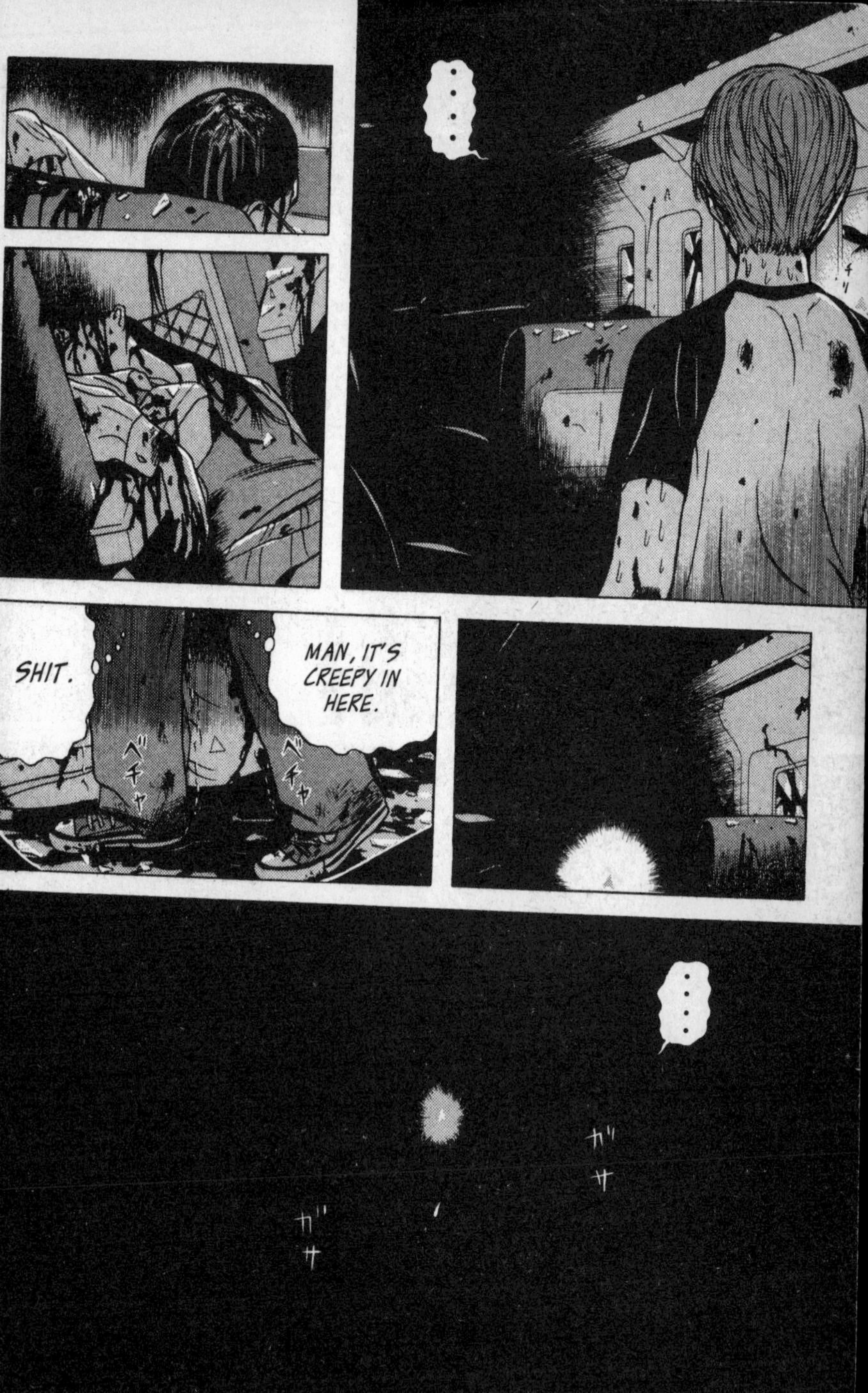
....
MAN, IT'S CREEPY IN HERE.
SHIT.
....

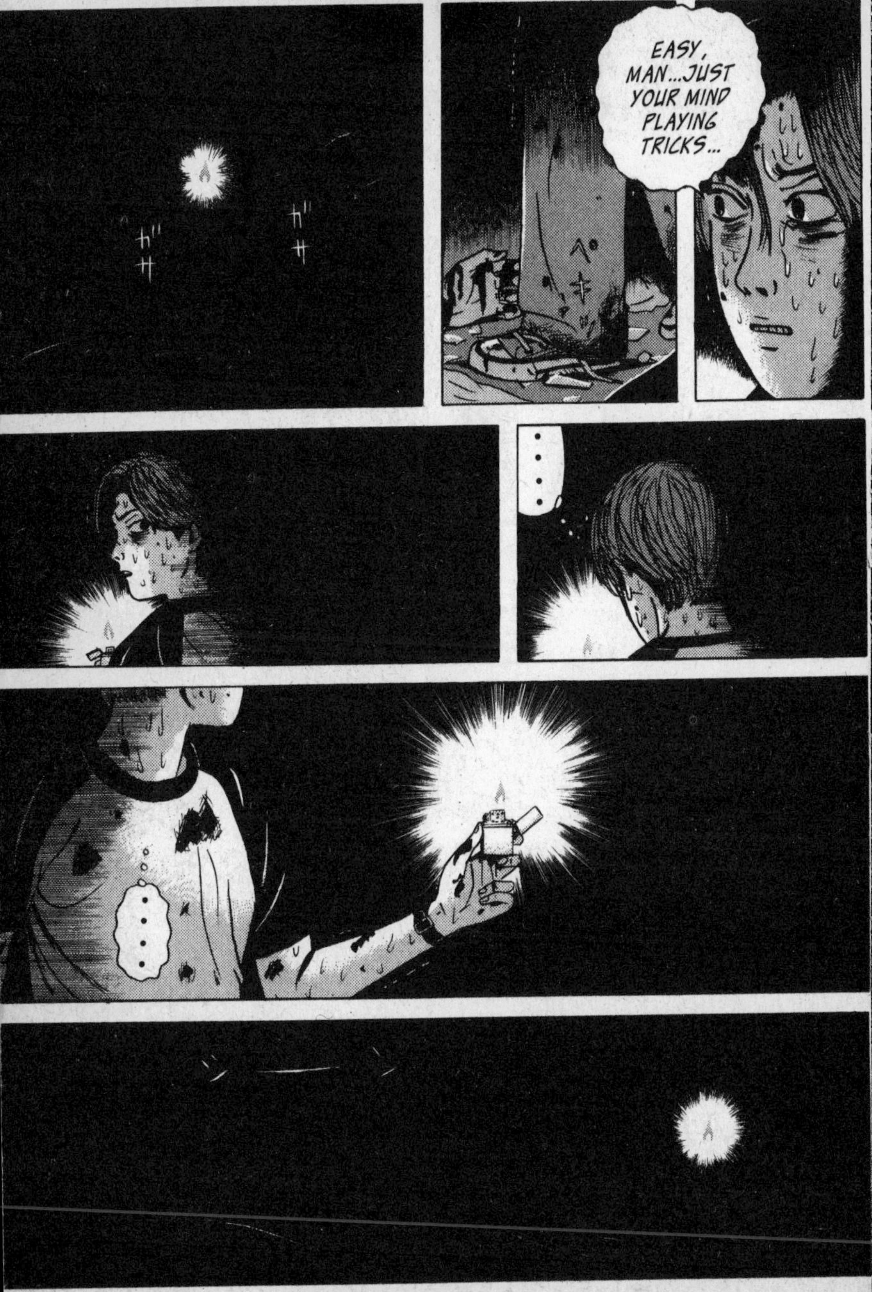
EASY, MAN...JUST YOUR MIND PLAYING TRICKS...
ガサ
ガサ
....
.....

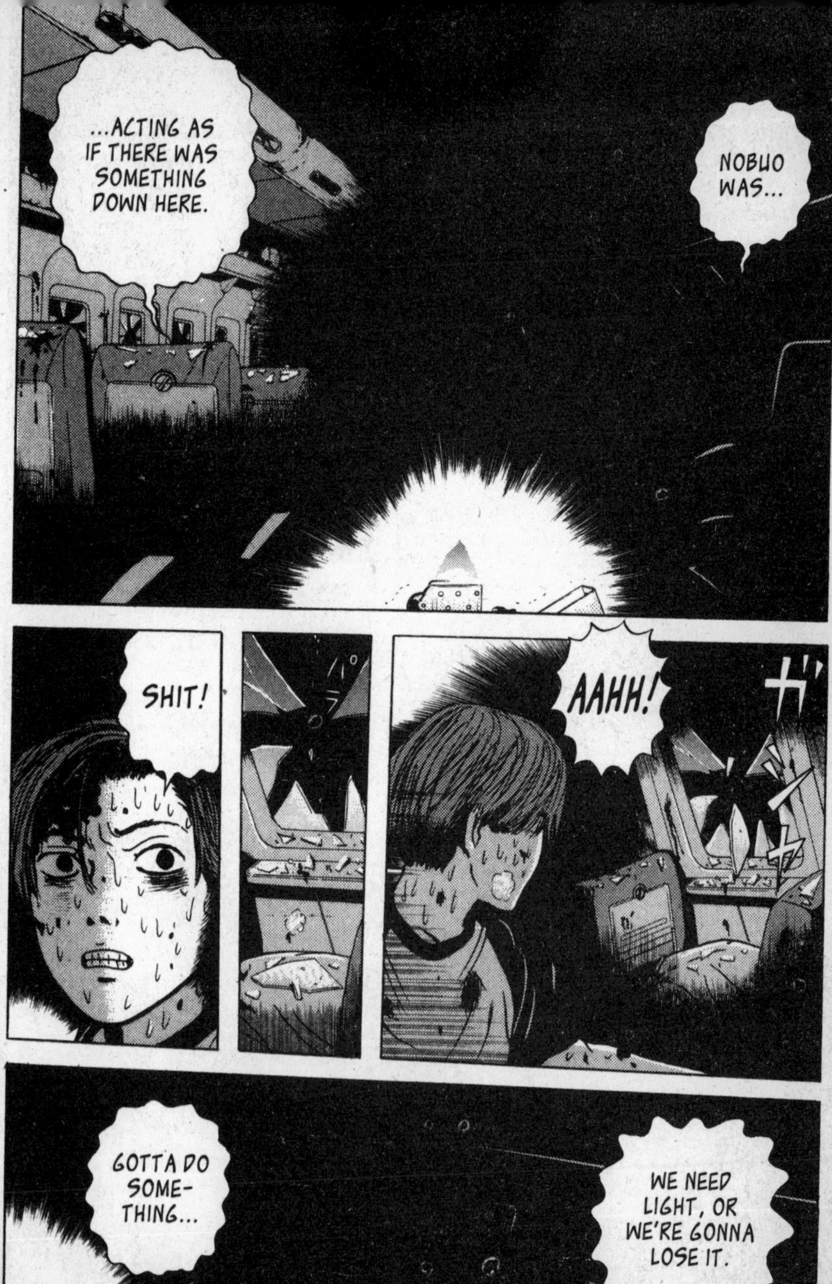
NOBUO WAS...
...ACTING AS IF THERE WAS SOMETHING DOWN HERE.
AAHH!
SHIT!
WE NEED LIGHT, OR WE'RE GONNA LOSE IT.
GOTTA DO SOME-THING...

NOTH-ING.

!

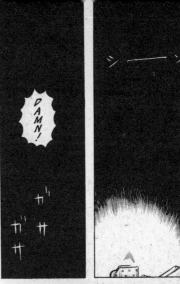

DAMN!

LISTEN! WE NEED TO MAKE SOME LIGHT!

HEY...

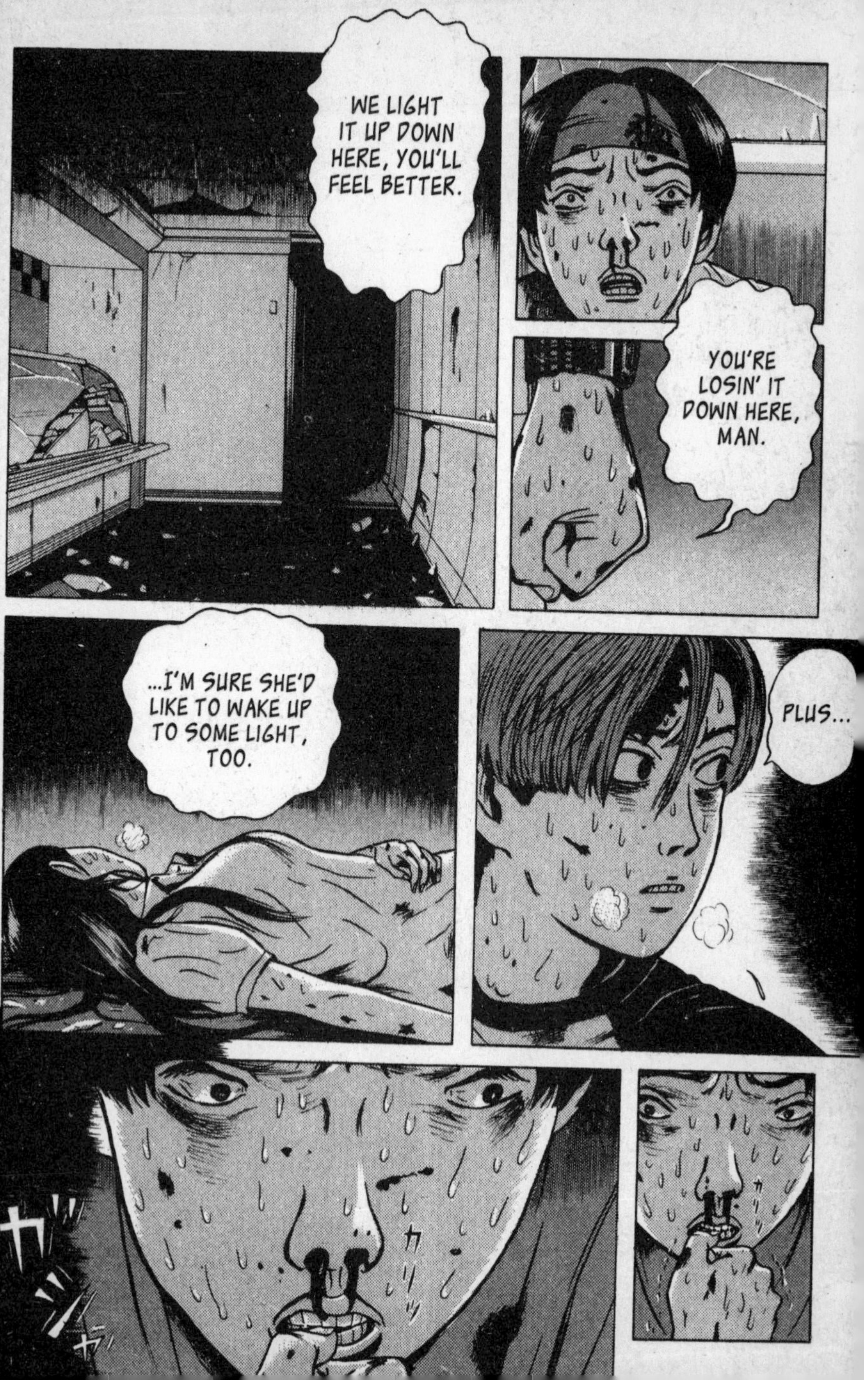
WE LIGHT IT UP DOWN HERE, YOU'LL FEEL BETTER.
YOU'RE LOSIN' IT DOWN HERE, MAN.
PLUS...
...I'M SURE SHE'D LIKE TO WAKE UP TO SOME LIGHT, TOO.

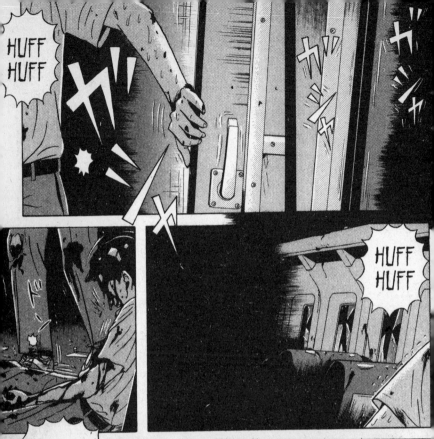

HUFF
HUFF

HUFF
HUFF

WH--WHO'S
THERE?!

UGH!

AAH!

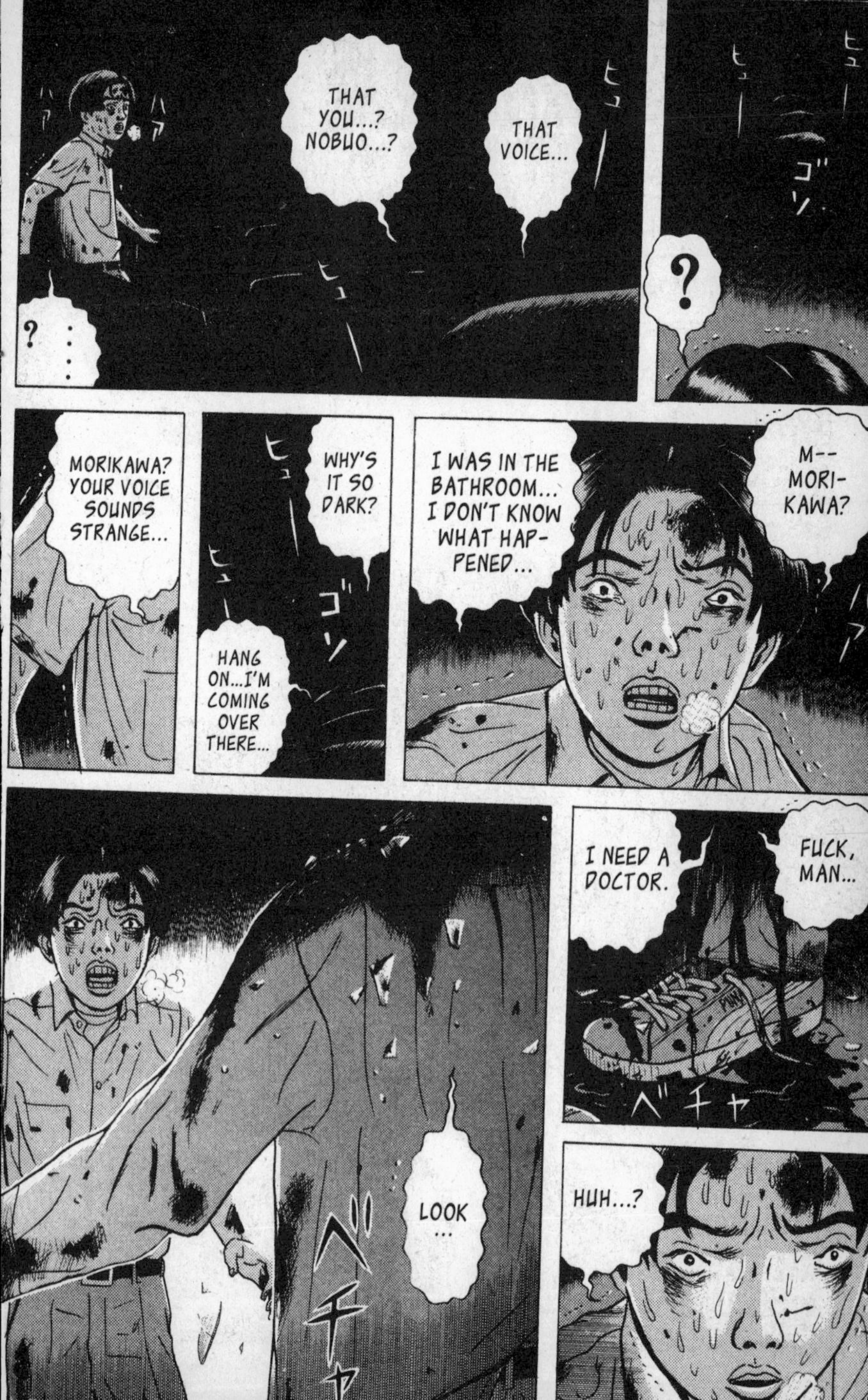
ヒュー
ゴツ
?
THAT VOICE...
THAT YOU...? NOBUO...?
ヒュー
? ...
M-- MORI-KAWA?
I WAS IN THE BATHROOM... I DON'T KNOW WHAT HAP-PENED...
WHY'S IT SO DARK?
ヒュー
ゴツ
HANG ON...I'M COMING OVER THERE...
MORIKAWA? YOUR VOICE SOUNDS STRANGE...
FUCK, MAN...
I NEED A DOCTOR.
ベチャ
HUH...?
LOOK ...
ベチャ

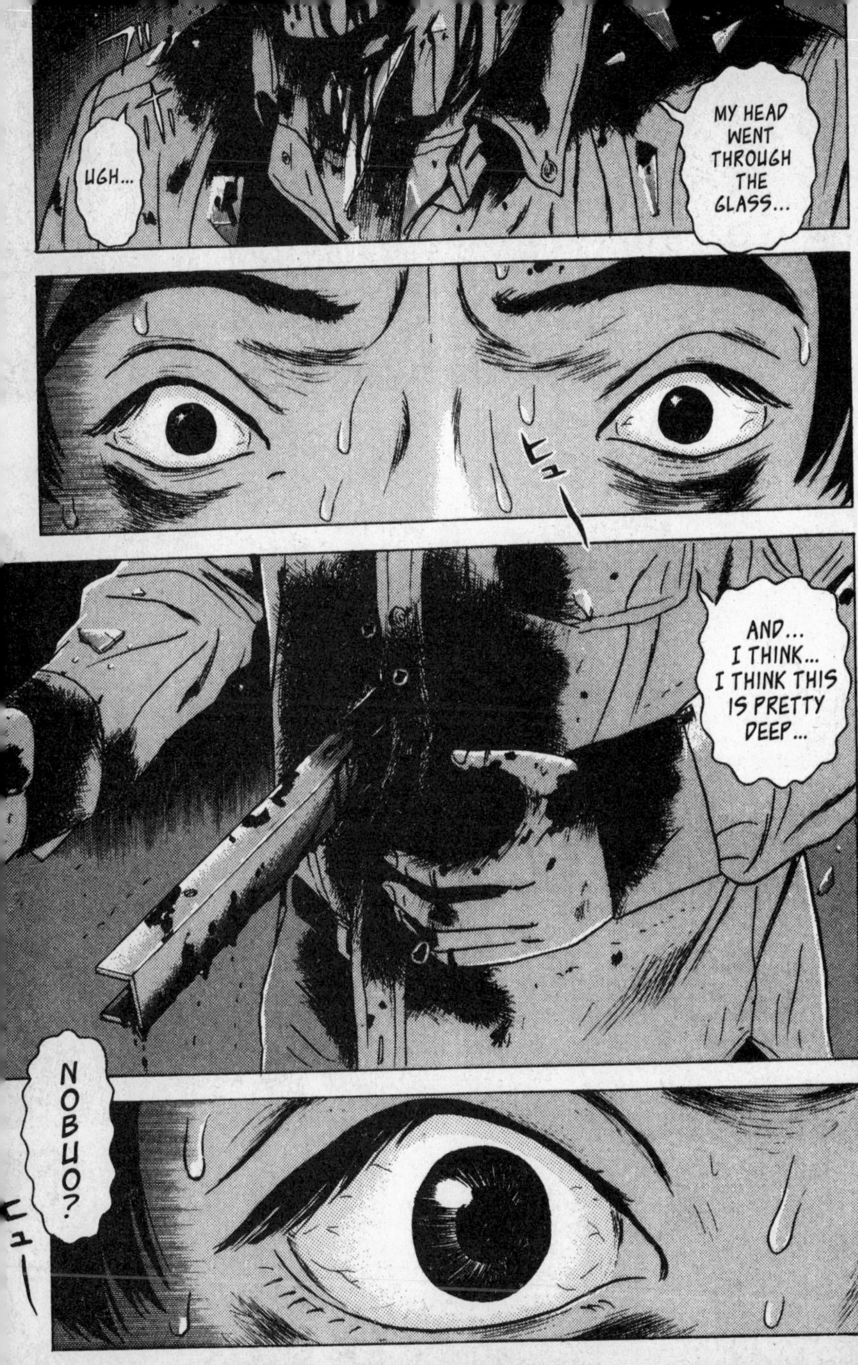
MY HEAD WENT THROUGH THE GLASS...
UGH...
AND... I THINK... I THINK THIS IS PRETTY DEEP...
NOBUO?

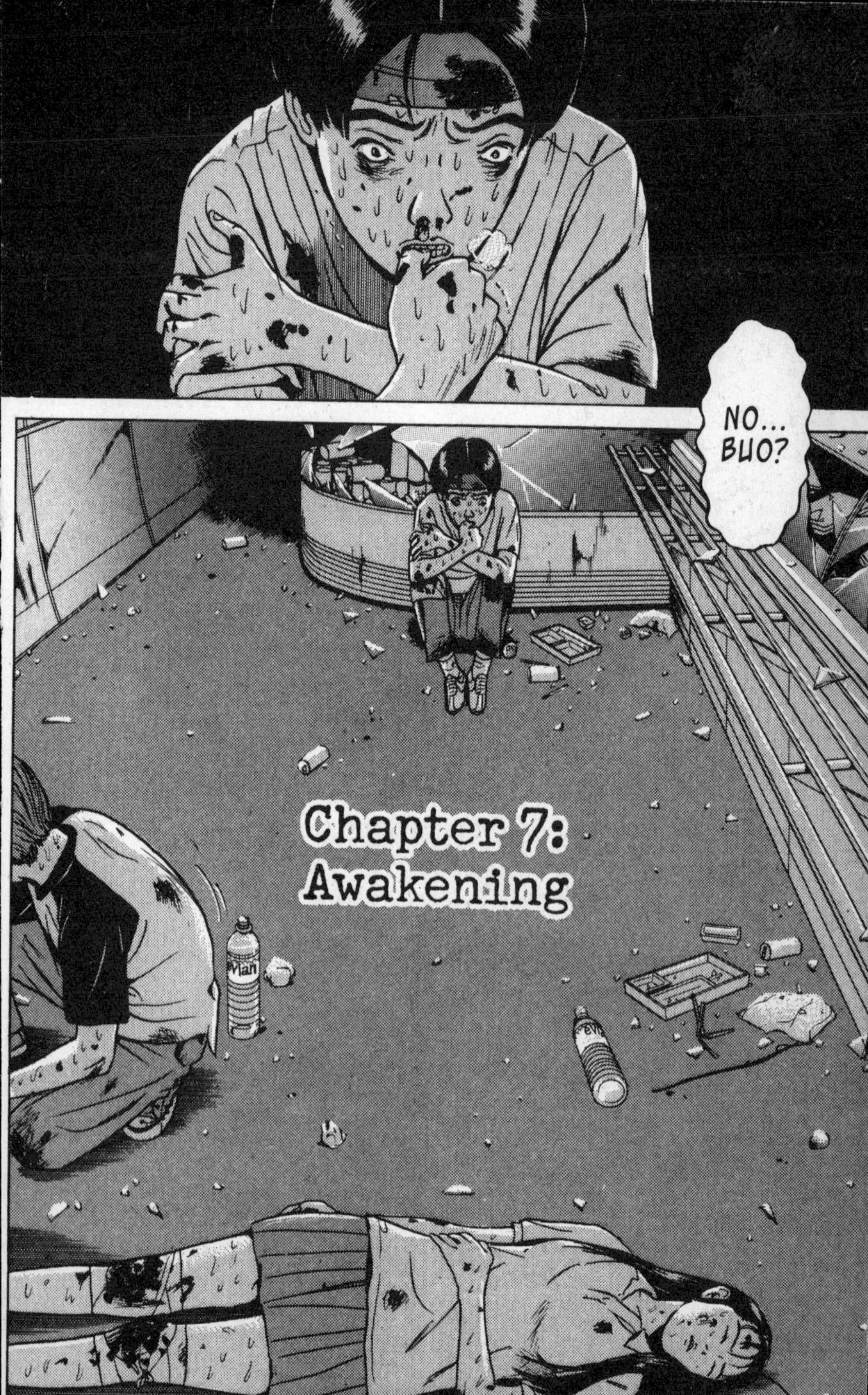
NO... BUO?
Chapter 7: Awakening

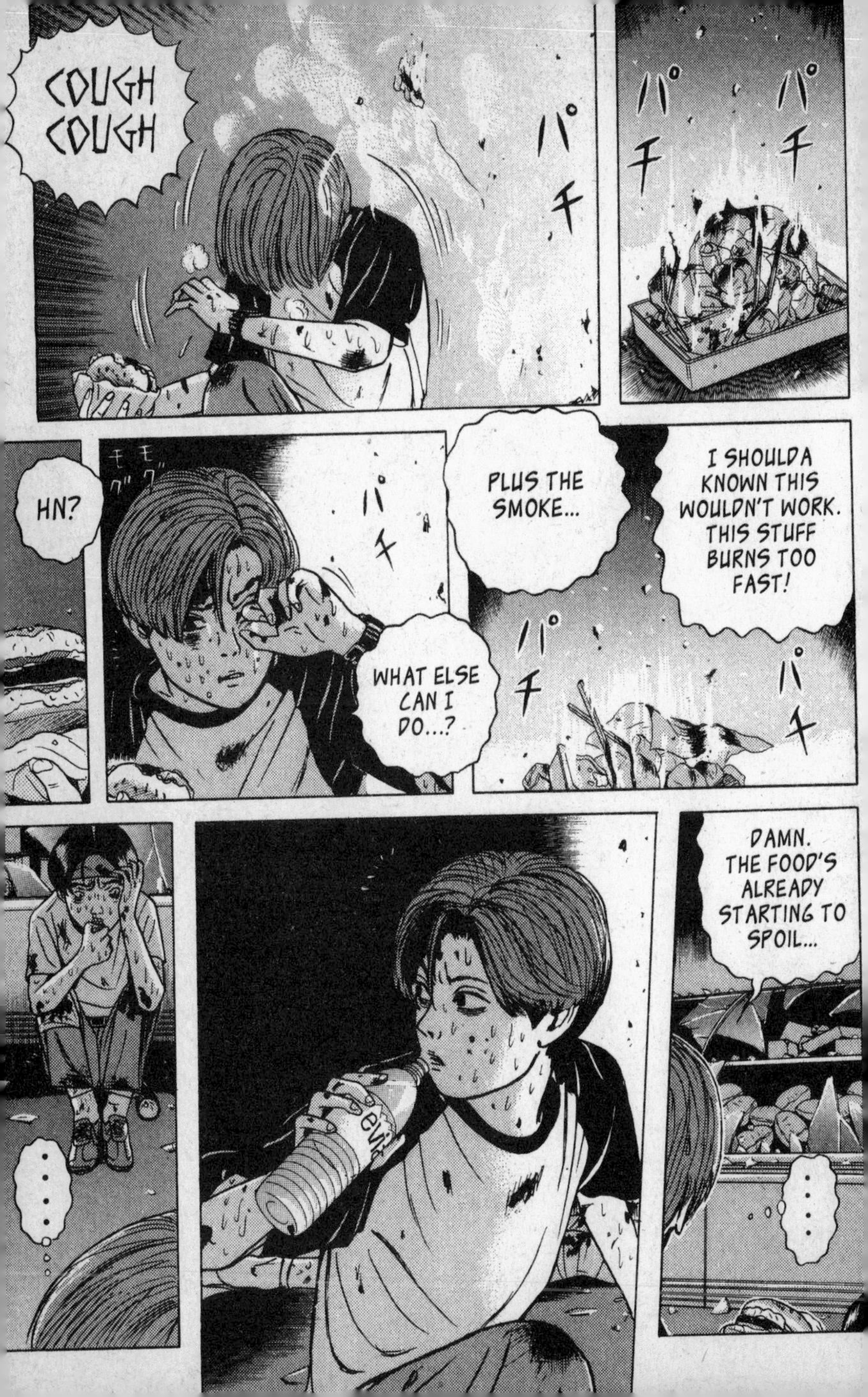
パチ
パチ
COUGH COUGH
パチ
I SHOULDA KNOWN THIS WOULDN'T WORK. THIS STUFF BURNS TOO FAST!
PLUS THE SMOKE...
パチ
パチ
パチ
WHAT ELSE CAN I DO...?
モグ モグ
HN?
DAMN. THE FOOD'S ALREADY STARTING TO SPOIL...
.....
.....

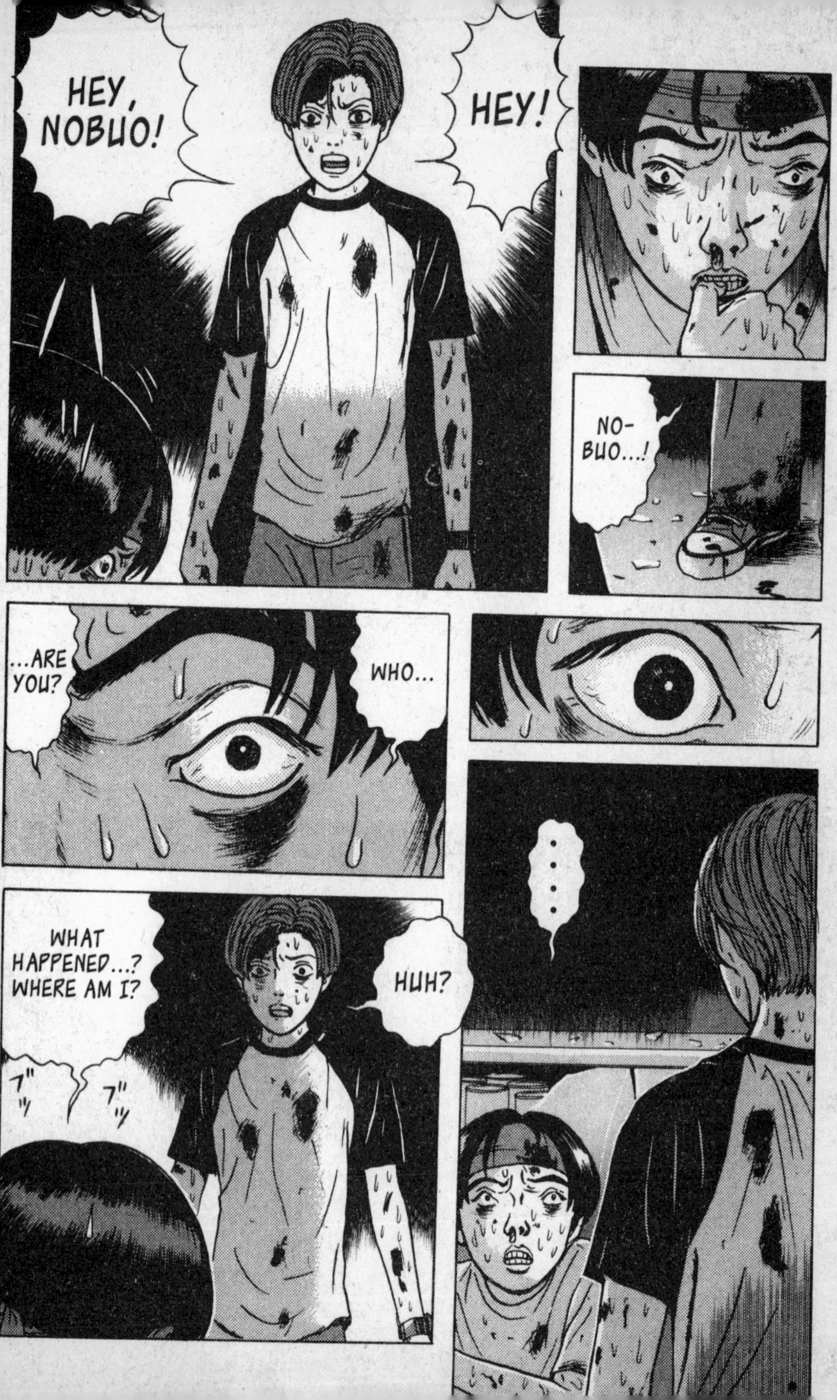
NO- BUO...!
HEY!
HEY, NOBUO!
WHO...
...ARE YOU?
.....
HUH?
WHAT HAPPENED...? WHERE AM I?
ブツ
ブツ

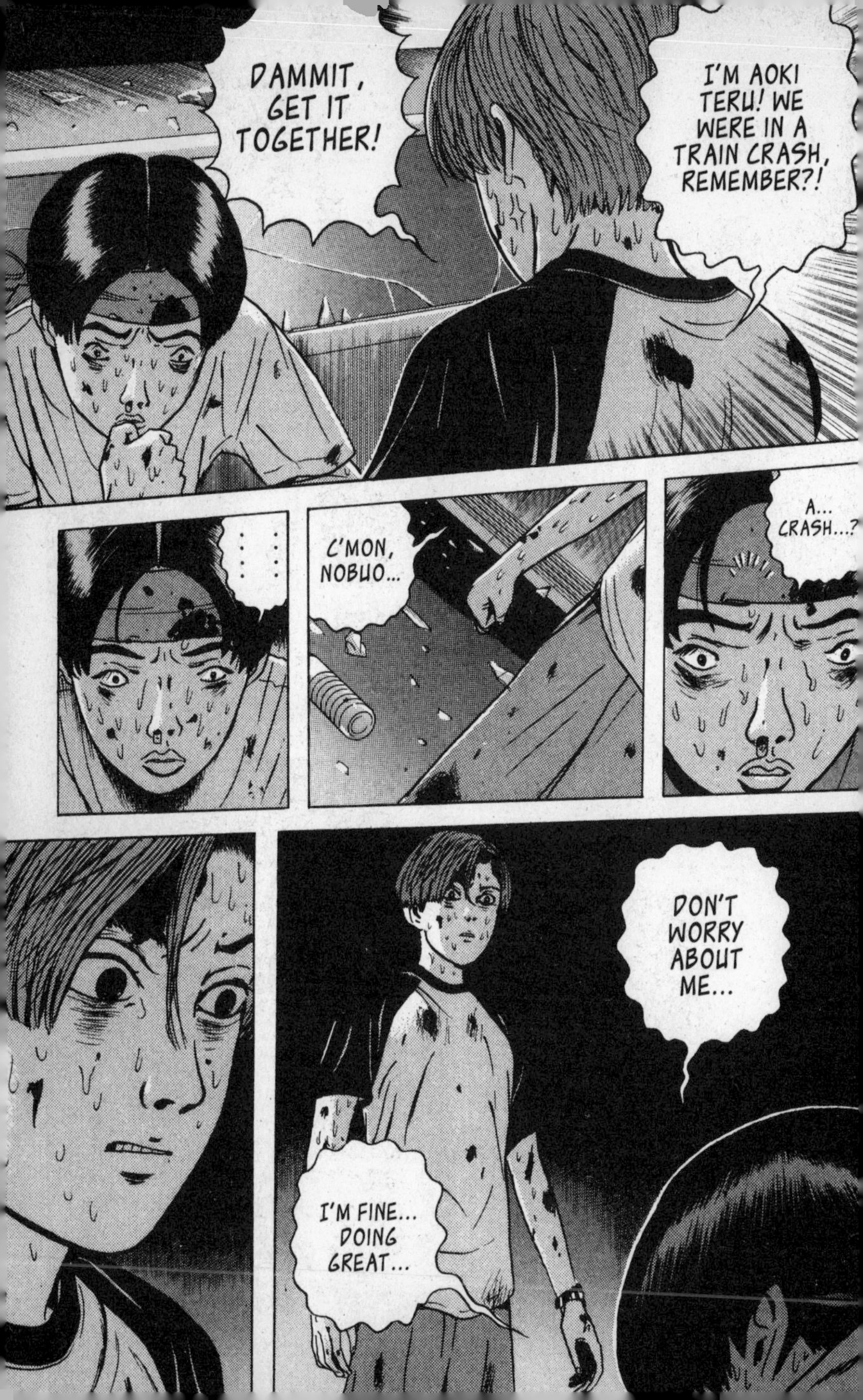
I'M AOKI TERU! WE WERE IN A TRAIN CRASH, REMEMBER?!
DAMMIT, GET IT TOGETHER!
A... CRASH...?
C'MON, NOBUO...
....
DON'T WORRY ABOUT ME...
I'M FINE... DOING GREAT...

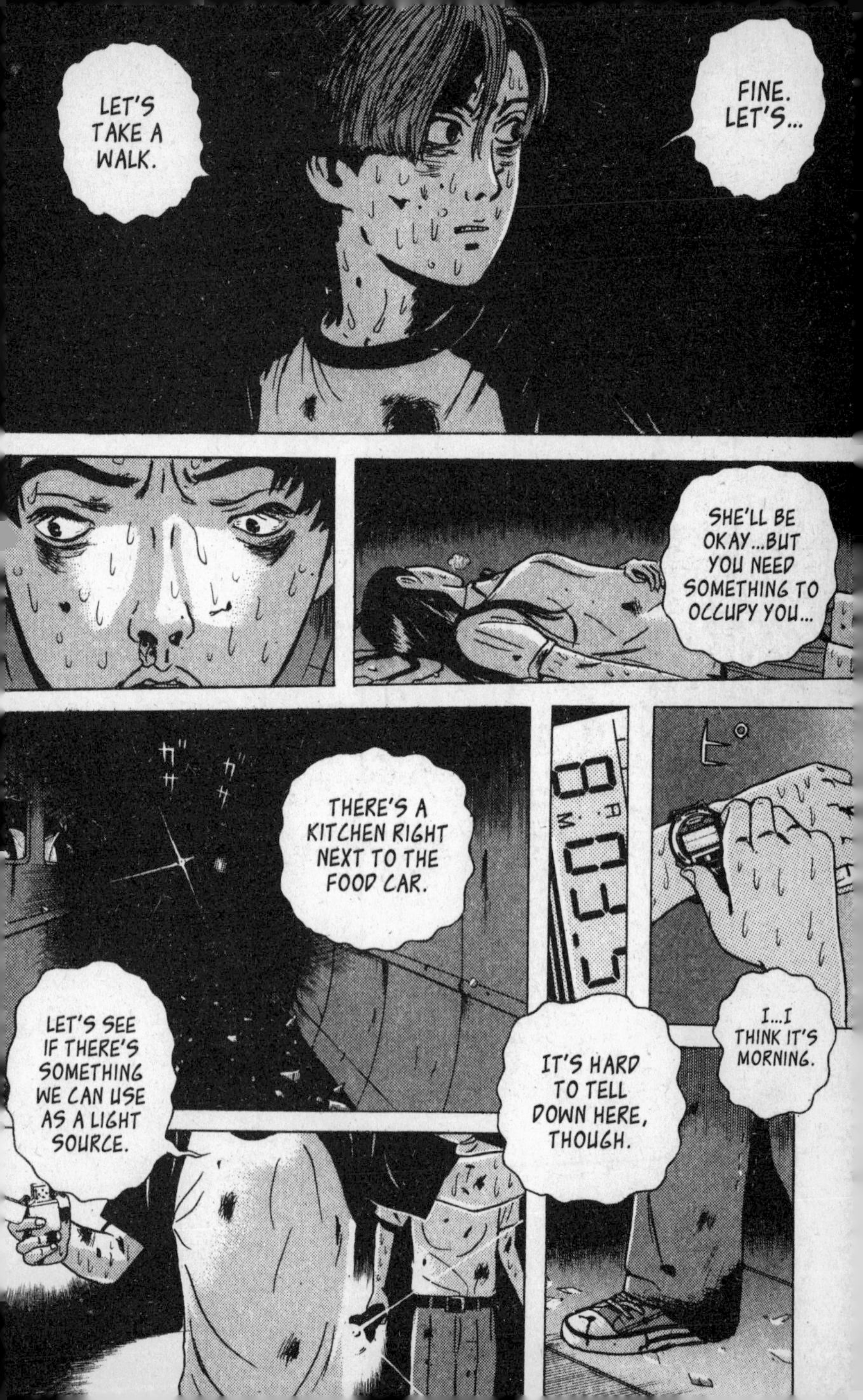
LET'S TAKE A WALK.
FINE. LET'S...
SHE'LL BE OKAY...BUT YOU NEED SOMETHING TO OCCUPY YOU...
I...I THINK IT'S MORNING.
IT'S HARD TO TELL DOWN HERE, THOUGH.
THERE'S A KITCHEN RIGHT NEXT TO THE FOOD CAR.
LET'S SEE IF THERE'S SOMETHING WE CAN USE AS A LIGHT SOURCE.

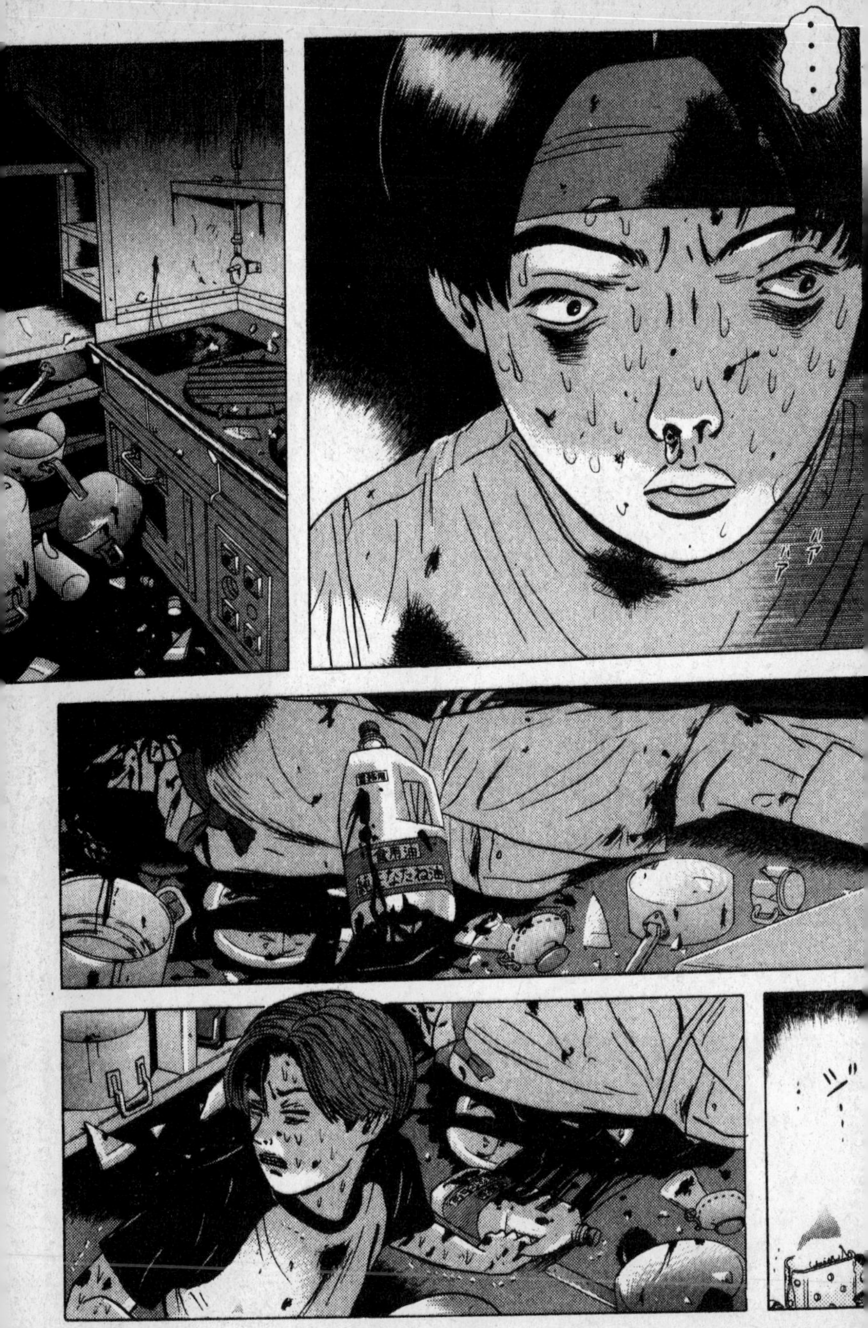
・・・・
ハァ
ハァ
食用油
なたね油

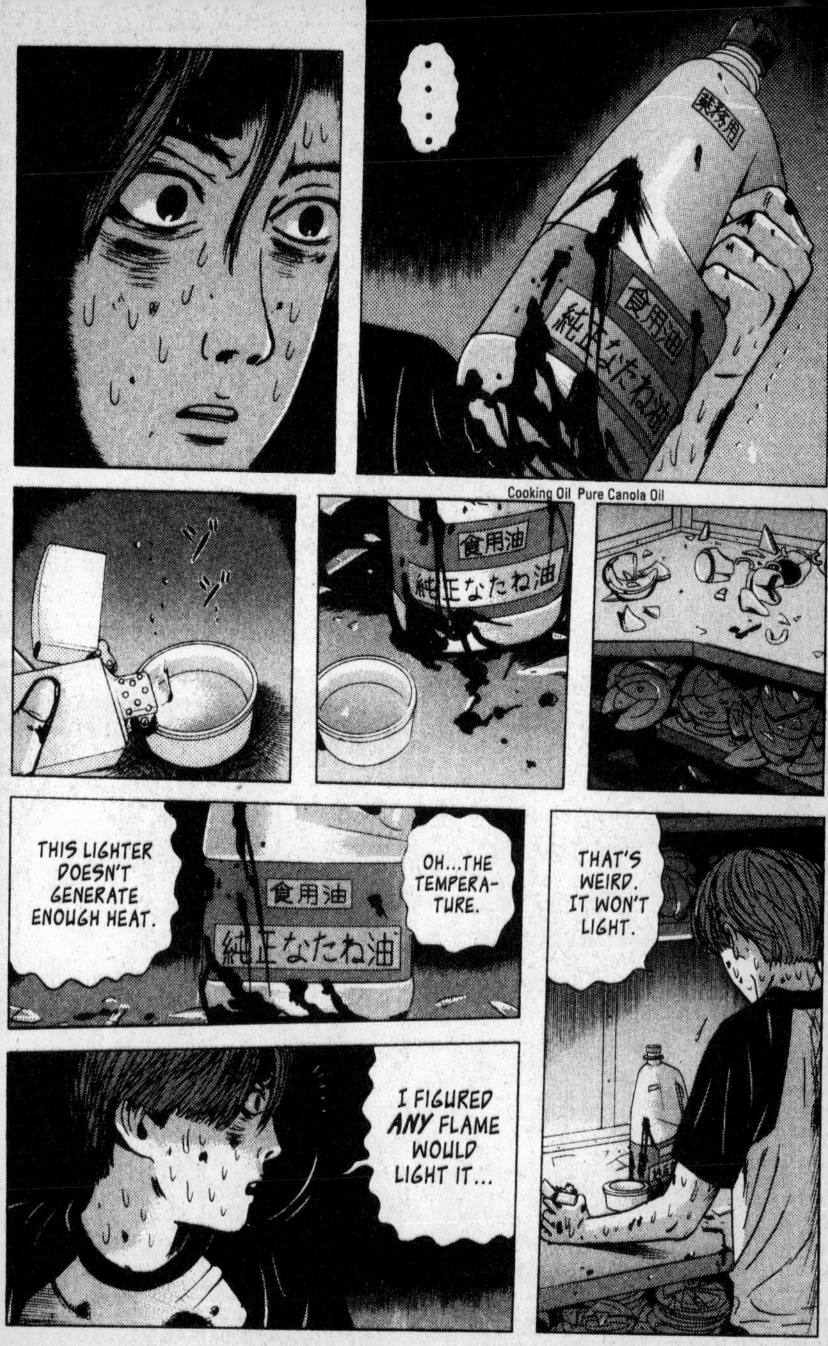

・・・・
業務用
食用油
純正なたね油
Cooking Oil Pure Canola Oil
食用油
純正なたね油
ジジ
THAT'S WEIRD. IT WON'T LIGHT.
OH...THE TEMPERA-TURE.
食用油
純正なたね油
THIS LIGHTER DOESN'T GENERATE ENOUGH HEAT.
I FIGURED *ANY* FLAME WOULD LIGHT IT...

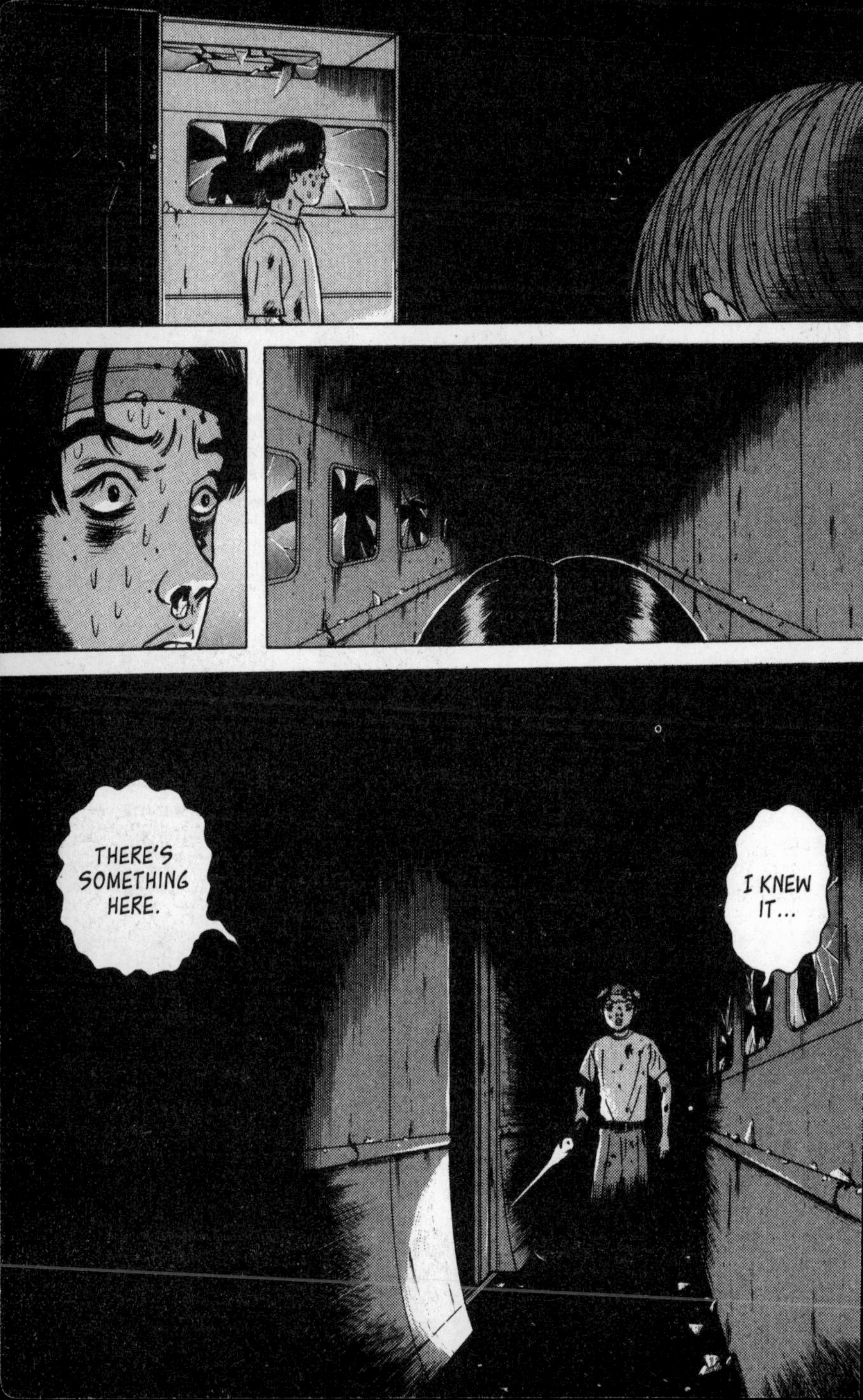
I KNEW IT...
THERE'S SOMETHING HERE.

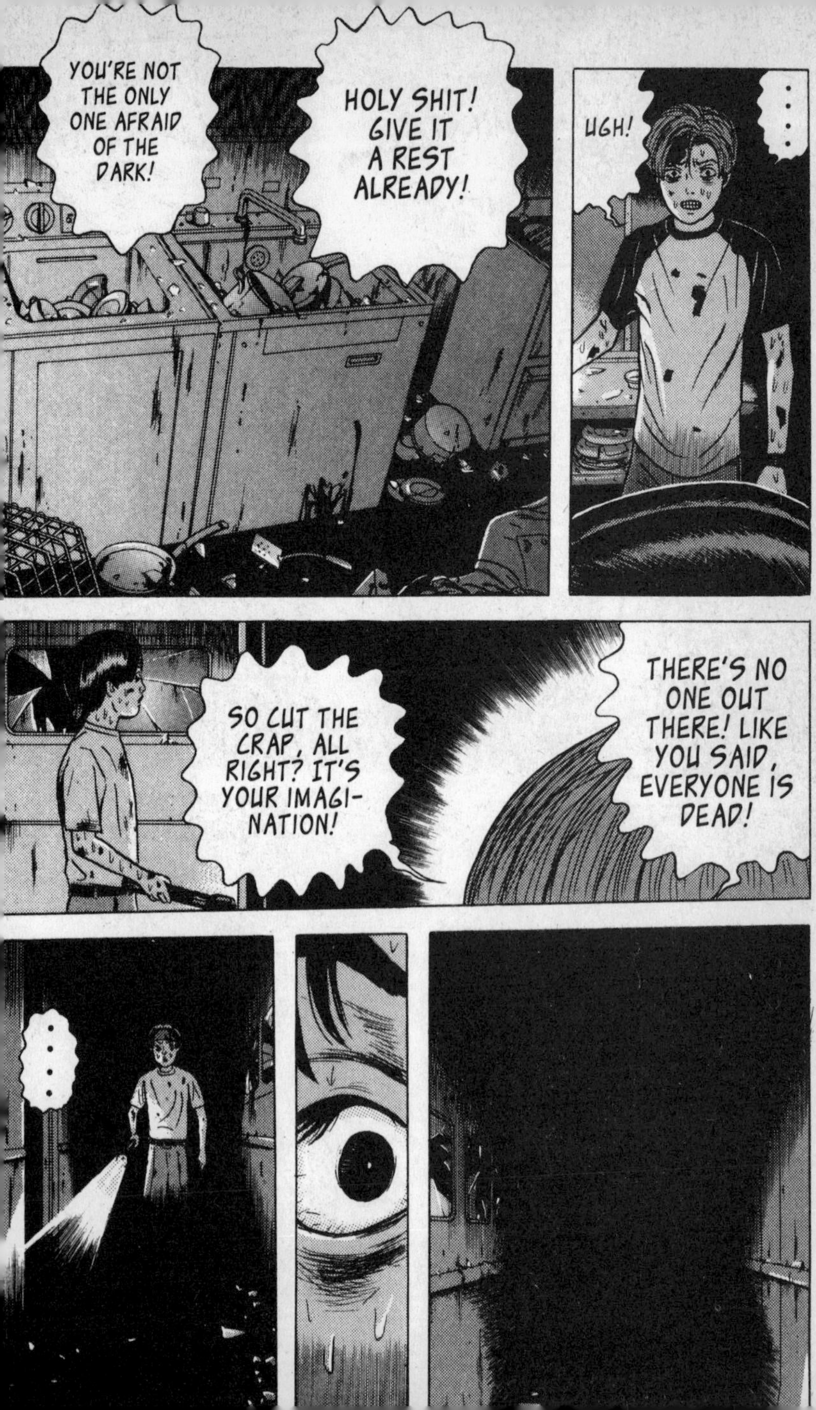
....
UGH!
HOLY SHIT! GIVE IT A REST ALREADY!
YOU'RE NOT THE ONLY ONE AFRAID OF THE DARK!
THERE'S NO ONE OUT THERE! LIKE YOU SAID, EVERYONE IS DEAD!
SO CUT THE CRAP, ALL RIGHT? IT'S YOUR IMAGI-NATION!
....

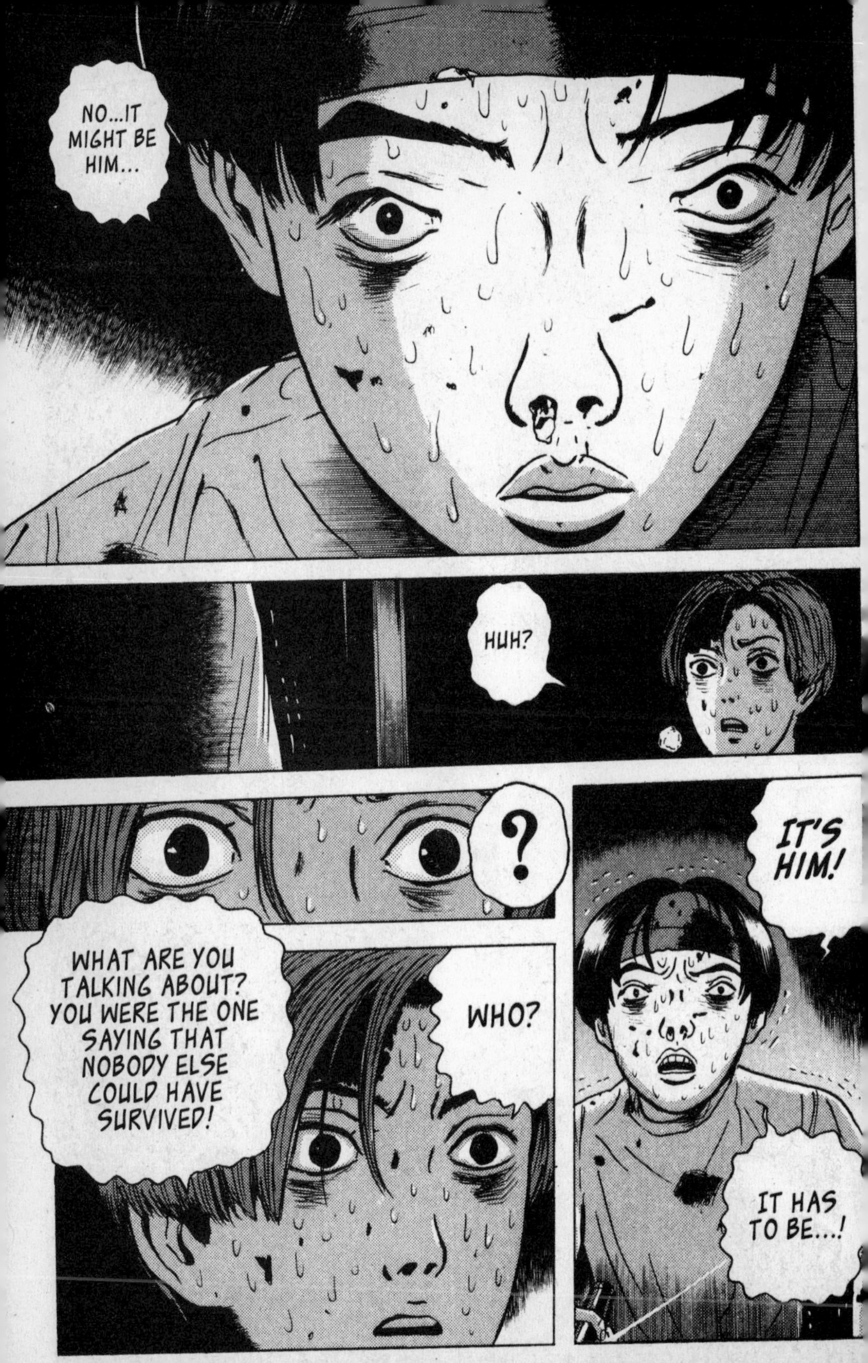
NO...IT MIGHT BE HIM...
HUH?
IT'S HIM!
IT HAS TO BE...!
?
WHO?
WHAT ARE YOU TALKING ABOUT? YOU WERE THE ONE SAYING THAT NOBODY ELSE COULD HAVE SURVIVED!

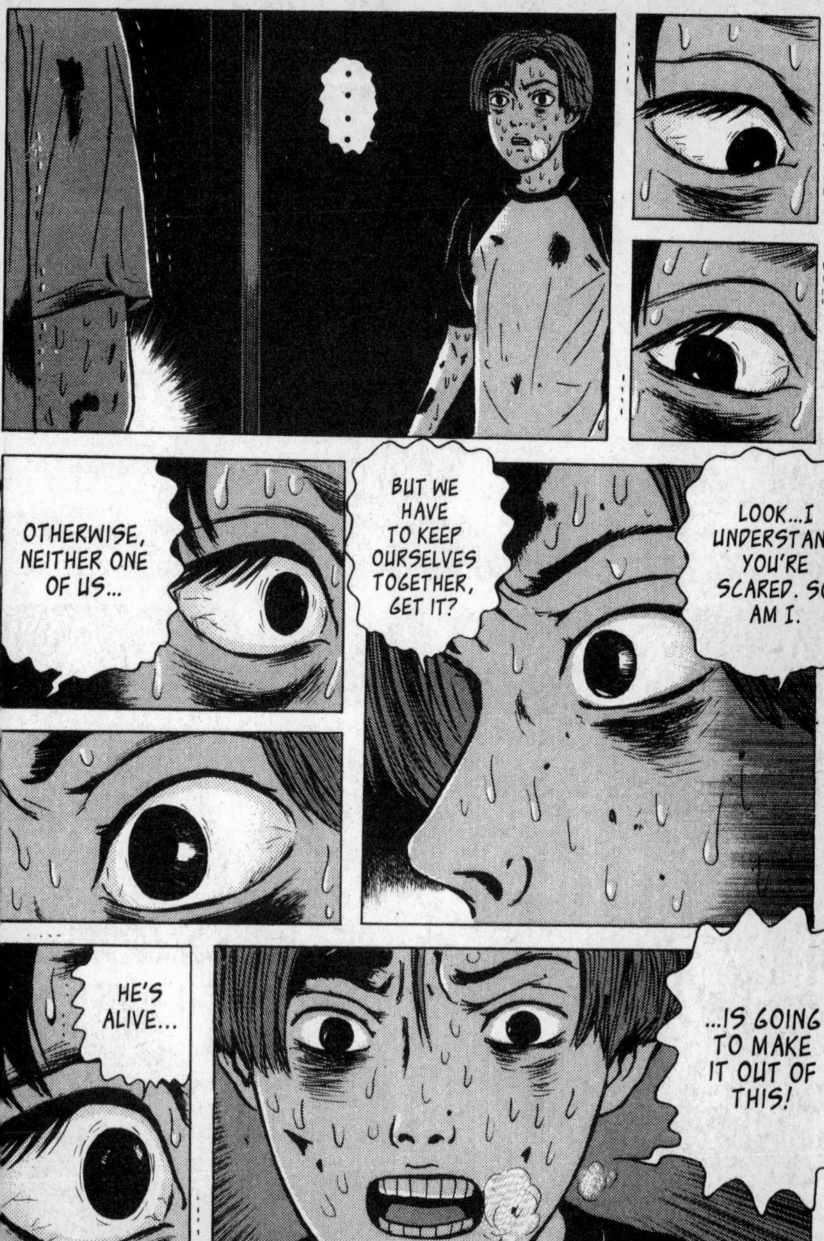
LOOK...I UNDERSTAND YOU'RE SCARED. SO AM I.
BUT WE HAVE TO KEEP OURSELVES TOGETHER, GET IT?
OTHERWISE, NEITHER ONE OF US...
...IS GOING TO MAKE IT OUT OF THIS!
HE'S ALIVE...

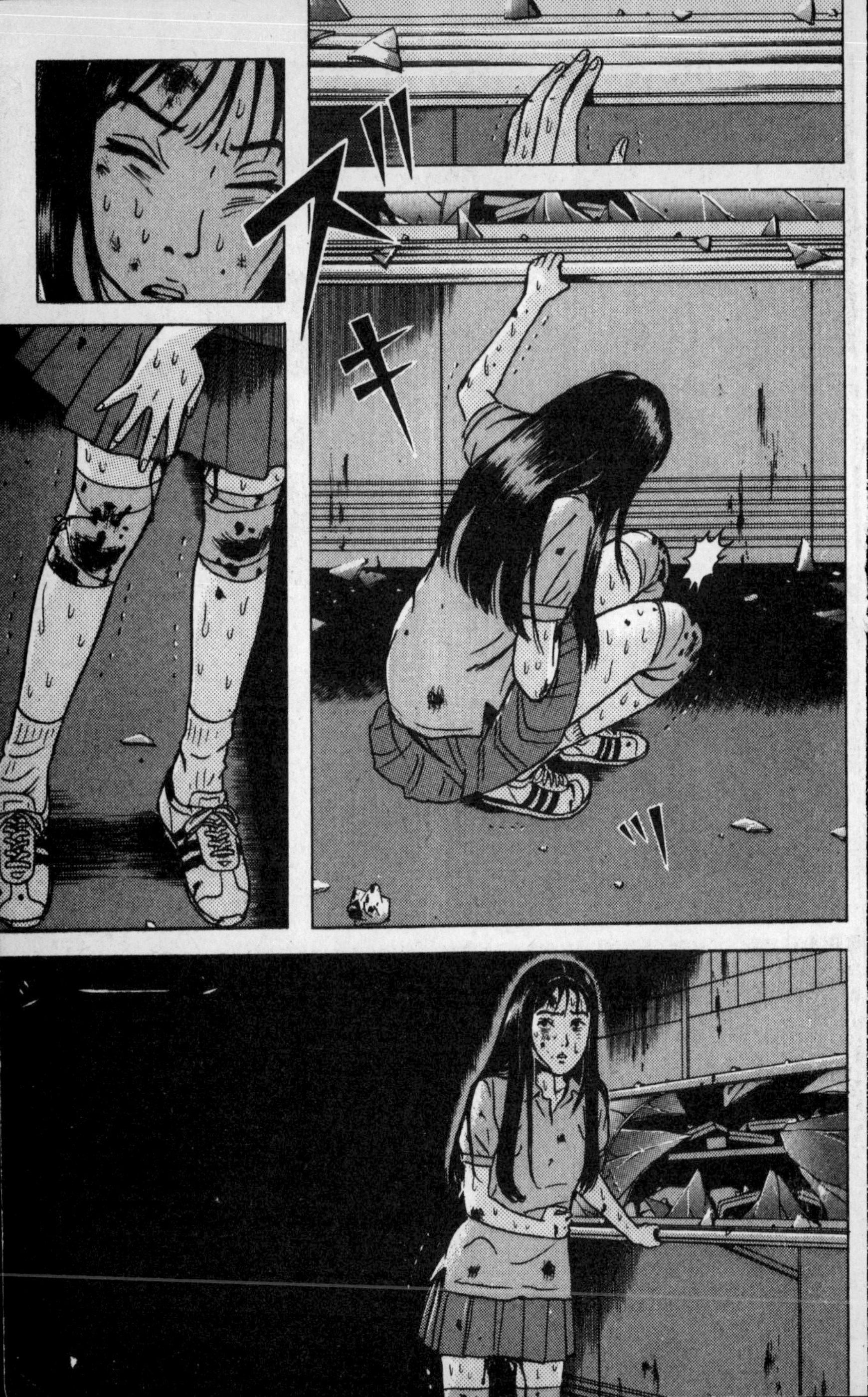
ズ
キ

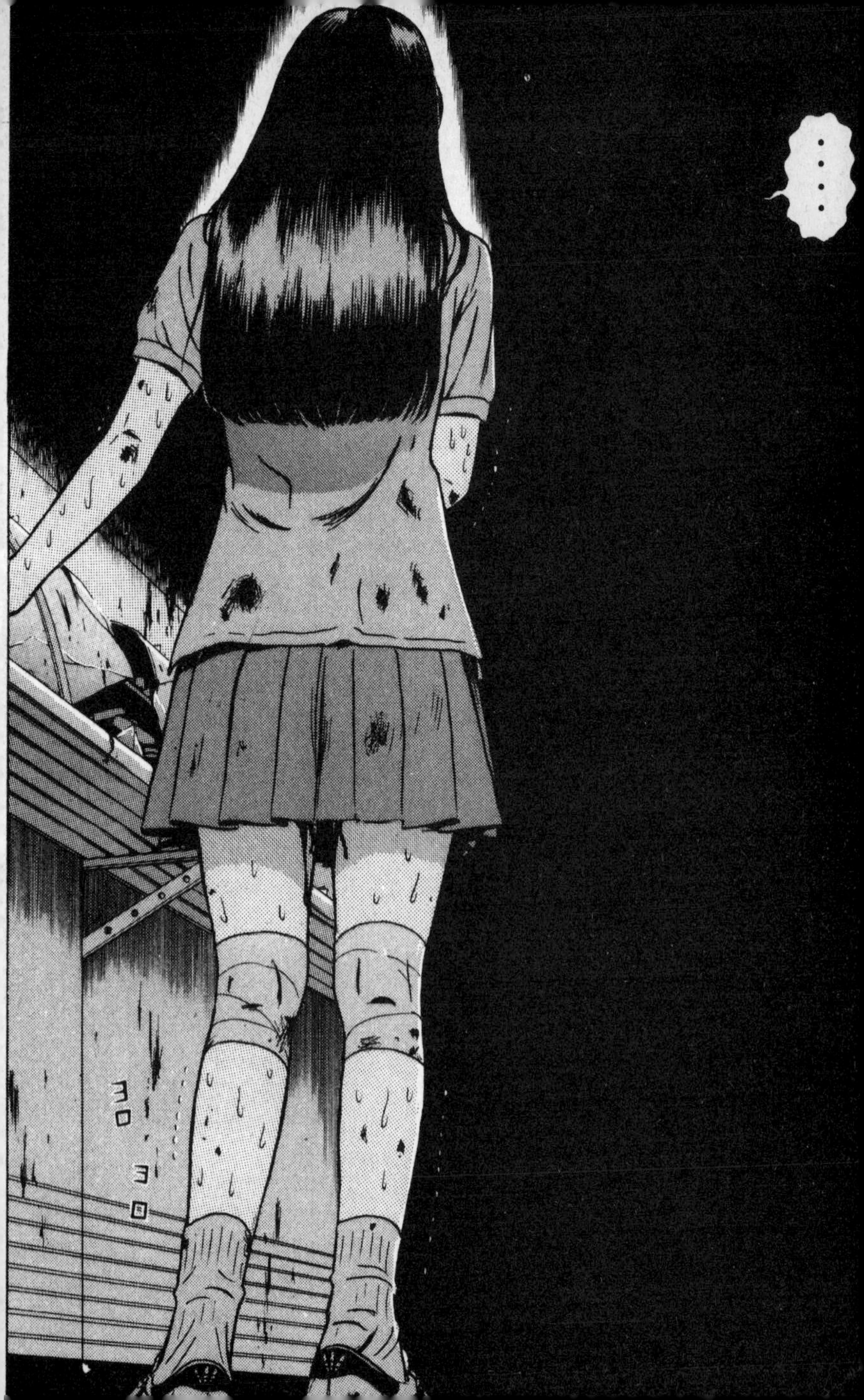
....
ヨロ
ヨロ

# Chapter 8: What Hides In The Mind

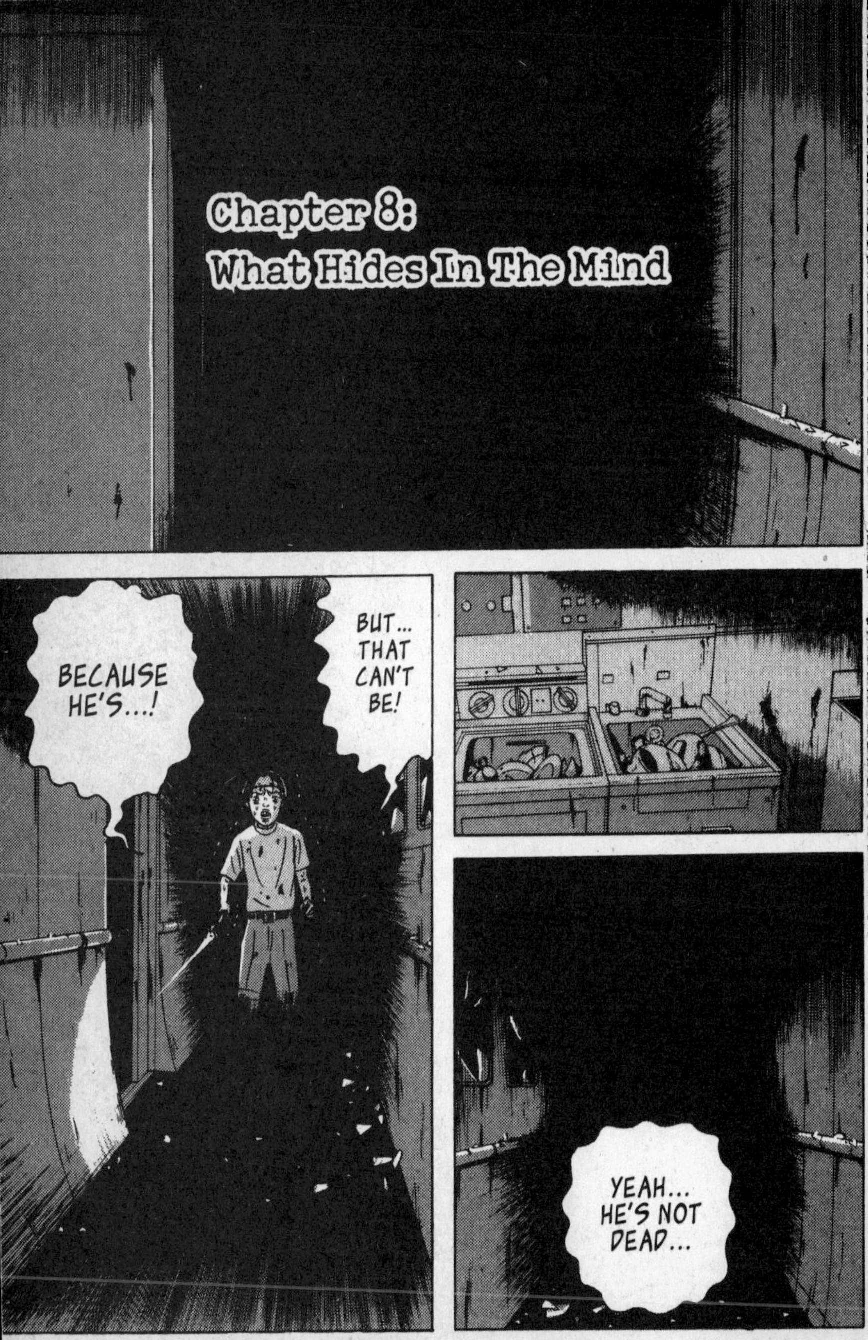
BECAUSE HE'S...!
BUT... THAT CAN'T BE!
YEAH... HE'S NOT DEAD...

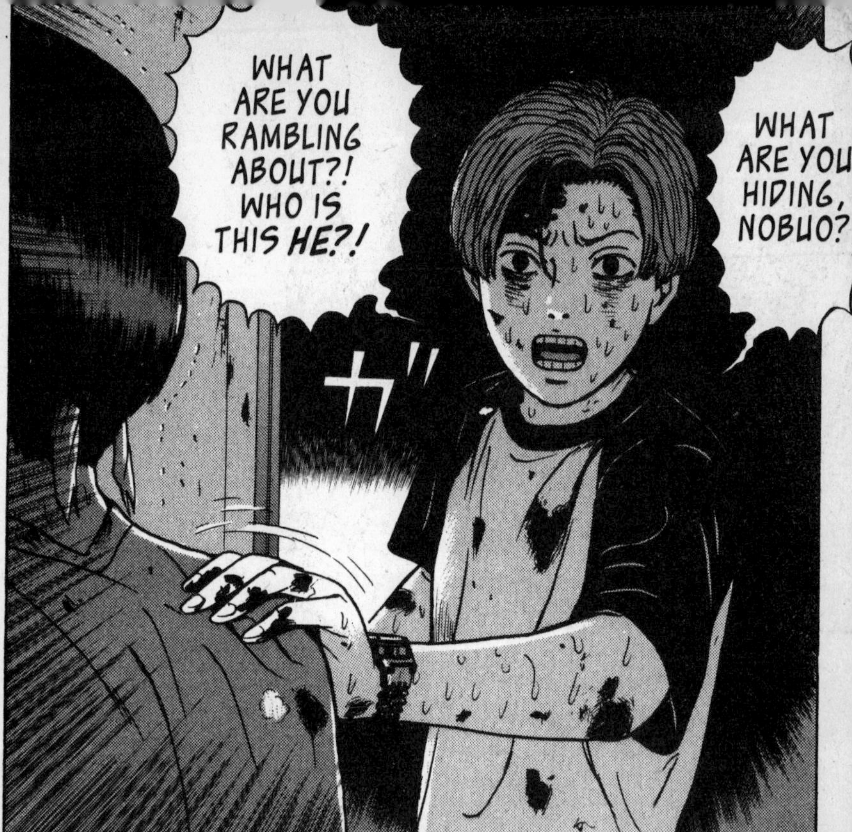
WHAT ARE YOU HIDING, NOBUO?
WHAT ARE YOU RAMBLING ABOUT?! WHO IS THIS *HE*?!

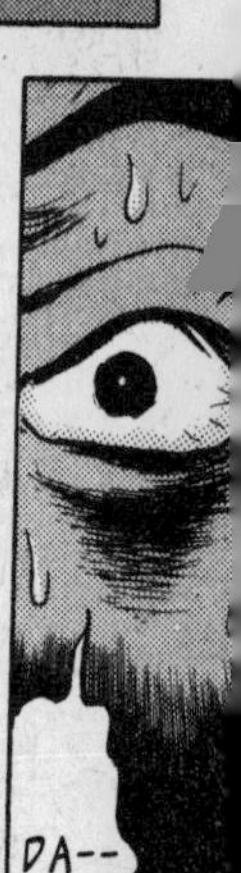
DA--

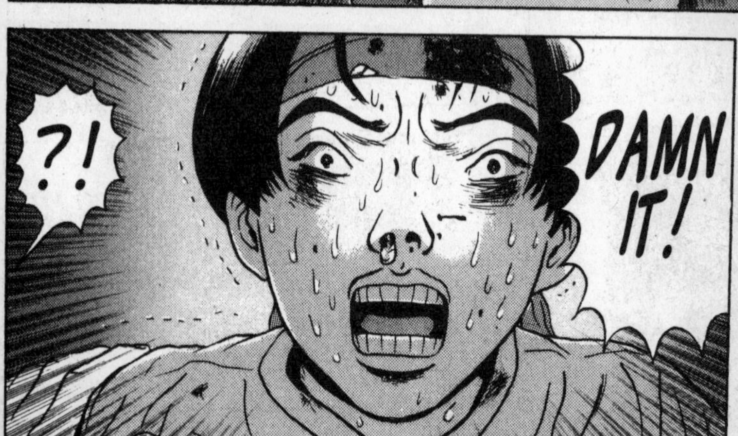
DAMN IT!
?!

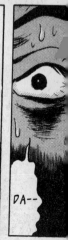

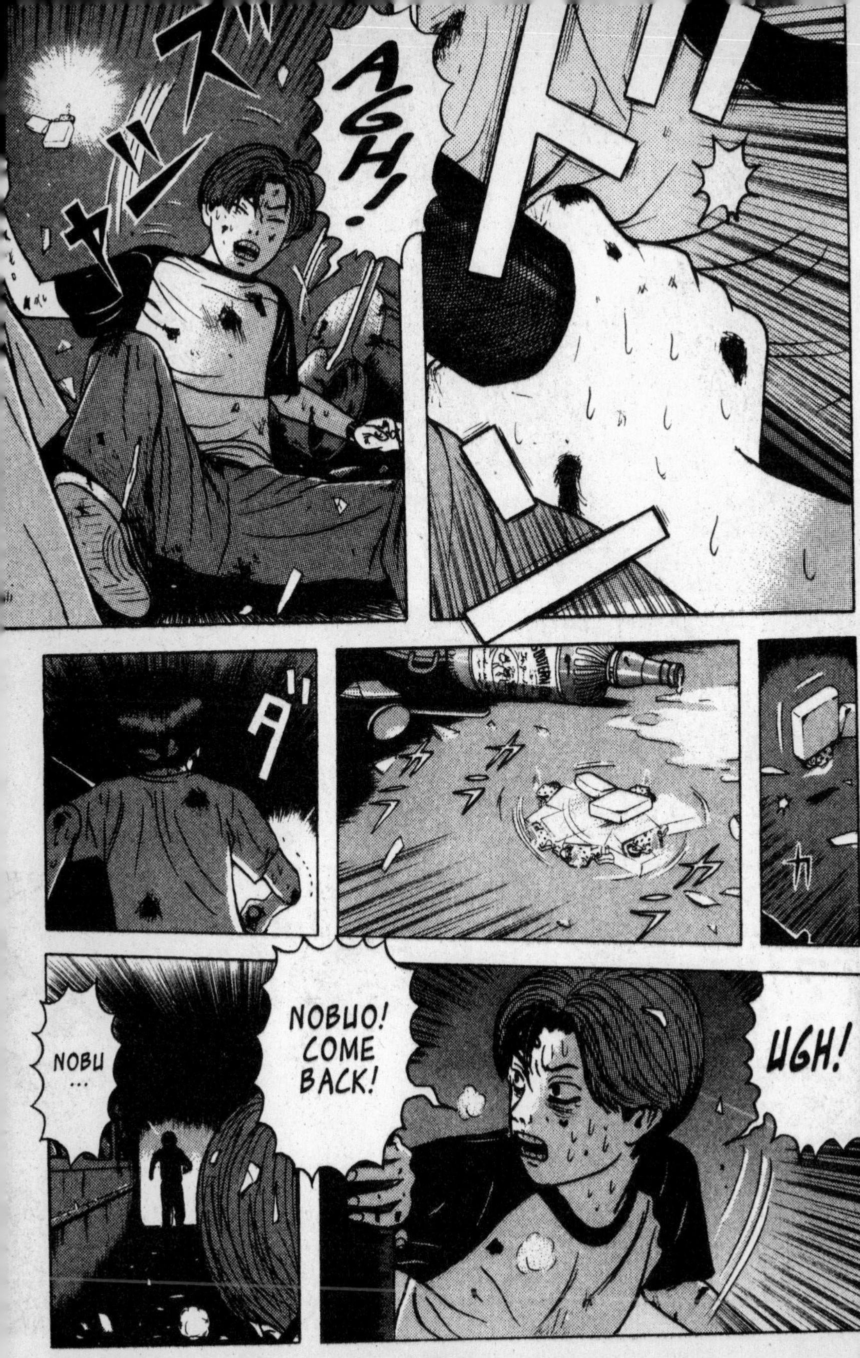
AGH!
UGH!
NOBUO! COME BACK!
NOBU ...

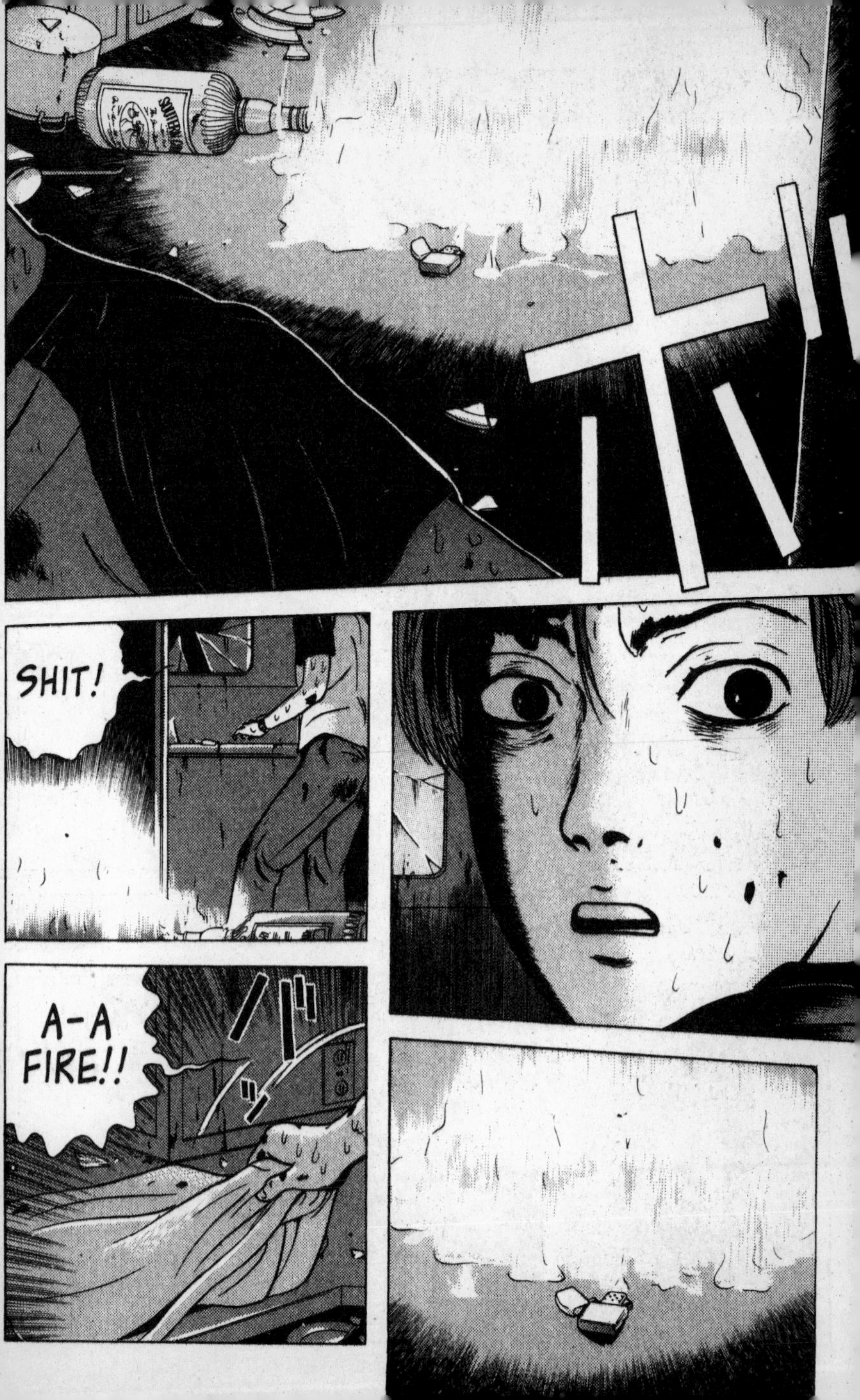
SHIT!
A-A FIRE!!

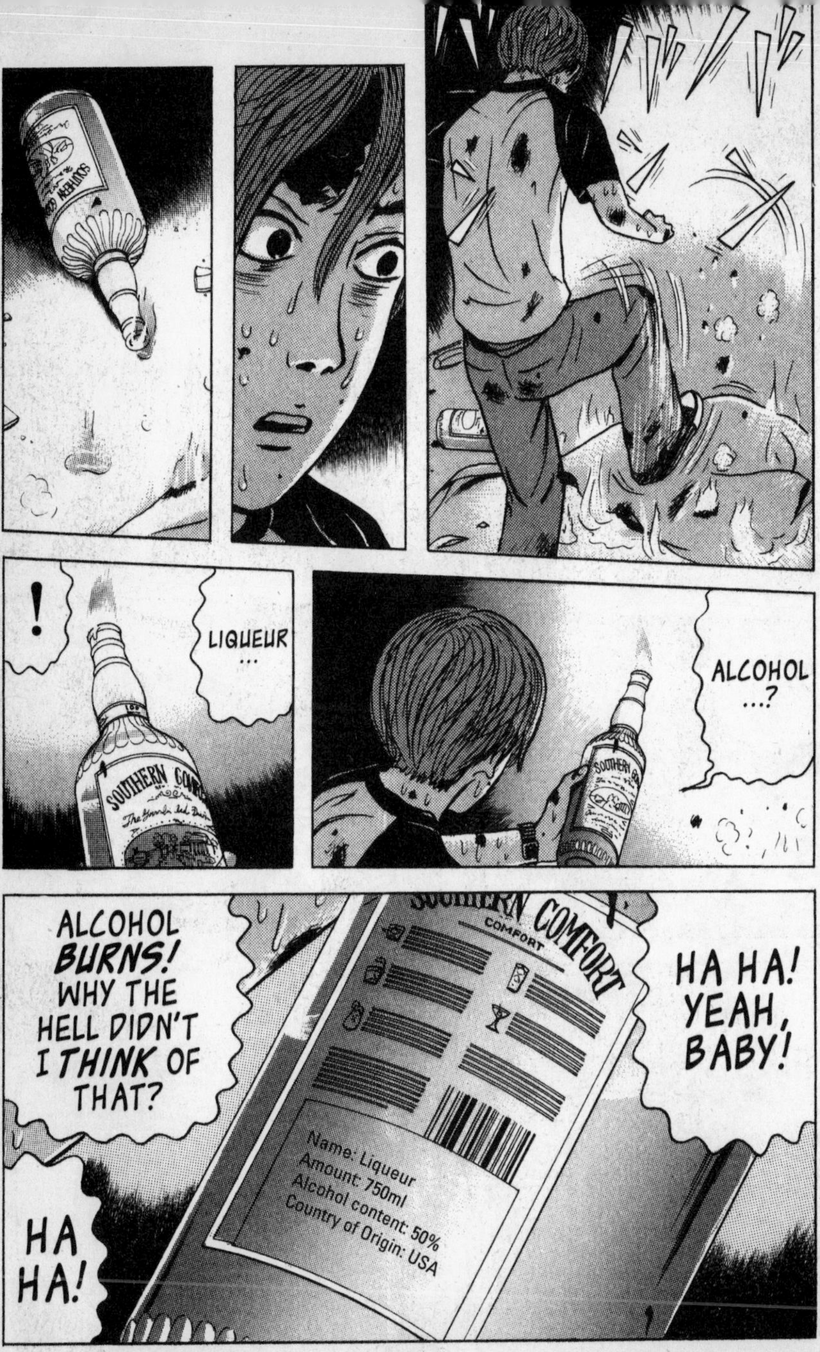
ALCOHOL ...?
LIQUEUR ...
!
HA HA! YEAH, BABY!
ALCOHOL BURNS! WHY THE HELL DIDN'T I THINK OF THAT?
SOUTHERN COMFORT
Name: Liqueur
Amount: 750ml
Alcohol content: 50%
Country of Origin: USA
HA HA!

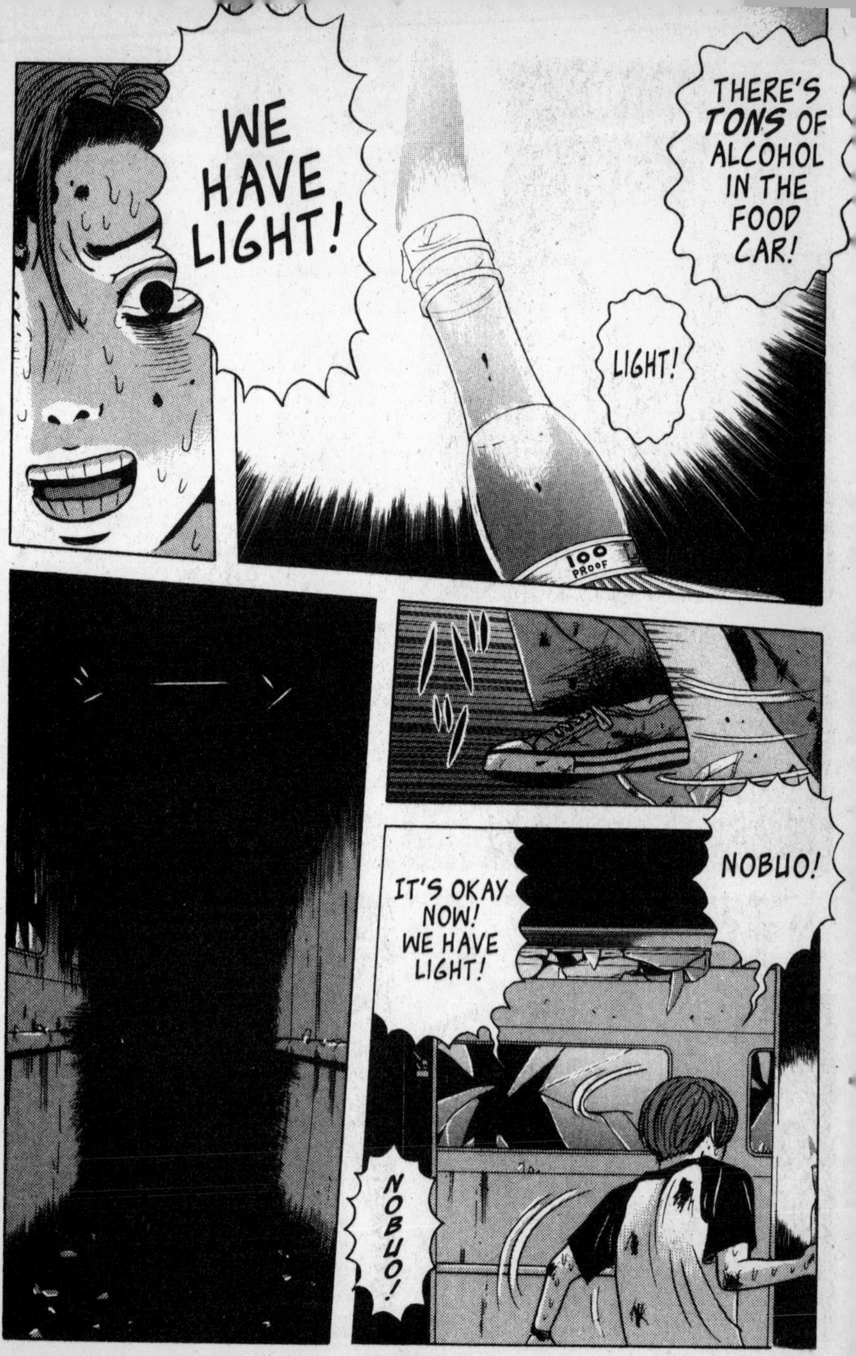
THERE'S TONS OF ALCOHOL IN THE FOOD CAR!
LIGHT!
100 PROOF
WE HAVE LIGHT!
NOBUO!
IT'S OKAY NOW! WE HAVE LIGHT!
NOBUO!

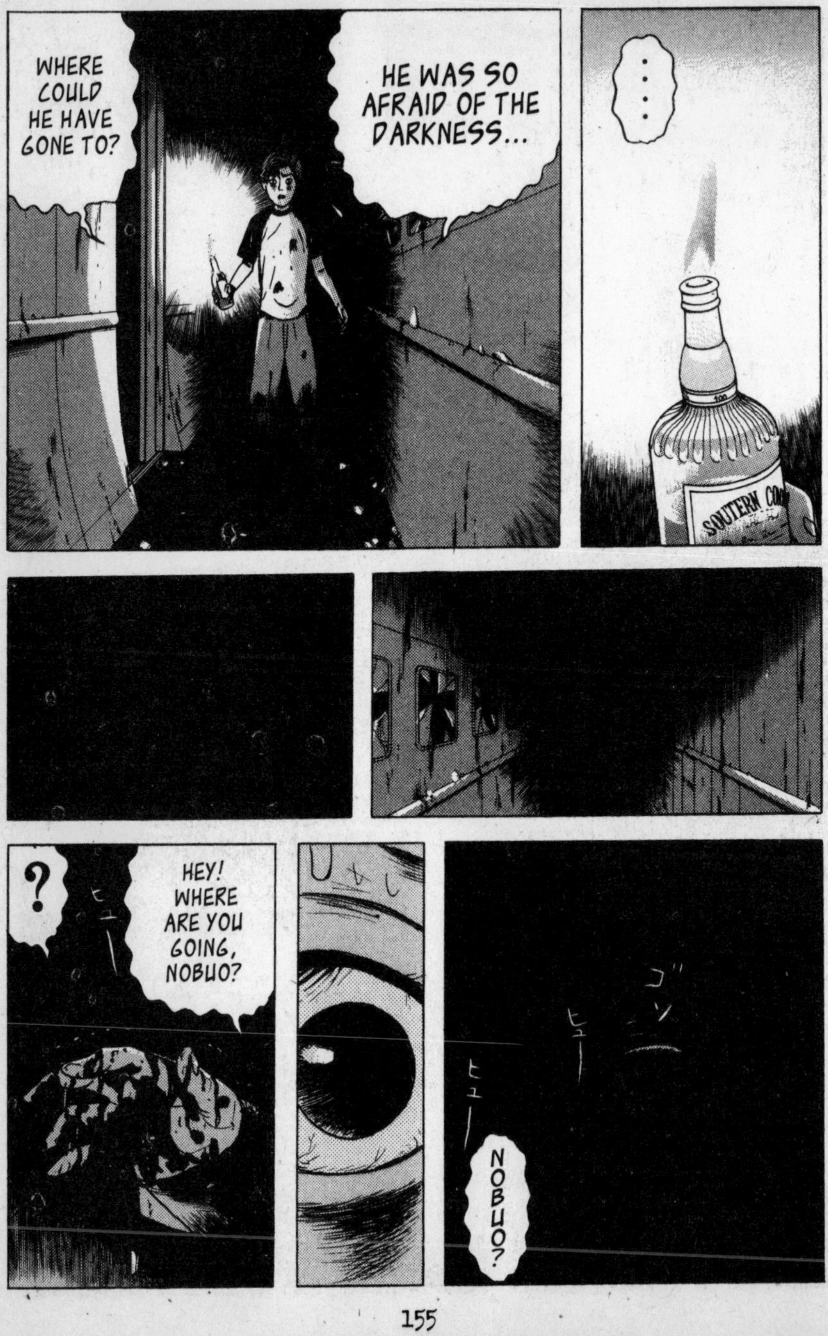
....
HE WAS SO AFRAID OF THE DARKNESS...
WHERE COULD HE HAVE GONE TO?
NOBUO?
HEY! WHERE ARE YOU GOING, NOBUO?
?

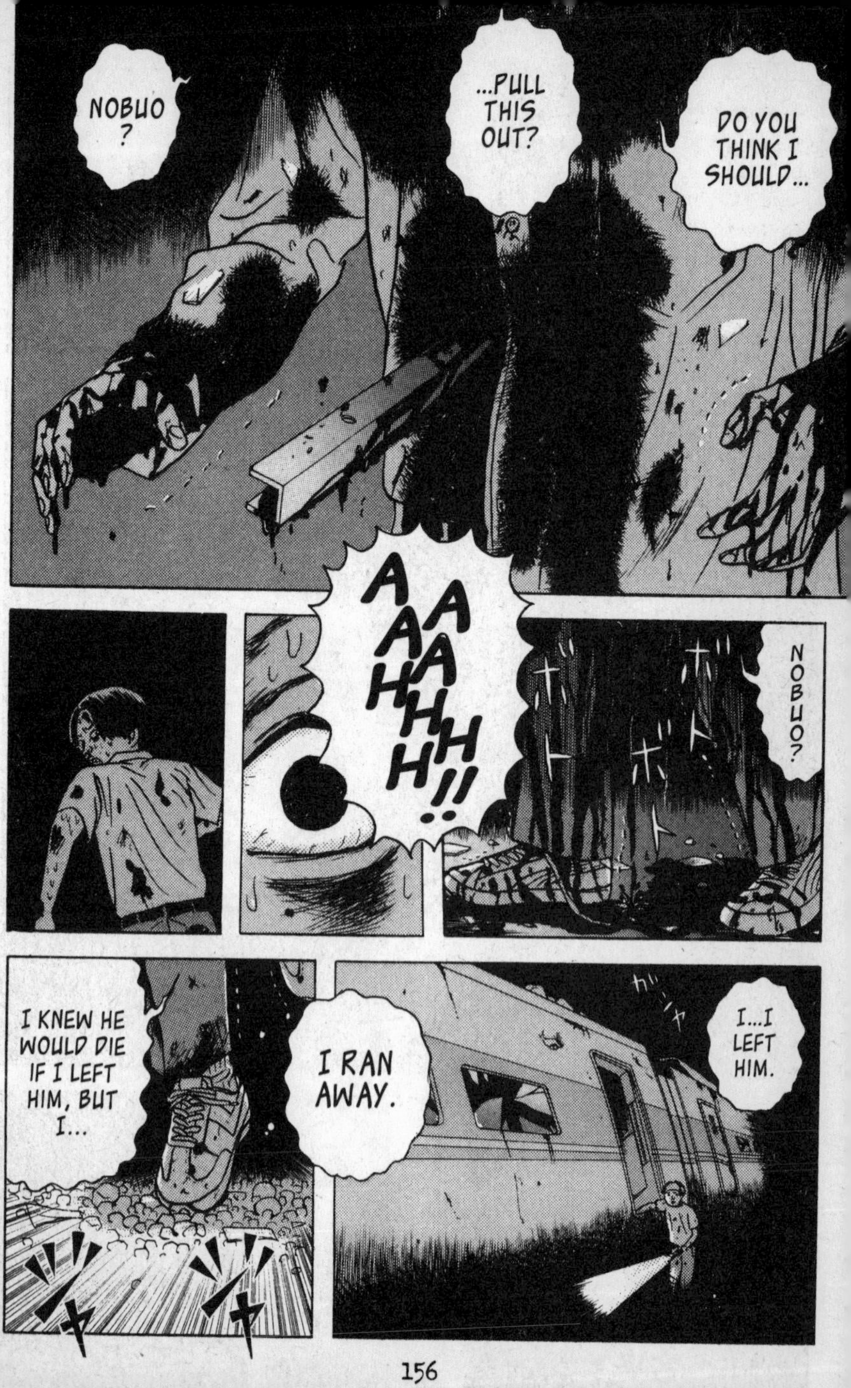
DO YOU THINK I SHOULD...
...PULL THIS OUT?
NOBUO?
NOBUO?
AAAAHHHHH!!
I...I LEFT HIM.
I RAN AWAY.
I KNEW HE WOULD DIE IF I LEFT HIM, BUT I...

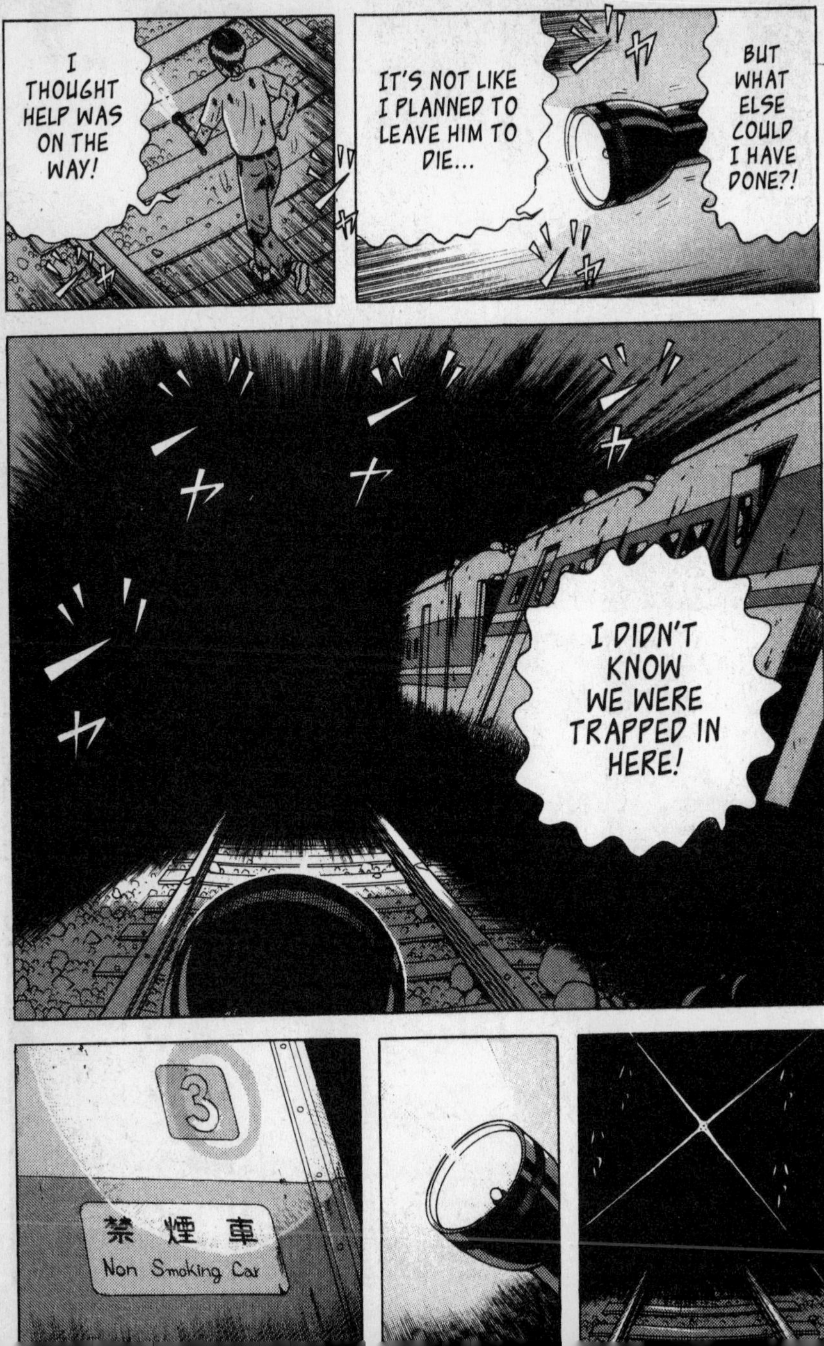
IT'S NOT LIKE I PLANNED TO LEAVE HIM TO DIE...
BUT WHAT ELSE COULD I HAVE DONE?!
I THOUGHT HELP WAS ON THE WAY!
I DIDN'T KNOW WE WERE TRAPPED IN HERE!
3
禁 煙 車
Non Smoking Car

THIS IS MY CLASS' CAR...

WHERE'S MORIKAWA?

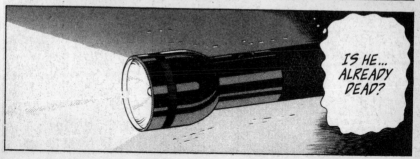

IS HE... ALREADY DEAD?

158

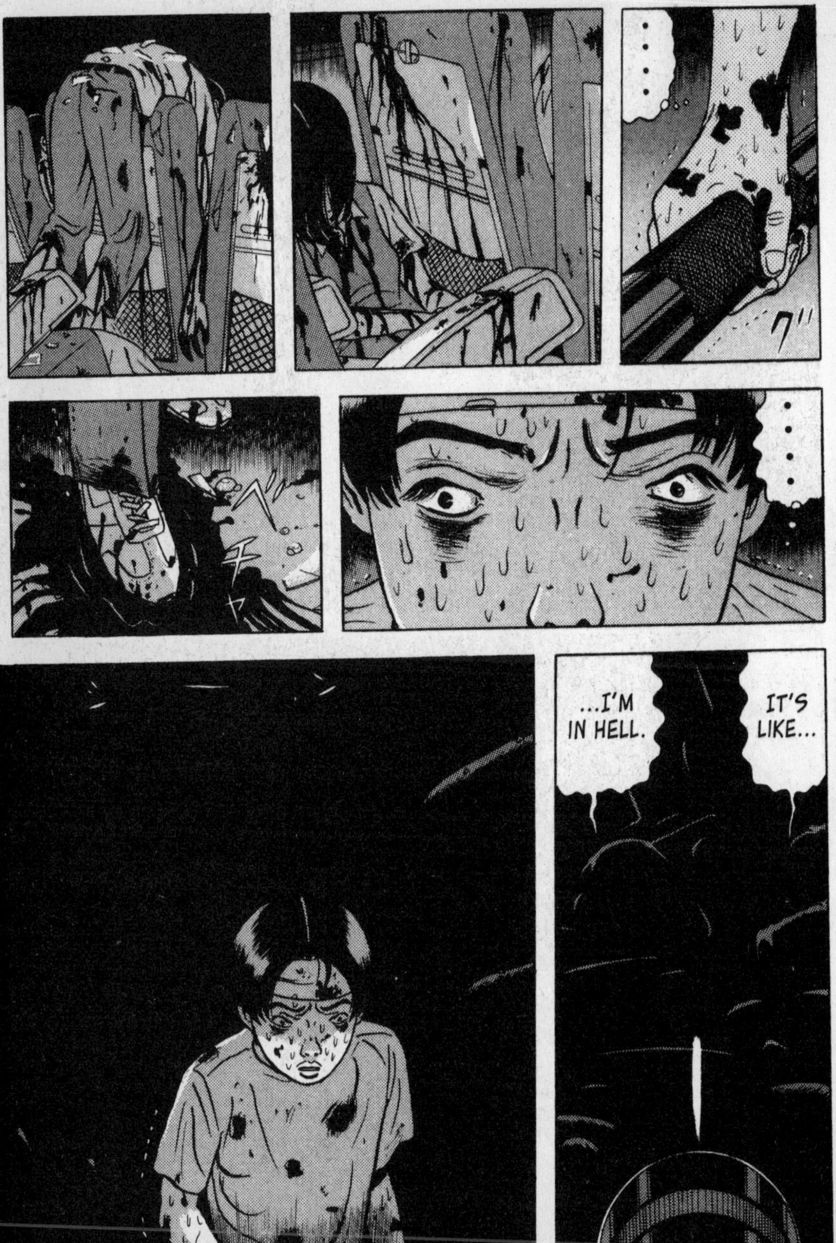
IT'S LIKE...
...I'M IN HELL.

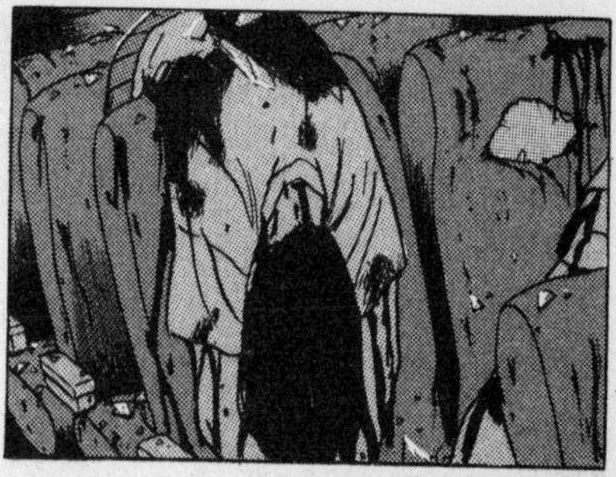
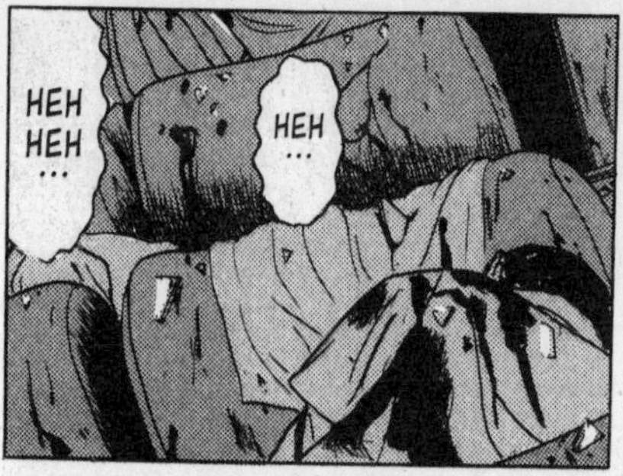
HEH ...
HEH HEH ...
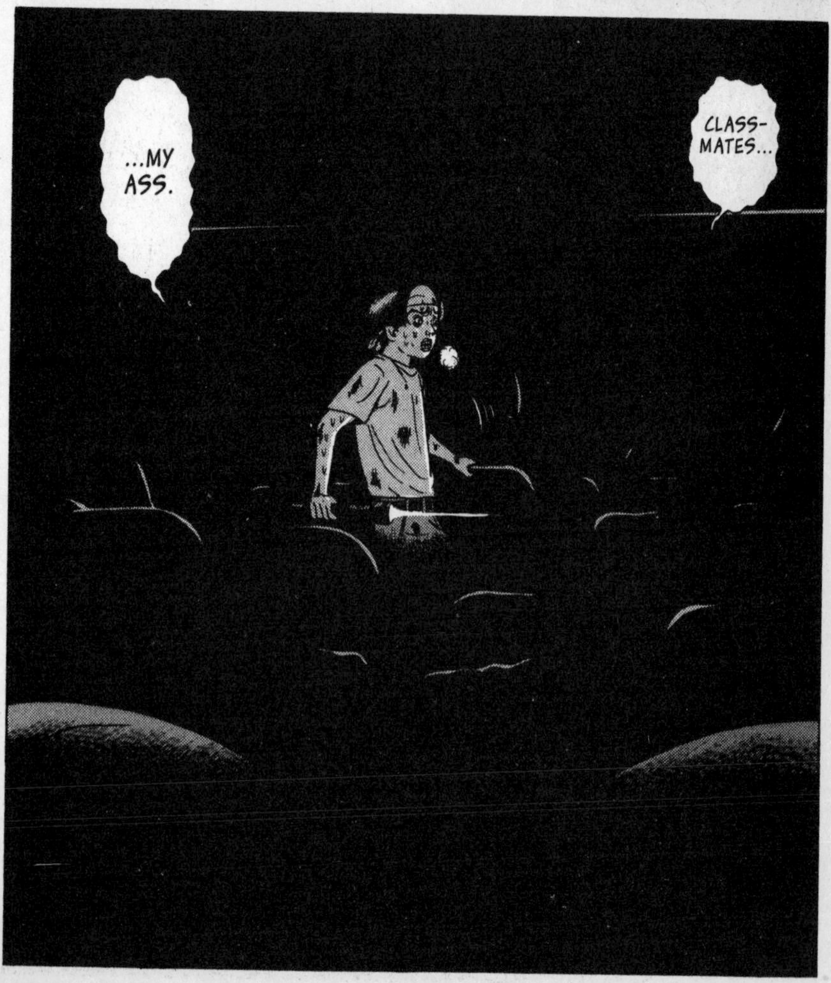
CLASS-MATES...
...MY ASS.

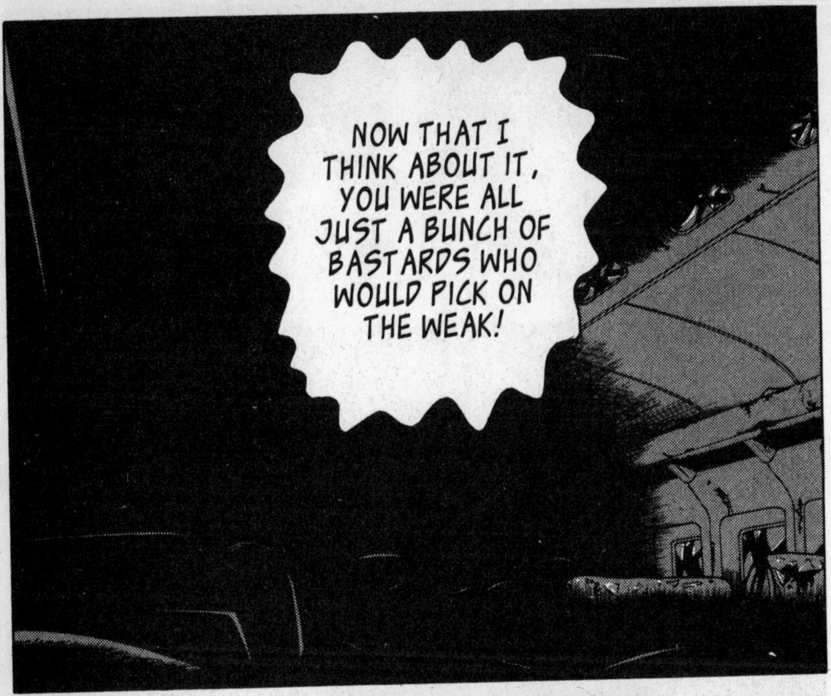
NOW THAT I THINK ABOUT IT, YOU WERE ALL JUST A BUNCH OF BASTARDS WHO WOULD PICK ON THE WEAK!

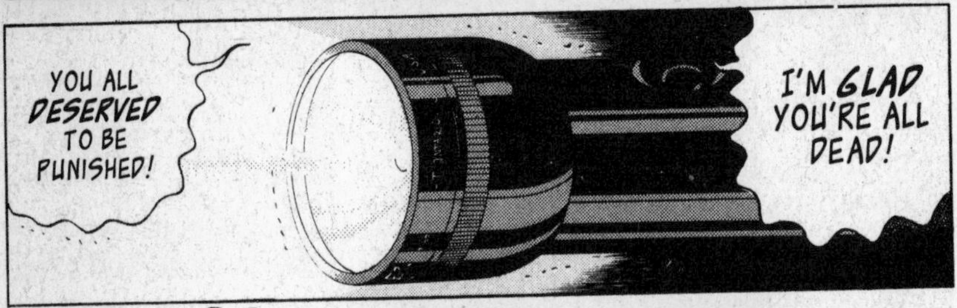
I'M *GLAD* YOU'RE ALL DEAD!
YOU ALL *DESERVED* TO BE PUNISHED!

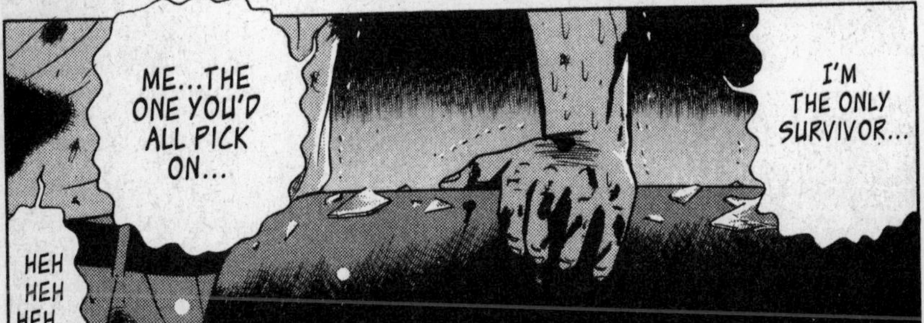
I'M THE ONLY SURVIVOR...
ME...THE ONE YOU'D ALL PICK ON...
HEH HEH HEH...

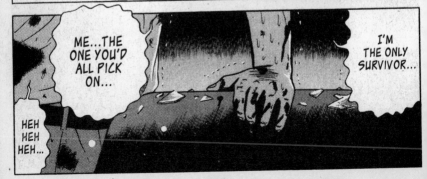

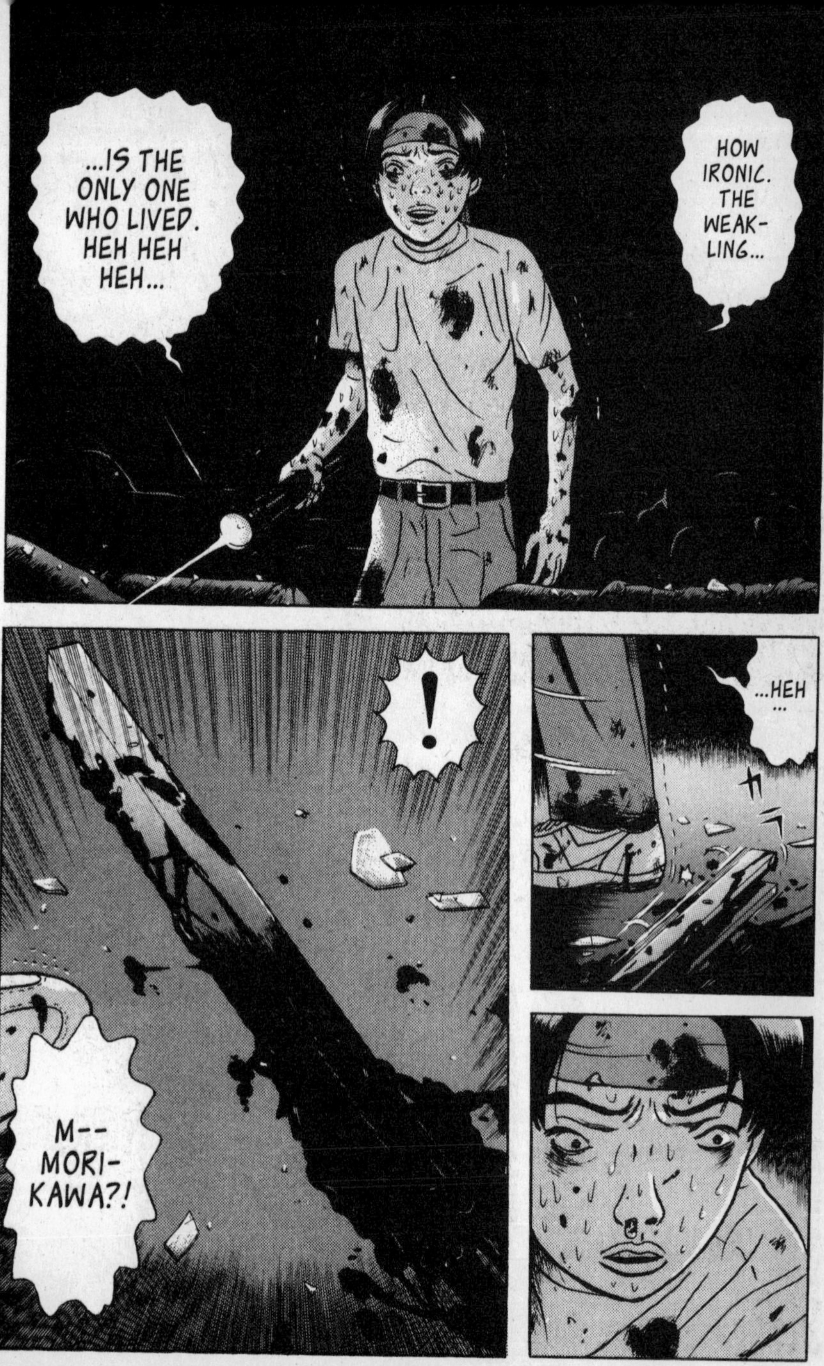
HOW IRONIC. THE WEAK-LING...
...IS THE ONLY ONE WHO LIVED. HEH HEH HEH...
...HEH ...
!
M-- MORI-KAWA?!

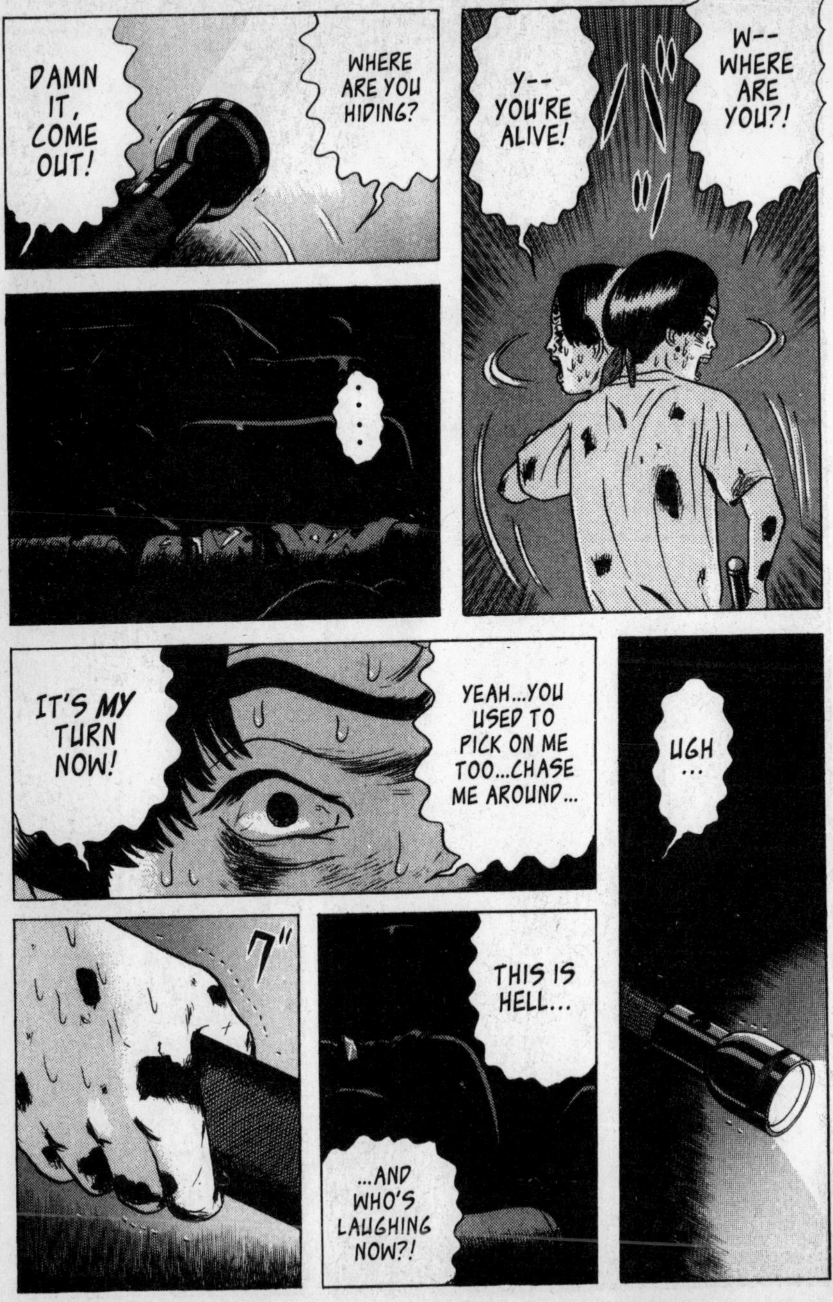
W--WHERE ARE YOU?!
Y--YOU'RE ALIVE!
WHERE ARE YOU HIDING?
DAMN IT, COME OUT!
....
UGH...
YEAH...YOU USED TO PICK ON ME TOO...CHASE ME AROUND...
IT'S MY TURN NOW!
THIS IS HELL...
...AND WHO'S LAUGHING NOW?!

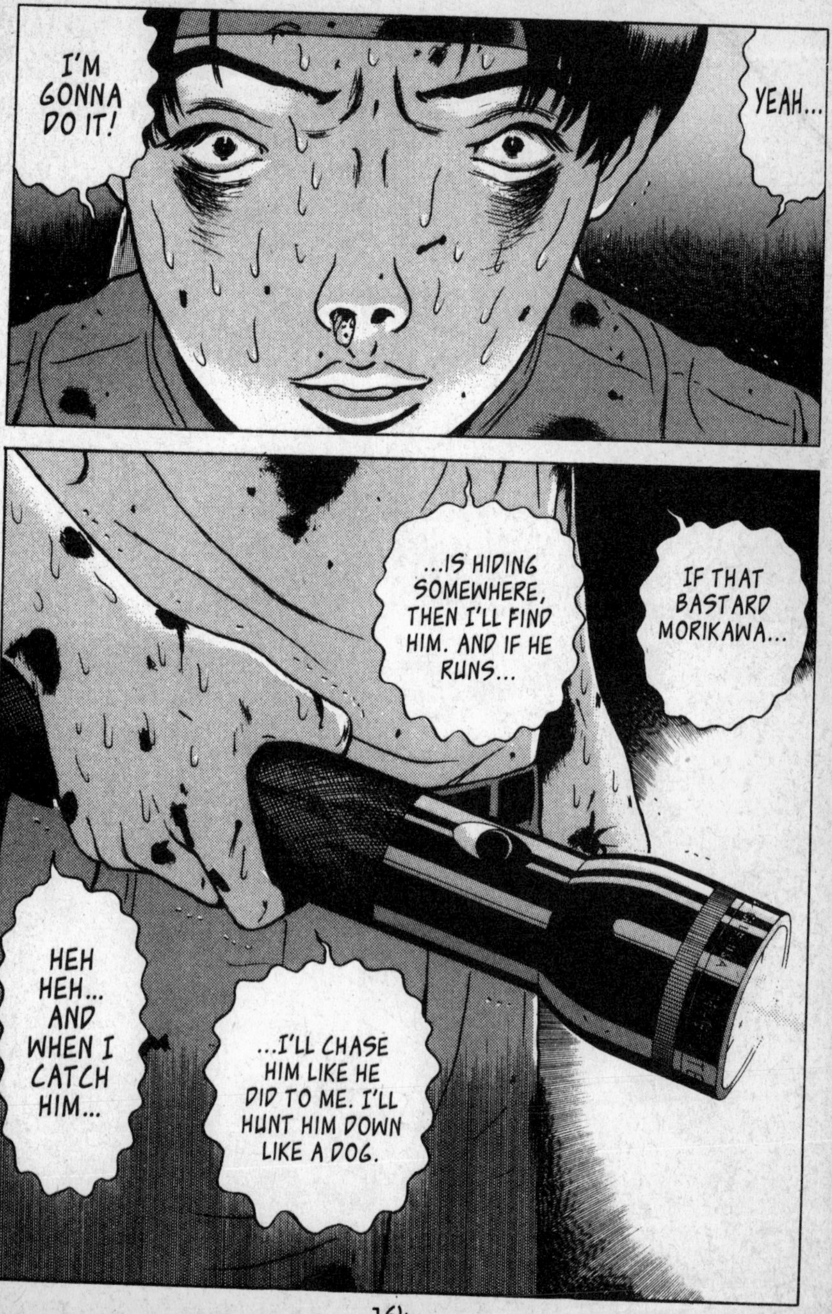
YEAH...
I'M GONNA DO IT!
IF THAT BASTARD MORIKAWA...
...IS HIDING SOMEWHERE, THEN I'LL FIND HIM. AND IF HE RUNS...
...I'LL CHASE HIM LIKE HE DID TO ME. I'LL HUNT HIM DOWN LIKE A DOG.
HEH HEH... AND WHEN I CATCH HIM...

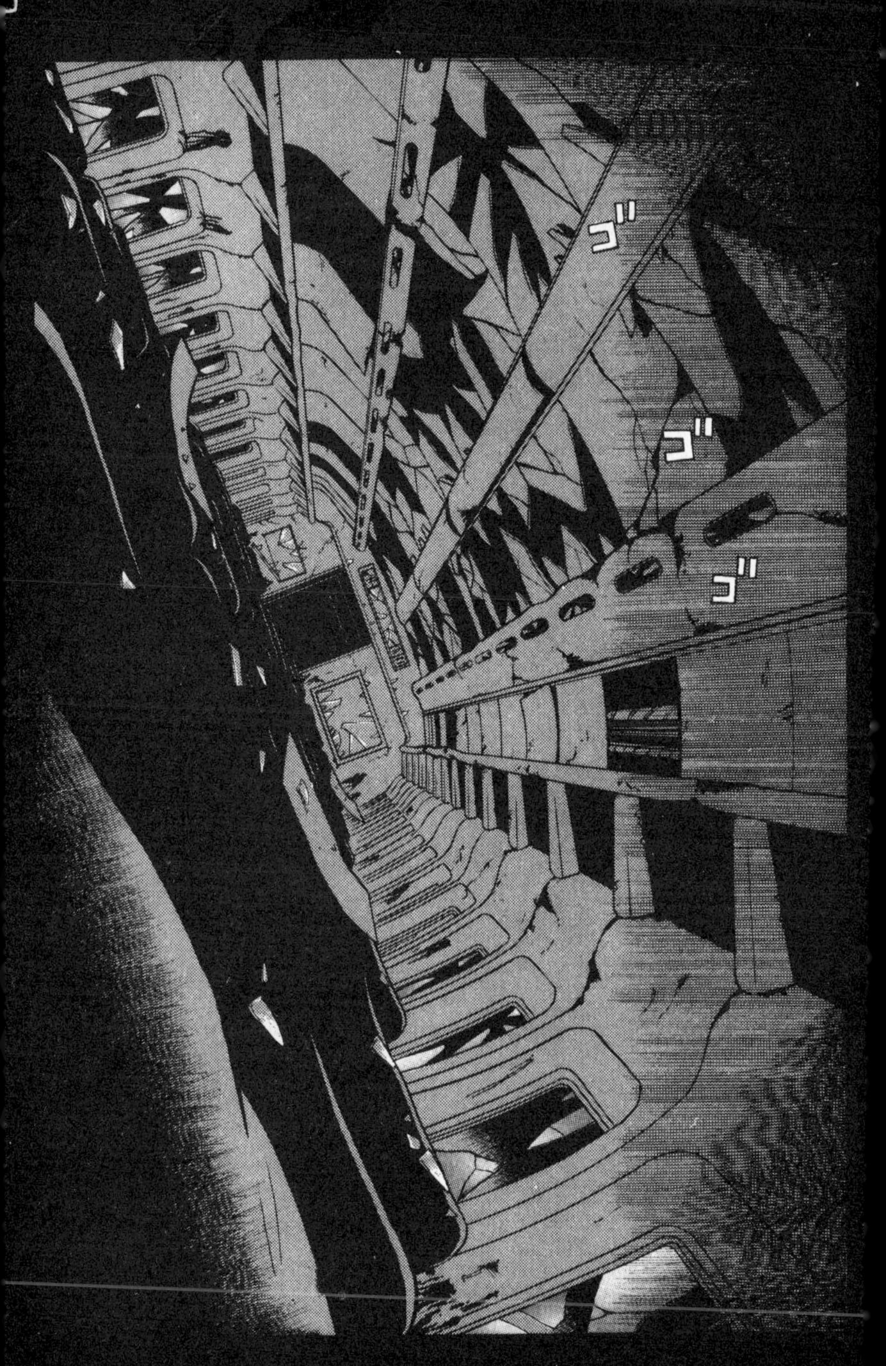
ゴ
ゴ
ゴ

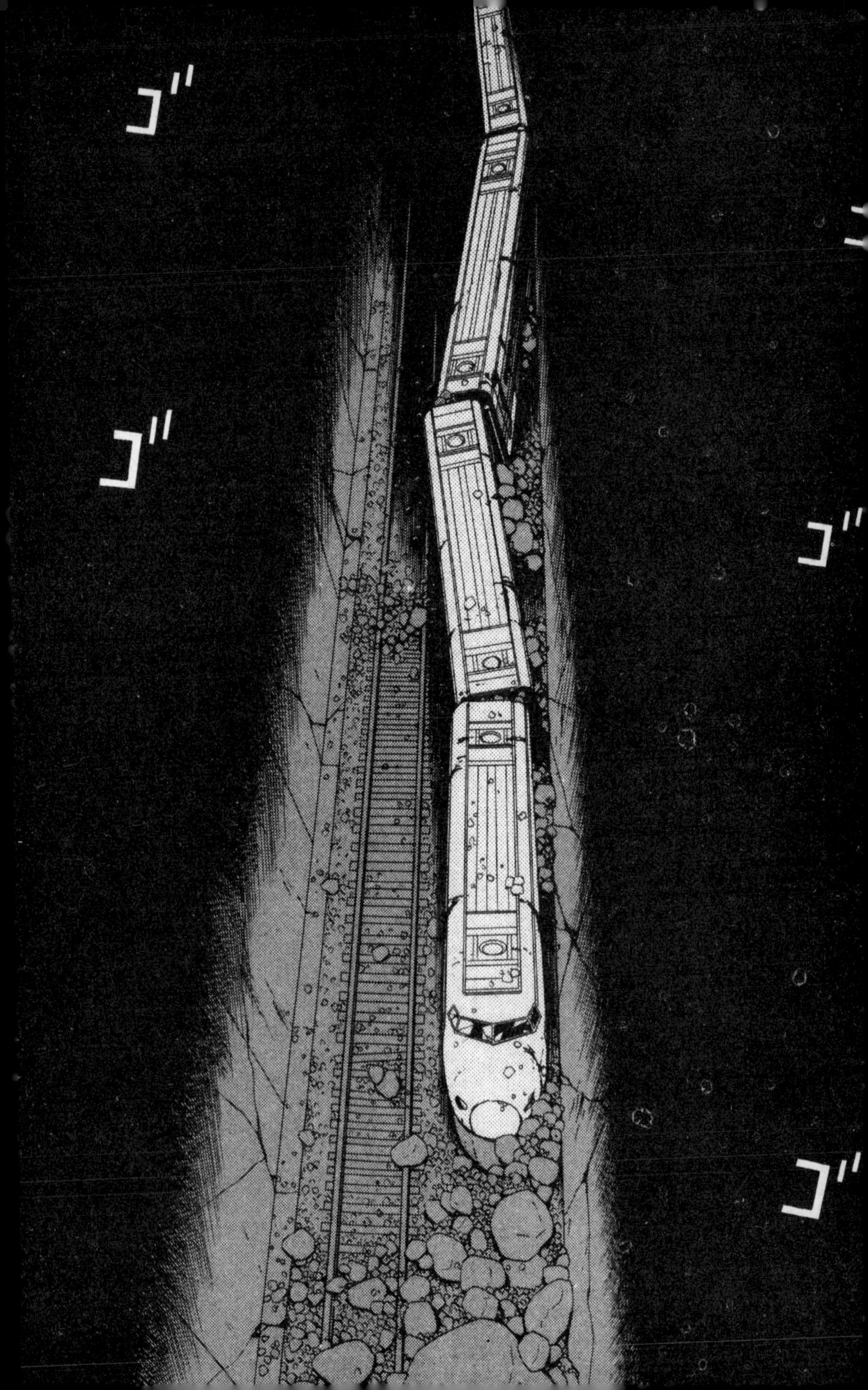
ゴ
ゴ
ゴ
ゴ

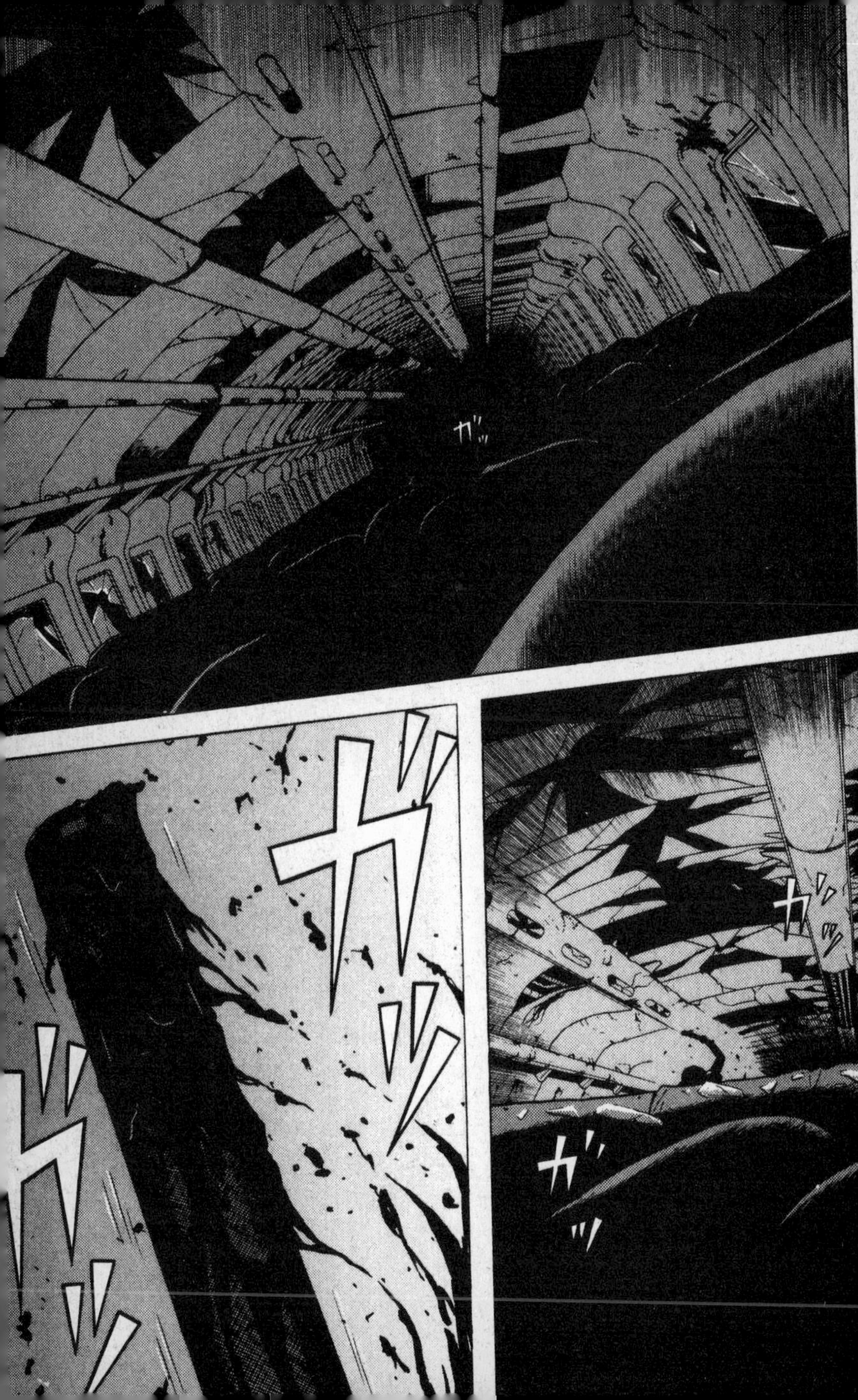
ガッ
ガッ
ガッ
ガッ
ガッ
ガッ

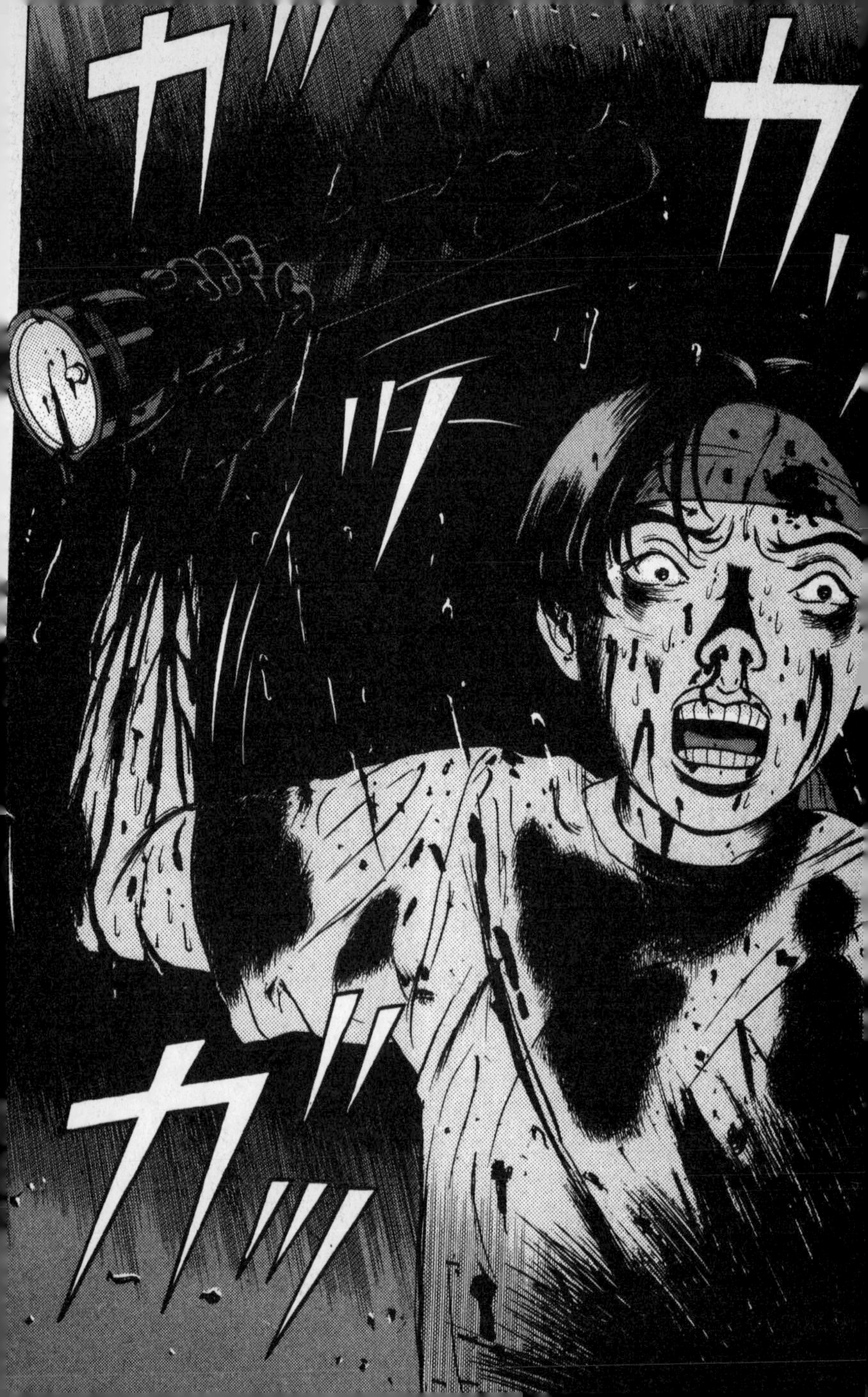
カッ
カッ
ッ
カッッ

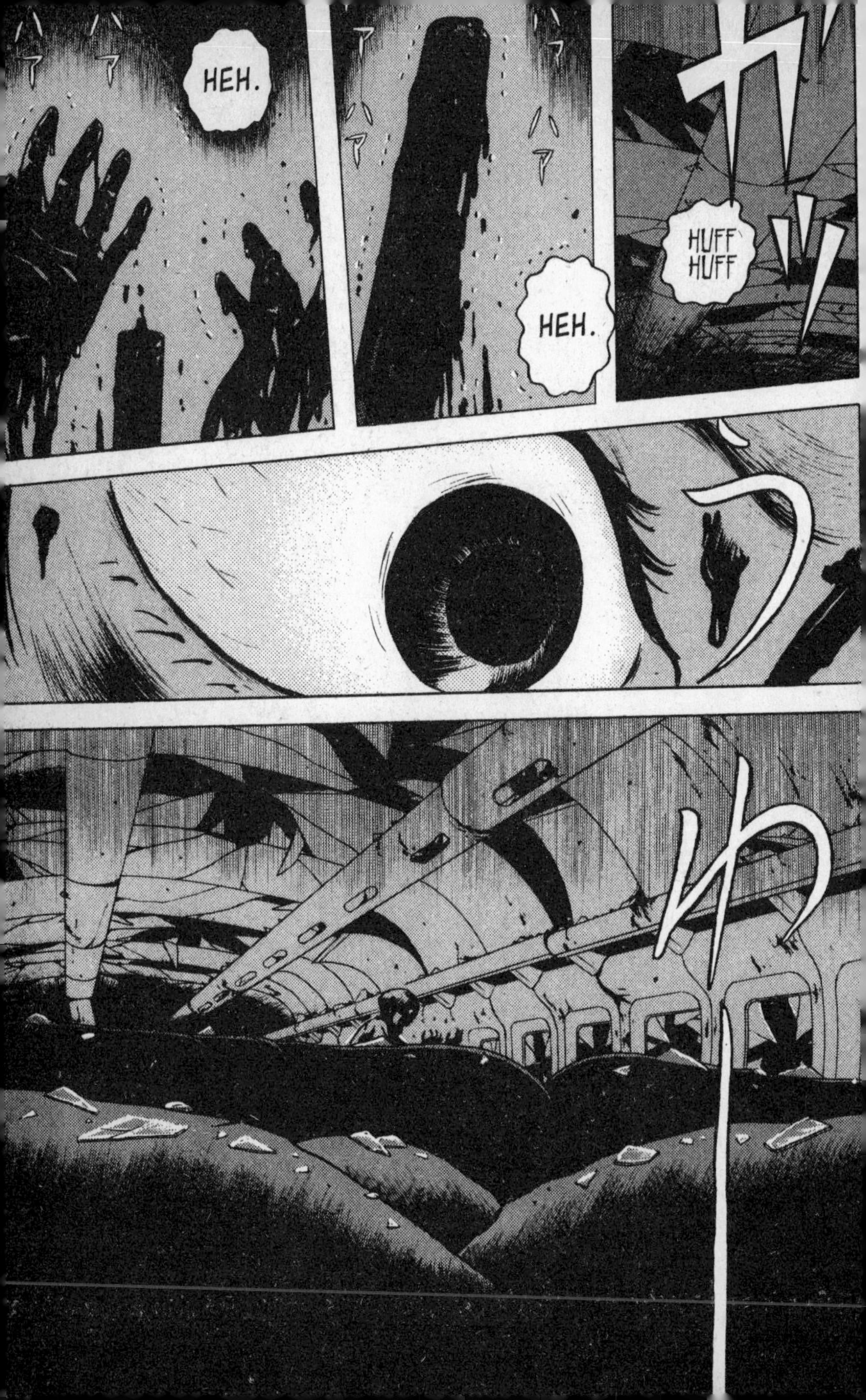
HUFF HUFF
HEH.
HEH.

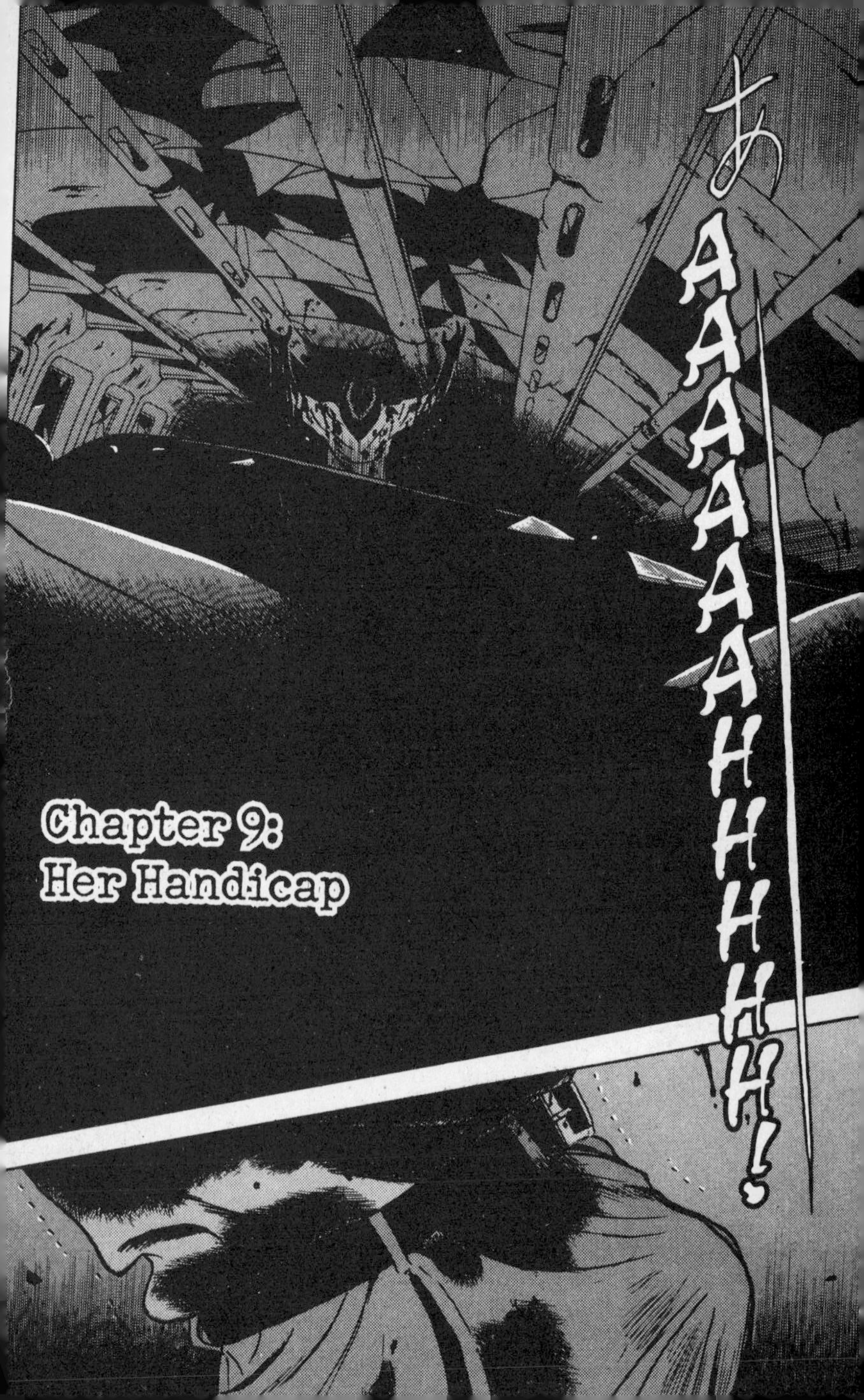
あAAAAAAAHHHHHHH!
Chapter 9:
Her Handicap

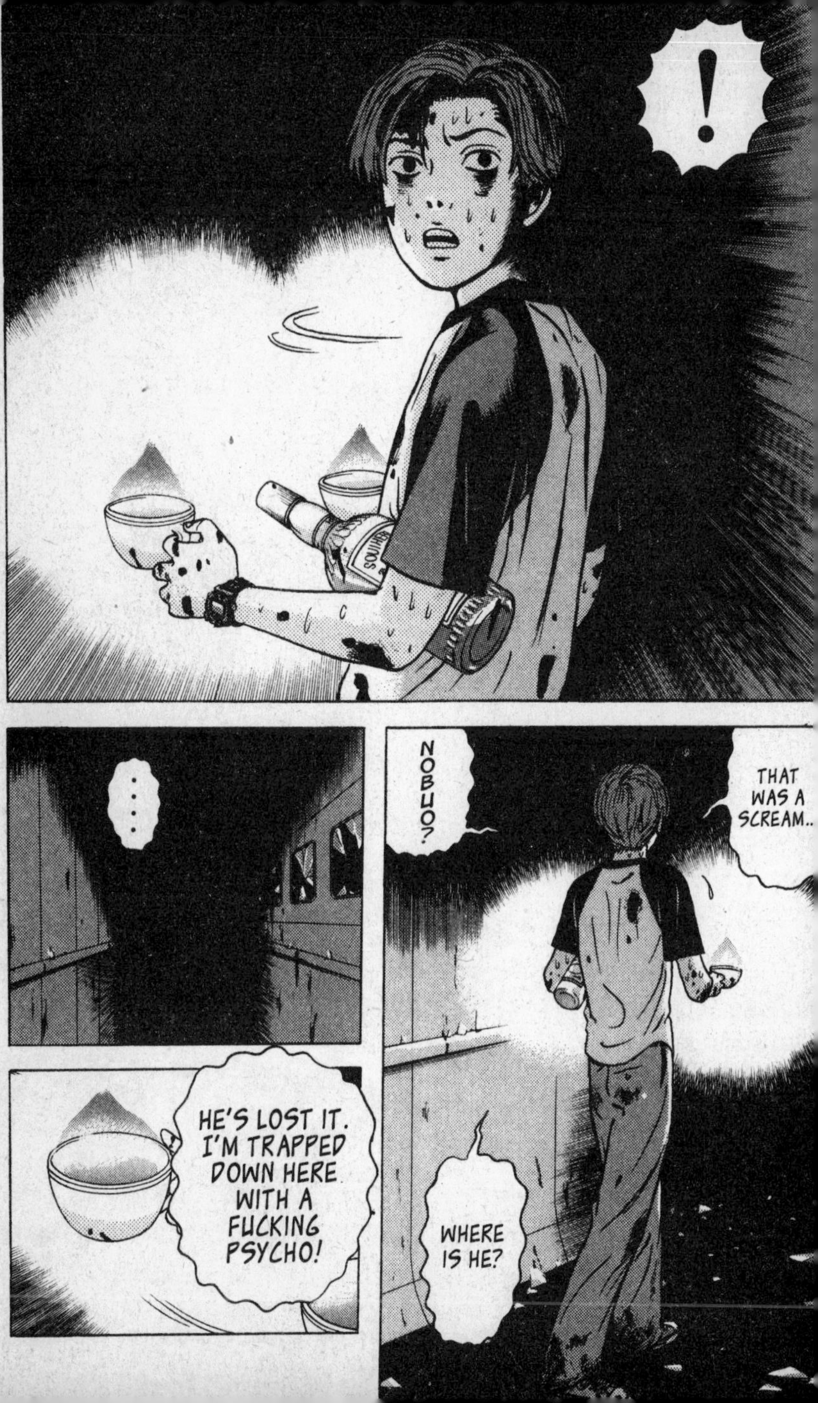
!
THAT WAS A SCREAM..
NOBUO?
WHERE IS HE?
....
HE'S LOST IT. I'M TRAPPED DOWN HERE WITH A FUCKING PSYCHO!

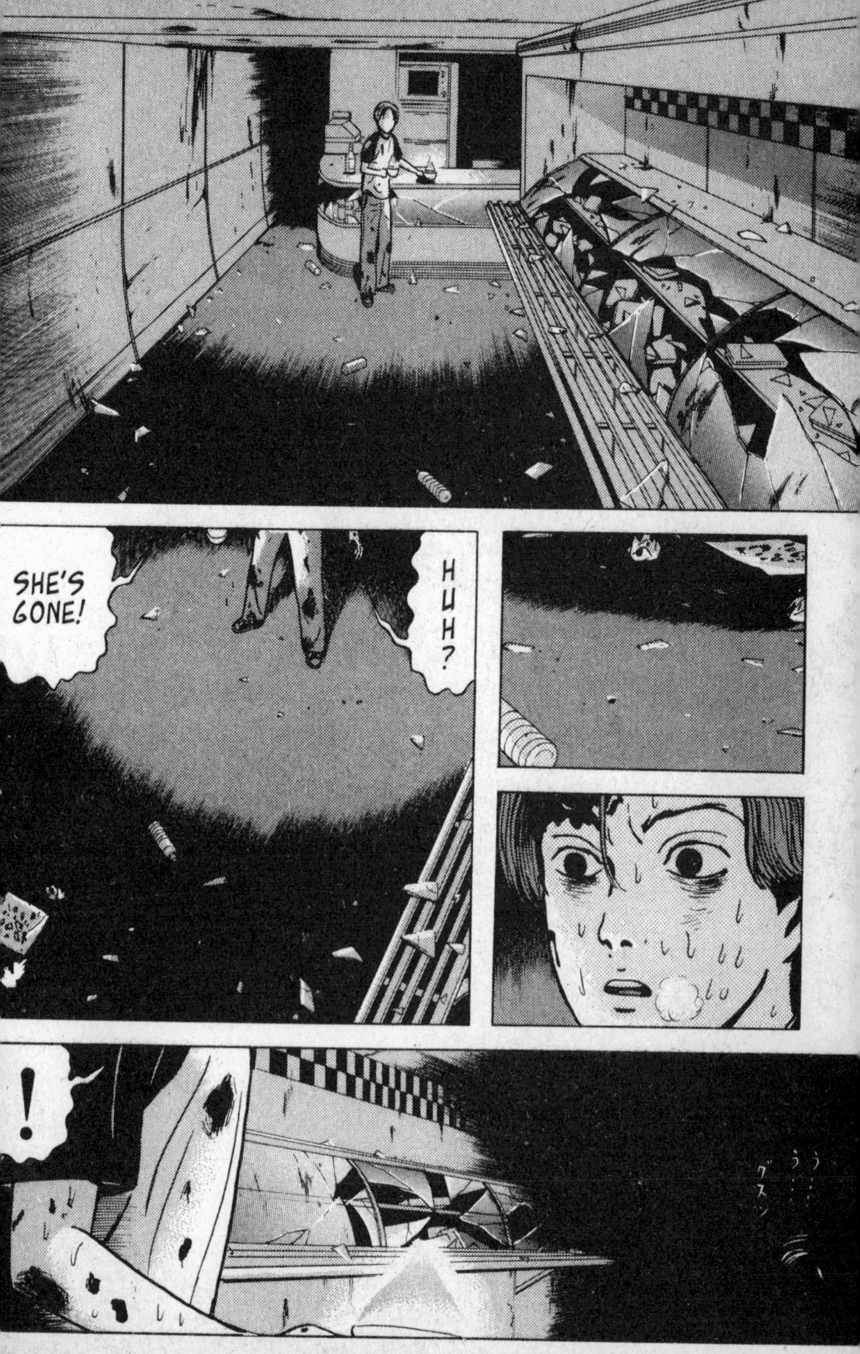
HUH?
SHE'S GONE!
うう…
グスン
!

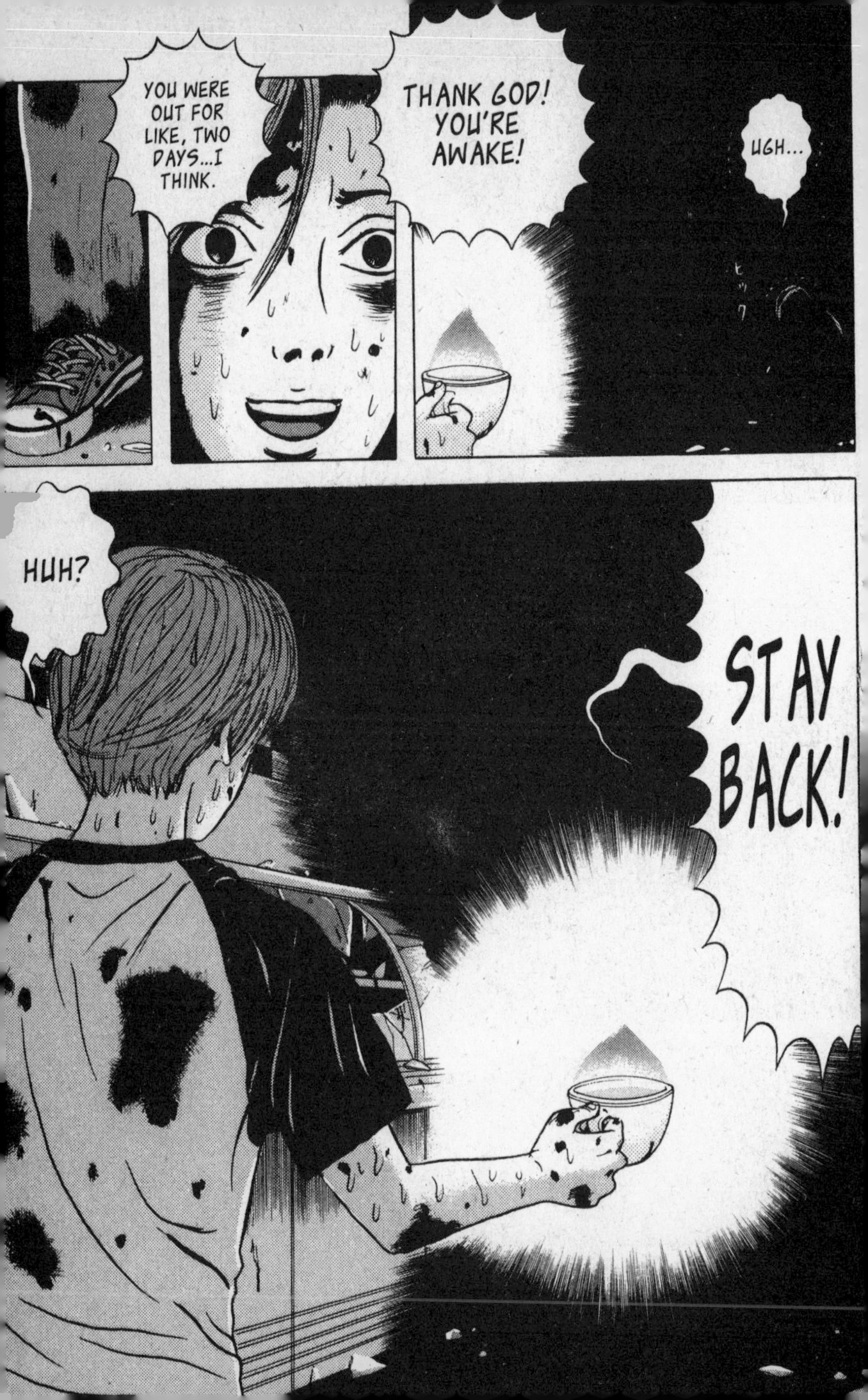
UGH...
ヒック
THANK GOD! YOU'RE AWAKE!
YOU WERE OUT FOR LIKE, TWO DAYS...I THINK.
STAY BACK!
HUH?

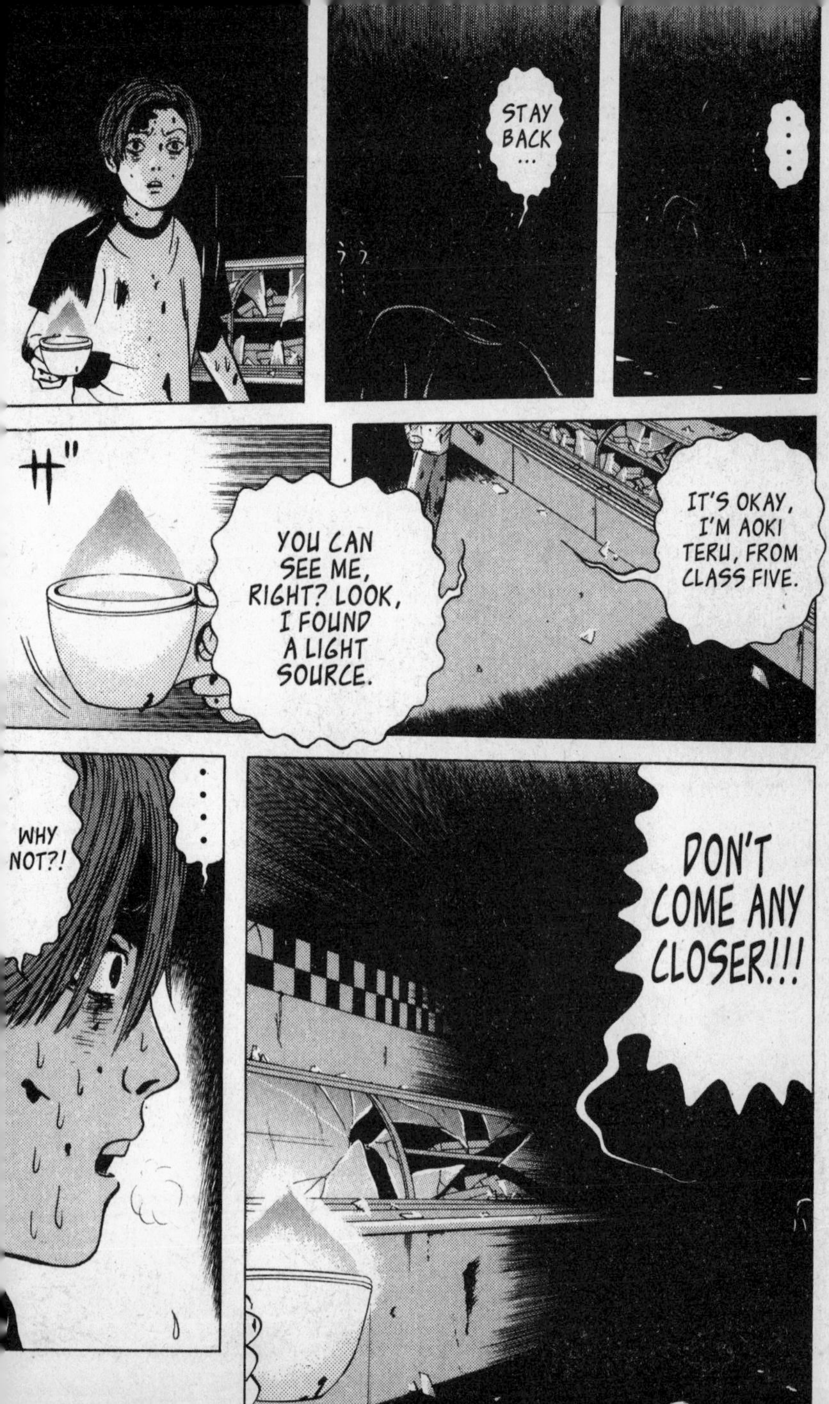
. . . .
STAY BACK ...
IT'S OKAY, I'M AOKI TERU, FROM CLASS FIVE.
YOU CAN SEE ME, RIGHT? LOOK, I FOUND A LIGHT SOURCE.
DON'T COME ANY CLOSER!!!
. . . .
WHY NOT?!

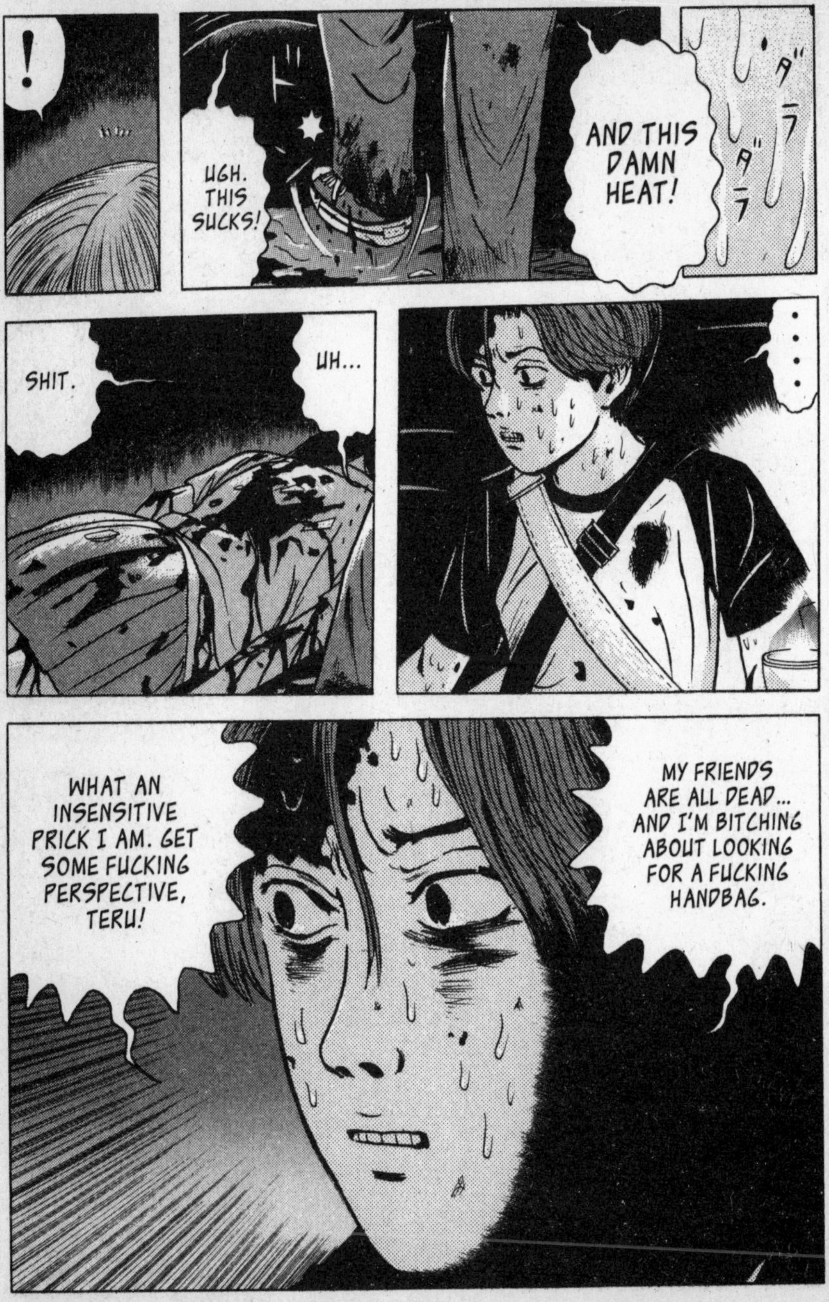
ダラダラ
AND THIS DAMN HEAT!
UGH. THIS SUCKS!
!
....
UH...
SHIT.
MY FRIENDS ARE ALL DEAD... AND I'M BITCHING ABOUT LOOKING FOR A FUCKING HANDBAG.
WHAT AN INSENSITIVE PRICK I AM. GET SOME FUCKING PERSPECTIVE, TERU!

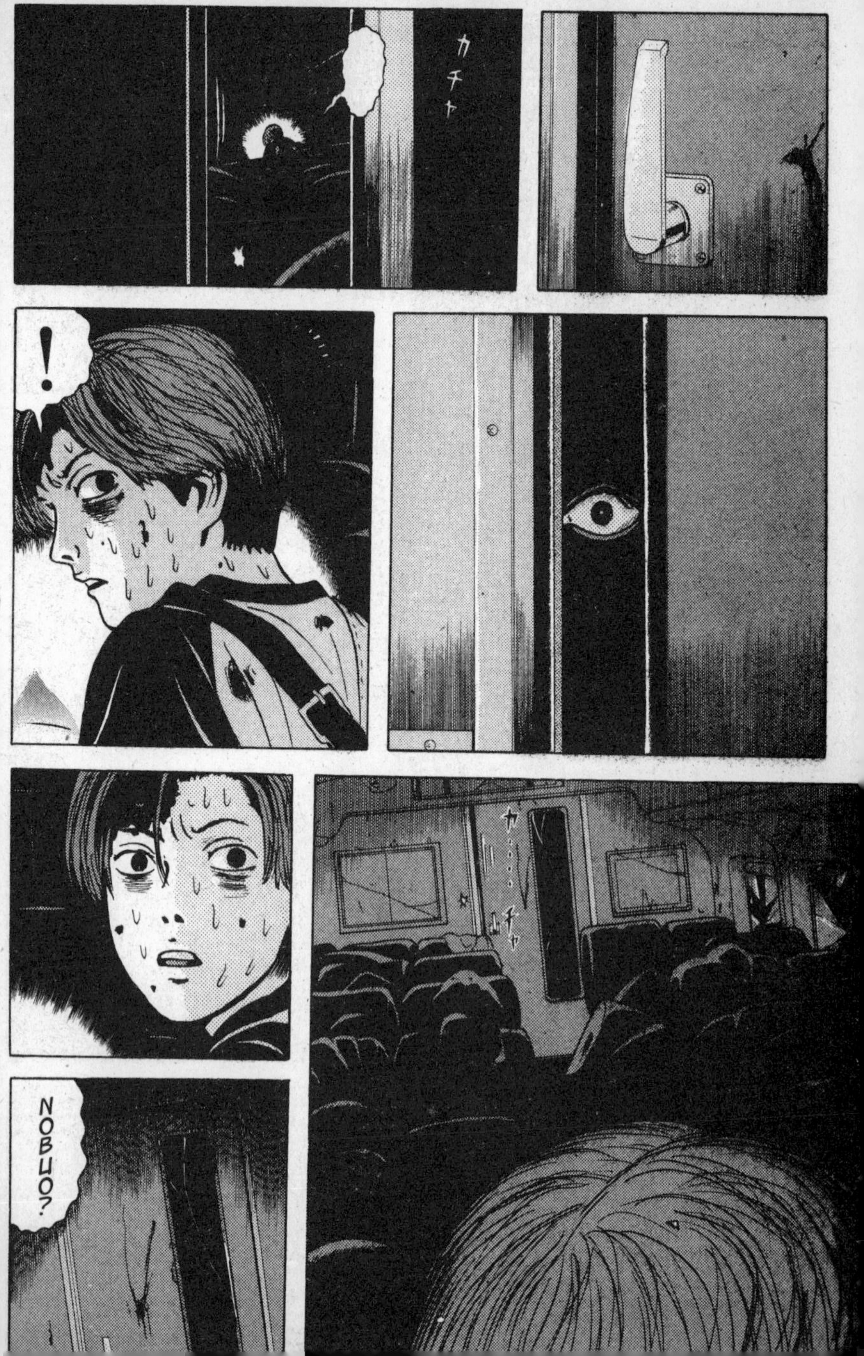
カチャ
!
カ・・・チャ
NOBUO?

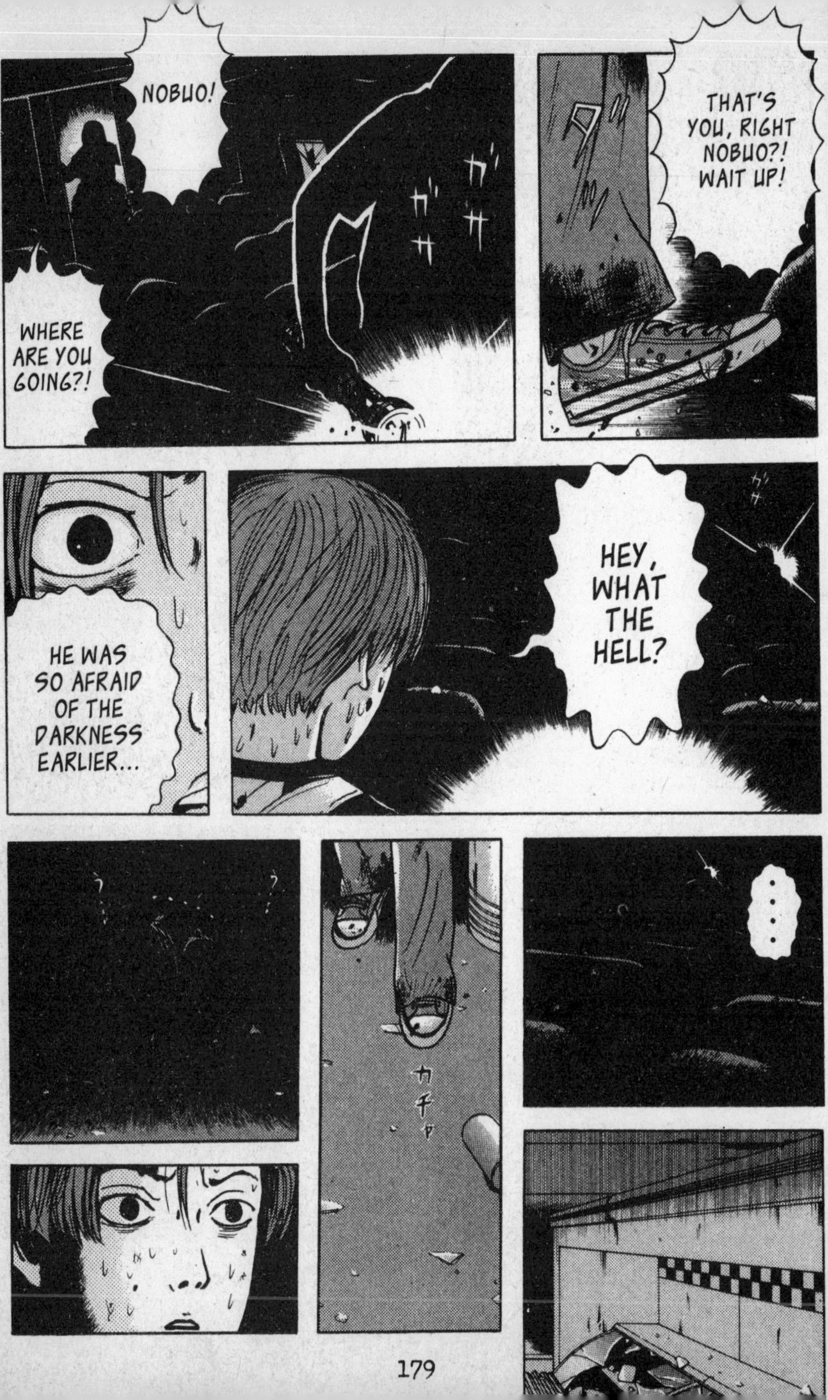
THAT'S YOU, RIGHT NOBUO?! WAIT UP!
NOBUO!
WHERE ARE YOU GOING?!
HEY, WHAT THE HELL?
HE WAS SO AFRAID OF THE DARKNESS EARLIER...
....

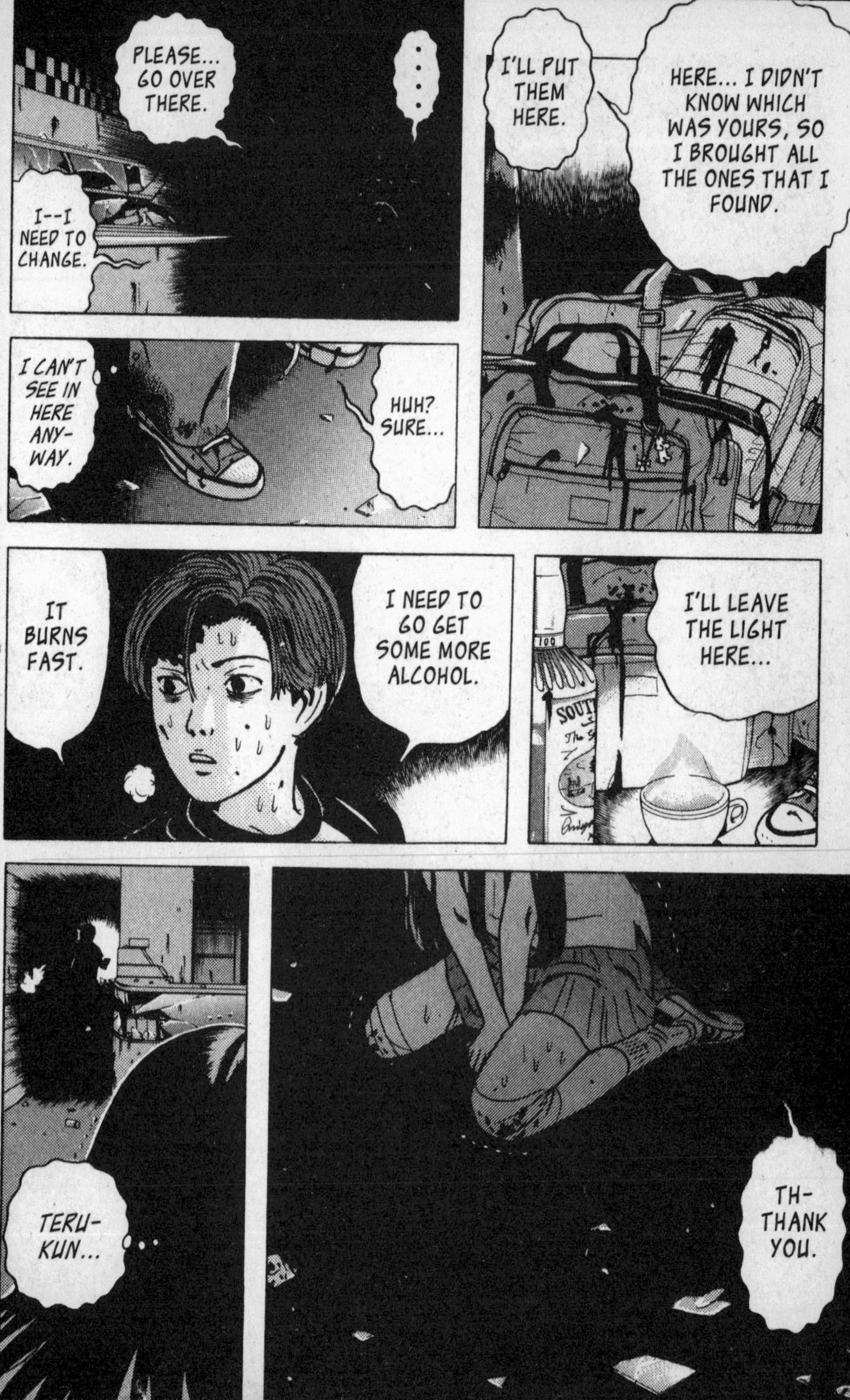
HERE... I DIDN'T KNOW WHICH WAS YOURS, SO I BROUGHT ALL THE ONES THAT I FOUND.
I'LL PUT THEM HERE.
...
PLEASE... GO OVER THERE.
I--I NEED TO CHANGE.
HUH? SURE...
I CAN'T SEE IN HERE ANY-WAY.
I'LL LEAVE THE LIGHT HERE...
I NEED TO GO GET SOME MORE ALCOHOL.
IT BURNS FAST.
TH-THANK YOU.
TERU-KUN...

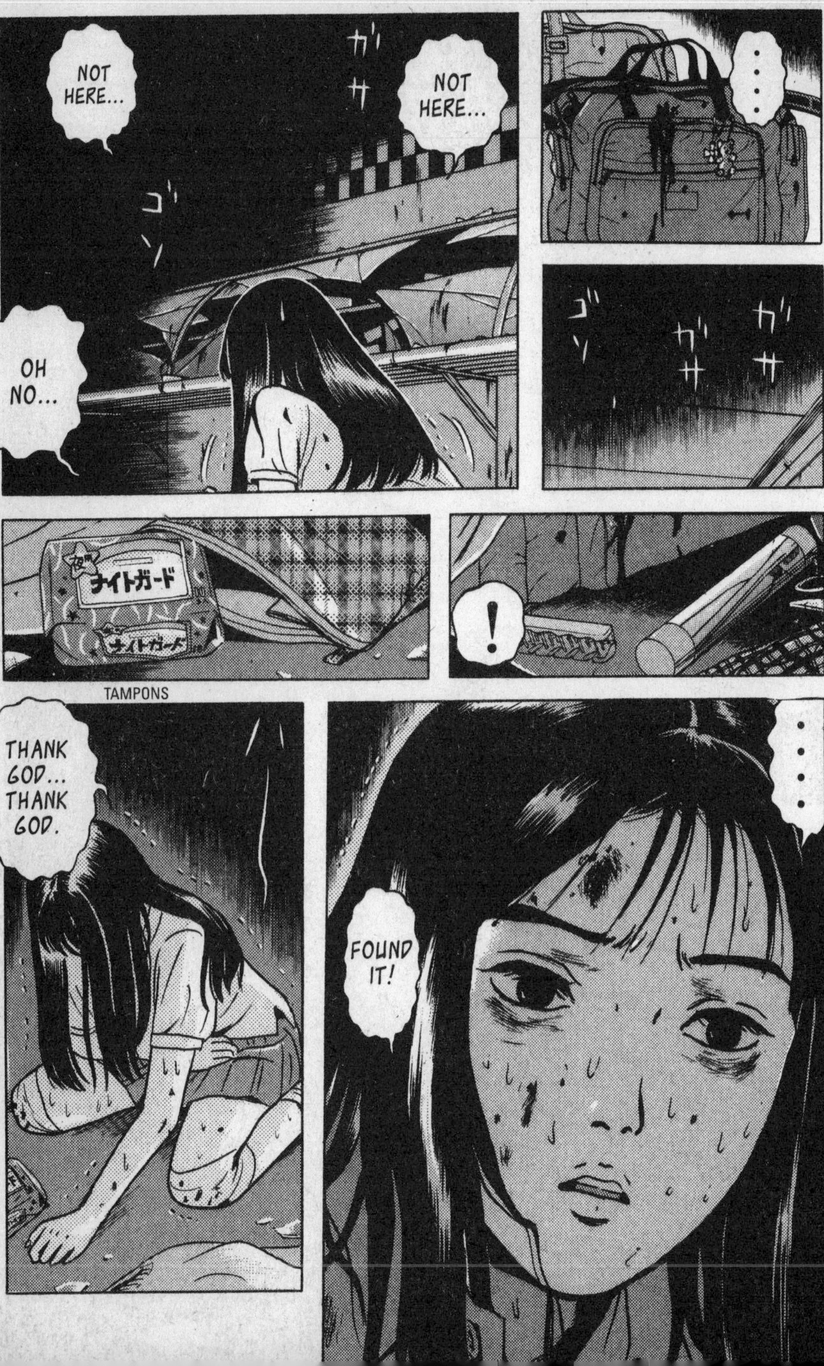
....
ゴソ
ガサ
ガサ
ガサ
NOT HERE...
NOT HERE...
ゴソ
OH NO...
!
夜用
ナイトガード
ナイトガード
TAMPONS
....
FOUND IT!
THANK GOD... THANK GOD.

I...
I NEED TO CHANGE ...
UNGH...
....
ポタ
ポタ

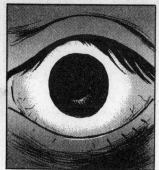

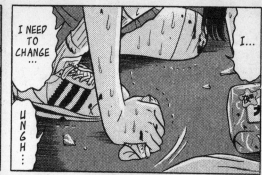

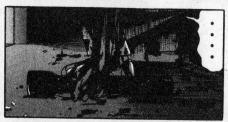

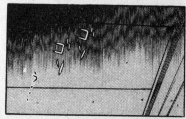

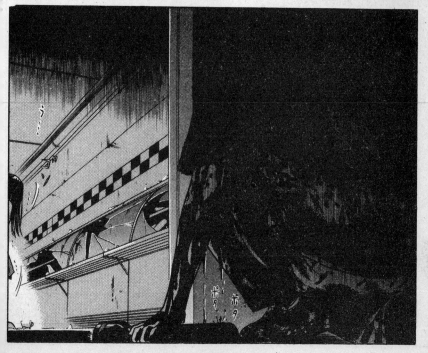

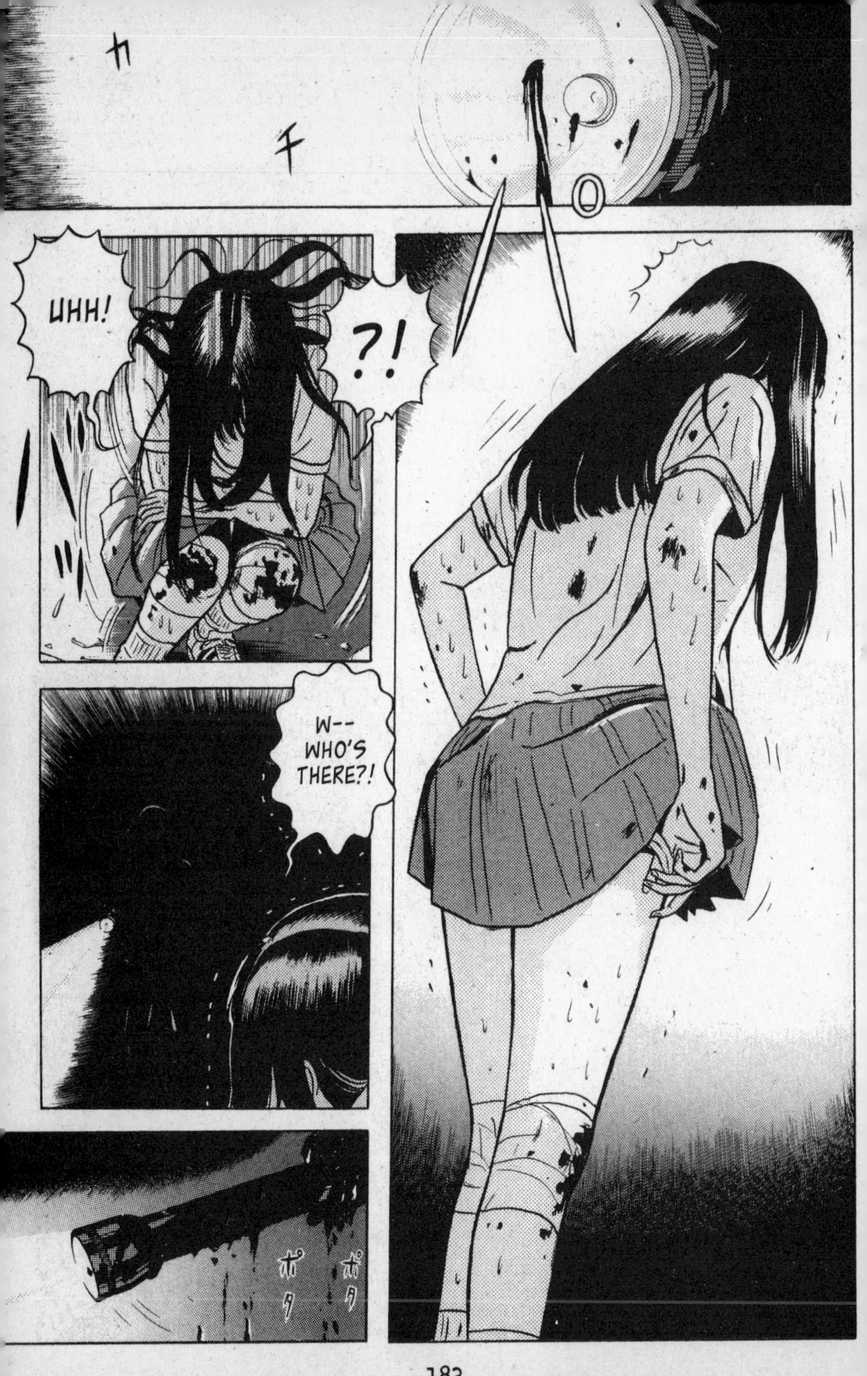
カ
チ
?!
UHH!
W-- WHO'S THERE?!
ポタ
ポタ

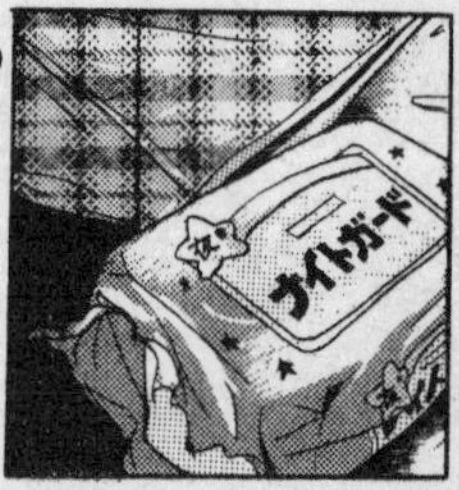
ナイトガード
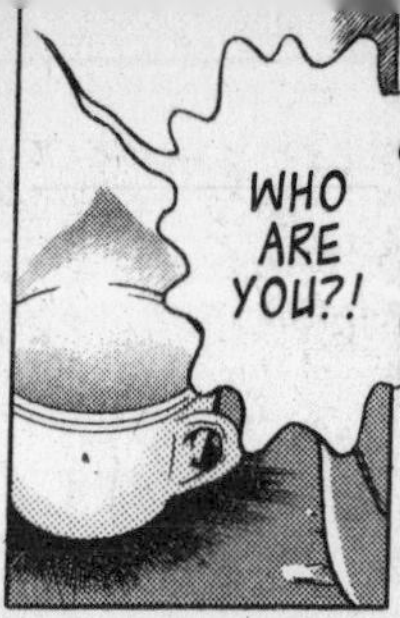
WHO ARE YOU?!
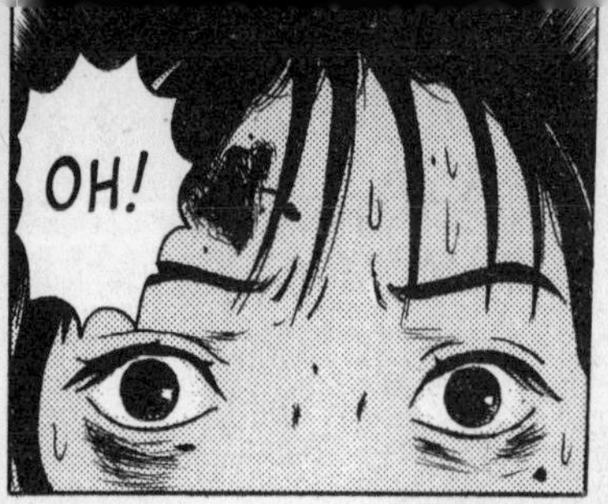
OH!
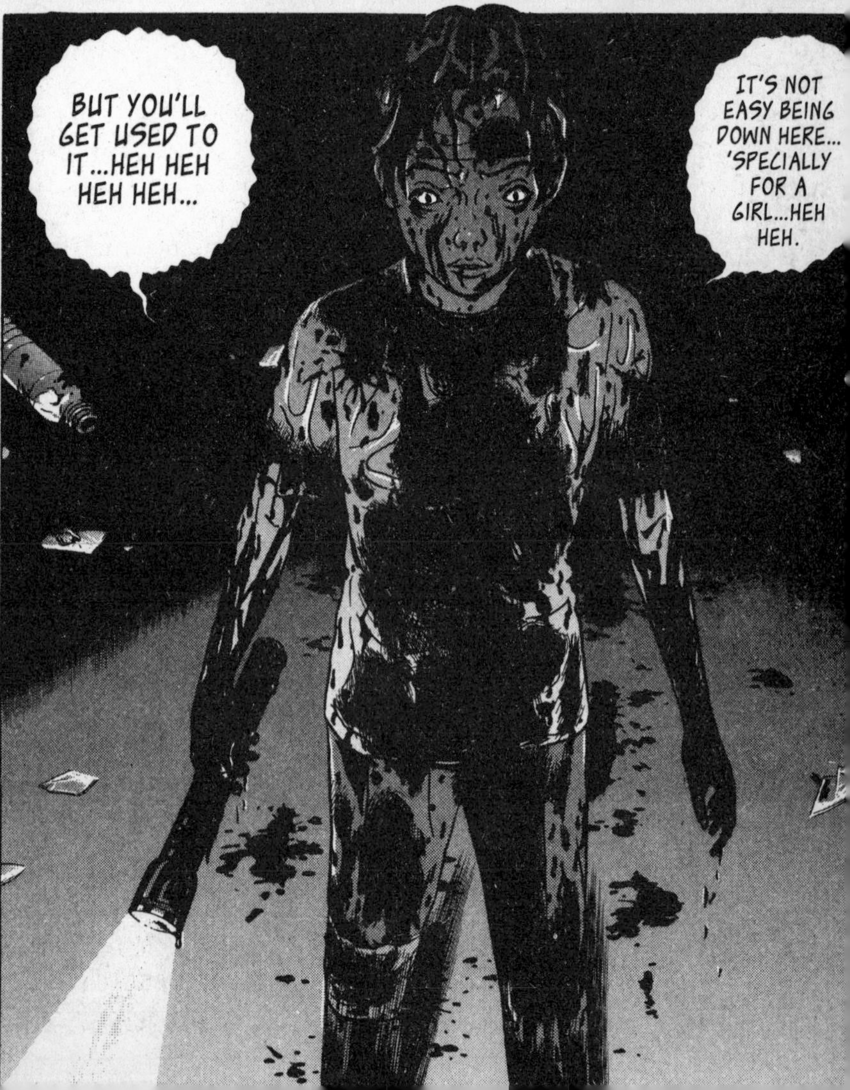
IT'S NOT EASY BEING DOWN HERE... 'SPECIALLY FOR A GIRL...HEH HEH.
BUT YOU'LL GET USED TO IT...HEH HEH HEH HEH...

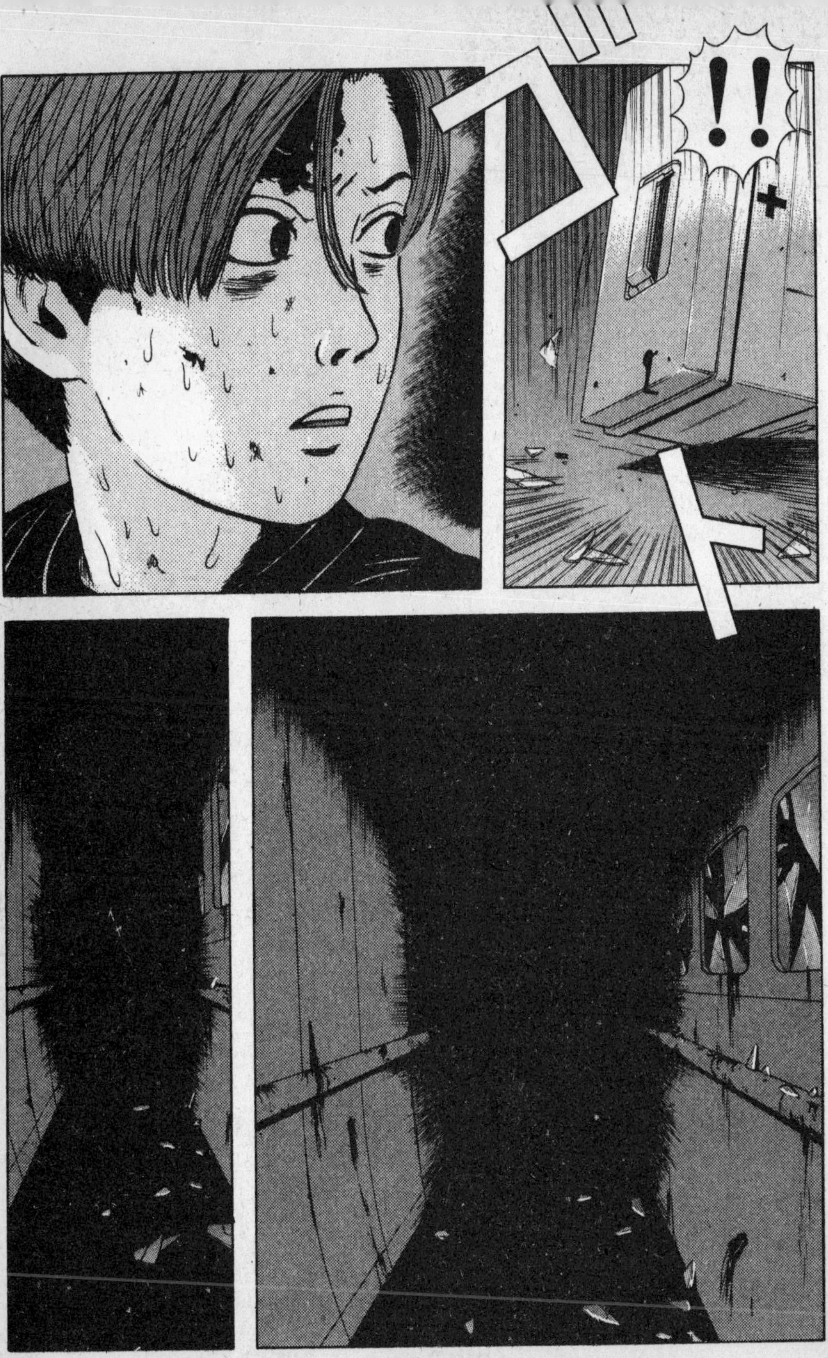
!!
ゴト

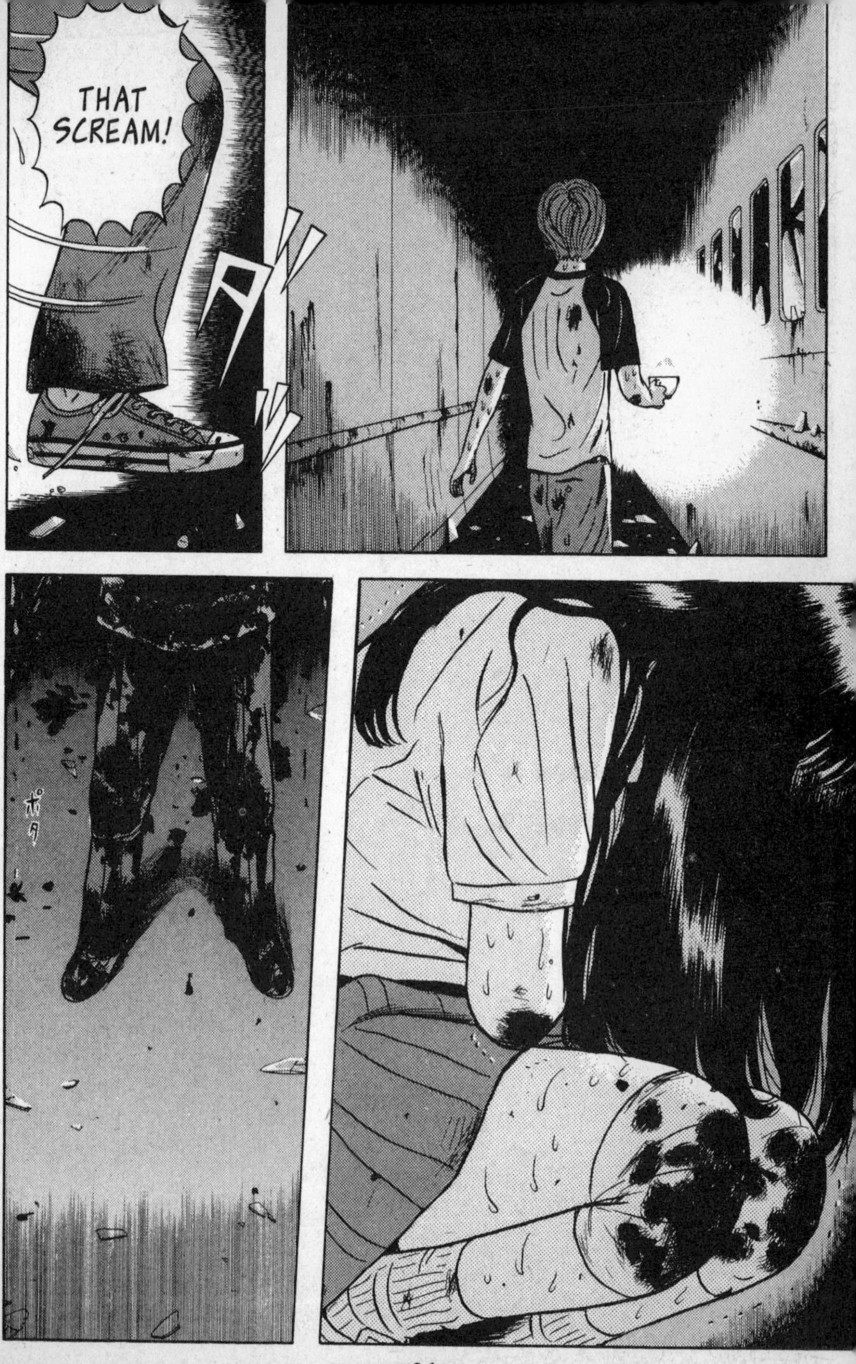
THAT SCREAM!
ポタ

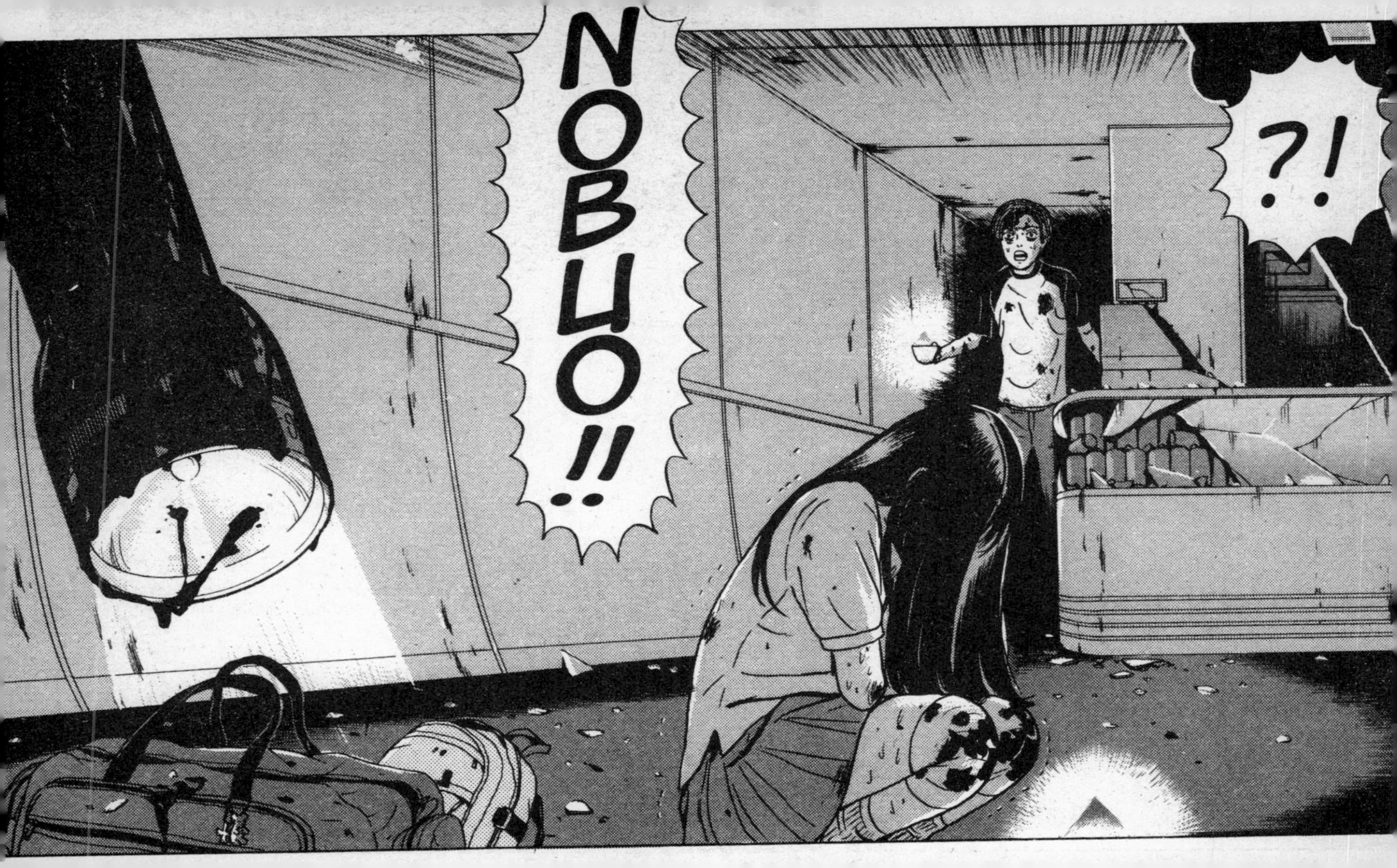
?!
NOBUO!!

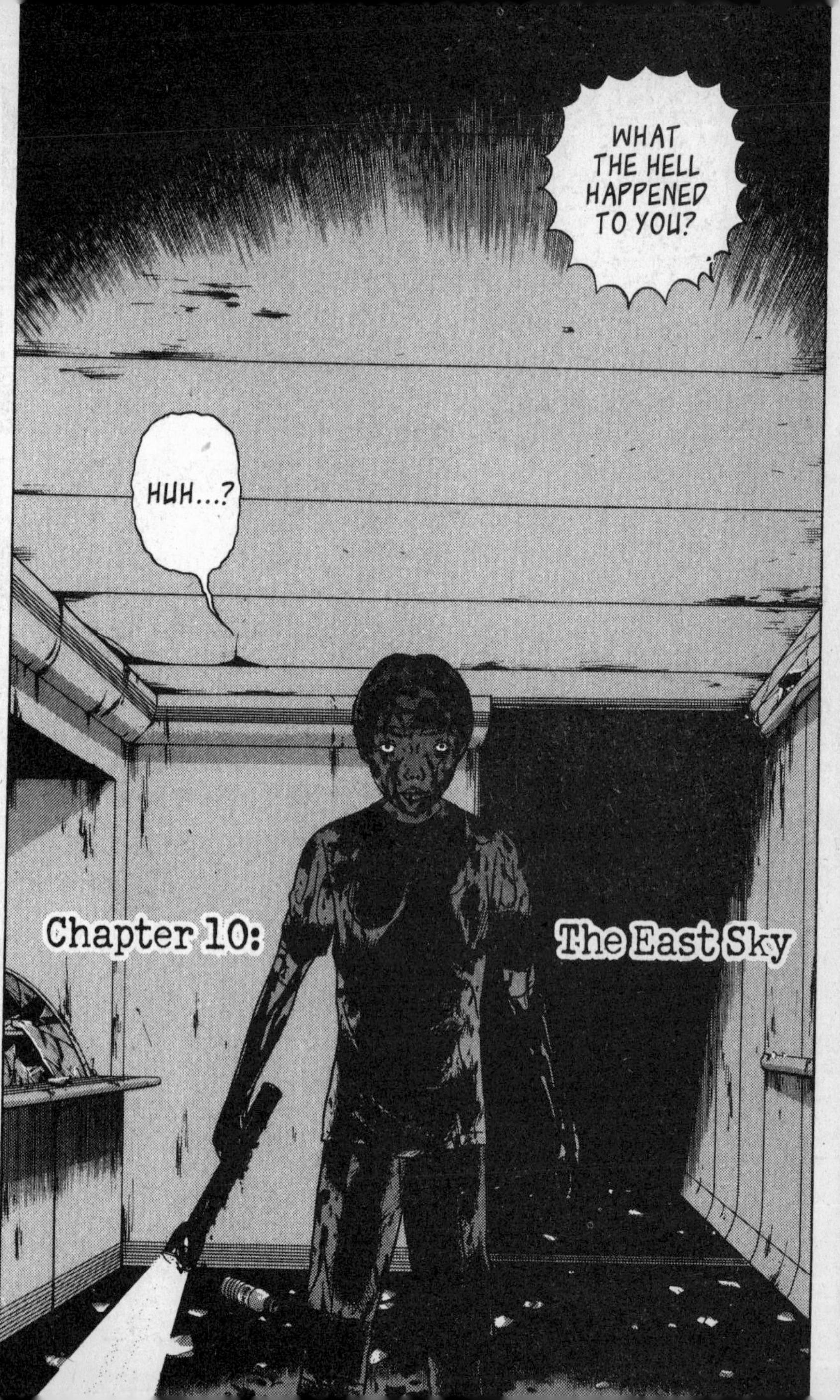
WHAT THE HELL HAPPENED TO YOU?
HUH...?
Chapter 10: The East Sky

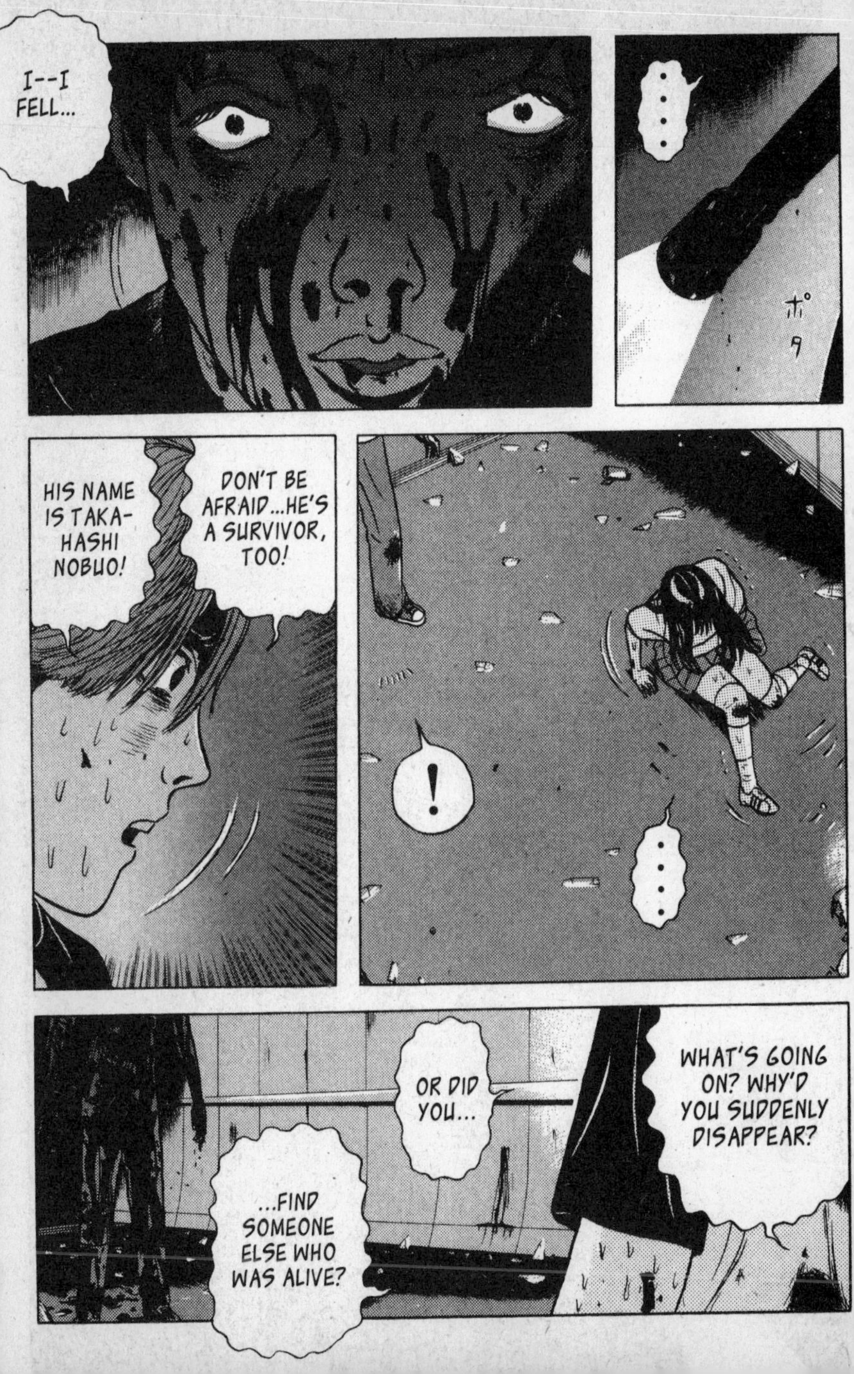
....
ポタ
I--I FELL...
!
....
DON'T BE AFRAID...HE'S A SURVIVOR, TOO!
HIS NAME IS TAKA-HASHI NOBUO!
WHAT'S GOING ON? WHY'D YOU SUDDENLY DISAPPEAR?
OR DID YOU...
...FIND SOMEONE ELSE WHO WAS ALIVE?

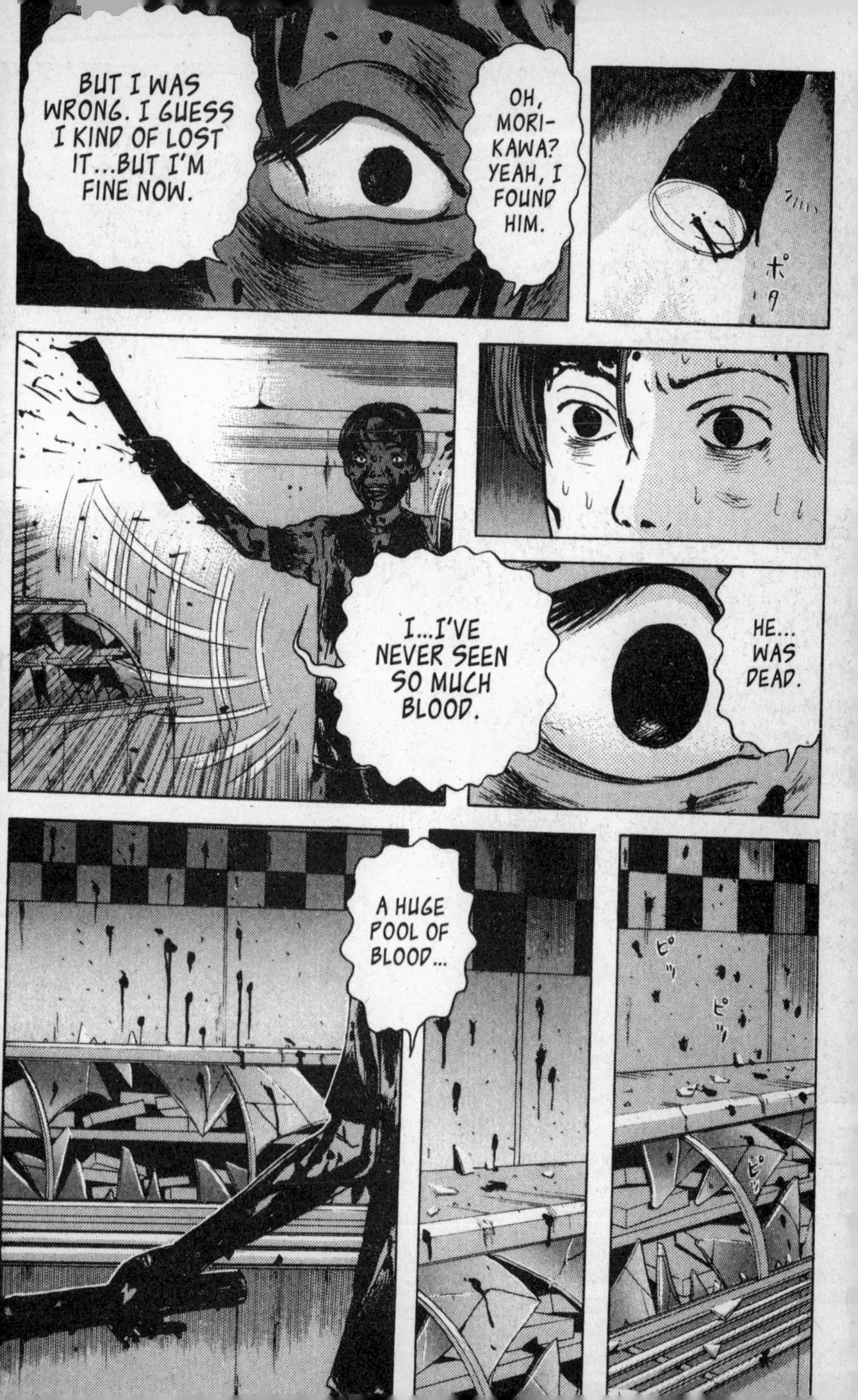
ポタ
OH, MORI-KAWA? YEAH, I FOUND HIM.
BUT I WAS WRONG. I GUESS I KIND OF LOST IT...BUT I'M FINE NOW.
HE... WAS DEAD.
I...I'VE NEVER SEEN SO MUCH BLOOD.
ピッ
ピッ
A HUGE POOL OF BLOOD...

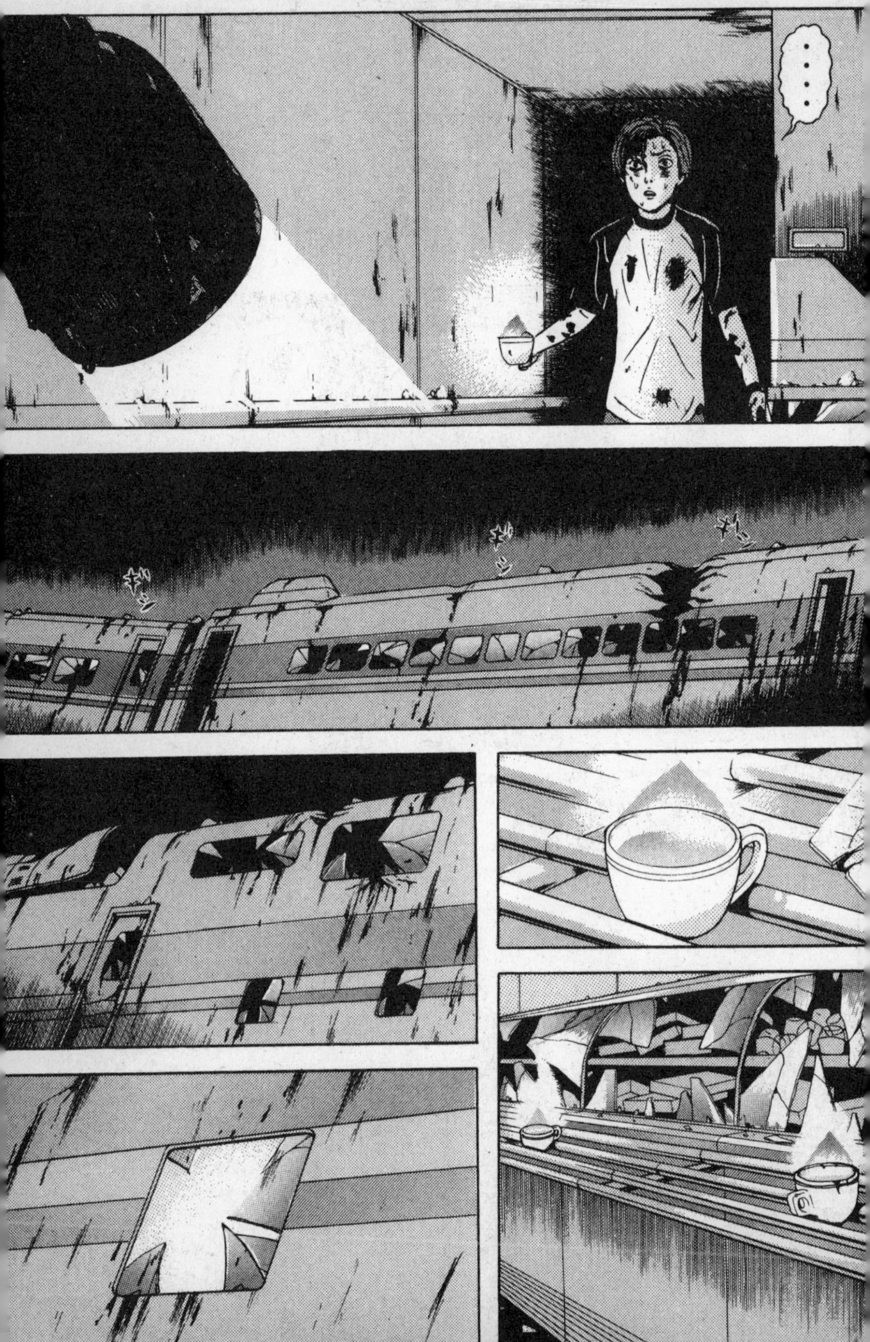
....

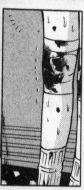

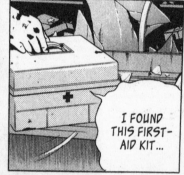

I FOUND THIS FIRST-AID KIT...

THANK YOU.

TERU-KUN...

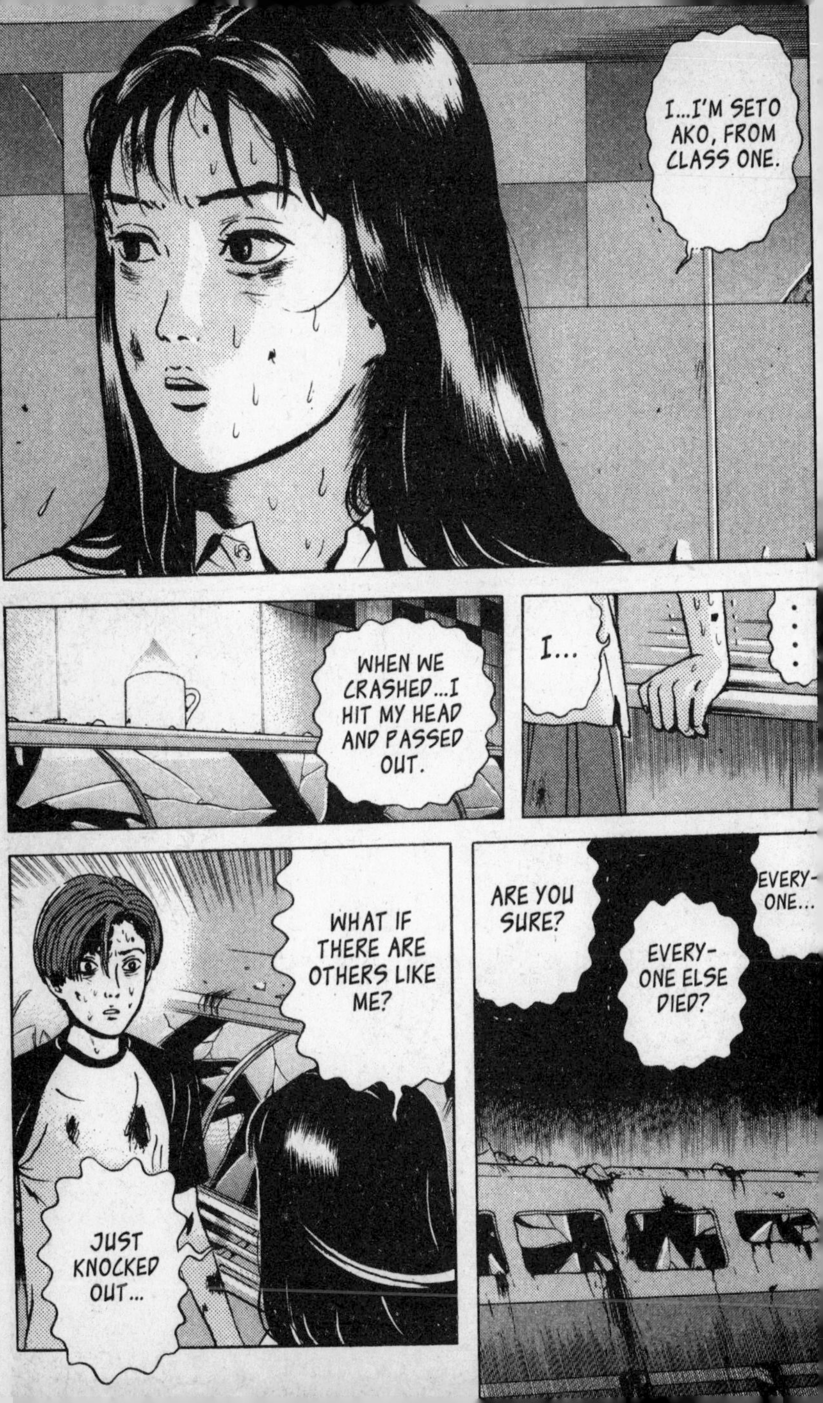
I...I'M SETO AKO, FROM CLASS ONE.
....
I...
WHEN WE CRASHED...I HIT MY HEAD AND PASSED OUT.
EVERY-ONE...
EVERY-ONE ELSE DIED?
ARE YOU SURE?
WHAT IF THERE ARE OTHERS LIKE ME?
JUST KNOCKED OUT...

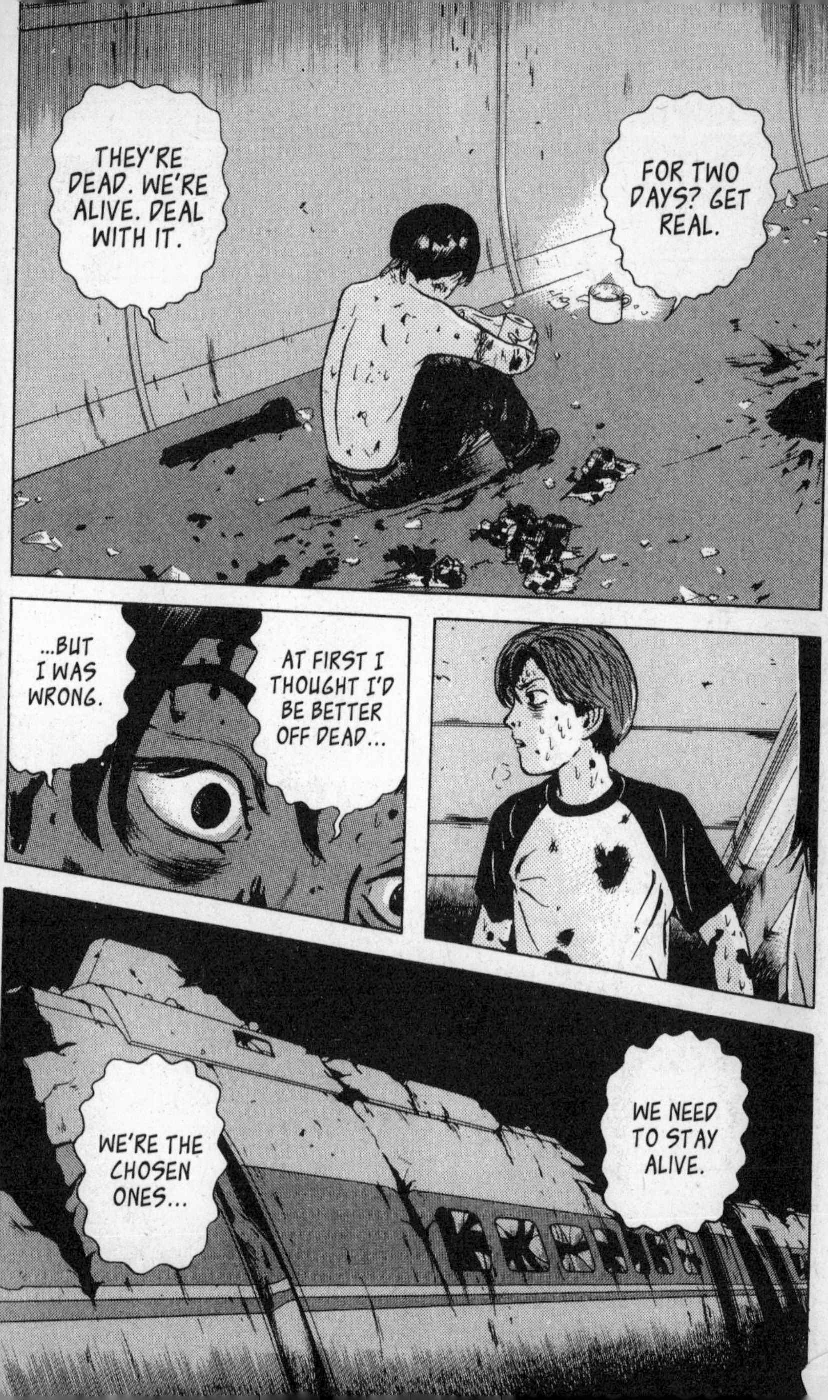
FOR TWO DAYS? GET REAL.
THEY'RE DEAD. WE'RE ALIVE. DEAL WITH IT.
AT FIRST I THOUGHT I'D BE BETTER OFF DEAD...
...BUT I WAS WRONG.
WE NEED TO STAY ALIVE.
WE'RE THE CHOSEN ONES...

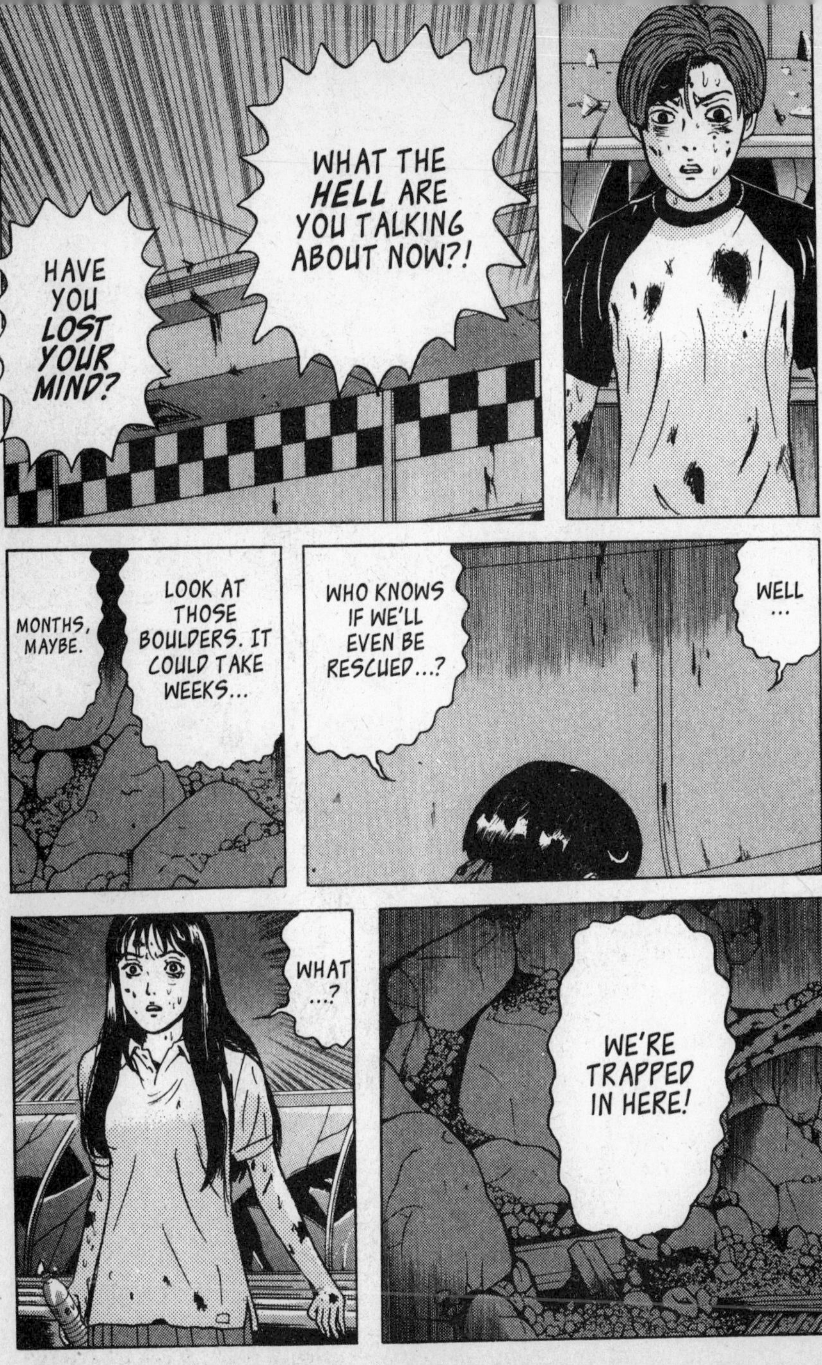
WHAT THE HELL ARE YOU TALKING ABOUT NOW?!
HAVE YOU LOST YOUR MIND?
WELL ...
WHO KNOWS IF WE'LL EVEN BE RESCUED...?
LOOK AT THOSE BOULDERS. IT COULD TAKE WEEKS...
MONTHS, MAYBE.
WE'RE TRAPPED IN HERE!
WHAT ...?

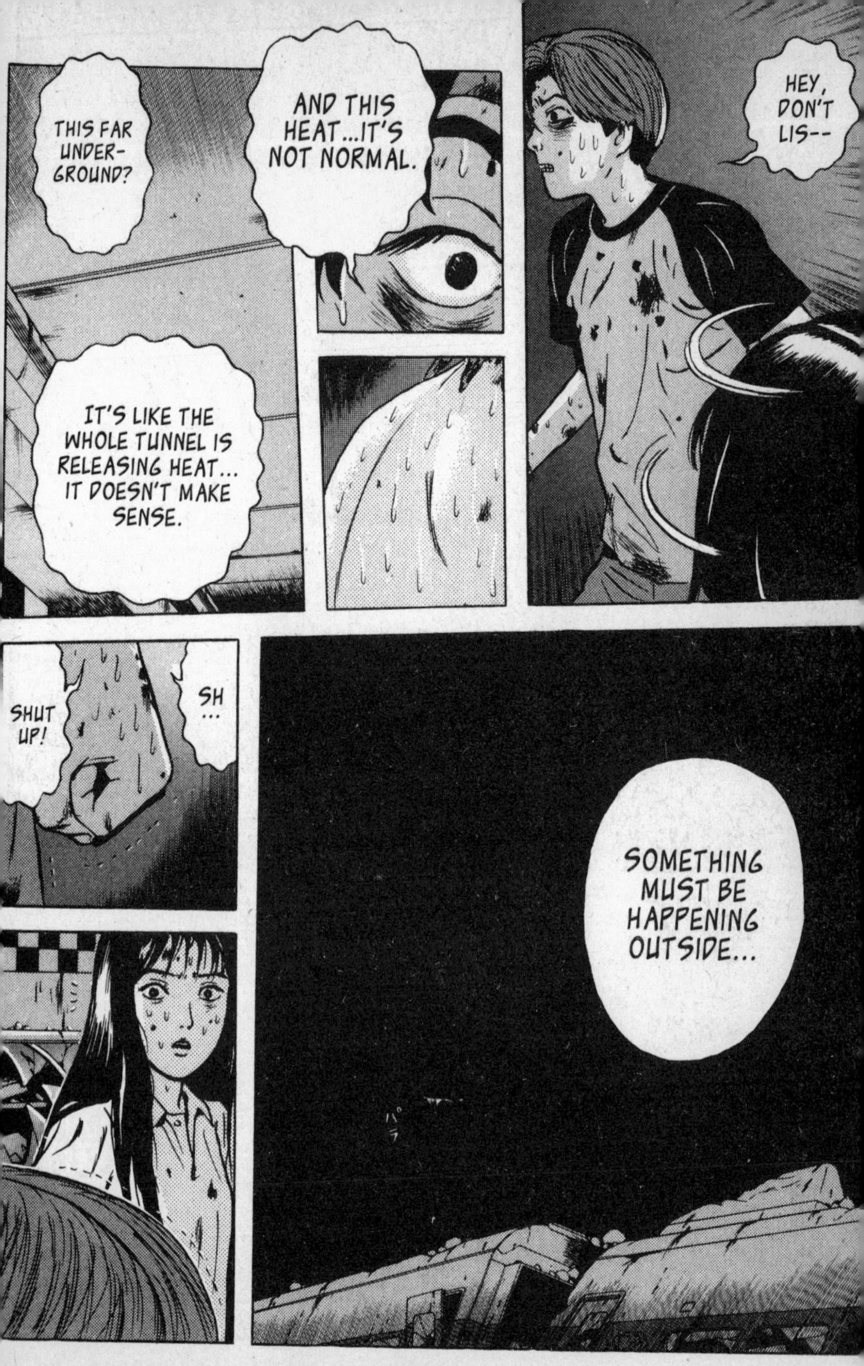
THIS FAR UNDER-GROUND?
AND THIS HEAT...IT'S NOT NORMAL.
IT'S LIKE THE WHOLE TUNNEL IS RELEASING HEAT... IT DOESN'T MAKE SENSE.
HEY, DON'T LIS--
SHUT UP!
SH...
SOMETHING MUST BE HAPPENING OUTSIDE...

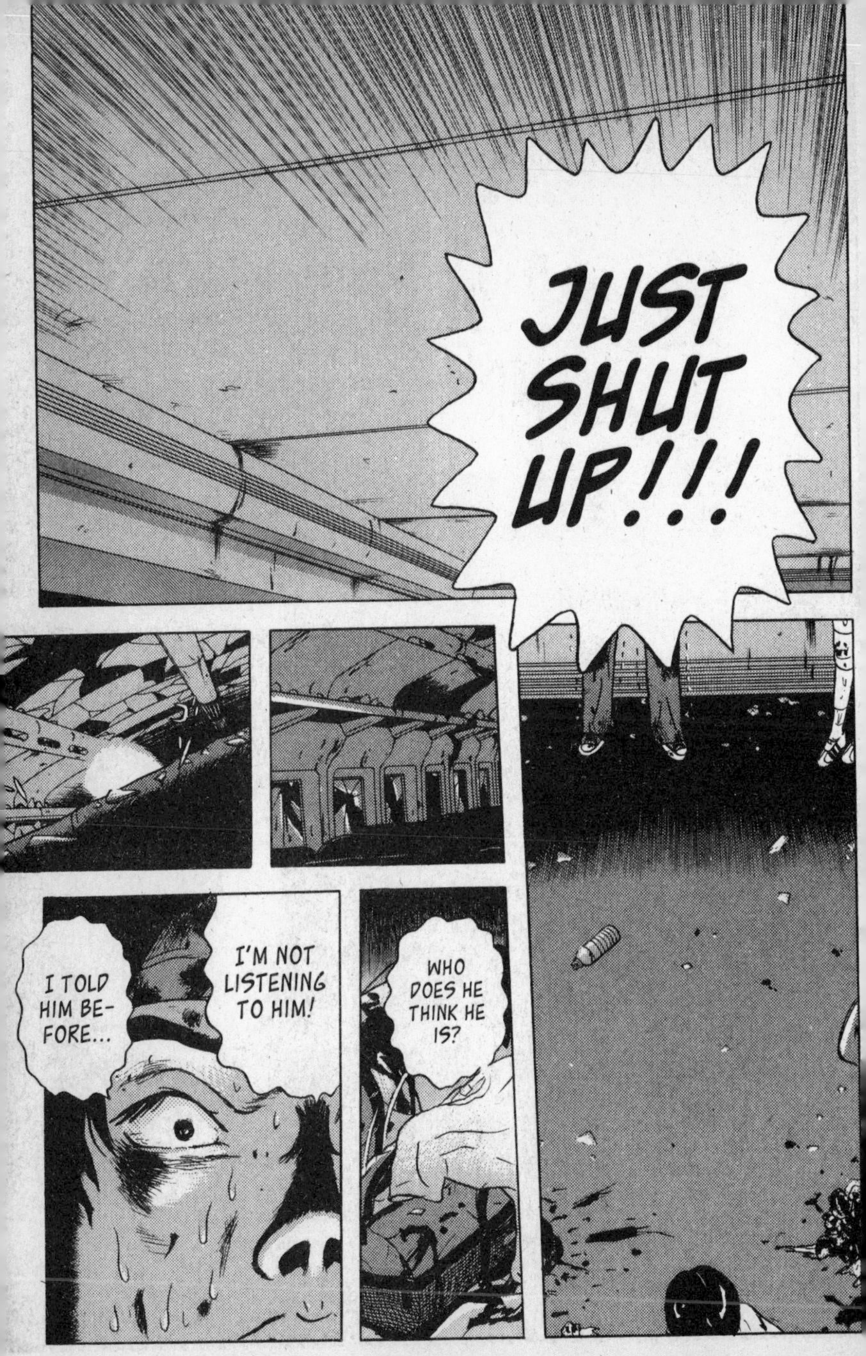
JUST SHUT UP!!!
WHO DOES HE THINK HE IS?
I'M NOT LISTENING TO HIM!
I TOLD HIM BE-FORE...

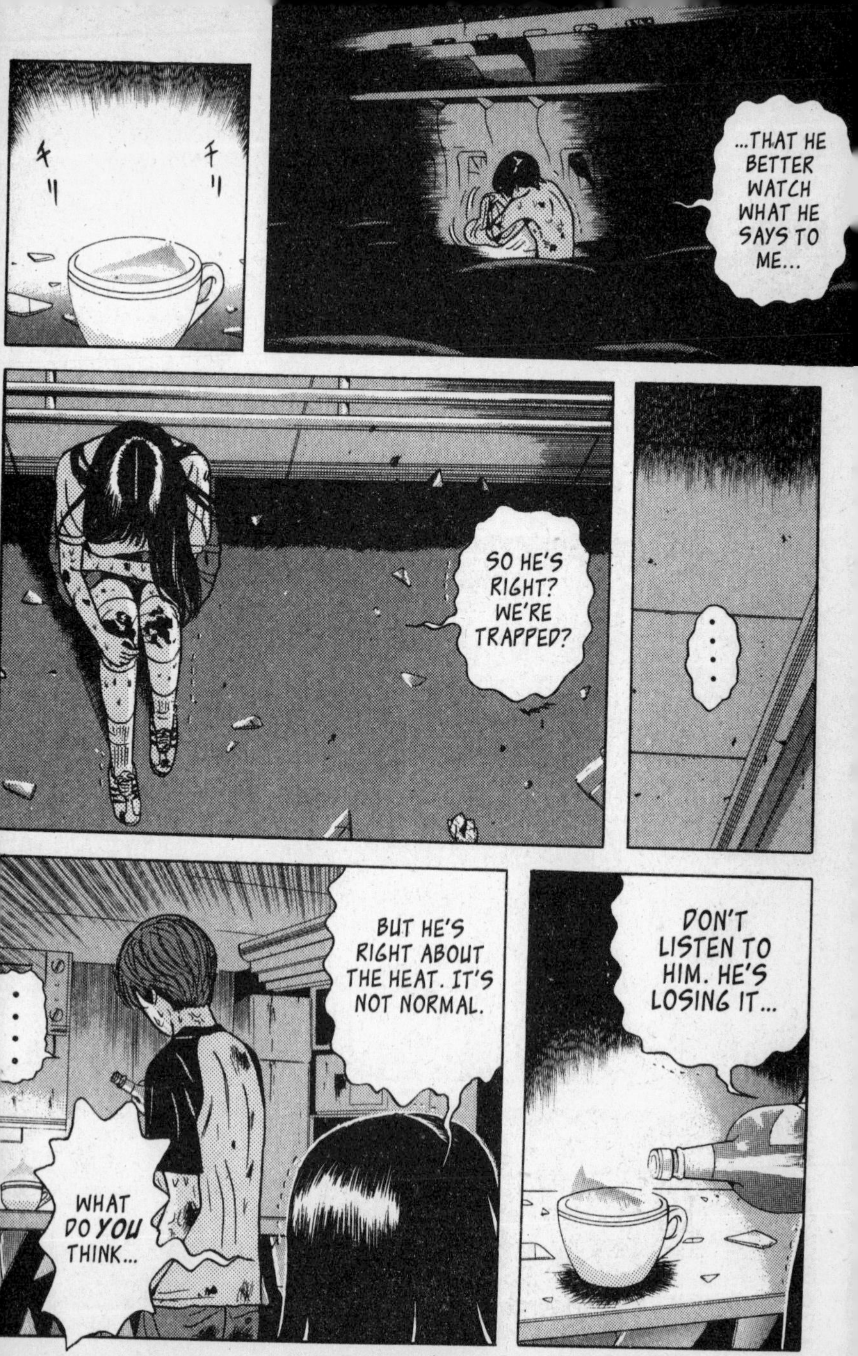
...THAT HE BETTER WATCH WHAT HE SAYS TO ME...
チリ
チリ
....
SO HE'S RIGHT? WE'RE TRAPPED?
DON'T LISTEN TO HIM. HE'S LOSING IT...
BUT HE'S RIGHT ABOUT THE HEAT. IT'S NOT NORMAL.
WHAT DO *YOU* THINK...
....

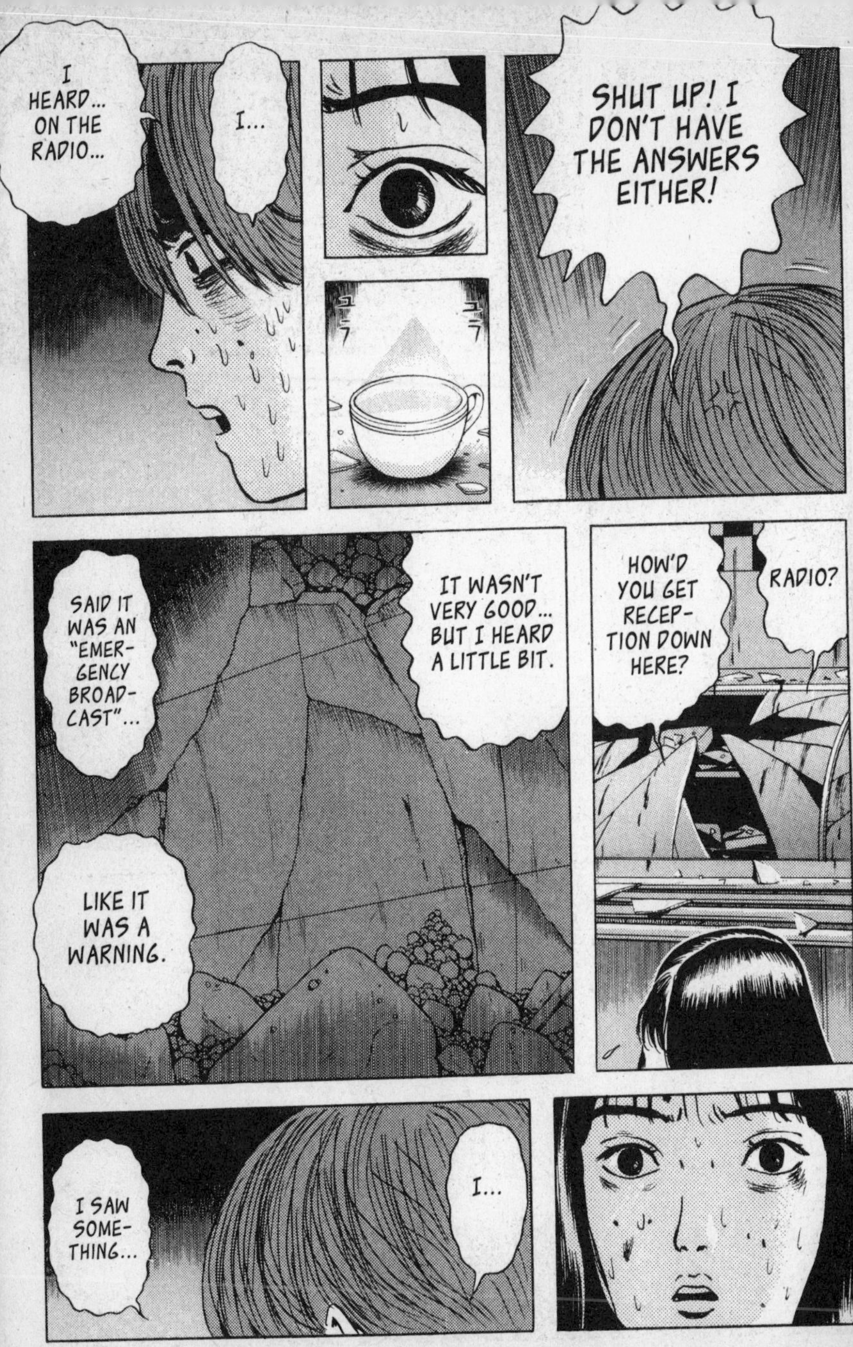
SHUT UP! I DON'T HAVE THE ANSWERS EITHER!
I...
I HEARD... ON THE RADIO...
RADIO?
HOW'D YOU GET RECEPTION DOWN HERE?
IT WASN'T VERY GOOD... BUT I HEARD A LITTLE BIT.
SAID IT WAS AN "EMERGENCY BROADCAST"...
LIKE IT WAS A WARNING.
I...
I SAW SOMETHING...

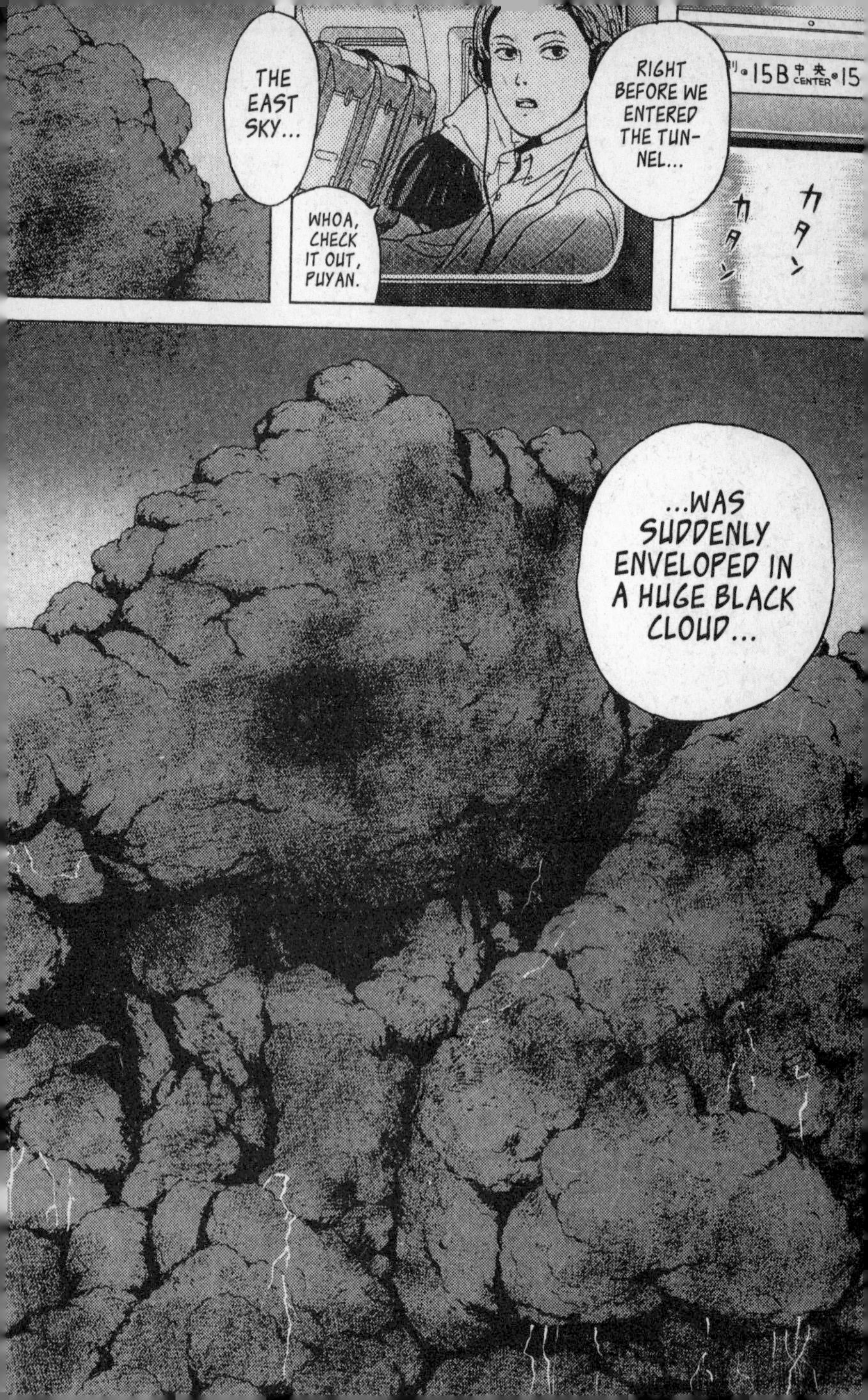
15B 中央 CENTER 15
カタン
カタン
RIGHT BEFORE WE ENTERED THE TUNNEL...
THE EAST SKY...
WHOA, CHECK IT OUT, PUYAN.
...WAS SUDDENLY ENVELOPED IN A HUGE BLACK CLOUD...

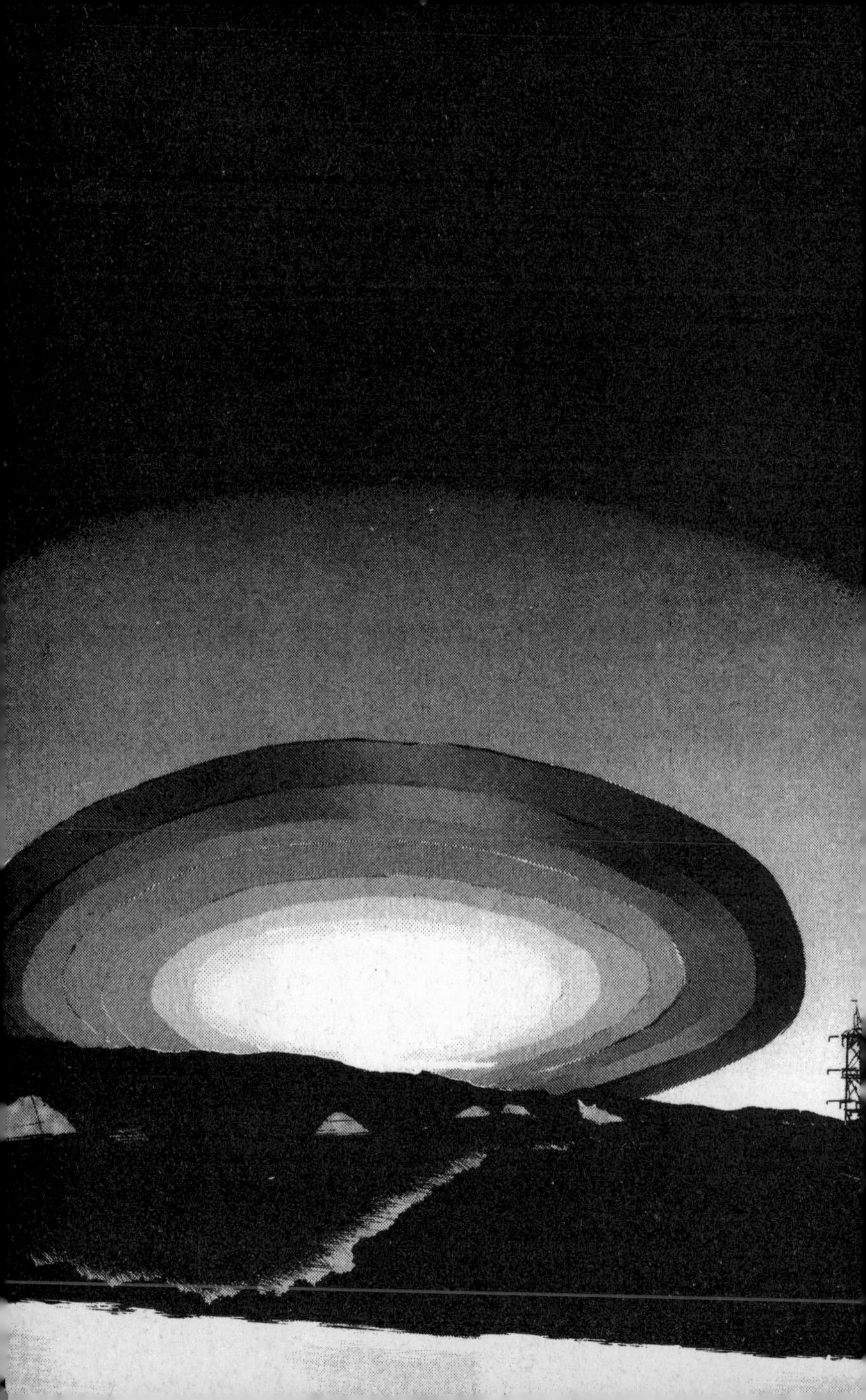

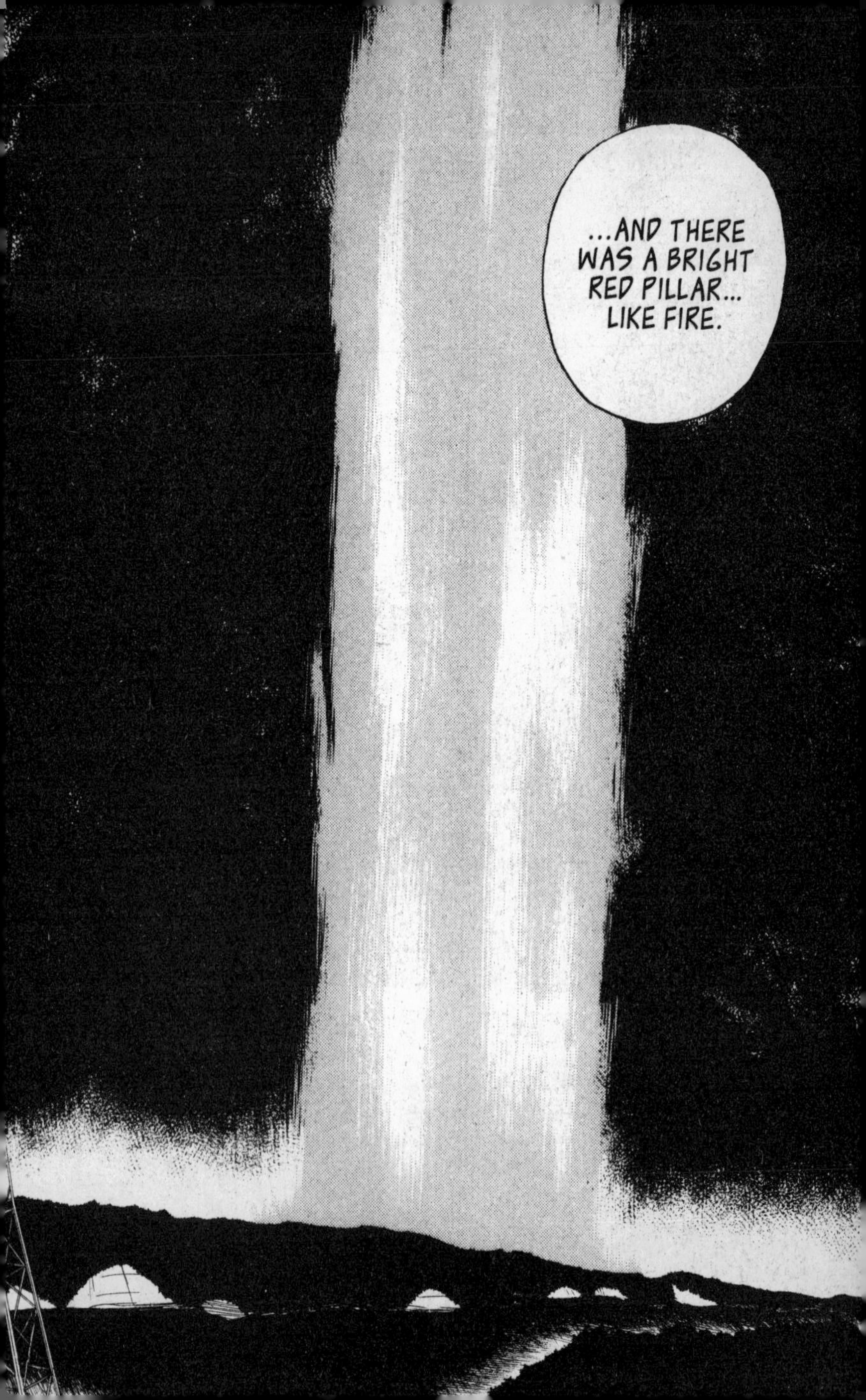
...AND THERE WAS A BRIGHT RED PILLAR... LIKE FIRE.

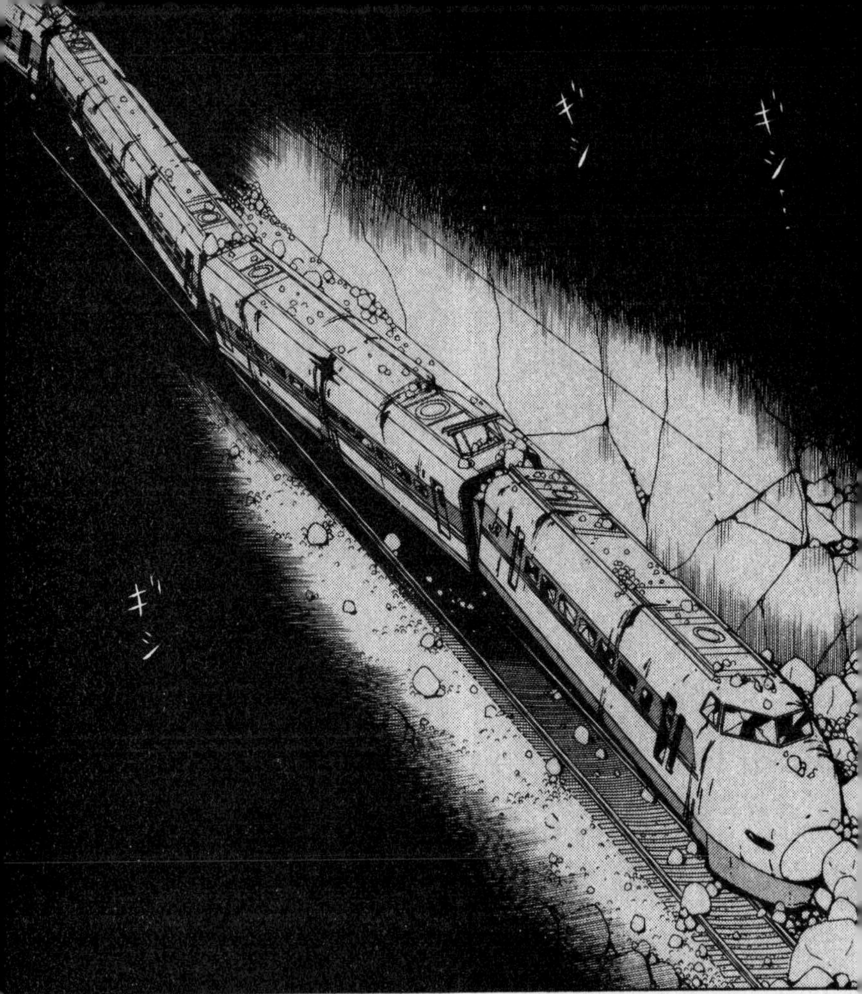
ギシ…
ギシ
ギシ
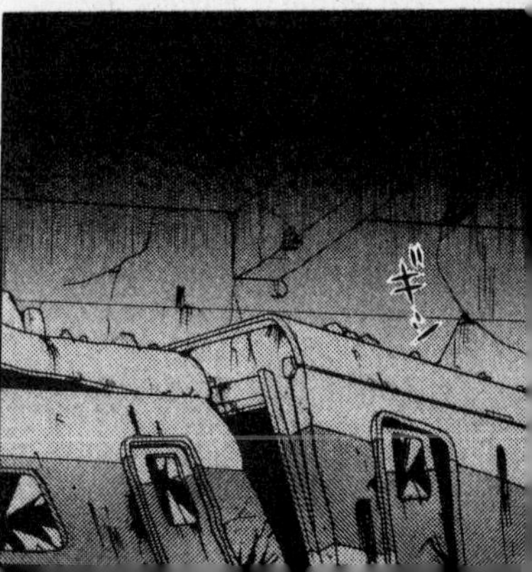
ギン
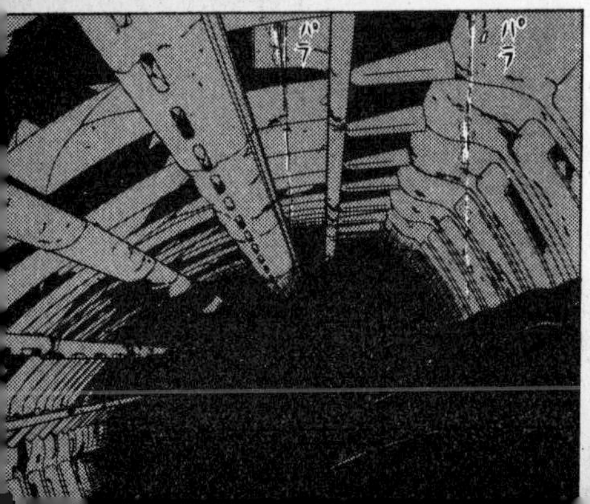
パラ
パラ

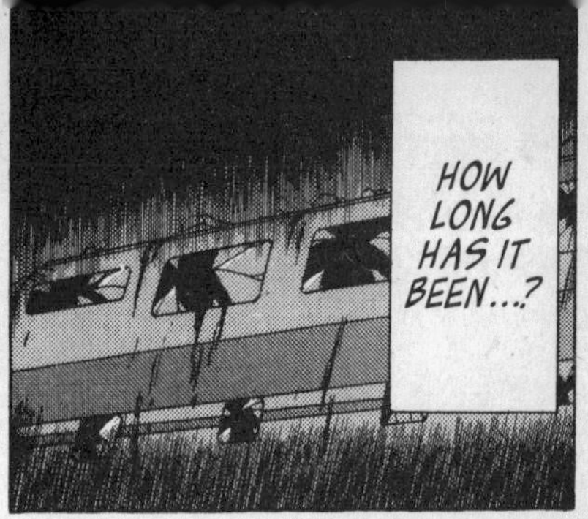
HOW LONG HAS IT BEEN...?
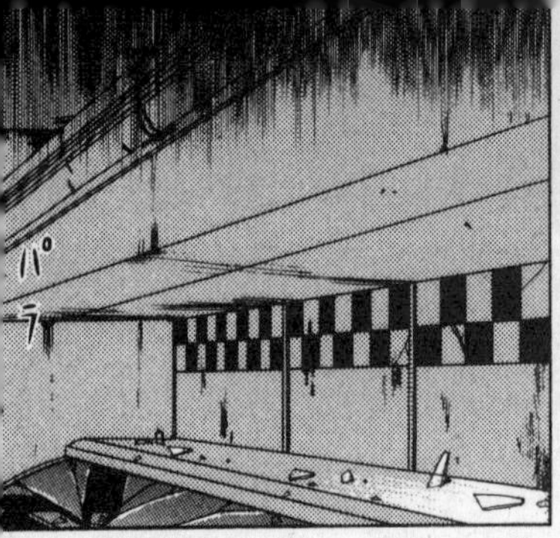
パラ
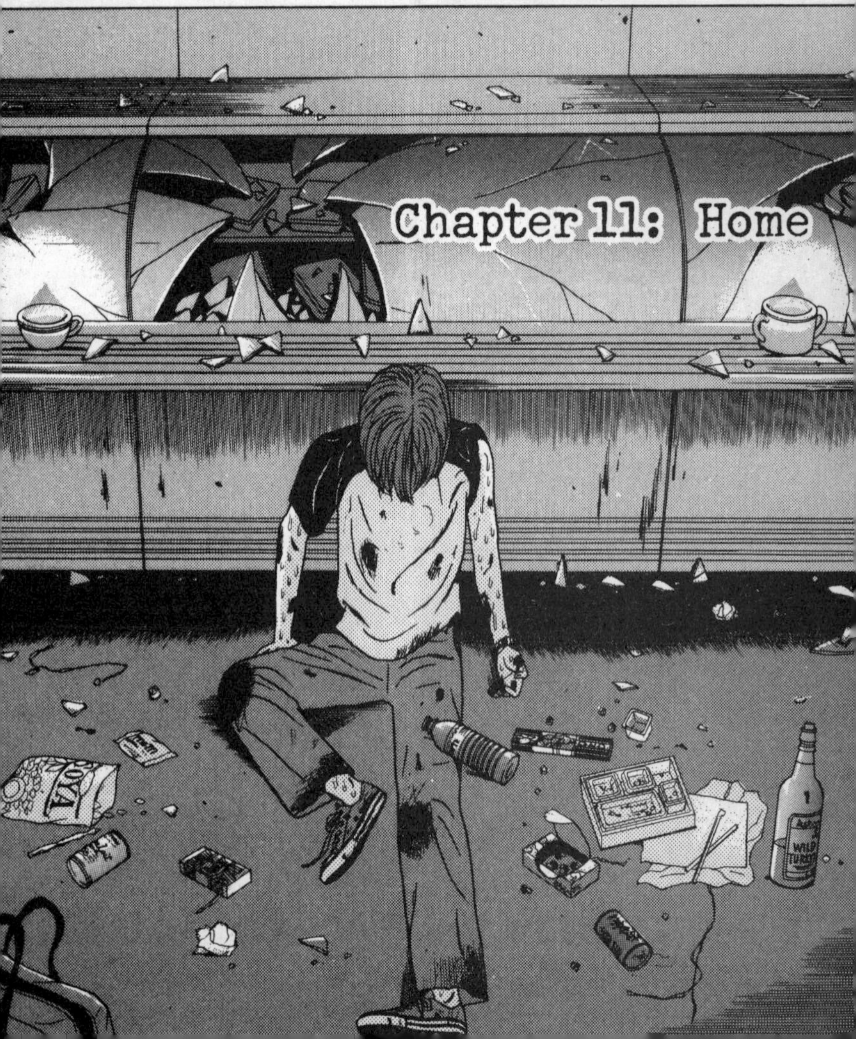
Chapter 11: Home

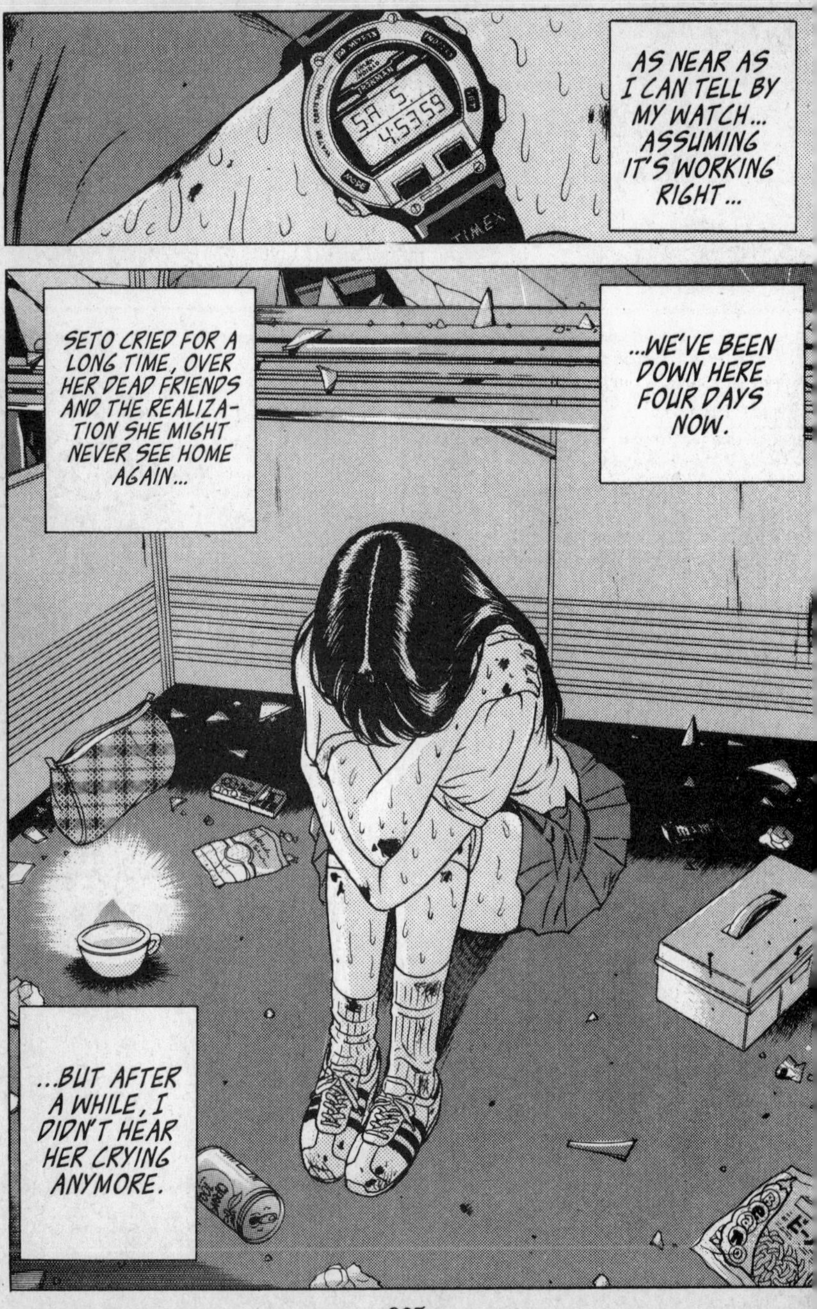
AS NEAR AS I CAN TELL BY MY WATCH... ASSUMING IT'S WORKING RIGHT...
...WE'VE BEEN DOWN HERE FOUR DAYS NOW.
SETO CRIED FOR A LONG TIME, OVER HER DEAD FRIENDS AND THE REALIZATION SHE MIGHT NEVER SEE HOME AGAIN...
...BUT AFTER A WHILE, I DIDN'T HEAR HER CRYING ANYMORE.

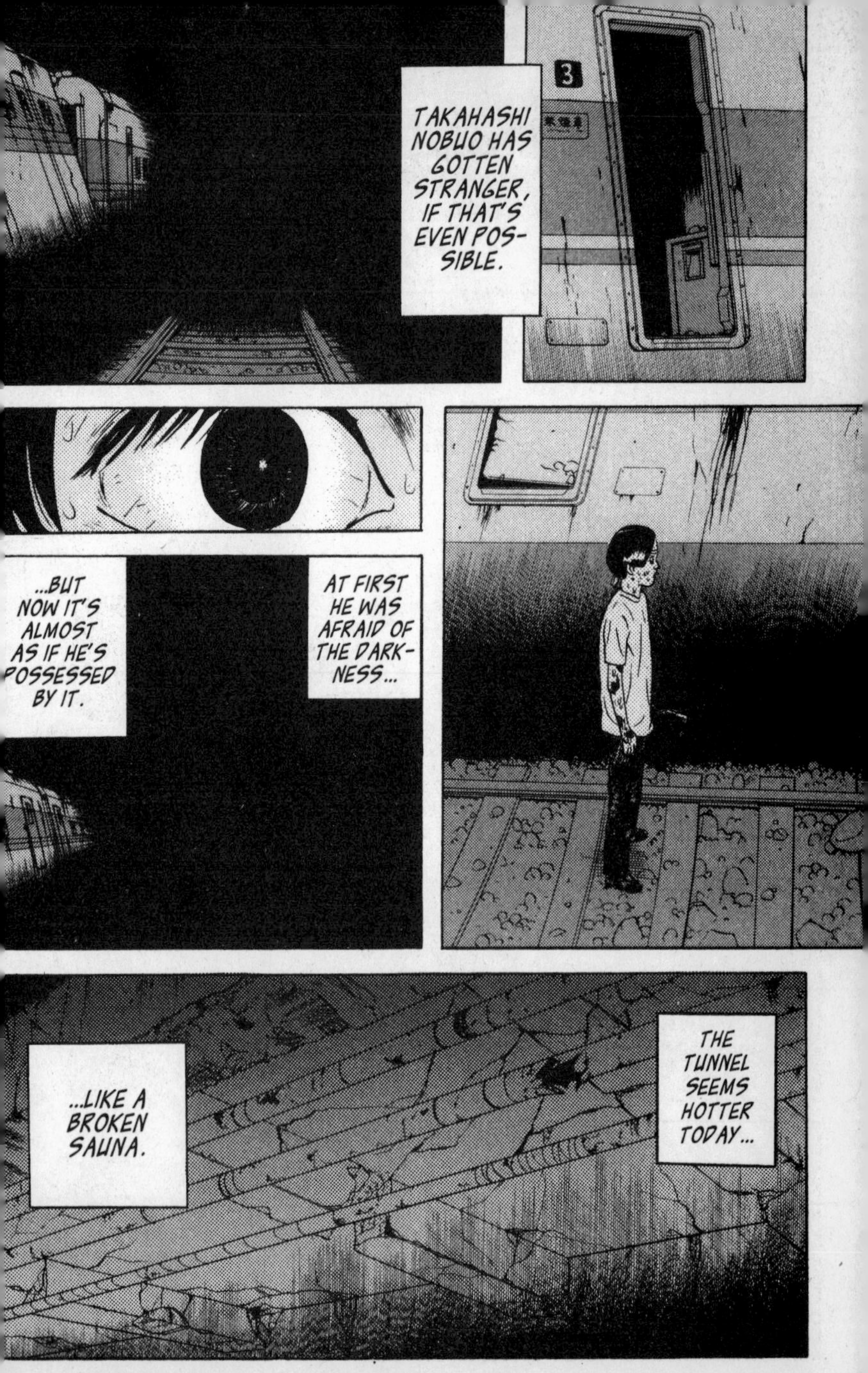
TAKAHASHI NOBUO HAS GOTTEN STRANGER, IF THAT'S EVEN POS-SIBLE.
AT FIRST HE WAS AFRAID OF THE DARK-NESS...
...BUT NOW IT'S ALMOST AS IF HE'S POSSESSED BY IT.
THE TUNNEL SEEMS HOTTER TODAY...
...LIKE A BROKEN SAUNA.

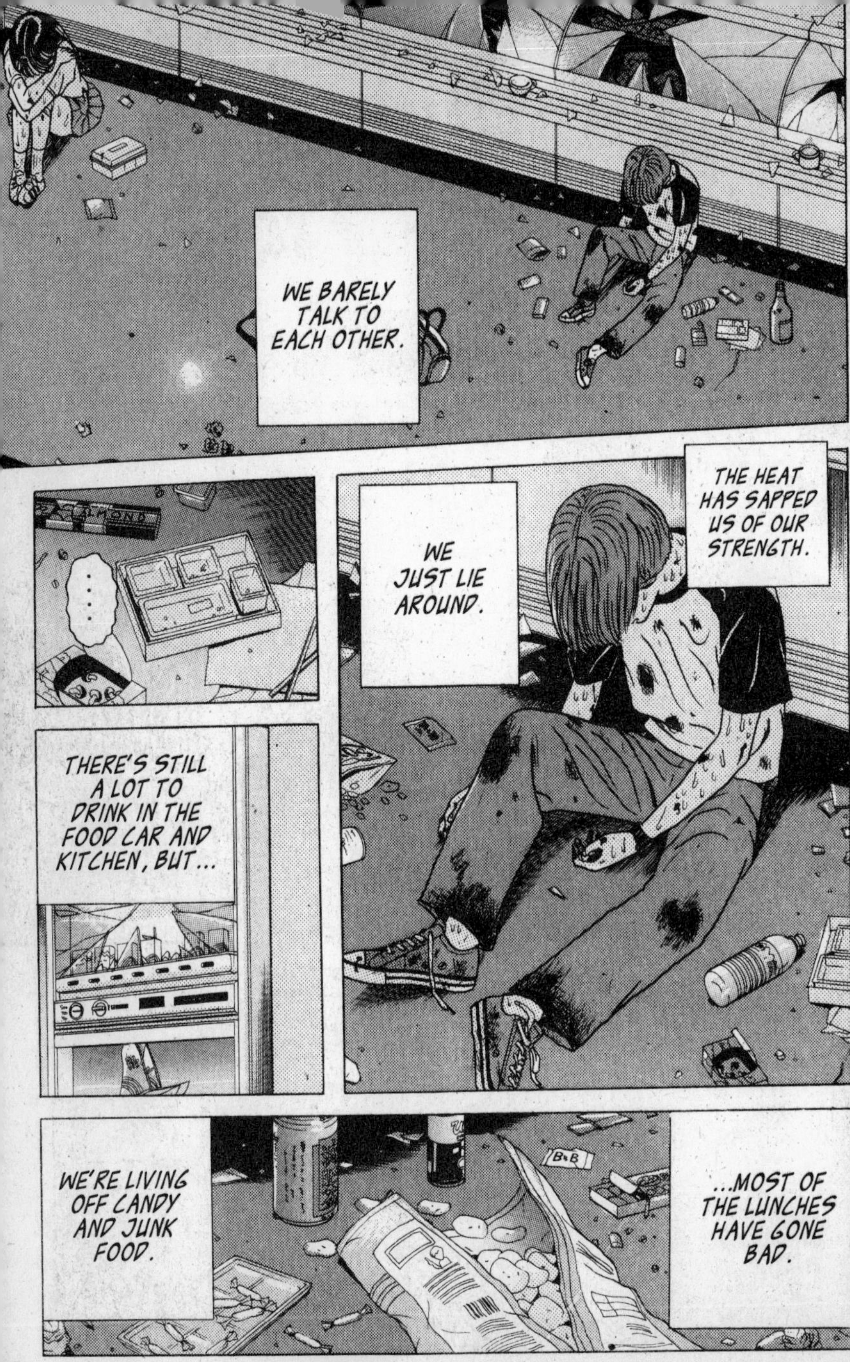
WE BARELY TALK TO EACH OTHER.
THE HEAT HAS SAPPED US OF OUR STRENGTH.
WE JUST LIE AROUND.
.....
THERE'S STILL A LOT TO DRINK IN THE FOOD CAR AND KITCHEN, BUT...
...MOST OF THE LUNCHES HAVE GONE BAD.
WE'RE LIVING OFF CANDY AND JUNK FOOD.

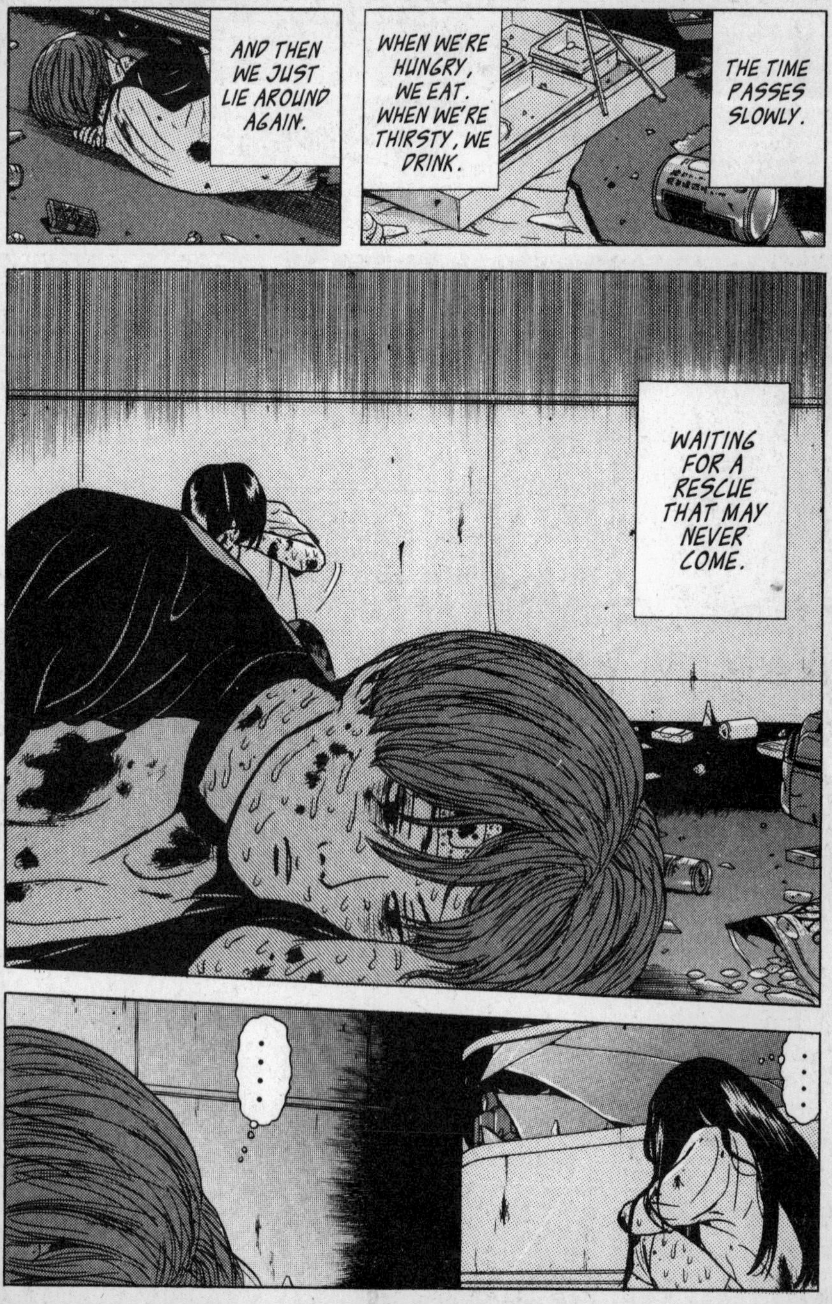
THE TIME PASSES SLOWLY.
WHEN WE'RE HUNGRY, WE EAT. WHEN WE'RE THIRSTY, WE DRINK.
AND THEN WE JUST LIE AROUND AGAIN.
WAITING FOR A RESCUE THAT MAY NEVER COME.
....
....

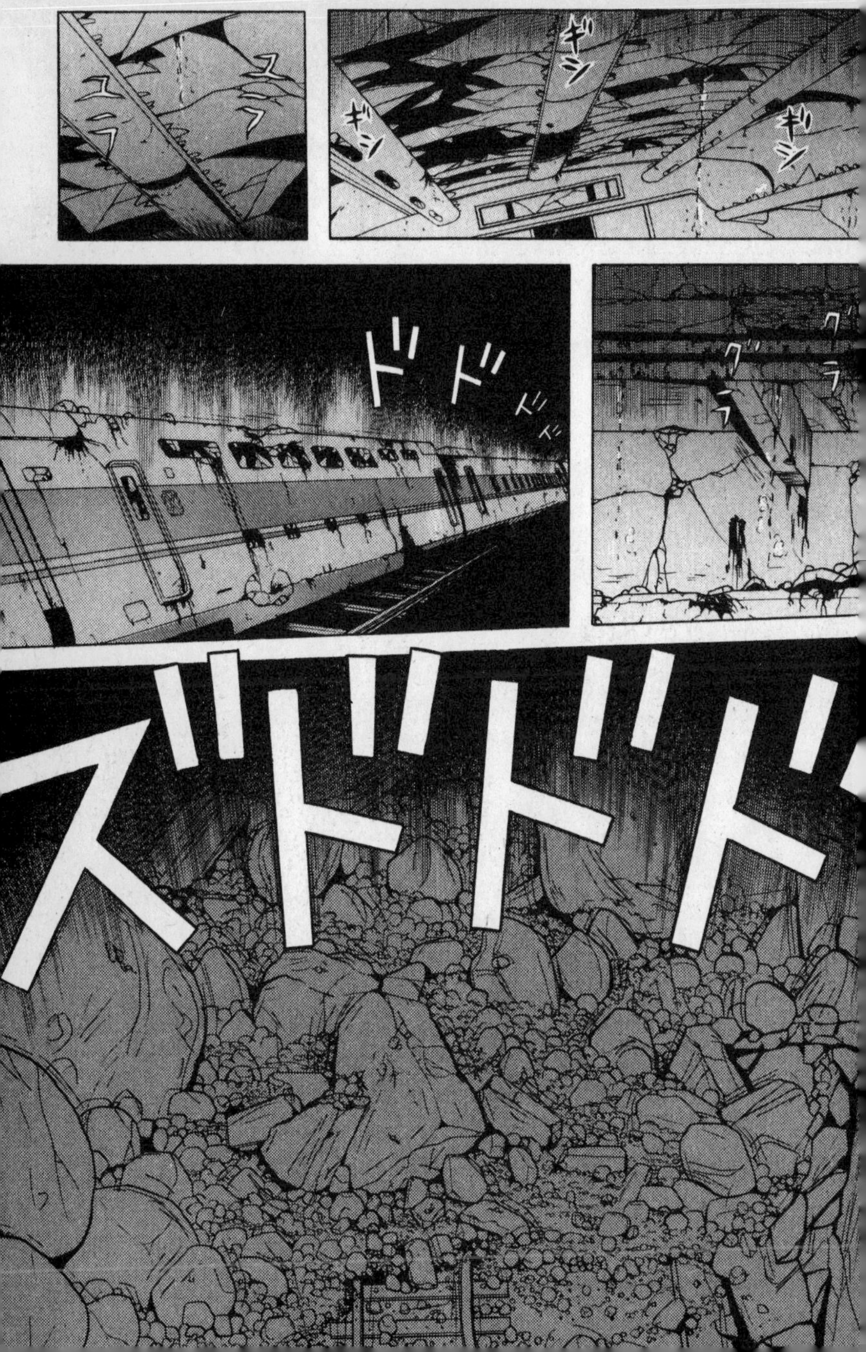
ギシ
ギシ
ギシ
ユラ
ユラ
グラ
グラ
ドド
ドド
ズドドド

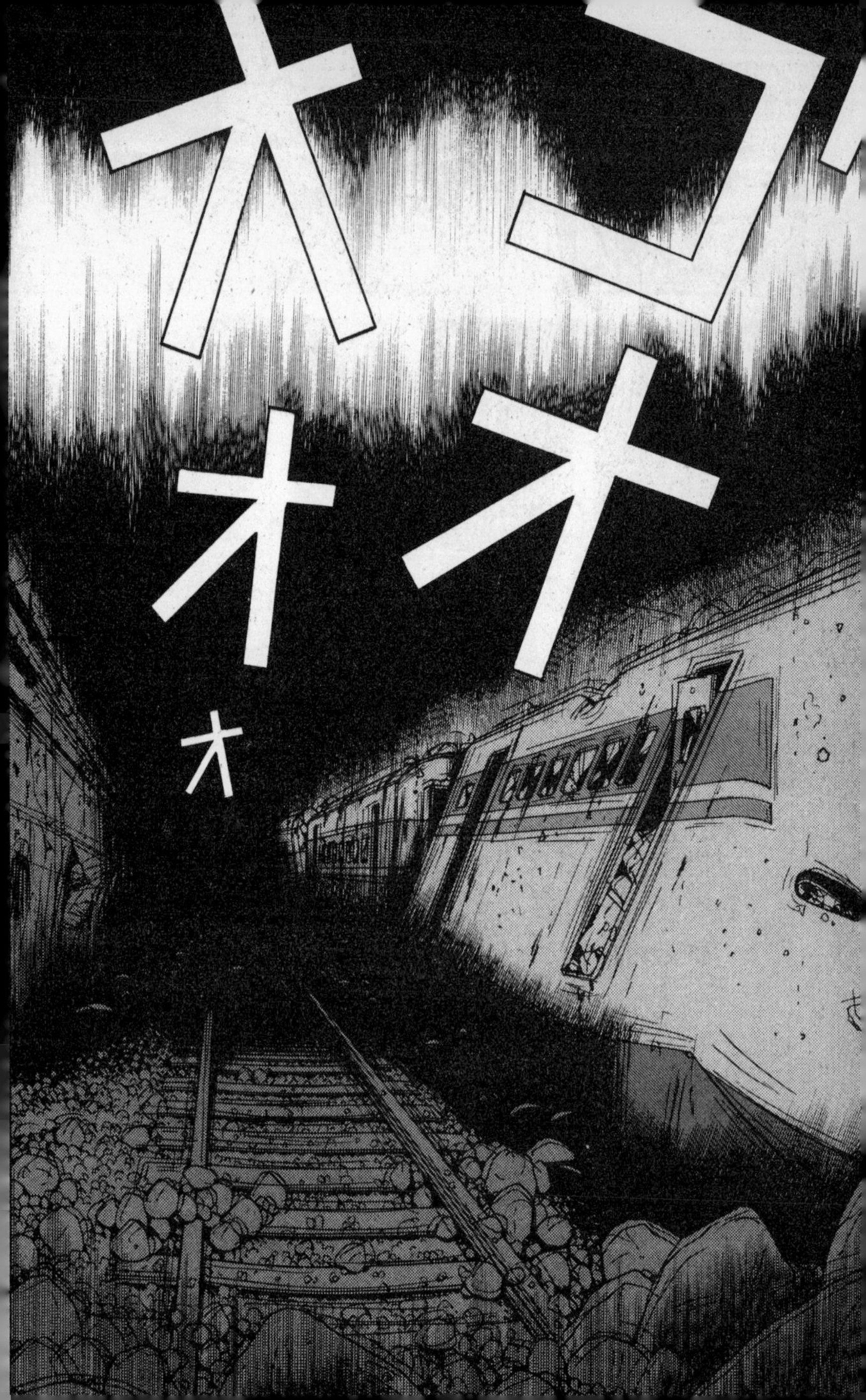
コオ
オオォ

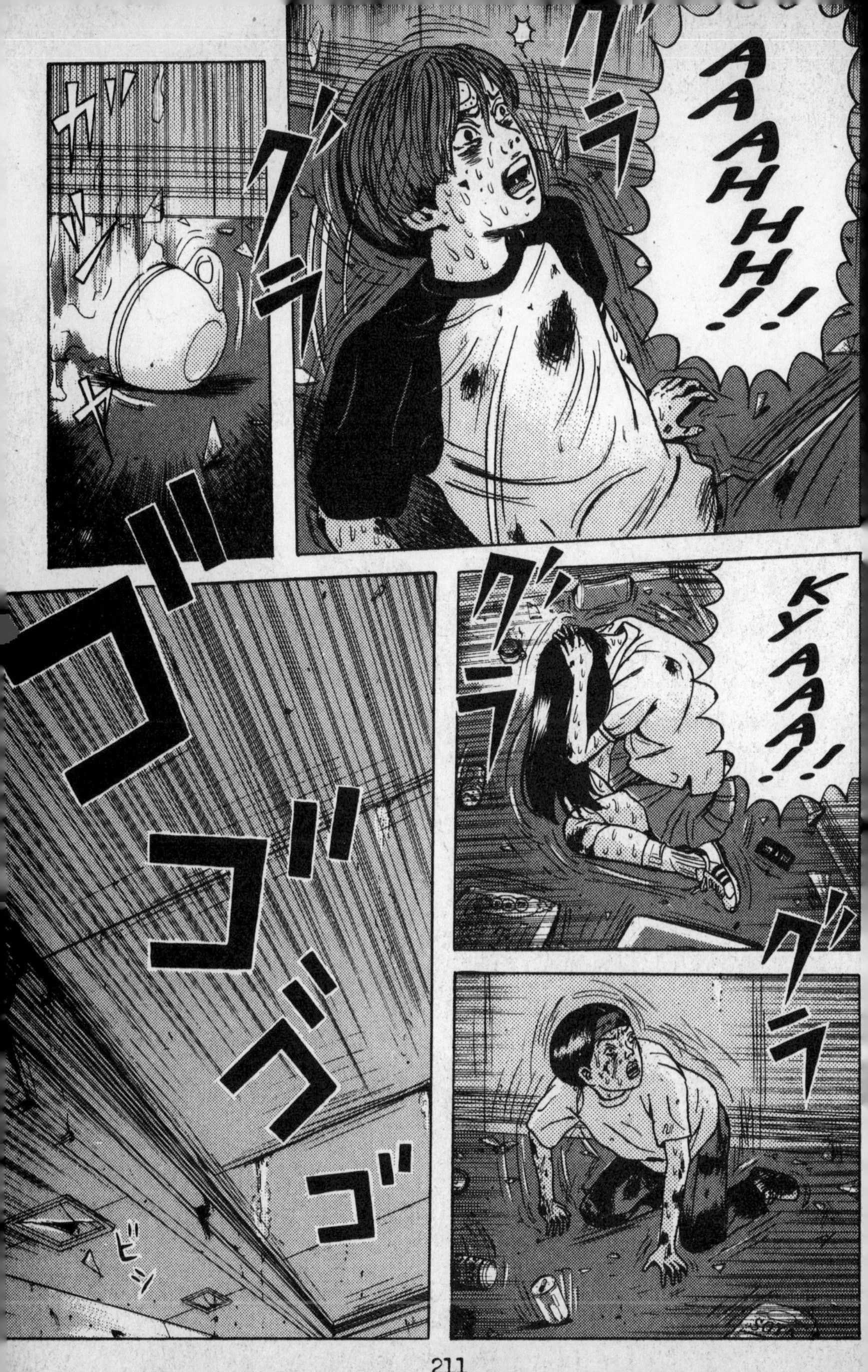
AAAHHHH!!
KYAAAAA!!

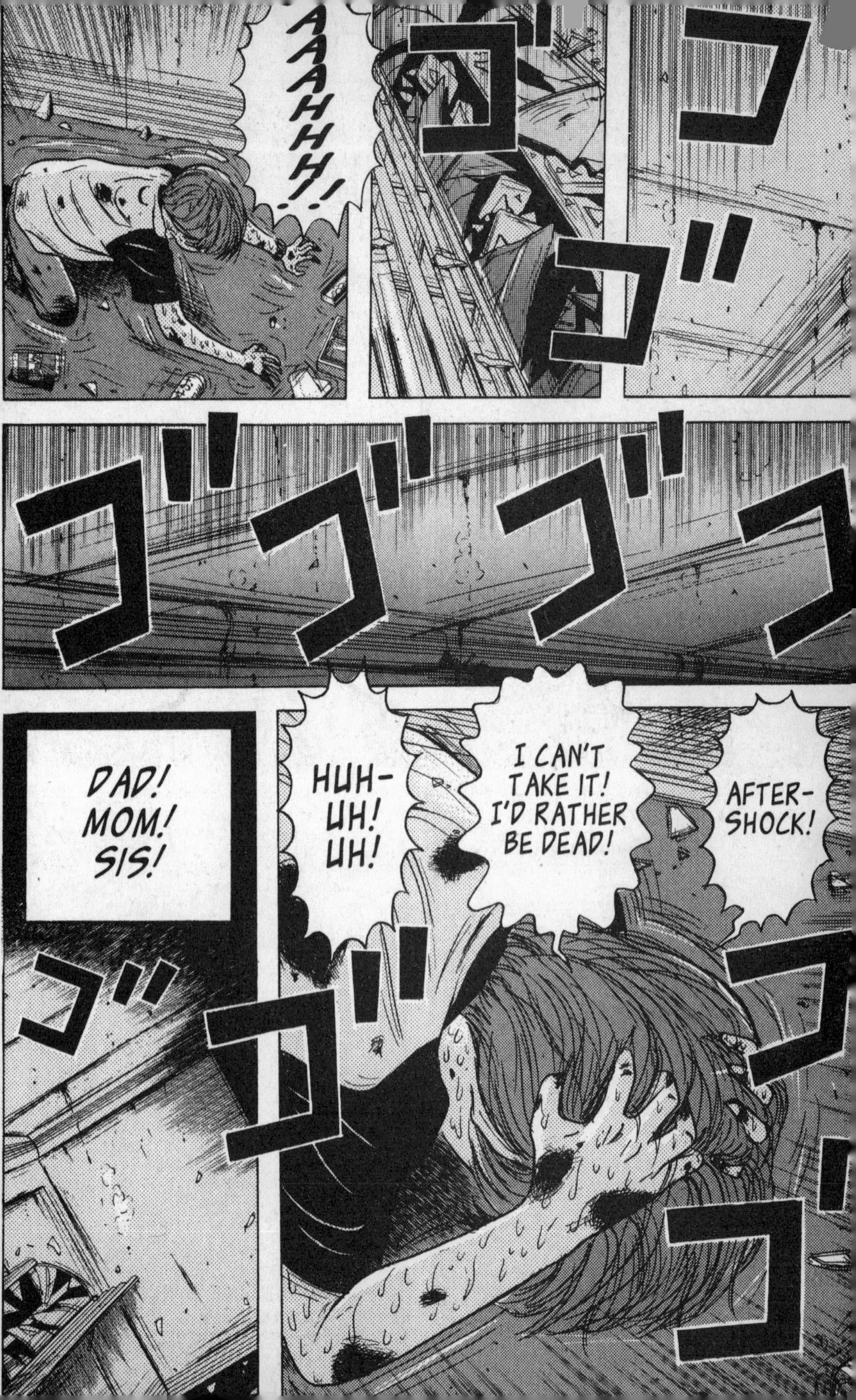
ゴゴ
ゴ
AAAAHHHH!!
ゴゴゴゴ
AFTER-SHOCK!
I CAN'T TAKE IT! I'D RATHER BE DEAD!
HUH-UH! UH!
ゴゴ
DAD! MOM! SIS!
ゴゴ

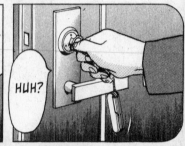

MOM GOT THE DAY OFF WORK?

NOT LOCKED?

HUH?

YEAH...

I'M HOME.

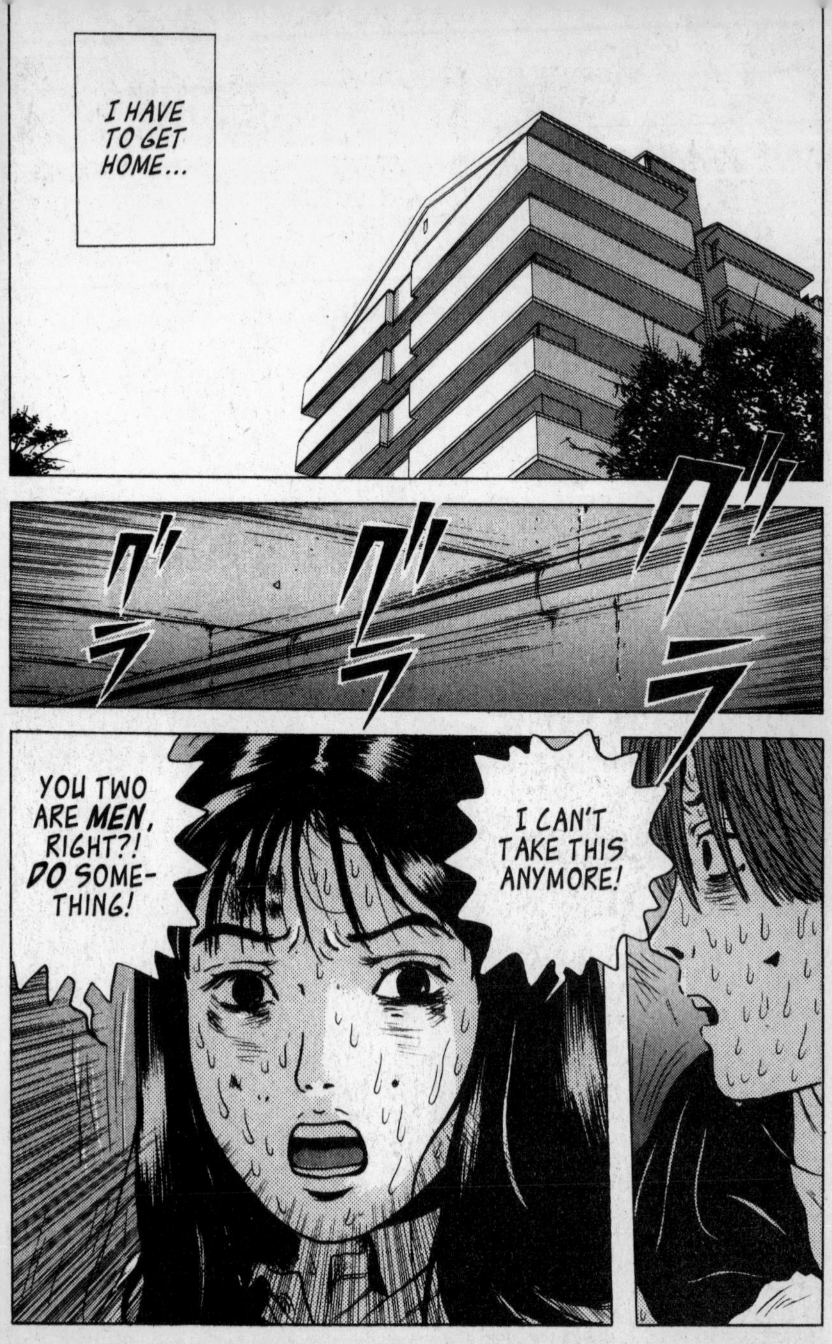
I HAVE TO GET HOME...
グラ
グラ
グラ
I CAN'T TAKE THIS ANYMORE!
YOU TWO ARE MEN, RIGHT?! DO SOMETHING!

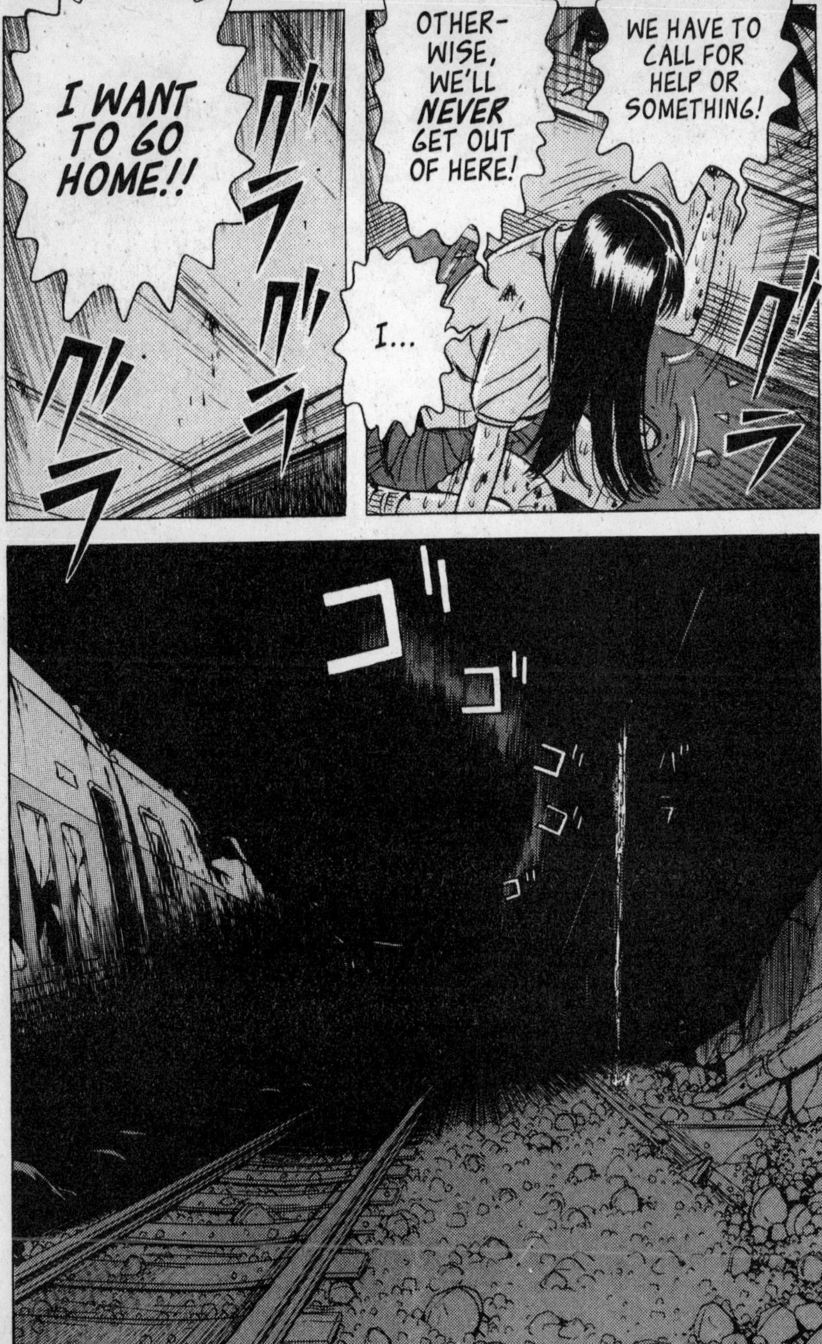
WE HAVE TO CALL FOR HELP OR SOMETHING!
OTHER-WISE, WE'LL **NEVER** GET OUT OF HERE!
I...
I WANT TO GO HOME!!

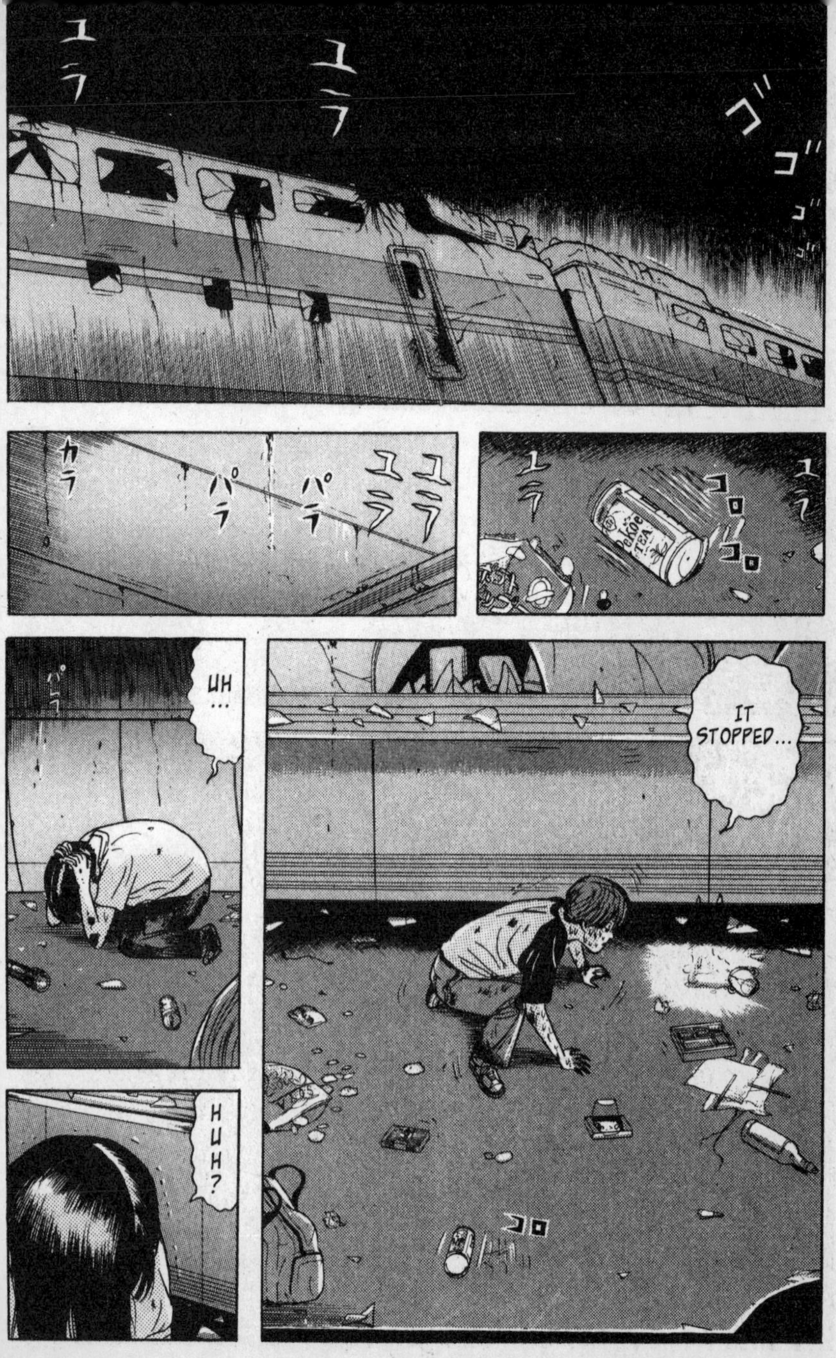
ユラ
ユラ
ゴゴゴゴ
ユラ
ゴロゴロ
ユラ
ユラ
ユラ
パラ
パラ
カラ
IT STOPPED...
UH...
HUH?

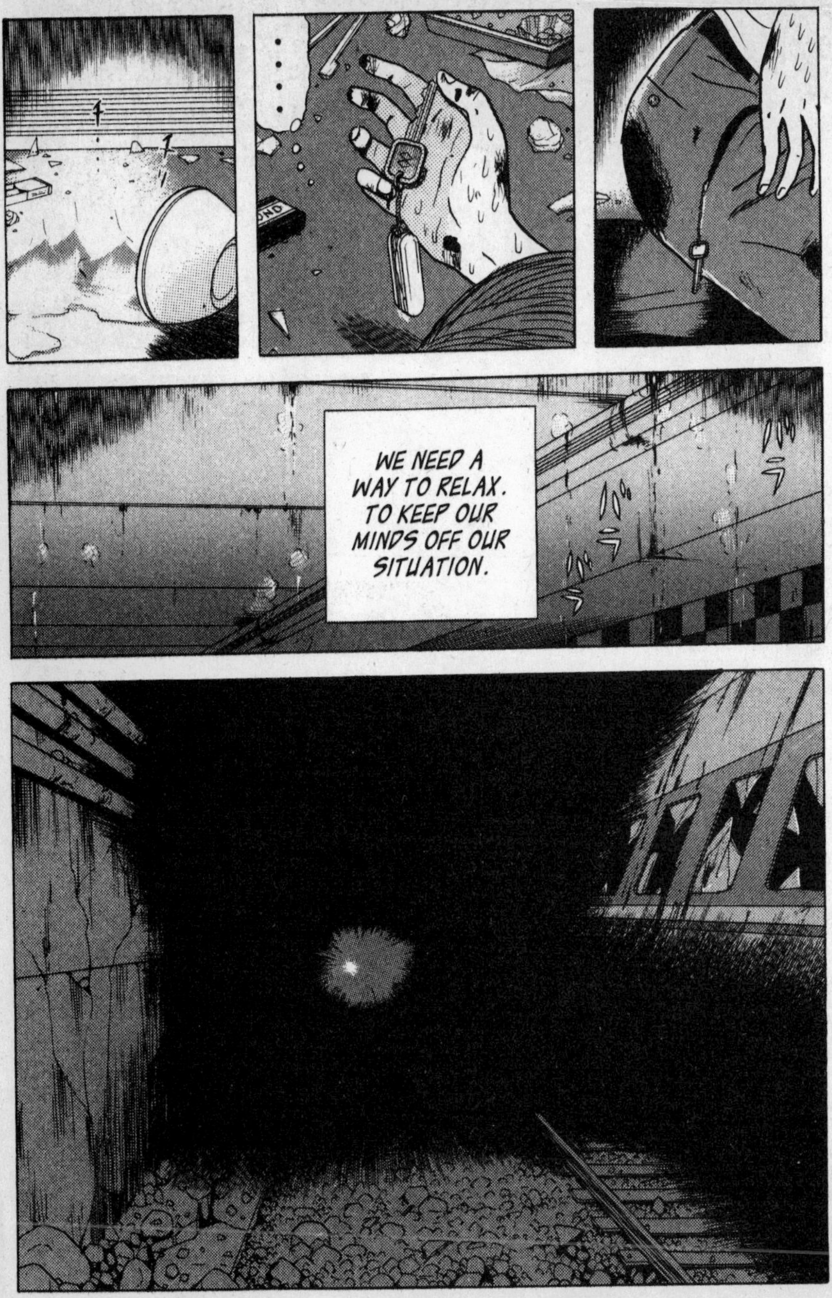
WE NEED A WAY TO RELAX. TO KEEP OUR MINDS OFF OUR SITUATION.

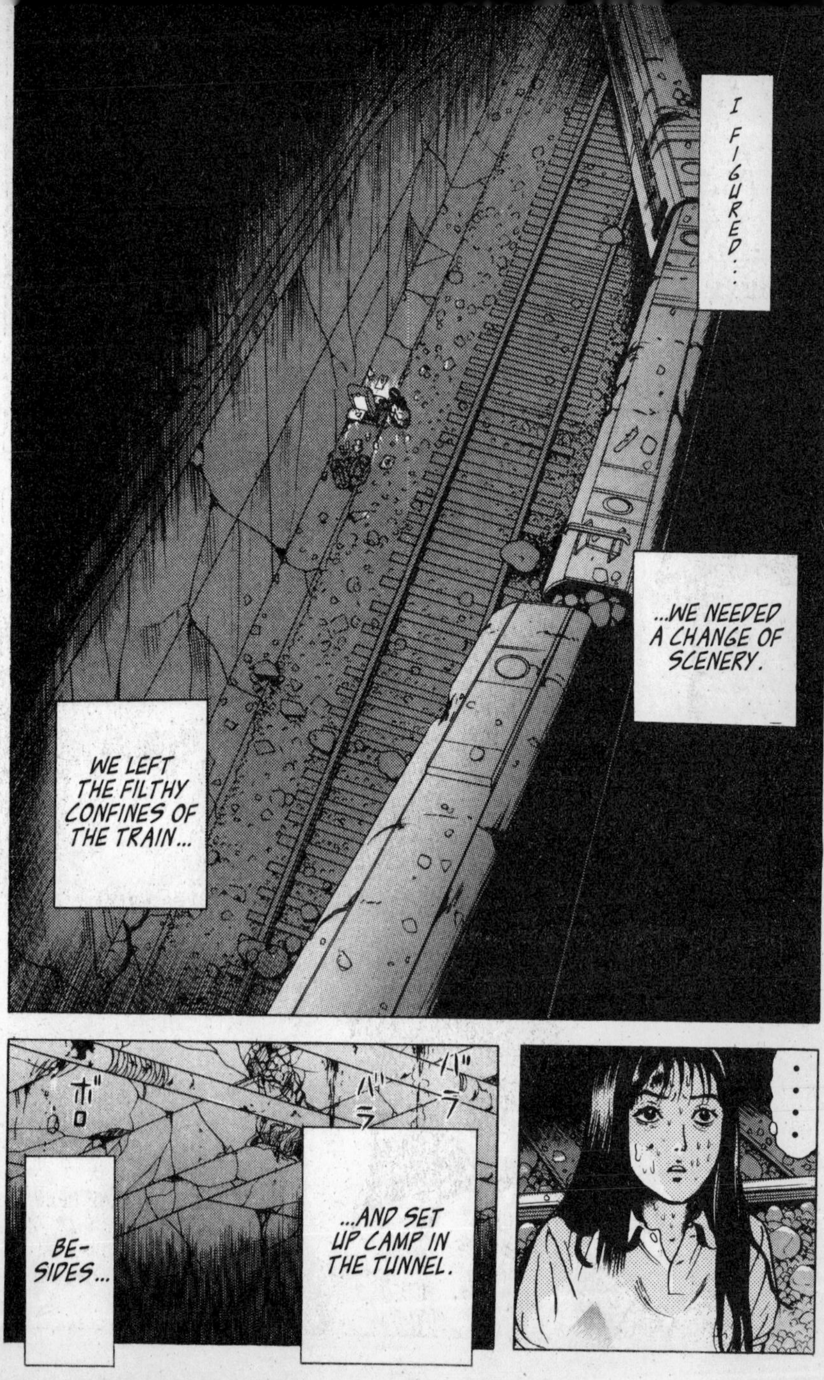
I FIGURED...
...WE NEEDED A CHANGE OF SCENERY.
WE LEFT THE FILTHY CONFINES OF THE TRAIN...
...
バラ
バラ
...AND SET UP CAMP IN THE TUNNEL.
ボロ
BE-SIDES...

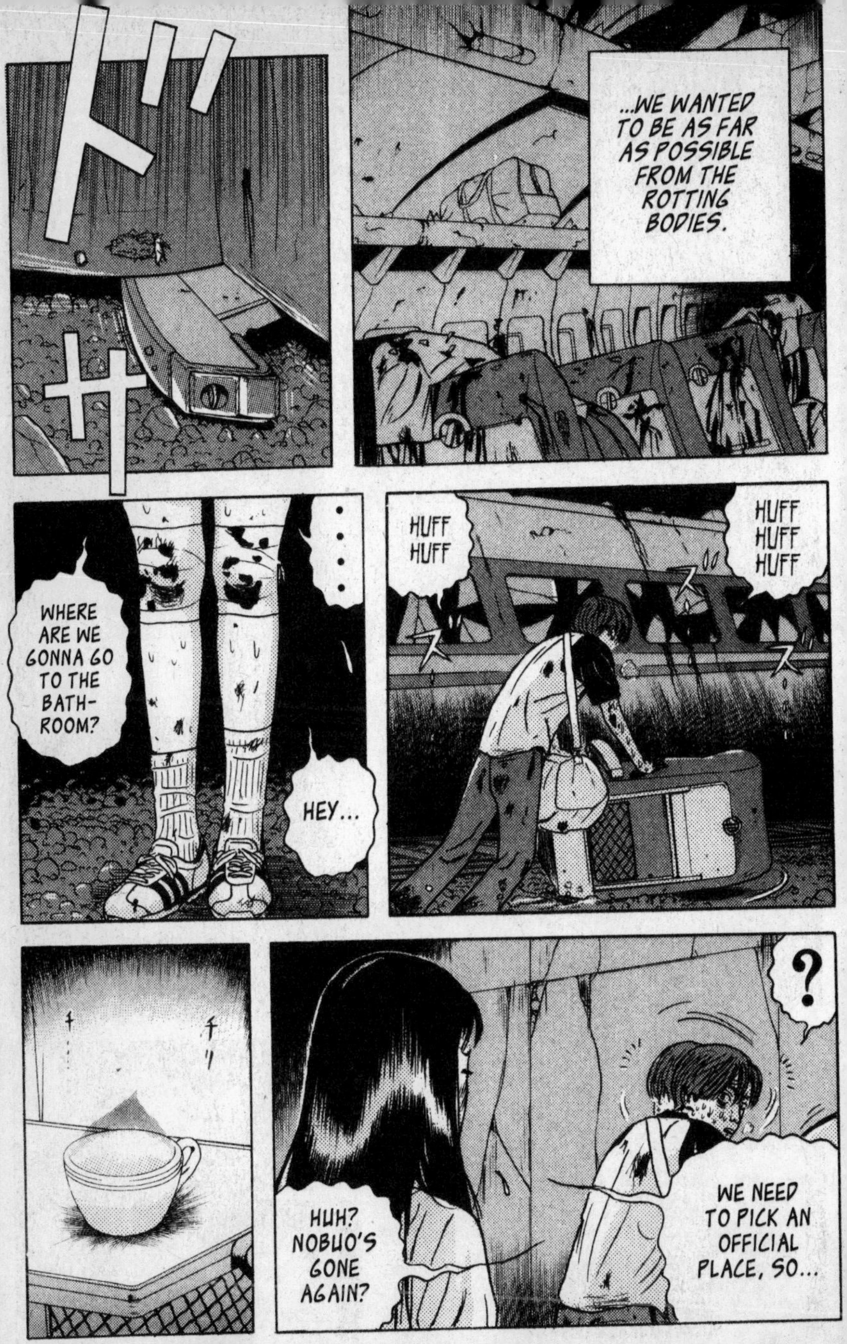
...WE WANTED TO BE AS FAR AS POSSIBLE FROM THE ROTTING BODIES.
ドサ
HUFF HUFF HUFF
HUFF HUFF
....
HEY...
WHERE ARE WE GONNA GO TO THE BATH-ROOM?
?
WE NEED TO PICK AN OFFICIAL PLACE, SO...
HUH? NOBUO'S GONE AGAIN?
チリ

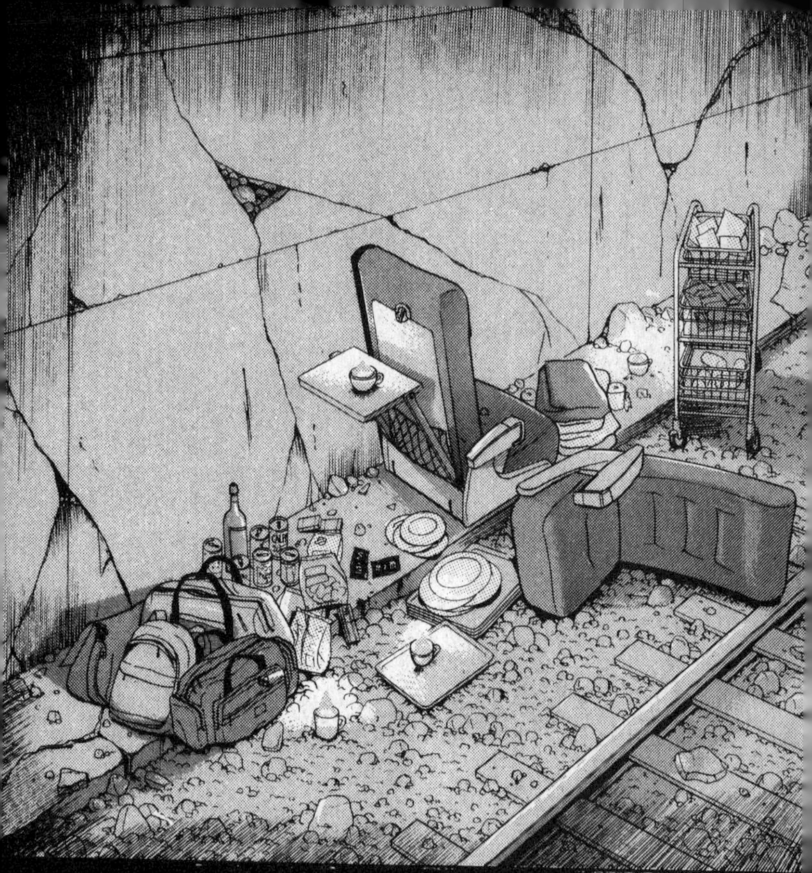

Dragon Head Volume 1 - END

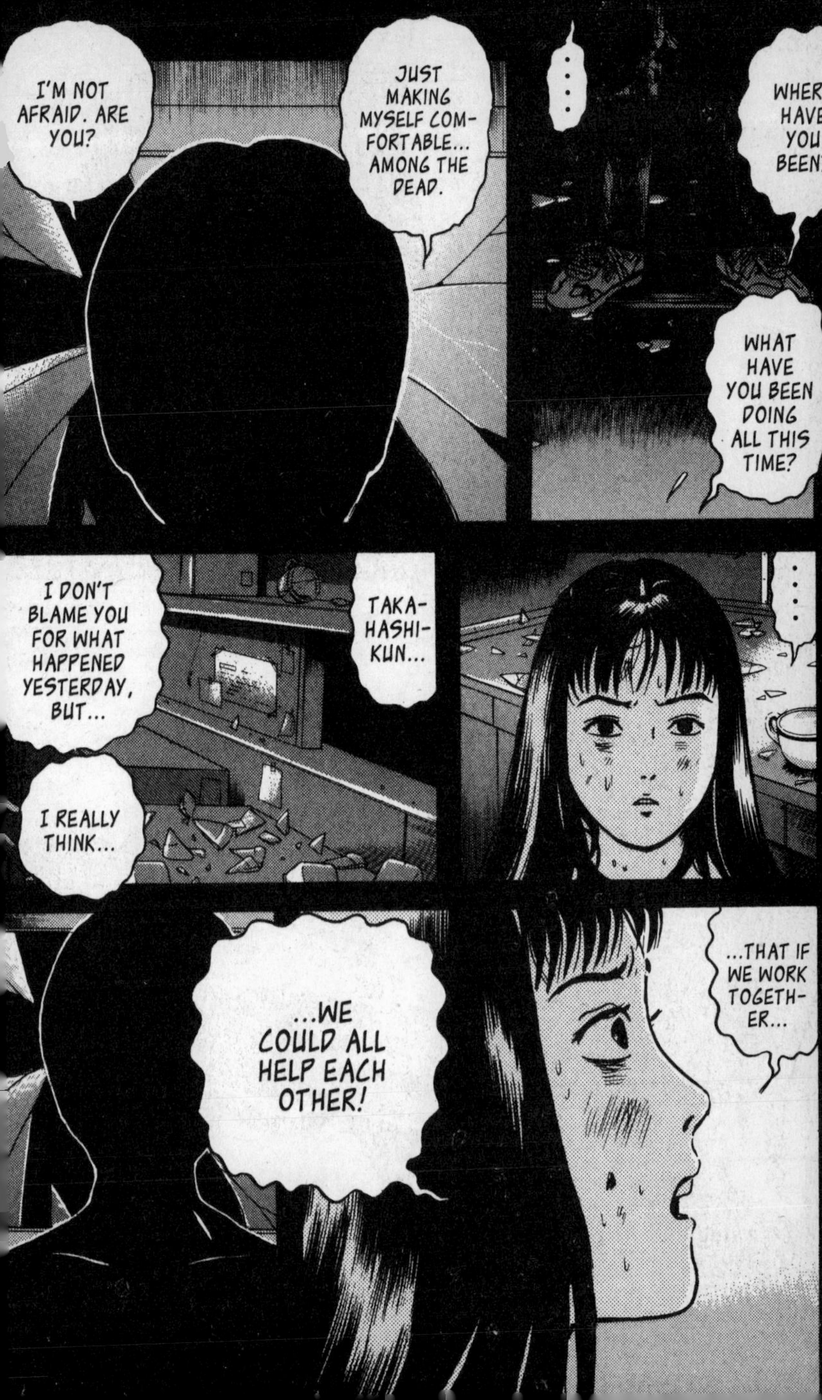
WHERE HAVE YOU BEEN?
. . . .
WHAT HAVE YOU BEEN DOING ALL THIS TIME?
JUST MAKING MYSELF COMFORTABLE... AMONG THE DEAD.
I'M NOT AFRAID. ARE YOU?
. . . .
TAKAHASHI-KUN...
I DON'T BLAME YOU FOR WHAT HAPPENED YESTERDAY, BUT...
I REALLY THINK...
...THAT IF WE WORK TOGETHER...
...WE COULD ALL HELP EACH OTHER!

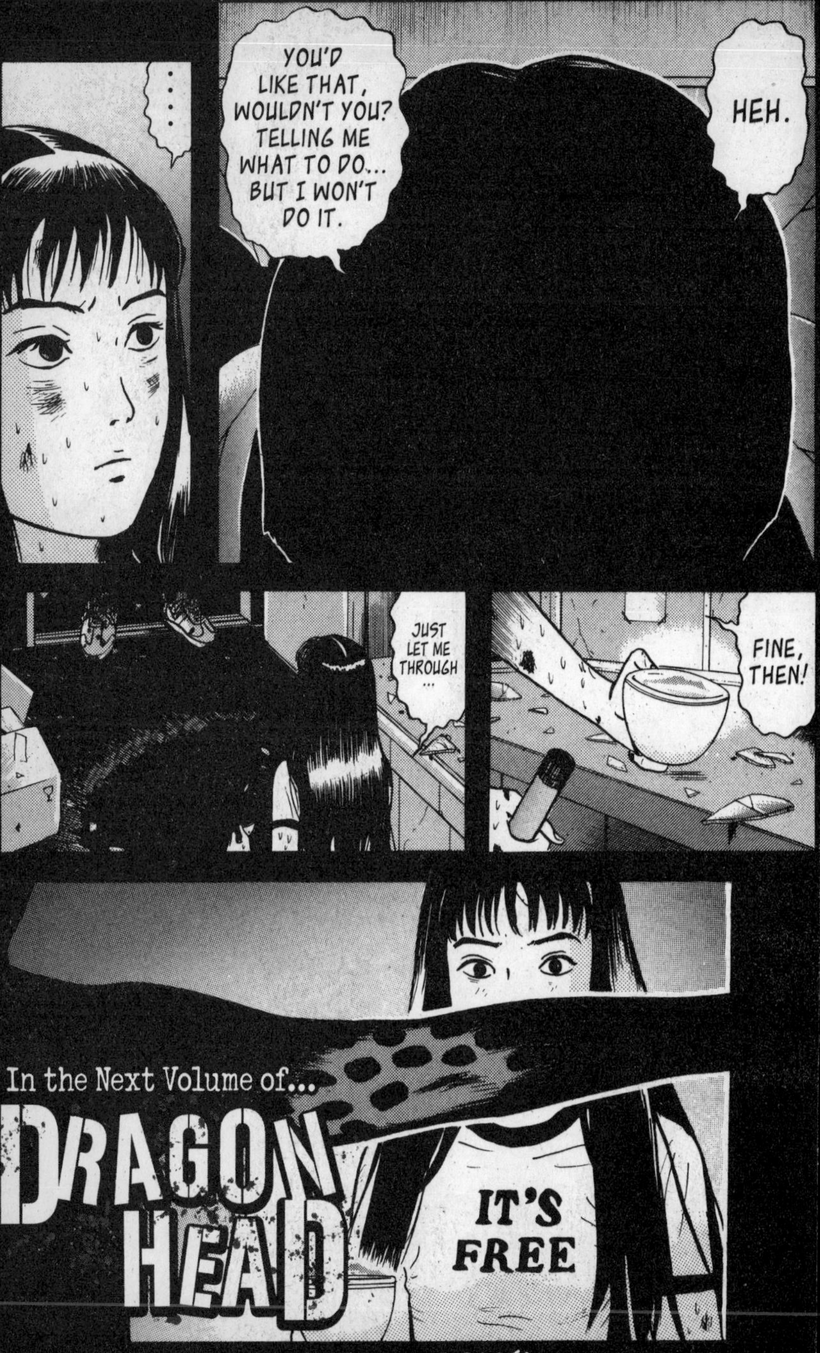
HEH.
YOU'D LIKE THAT, WOULDN'T YOU? TELLING ME WHAT TO DO... BUT I WON'T DO IT.
....
FINE, THEN!
JUST LET ME THROUGH ...
IT'S FREE
In the Next Volume of...
DRAGON HEAD

Available April 2006!

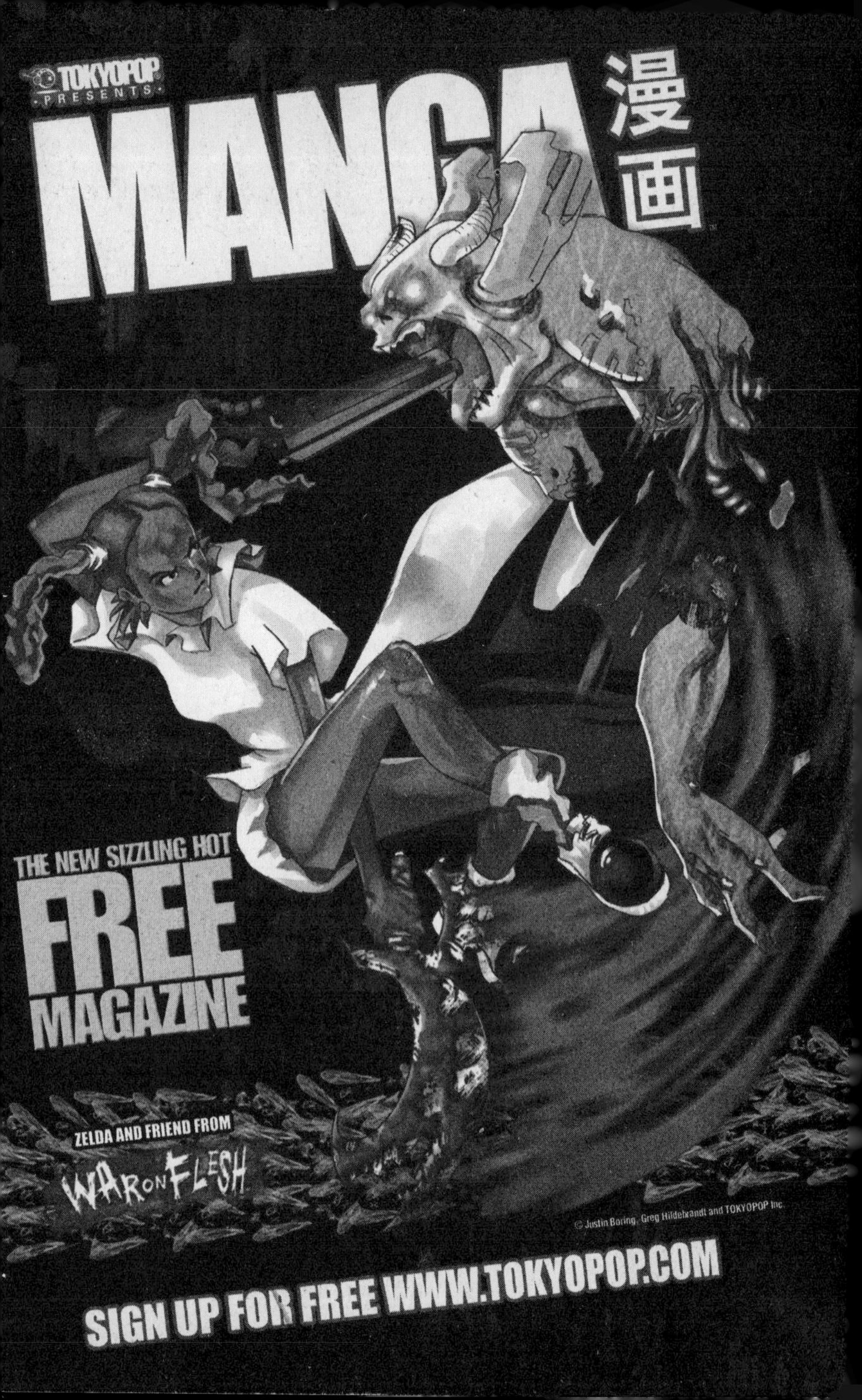
TOKYOPOP
PRESENTS
MANGA 漫画
THE NEW SIZZLING HOT
FREE
MAGAZINE
ZELDA AND FRIEND FROM
WAR ON FLESH
© Justin Boring, Greg Hildebrandt and TOKYOPOP Inc.
SIGN UP FOR FREE WWW.TOKYOPOP.COM

# TOKYOPOP SHOP

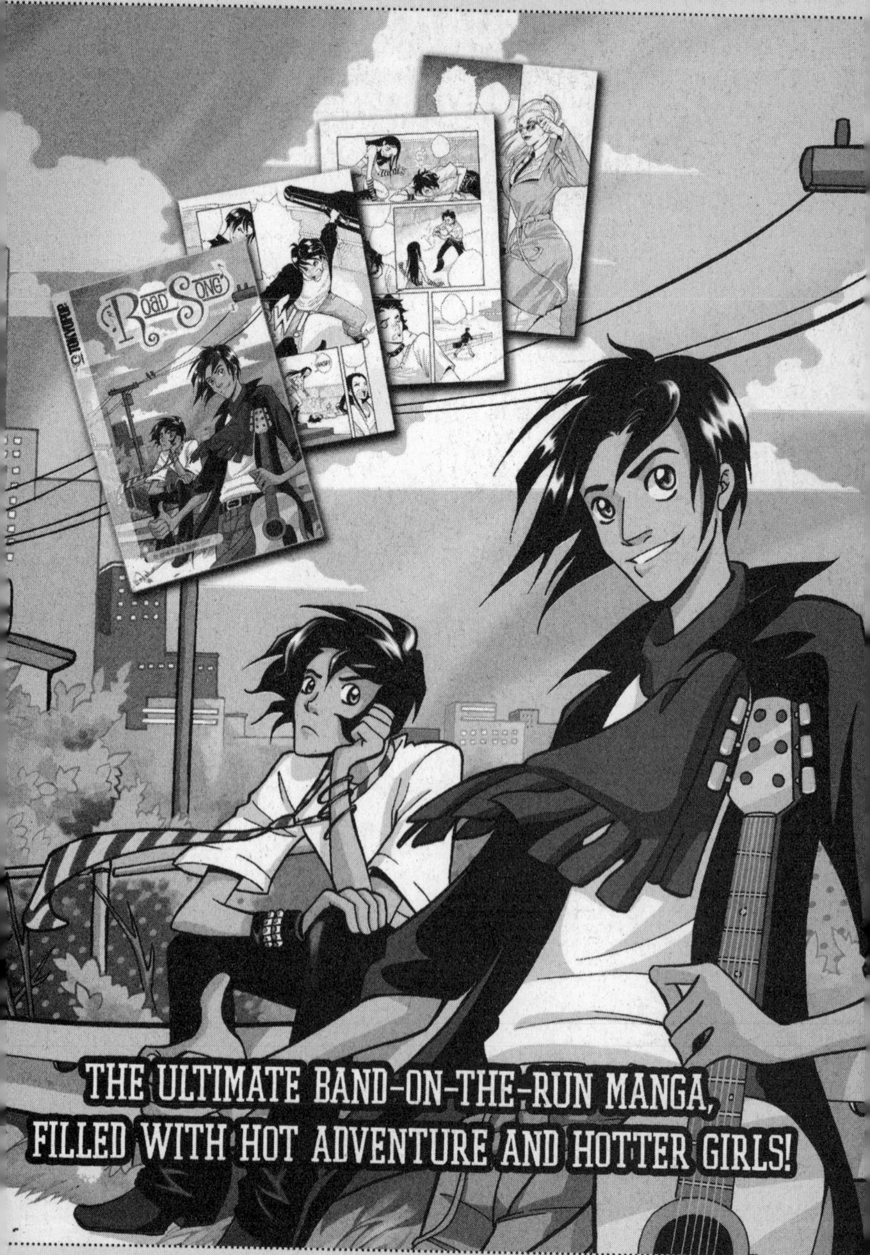
RoadSong
TOKYOPOP
THE ULTIMATE BAND-ON-THE-RUN MANGA,
FILLED WITH HOT ADVENTURE AND HOTTER GIRLS!

## Music...mystery...and Murder!

# RoadSong

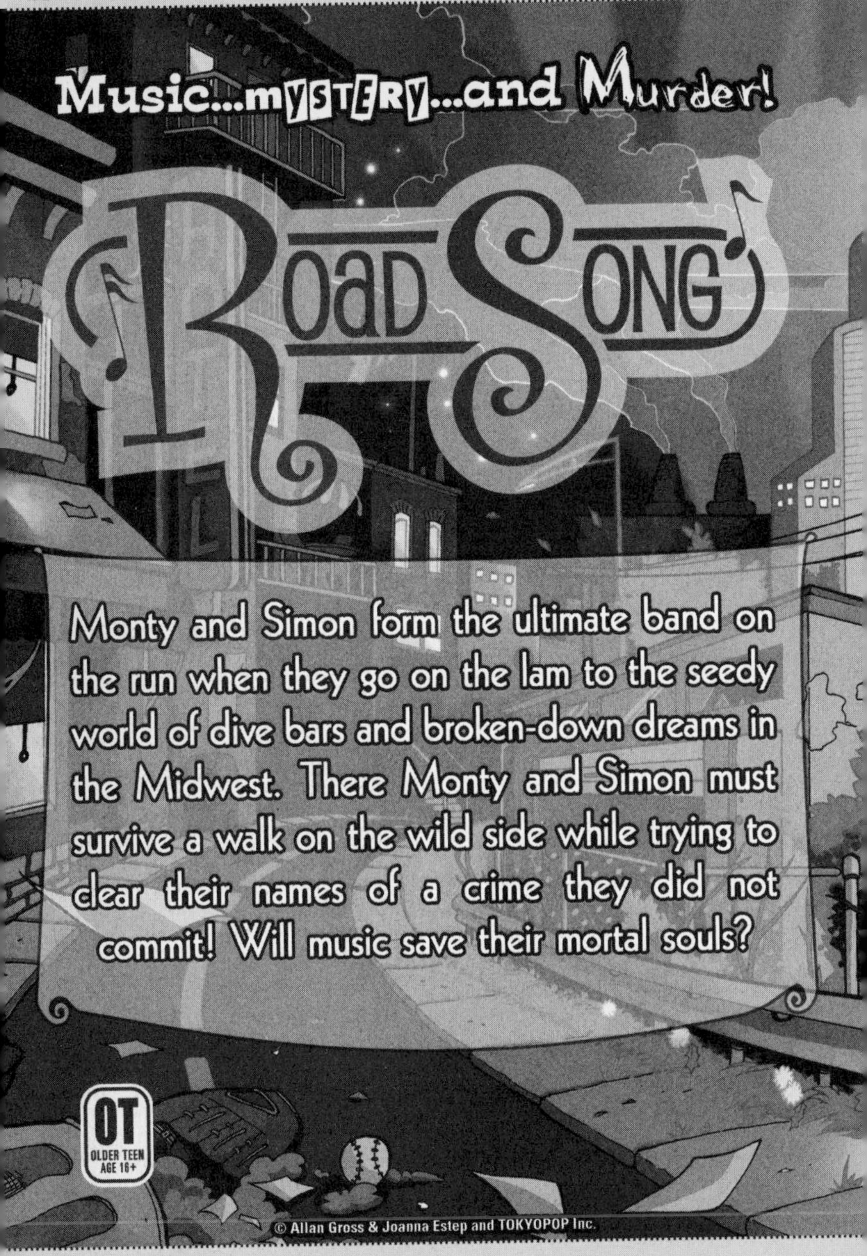

Monty and Simon form the ultimate band on the run when they go on the lam to the seedy world of dive bars and broken-down dreams in the Midwest. There Monty and Simon must survive a walk on the wild side while trying to clear their names of a crime they did not commit! Will music save their mortal souls?

**READ A CHAPTER OF THE MANGA ONLINE FOR FREE:**

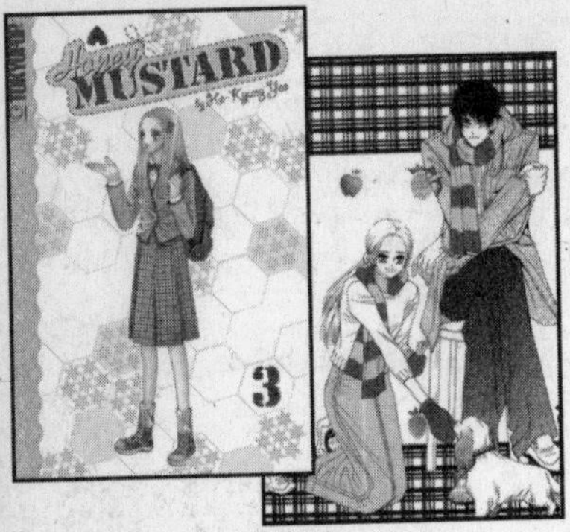
Honey
MUSTARD
3

BY HO-KYUNG YEO

## HONEY MUSTARD

I'm often asked about the title of *Honey Mustard.* What does a condiment have to do with romance and teen angst? One might ask the same thing about a basket of fruits, but I digress. Honey mustard is sweet with a good dose of bite, and I'd say that sums up this series pretty darn well, too. Ho-Kyung Yeo does a marvelous job of balancing the painful situations of adolescence with plenty of whacked-out humor to keep the mood from getting *too* heavy. It's a good, solid romantic comedy...and come to think of it, it'd go great with that sandwich.

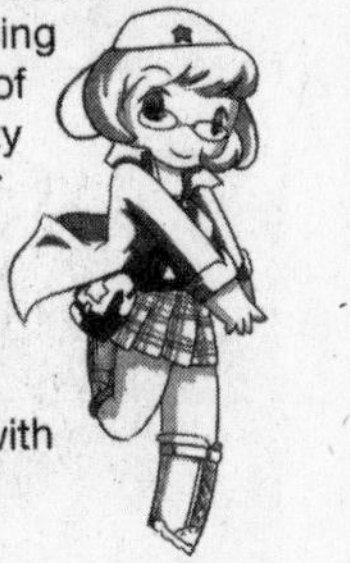

~Carol Fox, Editor

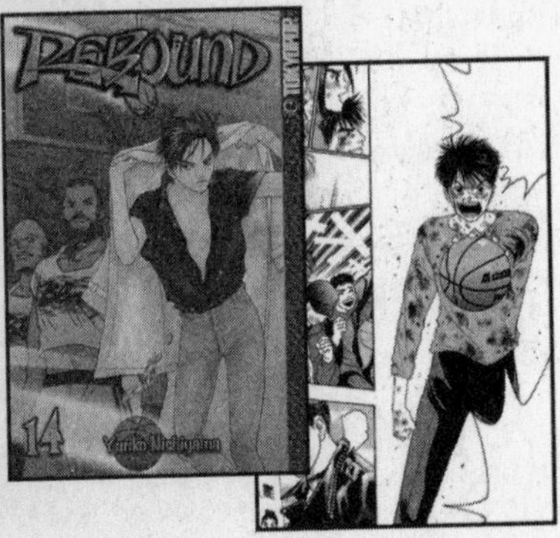
REBOUND
14

BY YURIKO NISHIYAMA

## REBOUND

At first glance, *Rebound* may seem like a simple sports manga. But on closer inspection, you'll find that the real drama takes place off the court. While the kids of the Johnan basketball team play and grow as a team, they learn valuable life lessons as well. By fusing the raw energy of basketball with the apple pie earnestness of an afterschool special, Yuriko Nishiyama has created a unique and heartfelt manga that appeals to all readers, male and female.

~Troy Lewter, Editor

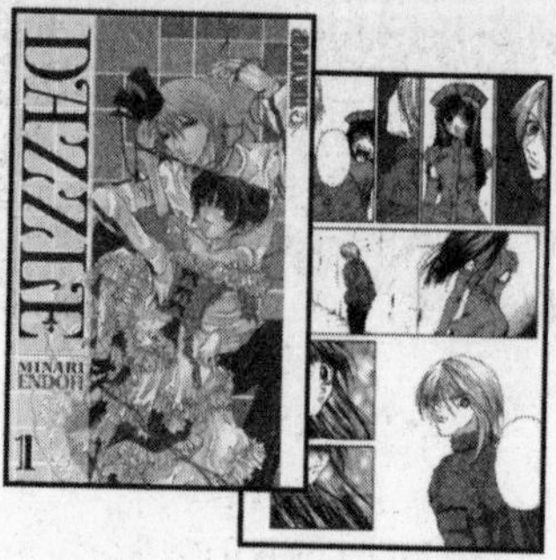
DAZZLE
MINARI ENDOH
1

© Minari Endoh/ICHIJINSHA

## DAZZLE

BY MINARI ENDOH

When a young girl named Rahzel sets out to see the world, she meets Alzeid, a mysterious loner on a mission to find his father's killer. Although the two share similar magical abilities, they don't exactly see eye-to-eye...but they will need each other to survive their journey!

**An epic coming-of-age story from an accomplished manga artist!**

T TEEN AGE 13+

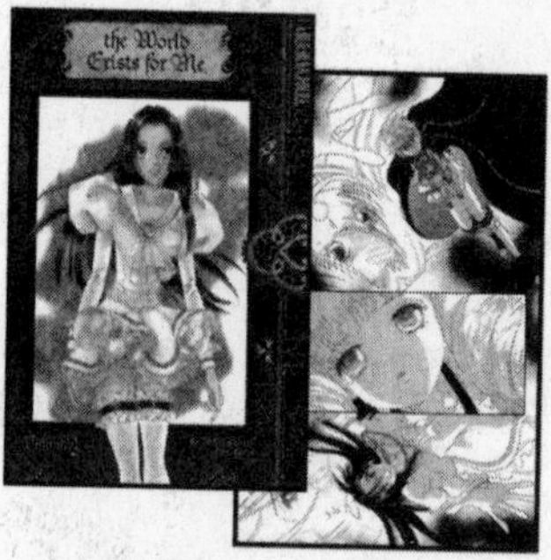
the World Exists for Me

© CHIHO SAITOU and IKUNI & Be-PaPas

## THE WORLD EXISTS FOR ME

BY BE-PAPAS AND CHIHO SAITOU

Once upon a time, the source of the devil R's invincible powers was *The Book of S & M.* But one day, a young man stole the book without knowing what it was, cut it into strips and used it to create a girl doll named "S" and a boy doll named "M." With that act, the unimaginable power that the devil held from the book was unleashed upon the world!

**From the creators of the manga classic *Revolutionary Girl Utena!***

T TEEN AGE 13+

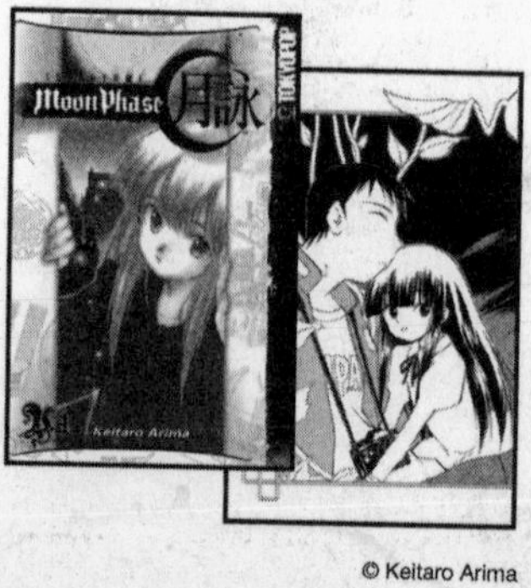
Moon Phase 月詠
TOKYOPOP
Keitaro Arima

© Keitaro Arima

## TSUKUYOMI: MOON PHASE

BY KEITARO ARIMA

Cameraman Kouhei Midou is researching Schwarz Quelle Castle. When he steps inside the castle's great walls, he discovers a mysterious little girl, Hazuki, who's been trapped there for years. Utilizing her controlling charm, Hazuki tries to get Kouhei to set her free. But this sweet little girl isn't everything she appears to be...

**The manga that launched the popular anime!**

T TEEN AGE 13+

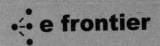

# STOP!

## This is the back of the book.
## You wouldn't want to spoil a great ending!

This book is printed "manga-style," in the authentic Japanese right-to-left format. Since none of the artwork has been flipped or altered, readers get to experience the story just as the creator intended. You've been asking for it, so TOKYOPOP® delivered: authentic, hot-off-the-press, and far more fun!

# DIRECTIONS

If this is your first time reading manga-style, here's a quick guide to help you understand how it works.

It's easy... just start in the top right panel and follow the numbers. Have fun, and look for more 100% authentic manga from TOKYOPOP®!

100% AUTHENTIC MANGA